CW01502263

About the Author

Kevin is a well-known and highly respected Martial Artist worldwide for forty plus years. At present, he runs his own training premises in his home town of Bristol named 'Impact Gym'. He also manages his own website www.kevinohagan.com

Kevin is now semi-retired and spends most of his spare time writing and travelling. He still teaches privately and on the seminar circuit.

When We Were Warriors

Kevin O'Hagan

When We Were Warriors

Olympia Publishers
London

www.olympiapublishers.com
OLYMPIA PAPERBACK EDITION

Copyright © Kevin O'Hagan 2017

The right of Kevin O'Hagan to be identified as author of
this work has been asserted in accordance with sections 77 and 78 of the
Copyright, Designs and Patents Act 1988.

All Rights Reserved

No reproduction, copy or transmission of this publication
may be made without written permission.
No paragraph of this publication may be reproduced,
copied or transmitted save with the written permission of the publisher, or
in accordance with the provisions
of the Copyright Act 1956 (as amended).

Any person who commits any unauthorised act in relation to
this publication may be liable to criminal
prosecution and civil claims for damage.

A CIP catalogue record for this title is
available from the British Library.

ISBN: 978-1-84897-815-7

First Published in 2017

Olympia Publishers
60 Cannon Street
London
EC4N 6NP

Printed in Great Britain

Dedication

For my parents, Joseph and Mary. God, bless you both. To Tina my lovely wife, my fantastic children, Thomas, Jacob and Lauren who have grown to be incredible people. To the next generation, my grandchildren to date, Logan, Eden and Brenen.

I hope this book serves as a blueprint for them and they grow up remembering what their granddad did for a living.

Acknowledgments

To each and every person who has taught, inspired and guided me in my martial arts journey. There are far too many to name but I thank you all. Special thanks to my training partners, fellow instructors and coaches for all your tireless work and dedication.

Remembering my teachers and peers sadly no longer here.

Love and thanks to my wife, Tina for her undying support and encouragement for all that I have undertaken. You are my rock always. When I was blazing a trail you and times were tough you unselfishly held the family together and ran a tight ship. You wholeheartedly deserve that recognition.

A special mention to my son, Tom for the cover design
www.apexfitnesssystems.com

Also, Matt Law for the front and back cover images.
www.mattlawphotography.com

Author Endorsements.

'Kevin is as real as real comes. I would like him by my side if faced with an ugly encounter.'
Jamie O'Keefe. Producer, actor, author and retired self-protection instructor

'I have known Kevin for some years now; he is a first-rate Martial artist and a man I admire.'
Geoff Thompson. Bafta award winning playwright, author, self-help and wellbeing coach, pioneering reality self-protection Instructor.

'Probably one of the best combat jujutsu men in the UK'
Dave Turton 10th Dan Goshinwai Combat. Martial Arts Hall of famer twice.

'Kevin is a British martial artist whom I highly recommend. You cannot only benefit from his technique but also his attitude of aggression tempered with good sense.'
Ed Beaumont US author of 'The savage science of street fighting' and many other combat publications.

'Kevin stands head and shoulders about even the most committed Martial artist when it comes to dedication to hard training.'
Peter Consterdine 9th Dan Black Belt in Karate and a former Gt. Britain and England International, Co-chief instructor of the British Combat Association

The Way of the Warrior

I see things through different eyes.
I see a bigger picture when others see grey skies.
Though many can't conceive it, I stand, facing the wind.
My bravery is not from my skills, but from my inner strength.
I am a warrior; I will walk the extra mile.
Not because I should, but because it's worth my while.
I know that I am different when I stand on a crowded street.
I know the fullness of winning; I've tasted the cup of defeat.
I am a warrior; they say I walk with ease.
Though trained for bodily harm, my intentions are for peace.
The world may come and go, but a different path I choose.
A path I will not stray from, no matter win or lose.

(Anonymous)

"Warriors aren't born, and they aren't made...
They create themselves through trial and error and by their ability to
conquer their own frailties and faults."

Philip J. Messina

"Everyone that lives, dies
But not everyone who dies has lived."

Dhaggi Ramanashi

Preface

When I initially developed the idea for this book, I sat down and thought long and hard about whether anyone would want to read about my life in the martial arts. After all, there were more experienced, talented and successful individuals in the martial arts world that hadn't yet put pen to paper, so why did I feel I had something different to offer?

With that thought in mind, I decided to put the project on the back-burner and go on with other activities in my life. I had too many doubts about the whole idea, so I tried to forget about it.

Fifteen months later, I revisited the project, and this time, I viewed it in a more positive light.

Firstly, I realised that I had presently devoted forty years to the martial arts. I can honestly state that, in all that time, there have been very few occasions when I haven't been training, trying to improve my abilities and absorb more and more information. There are few sportsmen or athletes who stay that long in their chosen disciplines. In this country, when a sportsman reaches thirty years of age, he is deemed 'over the hill'. If they continue beyond this, they are thought of as somebody special. My peers have bestowed me with accolades such as 'legend' and 'master'. Titles that I feel uncomfortable to wear but, at the same time, acknowledge because I have been around this planet half a century and more, and I would like to think that I can leave my mark and my legacy in the world of the combat arts.

I also noted how the martial arts had shaped my life and took me from a young, green and insecure fourteen-year-old boy, along an exciting, challenging and many varied journey to where I am now. I overcame a disability which hampered me not only physically, but also mentally, for a long time in my youth, and almost made me abandon my dreams because of it. But I didn't give up. As Nietzsche once said, "What doesn't kill us makes us stronger." This, in my case, was so true. I refused to give up or give in. Martial arts were my passion. They were my outlet. They were my release from my struggles academically at school, and from the bullies and piss-takers. It was my escape and I knew I could be good at it. I finally had found something I liked and could excel in.

Along the way, I have met some interesting characters. The good, the bad and the MAD! I have also made many loyal friends and have been inspired by people of genuine class. At one time, we were the new boys, the trailblazers, the warriors. Every dog has its day and I had mine.

I have experienced a multitude of combat systems, traditional, modern and eclectic and gathered vast quantities of knowledge and know-how. I have also sweated blood and tears for the cause and trained beyond what I thought a human being was capable of enduring.

As that young boy, I never dreamt that I could achieve the things I have done. On the grand scale of things, they may not seem important to those who have tasted greater and bigger success, but for me, from my humble beginnings, I have moved a few 'mountains'.

I was never the fastest, strongest, biggest or most gifted individual, but I had a determination to give something a good go. Win or lose, I never turned down a challenge that I set myself. I still carry this philosophy with me today. If I set my mind on doing something, I will follow it through to its conclusion whatever the outcome. You will learn why as you read through my story.

Martial arts gave me the confidence and belief to pursue other projects in my life that I probably wouldn't have thought I could achieve, and they also gave me the mental strength to face down and handle much adversity.

My success cannot be measured in riches and monetary gain, but from the inner satisfaction of having reached some of my long-term goals in life which have given me much happiness, belief, confidence and strength. I have fought and conquered many of my internal battles with fear and uncertainty and this, in turn, has given me a better life.

I have proven to my doubters that told me I would never make a living out of martial arts that they were wrong, and I have proven to myself that I have the guts to face adversity and handle it.

This book will track my time in the martial arts from humble beginnings right up to present day. I will tell it as near to chronological order as I can without jumping from one era to the next so you, the reader, can follow my journey accurately. I will tell it straight. No fabrication, no exaggeration and no outlandish claims. I will tell it how it was. No punches pulled. The good and the bad. The blood, sweat and tears. The highs and lows. The triumphs and the defeats.

Hopefully, you will find it entertaining and enlightening. Maybe it will also inspire you to pursue your dreams. Enjoy.

Kevin O'Hagan.
January 2016-01-04

Tough guy? Hard man? Animal?

"I class myself as none of these things. I am a warrior who chose the path of martial arts to forge my character, spirit and soul, and to face my fears. Yes, I have encountered violence, but I am not a violent man. At times, I did become the monster that I wanted to slay. Sometimes, you must go through the fire of adversity to come out the other side cleansed. I have been a fighter working towards the goal of winning a contest but, essentially, I am a martial artist and I live and breathe that in all areas of my life every day. I am a realist. We cannot stop the clock ticking. At one time, I was one of the 'new boys', 'the trail blazer'. Martial arts didn't make me invincible or give me special powers. For me, martial arts are an inner challenge of learning and self-discipline. I initially took up martial arts to learn how to fight. Now I know how to fight, I no longer want to. Peace."

Introduction

The date is June 19th, 2015. Today is my fifty-fourth birthday. I have been on this spinning planet for half a century or more. That is a sobering thought. I am a husband, father and grandfather. I have faced and experienced all the important things in life, good and bad. The things that used to give me sleepless nights when I was young have been faced down and beaten. The only thing left to face eventually is to meet the 'Big Man' in the sky... if I am lucky.

I am comfortable at the age I am now. I feel pretty much at peace with my life. I am semi-retired and enjoying not having to live life at full throttle these days. Don't get me wrong, I have much yet to do, see and experience, but on different paths to the one I have relentlessly pursued for forty years. Shit, that is a long time.

You see, martial arts have been my life and passion since a young boy of fourteen years of age. I fell in love with them, and that love affair has continued. Apart from my family, there has been nothing more important in my life. I have literally lived and breathed the martial arts in sacrifice for just about everything else.

The fire in my belly these days does not burn as brightly as it used to, simply because I have immersed myself fully in my passion to the point where I have nothing more to achieve. My head is metaphorically hitting the ceiling of my ambitions. I have been there, done it and got the t-shirt.

As a young man, I would watch in awe Bruce Lee, Chuck Norris, Jim Kelly, David Chiang and Jimmy Wang Yu amongst others on the silver screen, wishing I possessed their skills.

Then, I would follow the careers of hardened veteran martial artists as I began my own fledgling journey. Big names back then were the likes of Terry O'Neil, Andy Sherry, Joe Lewis, Benny 'the Jet' Urquidez, Bill 'Superfoot' Wallace, Ronnie Van Cleef, Gene Lebell, Larry Hartsell, Dan Inosanto, Brian Jacks, Jeff Smith, Jean Yves Theriault, Robert Clark, Ed Parker, Mas Oyama, Morio Higaonna, Keinosuke Enoeda, Tatsuo Suzuki and many, many more. All giants in their field and men I wanted to aspire to.

I also wanted my name to be honoured and revered in the martial arts world. I was ready to do whatever it would take. The blood, sweat, tears and sacrifice. I have trained through four decades and had to reinvent myself more times than Madonna. I have witnessed martial arts come and go as the flavour of the month. I have been around long enough for the seventies' invasion of kung fu, the eighties' explosion of taekwondo and kickboxing, plus the craze of the ninja. Into the nineties with Muay Thai becoming massive, ju jutsu having a re-birth and reality combat and cross training becoming the buzz words at the latter part of that decade. The millennium really heralded a martial arts revolution with MMA becoming massive and grappling arts coming out of the shadows, plus our great British martial arts of boxing and wrestling finally getting their deserved recognition with their Eastern counterparts. Brazilian ju jutsu has become a worldwide force and combat systems like Systema from Russia and Krav Maga from Israel amongst others have also appeared in the public eye.

I have been fortunate to train with experts in all of these aforementioned disciplines and others you may not have even heard of. I look back and realise just how many gyms, dojos and mats that I have been on all over the world.

Many of my peers and special individuals who have inspired and helped me have now gone to their graves. It does make you think of your own mortality and makes you want to seize every day and not waste it. Hence, the decision to write this book and document my story whilst I can.

I also realise that to write this book, I am going to have to dig deep into the memory banks to remember all the training and stories. I know I won't recall them all, and I know I will probably forget some important people's names along the way. So, I ask your forgiveness now.

I feel the time is right to catalogue my journey in writing and pass on my knowledge and thoughts to a new generation of martial artist. I would like to feel that, in my own small way, I have left an impression in the world of martial arts and done something worthwhile with my life. Martial arts certainly shaped the person I am and gave me discipline and direction. Otherwise, I may well have slipped off down another path which wouldn't have brought me any satisfaction or spiritual gain.

I hope you find my story inspiring and educational. It is an honest account of what I went through and achieved. It is not sensationalised or sexed up to curry favour. It is the truth, warts and all.

So, sit back, relax and enjoy the ride.

Prologue

My breathing is heavy and my heart is pounding. I work from my back, trying to get my opponent off me but he is fast and slippery. He has youth on his side; he is nearly twenty years younger than me. He has gained mount position and is ready to drop some big punches down on my head. I reach up and grab his waist and encircle it with both my arms. I pull him down towards me to deny him the leverage that he needs to inflict damage. But he pulls away with a surge of strength and throws a big elbow down which connects with my cheek bone. I register it, but with my adrenaline pumping at full throttle, I hardly feel it. I work to reverse my opponent, but it is not easy. At forty-three years of age, I am feeling the pace. People in some quarters had told me that I was too old to take this fight, but I was going to do my best to prove them wrong. This was another of life's challenges that I was willing to experience for my own personal growth. I was doing this for me. They say there is no growth without pain. They, whoever they are, are fucking right!

I am fighting in the cage in a professional MMA bout on the show 'Ultimate Combat 9 – The Rebellion' on the 28th March 2003 in my home city of Bristol. It is a welterweight European title eliminator against a young, up-and-coming fighter originating from Turkey named Sami 'the Hun' Berik. He is a San Shou British champion. He is no mug. He is here to fight.

I never would have believed that at the ripe old age of forty-three, I would be in the cage doing this. I had trained like a beast for this moment. I didn't want to let anybody down. There are so many people in the crowd willing me to win and a few hoping I will lose. The pressure is immense.

I am a veteran of pressure. Fear and its many guises has become a good mate to me. They have been one of my constant companions through my martial arts adventure.

I suddenly get an opening. I might not have youth on my side but I have experience. I bump my opponent off me and pass his legs to mount his chest. I push him right up against the cage. The tables have now changed. I rain down punches and hammer-fists on his face as the crowd cheer.

MMA can be a savage sport. I have no animosity towards him. It is just a professional fight. It's nothing personal. But it is strange how you can detach yourself.

My blows force my opponent to turn to his stomach. It's a bad move on his part. Face down in an MMA fight is not where you want to be. In fact, face down in any fight is not where you want to be!

I am on him like an anaconda and wrap my arm around his neck in preparation to choke him out. My arms are strong and chokes and strangles are my favourite grappling moves. I have put more people to sleep with them than a mug of Ovaltine or a Coldplay record.

I know the end of the round is close. I am tired and wondering if I have another round in me. The pace has been frantic and my lungs are burning. It is a testament to my fitness.

I decide that I have got to finish this now. If I can finish this, it will be another great milestone in a martial arts career that has spanned many decades. Hey, let's put this in perspective. It is going to be a big fucking achievement. I lock in the choke and begin to squeeze... The clock is ticking... I must make him tap out... Time seems to stand still... The roar of the crowd becomes muffled as if I were fighting underwater. I can feel and hear my heart pounding in my ears... *Keep squeezing*. My opponent is still struggling; attempting to get me off his back... I must hang on and keep squeezing. My arms burn with lactic acid build-up but I must ignore it... *Squeeze*!

Since a fourteen-year-old boy, I have trained in the combat arts and fought my many fears. I have faced many challenges and put my body through the extremes in my quest to learn the 'Way of the Warrior'. This is the ultimate test for me at this stage of a lengthy career.

It's been a hell of a journey to me being in the cage this night. I want to win this fight with every fibre of my being. I know I may never get the chance again. I also know I might never want the chance again. This is the time. It's now or never, as the Elvis Presley song goes.

Now all I need to do is squeeze tighter and beat that damn clock. *Squeeze*...

Early Seeds Planted

I had a great interest in sport when I was a youngster. I loved to watch it and to play it, although I wasn't born with the natural skills of an athlete. Back then, my first love was not the fighting arts.

I was particularly interested in football and avidly followed it with a great passion. In the seventies, I knew all the players from each first division team (old premier) and many of the other leagues. I collected all the magazines, football cards, old programmes; I was quite a fanatic around ten or eleven years of age. My favourite heroes of that time were George Best, Bobby Moore, Gordon Banks, Pat Jennings and later players like Kevin Keegan and Bryan Robson.

I grew up in a part of Bristol named Easton which meant, naturally, that I followed the blue half of the city which was Bristol Rovers. My dad took me to every home match when I was a young boy and then, for a good while later, my mates and I went. I witnessed some fantastic matches and legendary players at Rovers spiritual home, Eastville Stadium, which unfortunately, no longer exists. The famous, old ground is now an IKEA superstore. The standing joke is that IKEA gets more people through their doors each week than Rovers ever got through their turnstiles!

Back in those days, every kid was down the playing fields kicking a ball around. No sitting on the sofa with a computer game. We were playing for real. If I didn't have any mates to kick a ball around with, I would play alone in my back garden. Most evenings, after tea, I would be out there, homework conveniently forgotten about, lost in a fantasy world playing at Wembley, Old Trafford or Anfield.

Over a period of years, I wore the grass completely away and demolished my old man's 'bean sticks' and 'cabbage patch'. I just loved to play wherever and whenever I could.

I remember on Sunday afternoons, nagging my dad to bring me up to the local park to kick a ball around with me. Looking back now, my old man must have been knackered but he rarely let me down. He worked hard six days a week on the buildings, and Sunday lunchtime he enjoyed a few pints down his local pub. Coming back and going up the park to run around for hours was probably the last thing on his mind, but he was always there for me.

Although I was quite small, I was developing into a pretty good goalkeeper and enjoyed diving around all over the place. At school in the playground, I was constantly wearing holes in my clothes because I would dive at everything, no fear of the concrete.

I played for my school on a handful of occasions in goal and I did all right. Later, at fourteen years of age, I played many times for the local school youth club in eleven and five-a-side games. Up to a few years ago, I still played now and again for my local sports centre in five-a-side tournaments. You guessed it, in goal. Still throwing myself all over the place and not a mat in sight! The old reflexes are still sharp, and I put that down to the martial arts.

Tracking back again to around twelve years of age, I also developed an interest in wrestling and boxing. I used to watch the wrestling on ITV's Saturday afternoon 'World of Sport'. This was British wrestling and although the bouts were 'worked', it had a gritty reality to it, unlike the American stuff of today. Great wrestlers like Marty Jones, Mark 'Rollerball' Rocco, Fit Finlay, Pat Roach, Pete Roberts and Skull Murphy were some of the top boys from that era, and they really were tough men that could wrestle.

If rain stopped the Sunday afternoon kick around at the park, wrestling was next on the agenda! The living room floor was the ring and away Dad and I would go. I used to try all the moves that I had seen on the television on him and he would let me get away with so many and then suddenly pin me down. God, I worked up a sweat. Everything with me was one hundred percent full on. I always ended up red-faced and soaked in perspiration. I remember those times vividly. My mum used to be in the kitchen (the place where all mums seem to live), washing up the Sunday lunch dishes and shouting out, "What are you two doing? You'll wear a hole in that carpet. Stop it!" My mum was very house-proud and our wrestling bouts used to wind her up but having said that, she still let us both get away with it!

I would like at this stage to mention my parents, Joe and Mary. Both were born and bred in Northern Ireland. My dad lived later in Scotland for a time before coming to England and then brought my mum over. They settled here in Bristol and my sister, Brenda, and then later myself, were born. They were always hardworking, active and down-to-earth people. They both could be gentle or hard when needed, and I suppose this is where my Irish fighting blood comes from and my steely determination to succeed in whatever I do. Our background is working class. Although we lived simply and times could be tough, my childhood was generally a happy one.

My dad was tough but fair. You couldn't pull the wool over his eyes and sometimes he had to be cruel to be kind. But under his tough exterior was a heart of gold. But you would have to dig deep sometimes to find it. He passed away a few years back now and I do miss my chats with him. He always liked to hear what I had been up to. I wasn't always sure what he thought about me eventually teaching martial arts for a living as he never said much. Then one day I was in Bristol town centre in W.H.Smiths and I saw him browsing the martial arts magazines. I didn't approach him but later mentioned it to my mum. She told me that every month he would walk into town (about three miles there and back) and check if I was in any of the magazines. If I was, he bought it and then would bring it down the local pub to show his friends. He never mentioned this. About a month before he passed away, he finally told me that he was proud of me and what I had achieved. That was like gold dust to me. I had waited a long time to hear that from him. I am only sorry that he left it so long. But maybe that is why it meant so much.

Mary, my mum, was soft and gentle and oh-so very kind. She had a tough upbringing, losing her mum at an early age and having to help bring up her brothers and sisters and look after her dad. I had so many laughs with her, she shared my wicked sense of humour.

Today, she is in a nursing home. She had two major life-threatening strokes over a period of years which left her with physical and mental defects. She now has dementia. She battles on gamely but she is only a shell of the wonderful woman that I called Mum.

It saddens my heart every time I visit her to see such a wonderful mother ended up this way. Life can be cruel. Both my parents lived fighters' lives and I owe them much.

Both my parents instilled in me, at an early age, the difference between right and wrong. Also, that God helps those that help themselves. In other words, don't sit moaning about what you could have done, get out there and do it! My dad worked hard all his life in the building trade. Mum tirelessly worked in the NHS. Both grafted relentlessly for what they achieved in life. They were always there for me with help and advice and I would like this chance to thank them both in print. I love them and they will always be in my heart.

Okay, back to my early combat influences. At the same time, I was enjoying the wrestling, I also started watching some of the big boxing matches on television. Muhammad Ali was the main man in those early seventies, although my old man would tell me stories of Jack Johnson, Jack Dempsey, Joe Louis, 'Jersey' Joe Walcott, Ezzard Charles, Rocky Marciano and the fearsome Sonny Liston.

When I was young, I hated Ali and longed for him to be beat. I suppose at twelve or thirteen years old, you wondered who this loud-mouthed, cocky and brash boxer was, and I could remember being over the moon when the excellent Ken Norton beat Ali and broke his jaw. I also recall the epic encounters he had with 'Smokin' Joe Frazier. Brutal fights that wouldn't have been allowed to go on now currently in this era. Later on in life, I realised just how good Ali had been and what an influence he had on the boxing world.

Around this time, I was bought a pair of boxing gloves and a punch ball on a stand for my twelfth birthday. I loved it and whacked away at it daily, although it used to whack me back just as much!

Also, my parents had a spare mattress for their bed up in their bedroom and I used to go in there, put it up against the wall and punch the hell out of it for ages, working up a great sweat. An old mattress was a staple standby in those days if you didn't have a punch bag!

Then, come Sunday afternoon, the front room would suddenly transform into Madison Square Gardens! I would fire away at Dad, working up lather, but usually it would end up in a wrestling match with me still firing punches on the floor. Come to think of it, that could have been the birth of Mixed Martial Arts and cross training, although I didn't really have a clue what I was doing at the time!

These early memories show that I must have had a subconscious liking for the fighting arts, but football was always my first love. Although I had a passion for all sports, I was hindered from developing fully in any of them and really missed my chance to excel. I will explain to you why.

I was born with my right leg slightly shorter than my left. This has caused me to walk with a slight limp all my life. When I was very young, I hardly used the leg and dragged it along rather than throw it out to walk correctly. I constantly wanted to be carried or wheeled around in a pushchair (slightly embarrassing when you're sixteen years old… Only kidding!). Because of this, I suffered muscle wastage to the leg and that has stayed with me to present day, even after intense exercise to build it up.

There was a point in my young life where my dad decided to lay the law down and try to correct my walking. He used to take me out for long, and I mean long, walks. He would constantly remind me to step out and use the right leg. He, as I mentioned previously, had to be cruel to be kind, although at the time I didn't always realise the fact and hated every minute of it.

On occasions, I would be angry, frustrated or cry. It was tough being constantly reminded to walk correctly whenever you stepped out of your front door. But I was developing a steely determination, so I persevered at it.

I also had to visit a specialist that manipulated my foot, ankle and rest of my leg in some weird and wonderful positions and gave me a series of exercises to be performed every day.

The ritual would be to do these exercises before I went to bed. I loathed them and again, there was much frustration, rebellion and tears. But once more, I stuck at them.

Being reminded at home of your slight disability was tough enough, but it didn't compare to the ridicule and piss-taking that I received at school and the neighbourhood. Kids can be very cruel and heartless and I experienced my share of this, especially at sports time. It got me into many fights, just out of pure frustration.

This began to drive me more inward on myself and to become ever more self-conscious about my problem. I became one of those kids at the back of a line to be picked for football, rugby, etc., when I desperately yearned inside to be at the front. But all my self-confidence had been knocked for six. My self-belief system was taking a battering. Looking back, if I had been mentally stronger, I could have done well in any sport as I proved later in my life, but then, I was aged between eleven and fifteen and it was a tough time, as there seemed to be a piss-taker at every corner I turned. Teachers didn't really help and I kept this all bottled up inside and never told my parents. You just didn't talk about these things back then and most people were not really understanding. My release at the time was reading Marvel comics. I would fantasise that I was Spiderman or Captain America. I wanted to be a fearless superhero who could take on the 'baddies' and crush them effortlessly. Oh, how I wished that to be true, but I began to realise that real life wasn't like that. So instead of facing the bullies, I mainly ran away or hid from them.

Through all this, there was a part of me determined to fight back and overcome the disability and the fears that went with it. Currently, people are a lot more tolerant and respectful of those that might be hindered physically and show a great deal of empathy. In the seventies, there was no such thing. Political correctness didn't exist. It was a dog-eats-dog time at school. Shouts of *spastic*, *peg leg* or *cripple* were common. There was no running to the teachers or authorities with cries of bullying, no wearing of pink ribbons and no racial or prejudice claims. Either you hid or avoided the bullies, which initially I did, or you had to fight them, which gradually I resorted to.

As previously mentioned, I also grew up in Easton which had a tough multi-racial presence. You had to be able to look after yourself or know people who could look after you. I found those early years tough going.

I recall a family who lived at the bottom of our street. They were notorious for bullying and violence. I would try to avoid walking down the street on my own at any costs and would take a longer route just so I didn't bump into them. Normally, this worked okay but other times, you would get caught out.

Once I was walking down the street and couldn't see them hanging around by their front gate, which they normally did to intimidate anybody passing by. I thought to myself, "Great, I will be okay today." As I was physically and mentally relaxing, three of the boys walked around the corner. I saw them early and crossed the road, but they had spotted me and like a pack of wolves crossed the road as well and headed me off.

I was pushed against a wall. They closed in on me. "You need to pay us to walk down this street," one of them snarled. I smiled, thinking that it was a joke. The punch in the mouth that I received for smiling told me it wasn't a joke. "You think it's funny, do you? Give us your fucking money!"

I only had fifty pence on me. Not a fortune but, hey, it was mine. I was on the way to buy my weekly comic and a few sweets. So, I told them that I didn't have any money. Seemingly, out of thin air, I was suddenly looking at a ten-inch carving knife pointing at my stomach. This crazy bastard must have just lifted it from his kitchen, as it still had the remains of what looked like steak and kidney on the blade. I was roughly searched and relieved of my meagre pocket money. "You come down here again and we will do the same, got it? Next time, we'll fucking stab you."

They waited whilst I walked back up the street, after receiving a sharp kick up the ass to reinforce what they said. They continued shouting threats and abuse at my back. I was glad I was still in one piece, albeit with a sore mouth, but I was more humiliated. I fucking hated those kids with a passion. I would lie in bed at night and fantasise about destroying them. I would picture myself armed with superhero powers and blasting the bastards to oblivion. I invented the most ingenious ways of killing the motherfuckers. Some of my thoughts amazed and shocked me at the same time!

I didn't want to live in fear of them or anybody like them, but I didn't have the confidence or the fighting skills to deal with them. So, I became very good at avoidance.

There was another horrible little fucker that used to prowl around my neighbourhood. He was another bully. We had crossed paths a few times, but I had always managed to get away unscathed.

One day, I was coming home from school and had been on a school trip. In the bag that I was carrying was an empty sandwich box and an empty Corona lemonade bottle. It was one of those old-school glass jobs.

This bastard stopped me and demanded I show him what I had in the bag. Now, on that day I don't know what was different about me, but I guess I saw through this kid for the first time. Standing right up close in my face, he didn't seem so big or frightening. He demanded again to see what was in the bag or he would 'fill me in'.

I took my bag off my back and opened it. I took out the lunchbox which he threw on the ground and asked what else I had. I took out the empty bottle informing him that was it. His face twisted into a look of pure hatred. "I'm going to fucking smash you in," he screamed. I didn't fancy the sound of that, so I hit him on the side of the head as hard as I could with the chunky lemonade bottle. BANG! It just happened. No real thought process. Down he went like a sack of shit. Hell, that is being disrespectful to a sack of shit! He hit the pavement now screaming in pain and no doubt, surprise. I was tempted to give him another shot, but I 'legged' it instead. After all, I wouldn't have got the cash refund on the bottle if I had broken it!

From that day, he never gave me any trouble and the word went around that I was not to be fucked with. It was a small victory for me, but I still hated confrontation and violence. As one arsehole disappeared into the horizon, there always seemed to be another one ready to take his place. As Clint Eastwood's 'Dirty Harry' might say, "Too many arseholes, not enough bullets."

At school one day, I got into a bit of a playground scrap with another lad who was bigger than me and a bit of a bully. Here, I learnt my very first lesson about pressure points, although at the time I didn't have a clue what I had done.

During a standing struggle, he was attempting to apply some sort of crude strangle or headlock upon me when I managed to pull free and swung around and quite by chance, I 'clocked' him one with the back of my fist on the side of the neck.

I saw the shock register on his face (he must have also seen the bigger shock on mine!). I, then, saw pain register and that closely followed by fear. He held his neck as his face paled and mumbled something about 'next time' and wandered off on rather unsteady feet. I never really had much more trouble out of him after that episode. I didn't realize then that I had used an attribute so often taught in martial arts systems.

When I hit him, it wasn't because I had suddenly become bigger, stronger or harder. That wasn't the reason that made him back off. It was because I had hit (totally by accident) on a vital point on his body (the carotid artery) that hurt and confused him and he didn't fancy getting another! What a stroke of bloody luck for me!

Years on, in my martial arts journey, I began to learn about weak spots, vital points and pressure points. I began to understand that, no matter how big or muscular a person is, these areas are vulnerable on everybody.

I was curious and enthusiastic to learn as much as I could on this topic, as most of the people I began to encounter in my life were larger than me. More on this later.

I did find some respite from my fears and disadvantages by getting a chance to play in goal for my school. As I mentioned earlier, I had no fear of diving around, so I did quite well and was picked to be goalkeeper on many occasions. Amazing how one bit of talent can make people forget about your other shortcomings. The hours up the park with my dad had certainly paid off. But inwardly, I felt slightly cheated when some of my mates were picked constantly for the school football, rugby, cricket or athletic teams. I felt it could have been me but for different circumstances.

I grew to live with my problems. I found balancing on the right leg hopeless, kicking a ball useless and things like climbing extremely difficult. I was ever conscious of these facts. To cap it all off, I also had three bad injuries to the right ankle during my school days, which further weakened the leg and caused more problems. I have fractured my ankle, torn the ligaments, broke toes and sprained it countless times.

On one of these occasions, I jumped off a high wall whilst being chased by a gang of lads. I landed badly and struggled to regain my feet. As the gang got closer, I waited for the inevitable 'kick in', but I was spared, as my two mates that were with me at the time came back for me and dragged me to safety like an injured soldier on the battlefield in Vietnam! I had badly damaged my ankle. These weren't to be my last injuries to my ankle either. In recent times, I cracked the bone in the right foot trying to escape a foot lock. A very painful experience, I can tell you. Foot locks suck if you are on the end of them.

I was never what you could call a constant target for bullying at school, but I did experience it on more occasions than I care to remember. Being small for my age didn't help and bigger kids thought they could take advantage. I still lacked confidence and self-belief. I still hated confrontation. I hate bullies even to this day. Later in life, many made the mistake of misreading me and paid the price. At school, for all my problems, I was a bit of a joker and enjoyed a laugh. I certainly could have achieved a lot more in my schooling, but I was too easily led into other things. I was never a troublemaker, more of a joker.

My reports always read on a regular basis, 'Could try harder', 'easily distracted', 'could do better', etc. I liked English and Art. These subjects, funnily enough, helped me considerably later, and I trained myself to make reading become a habit, which I am so glad I did because reading can open a treasure-trove of information. As someone once said, I can't recall whom, "Books give a soul to the universe, wings to the mind, flight to the imagination and life to everything."

Over the years, I have re-educated myself by reading. I read just about anything of interest I could get my hands on, particularly martial arts and fitness. I am proud of that fact. I also never dreamt I would end up writing magazine and internet articles and then, books.

Apart from the subjects mentioned, I didn't really have much interest in school. I just lived for the day and never really looked further than that. I hated homework and preferred to be in the back garden recreating another cup final or hitting my punch ball. I was quite smart when I put my mind to it but only if the subject interested me!

At fourteen years old, coming rapidly towards the end of my school career, I didn't really have an idea what to do and just drifted along quite merrily. I was concerned that I was small for my age and also, I became more aware of my body (in more ways than one) and I decided I wanted to build it up. I inwardly believed that a few muscles would get any bullies or piss-takers off my back.

I persuaded my dad to pay for the old Charles Atlas dynamic tension body building course. Remember the adverts in the comics of the bully kicking sand in the wimpy kid's face? Then, this lad would take the course and build himself up and then go back to the beach and 'chin' the bully. I fancied some of that!

The exercise programme arrived through the post every month and I worked hard at them. Did it transform me into Arnie? No, but what it did do was spark my desire to train, and this simple little course changed my way of thinking forever.

I wanted to be tougher and stronger, and I decided to do something more about it. I was determined to succeed. Now, a mate of mine, Robert Shepherd, told me that he was going to join a local gym in Bristol called the 'Empire Club'. This gym was one of the first and original in Bristol. It still exists today as the 'Bristol Boxing Club'. Back then, it was a typical spit and sawdust gym. No fucking power plates, spin bikes or fit balls in this place. If you had walked in the gym sporting Lycra, you would have been leaving again sharpish via the nearest window. It was home for body builders, weight and power lifters and it also had a boxing gym where a young Chris Sanigar did his training. Chris went on to have a successful professional boxing career and later, as a promoter. Olympian weight lifters, Precious McKenzie and Newton Burrowes, were big names in the gym around this time in the mid to late seventies. It was a place of many weird and wonderful characters. All very exciting for a young, wide-eyed lad, I must say.

There were some very tough characters in the gym. Also, there was a good deal of racial tension. It was a melting pot of cultures. Many got on well together and many didn't.

It wasn't the sort of gym to fuck about in. If you were there, you were there to train, otherwise you would be asked to leave or if that failed, you were chucked out. There was no shortage of takers for the chucking-out job. The place was full of big guys, street fighters, doormen and powerlifters.

Although these guys were hard men, if you showed a genuine interest in training, some of them were happy to give you advice and their time. I learnt much just from being around these men and listening and watching what they did.

I was certainly keen to join and I told the then owner, Dennis Welch, that I would try and get the money together to pay the membership fees. Dennis was a good man, but also scary. He didn't have any nonsense in his gym and would have no problems sorting it out if he did. His son, Kevin, was also a very accomplished and respected Olympian weightlifter. I have some great memories of training there, and some nightmare ones. More about the 'Empire' coming up later!

During this period in my life, I suddenly came across somebody who would set about changing me for the rest of my life. I didn't realise the impact and influence that he would have on me but he did big time. This was the start of my martial arts journey. 1975. What was the name of the man that started me on the road? The one and only: Bruce Lee, of course.

'From little acorns, mighty oaks grow.'

Kung Fu Fighting

I was in the changing rooms at school before a PE session when I noticed a group of lads huddled around reading something. Hold up, I thought. It must be another one of those girlie magazines doing the rounds again! As I drew closer, I heard gasps of amazement and voices exclaiming, "Look at that body" and, "Wow, I never realised you could do that!" Getting a little excited, I thought, this is one of those girlie magazines! But no. As I peeped over one of the lad's shoulder to get a look at what it was that they were raving about, I saw something very different to what I expected. I saw images of this small, incredibly fit-looking Chinese man performing amazing kicks and strange-looking postures. I asked who this man was. Bruce Lee was the reply.

I can't recall having heard his name mentioned before this time and this was after he had, unfortunately and tragically, passed away. Surely, I should recall his funeral on the news or pictures in the newspapers? But I couldn't. Sadly, I only got to really know about him after his death.

So here I was suddenly transfixed, looking at this magazine. Incidentally, it was called 'Kung-Fu Monthly'. Remember the one that used to open out into a poster of Bruce. I'm sure that all of you seventies martial arts veterans will recall it!

I wanted to read it fully, but the lad who owned it had already promised it to another three guys first. So, I had to wait my turn. My turn came the following Friday, which was good because I got to bring it home for the weekend. I read every inch of it, absolutely amazed that this little man had such speed, power and ability. Before this, I just presumed that you had to be a big, well-muscled guy to look after yourself, as portrayed in all the films and TV shows. But here was somebody different. It gave me hope. It gave me purpose. I knew then and there that I had to practise Kung-Fu and I wanted to be the next Bruce Lee (yes, I was young and naïve), but that wouldn't dampen my enthusiasm.

Up to this point in time, which was 1975, I had heard very little about martial arts. I had seen snatches of judo on the television and little bursts of karate in some films (mostly badly demonstrated). But after discovering kung fu, martial arts seemed to be popping up everywhere. This was the seventies' kung fu boom.

The TV series 'Kung Fu' starring David Carradine arrived on TV! More magazines and books began to appear in the shops. Remember the Bruce Tegner series of books? The record 'Kung Fu Fighting' shot to the number one spot in the music charts and everybody who ran the local Chinese takeaway was a secret kung fu master. It was crazy but exciting times for me.

I remember Bruce Lee's film, 'Enter the Dragon,' playing at a local cinema and I just had to see it. The film was an 18 certificate and I, of course, was only fourteen! So, on went the platform shoes and big overcoat, two weeks' worth of bum fluff on my chin making me apparently look older and away I went. Amazingly, I got in to see it! The film was on a double bill with 'Freebie and the Bean,' starring James Caan who, incidentally, is also a fanatical martial artist.

I sat through that film, the commercials and the interval without moving. I didn't risk going to the toilet or buying a drink in case somebody suddenly discovered I wasn't old enough and threw me out.

When 'Enter the Dragon' eventually came on, I sat totally transfixed. To see my hero on the big screen was an incredibly exciting moment. Bruce Lee had a screen presence and charisma that I personally don't think has ever been equalled in this genre of film. Even now, when I watch one of his movies, his screen presence and class just shines through. When I exited the cinema, I was in a daze and I walked home in a trance. The film had been everything and more to me, and I was completely sold on martial arts. I wanted there and then to take on a gang of bullies with a series of chops, kicks and blood-curdling screams. I wanted to rip off my shirt and expose the lethal claw marks on my muscled torso. Shit, I wanted to join the Shaolin Temple! I was well and truly a convert. I might even start enjoying a Chinese takeaway!

I was absolutely determined to start training and when I saw an advert in my local newspaper for a kung fu class starting soon in my home city of Bristol, I knew I just had to go. I persuaded my mum to lend me the money for my first session and away I went at fourteen years of age into the unknown.

Unfortunately, the first experience of kung fu came to an abrupt halt when after the first session; the instructor told me that if I wanted to come back next week, I would have to bring a twenty-five-pound joining fee. That was a lot of money in those days and my parents couldn't afford it. Plus, they were apprehensive, as the national newspapers had run a few articles about bogus kung fu instructors taking joining fees and then disappearing into the night! So, I never went back to that class. But I did remember and practise the moves I had been shown.

About six weeks later, another advert appeared in the local paper. Once again, a new kung fu class was being opened in a church hall in the centre of Bristol by the bus and coach station.

Again, I asked my parents if I could go, and they finally agreed after my constant nagging. This time, the experience was altogether different. The club was looking for new members, but it had already been established for a while. When I entered the hall, there was a small group of people waiting. We could see the class through the open door and it looked great. It was mostly guys, all in black gis with various coloured sashes around their waists, practising their moves.

The system was a Southern Shaolin style called Pak Mei (White Tiger). It was very little known outside China. The instructor was Sifu George Taylor from Birmingham. He had classes all over the country and travelled down to Bristol on a Friday for this class.

I found out, as time went on, that Sifu Taylor was the 'real deal' in this art and was certainly no paper tiger. His training was very tough and extreme. Currently, you wouldn't get away with it. On reflection now, some of it bordered on barbaric! This type of kung fu was not some 'wishy washy' system. It was designed for combat.

On seeing the class, I was eager to join. This time, there was a modest membership fee for which you got a black t-shirt and black gi bottoms and a membership card. "Come back next week," I was told, "and you can start." I couldn't wait.

The next week, I was there and ready to go. A few of my schoolmates had also said that they would start, but at the last minute, they let me down. My best mate, Robert, had decided to join the 'Empire Club' after all, and he went on over the years to win umpteen weight-lifting championships at school and senior level. He even lifted for Wales in the Commonwealth Games. He practically lived at the 'Empire' and the then owner, Dennis Welch, treated him like another son.

It all got a bit much for Rob later in his career. It was too much too soon, I think, and he gave it all up for a time. I feel that he had the potential to be an Olympic champion if he had stuck at it. He was very good and we had some tough times at the 'Empire' together, which I will outline shortly.

So basically, I was now on my own and the youngest guy in class. But although part of me was scared shitless, the overriding need to do this outweighed the fear. I was in and going to see it out whatever it took.

Those days, the training was basic and hard. The class ran from six p.m. to nine p.m. The first hour was pure conditioning. Hundreds of standard and bouncing knuckle press-ups on the wooden floor, sit-ups, leg raises and deep knee bend squats. These would be repeated in cycles.

Being a young lad, my muscles used to be screaming with fatigue. I can remember being at the back of the large class one week. My position was right by a table where Sifu Taylor's wife collected the weekly fees. Under the table, lay her two dogs. I don't recall what breed they were, but they were big and ugly! I swear that every time I stopped doing a push-up or a sit-up, they would growl directly at me, as if to say, "Get on with it, you lazy bastard, or we will tear your throat out!" I tell you, there is no better motivation to keep going than when your head or ass was so close to those dog's teeth! Other training would involve hard body conditioning and continuous blocking to condition the forearms. Sometimes, I left the classes and my arms were purple. I would have a job to hold a pen or a knife and fork for days after. Also, you would be kicked around the legs and punched and kicked in the body. This was all to build up physical and mental toughness. This was not too bad, unless you ended up with a partner who had no control! Sparring was rough and brutal, and I used to initially dread it, but I suppose that after numerous beatings, your ego and fears diminish. For a young lad, fighting grown men was a tough experience, but I kept coming back. Black eyes, nose bleeds and a kick in the bollocks were standard in these classes.

The class was filled with many weird and wonderful characters. All wanted to be the next Bruce Lee. Some nights, there would be sixty or seventy people crammed into the hall, sweating and shouting, going through punches, kicks and strikes up and down in lines.

Another one of Sifu's little ploys was to start the class off with a 'little run'. Now, bear in mind that the venue was close to the main Bristol city centre and nightlife, and that most people on a Friday evening were in town for a drink and a night out. Next minute, they would see a group of 'black pyjama' clad men running along with kung fu badges emblazoned on their uniforms. They didn't know whether to be frightened or laugh. Personally, I kept tight in the middle of the group to save ridicule or getting the shit beaten out of me! Nobody really wanted to be separated from the herd. Oh, I forgot to mention that Sifu liked you to do the run in bare feet!

Circuits were another love of George Taylor. We would do an hour of this, running from station to station in the hall. The stations were all different. Punch bag at one, kick shields at another, free-weights, callisthenics and partner drills, etc., etc.

At one end of the hall was a stage with steps leading up one side and down the other. One trick was to run up those stairs with a partner on your back or shoulders and come down the other side. Now, I had a job to get somebody on my back, let alone climb the stairs! Plus, my bad leg was just too weak. A few times, I tried and failed miserably. It became my nightmare every time when circuits were mentioned, and I dreaded it. All those feelings of insecurity came flooding back, which I hated. But there were some good guys who helped and encouraged me. It was good of them to spend time with a youngster.

One guy, whose name I can't recall, became my training partner. He only had one arm and had a special light weight metal one made so he could do his moves and his push-ups. I really admired his resolve and spirit to train and if he accidentally clocked you with his 'bionic arm', you certainly would know about it! Much later in life, I had a senior black belt in my ju jutsu system called Darren Sim who also had one arm, but you just wouldn't realise it as he adapted so well to techniques and would also box and wrestle competently. He is also an accomplished and high-ranked aikido instructor in Bristol at the Templegate dojo.

Sifu Taylor used to keep dreaming up different drills for us to test ourselves. Another one of his tortures was to pile up a small stack of metal-backed chairs and get us to practise high kicks over the top of them. As we became more proficient, he would add another chair. This all had to be done in bare feet. Many a toe was stubbed, foot smashed or shin cut doing this demanding drill (I can personally testify to all the above injuries). Also, he would get you to try flying kicks over the chair backs. This was another of my nightmares, often ending in a tangle of metal, arms and legs. For all this, I enjoyed the classes! They certainly sparked my interest in fitness, built my confidence and gave me a chance to practise my beloved kung fu.

Sifu Taylor was a good instructor and he had a few good senior lads as well. Two bright and up-and-coming stars were the Davies twins, Andy and Chris, who have gone on to very high achievements within the world of taekwondo and kickboxing. Andy, ironically, now runs his 'Elite Black Belt Academy' out of my own 'Impact Gym'. We have hooked up again after many years. It is a funny, old world. We will have a laugh and reminisce about those early training sessions.

Another episode that sticks out in my mind vividly was when we would all run through punches, kicks and stance work as a class. Sifu would halt you in your stance and come around to check your posture. He was brutal and unrelenting in kicking or sweeping out anyone's legs if they weren't in the right position. I must admit that I didn't like or agree with this, but this was how it was done back then.

One night, we were all brought to a halt and Sifu began walking around the lines. He started at the back of the class and worked his way forward. That evening, I was at the front of the class (at least I was away from those bloody dogs!). I could hear bodies hitting the wooden floor like skittles. You daren't look back. You just had to wait and sweat. I could hear him getting closer. I heard a grunt and a slam behind me as another one bit the dust! Next to me were a young couple that had started that evening. They were husband and wife, I believe.

They were standing, understandably, in the wrong posture, but then again, it was their first night. I felt sorry for them, but I had more important things on my mind like avoiding a trip to the floor myself. Suddenly, Sifu appeared by my side and then proceeded to circle me like a big fucking panther. Could he sense the slight tremor in my body? I hoped to God that my legs would not shake. I tell you, I was so nervous that you wouldn't have been able to slip a cigarette paper between the cheeks of my ass! I gritted my teeth waiting for the impact. I had been there before. But no, he had moved on. I breathed a sigh of relief. Then he was by the young lady who had started that night and without a word, he just swept her leg out and she crashed to the floor in a heap. Her husband looked down at her, and then at Sifu Taylor, and for a moment, I thought that he was going to have a go at him, but I think that something in Sifu's eyes made the man change his mind.

These were tough times in martial arts classes. The fighting was hard. No pads or protection, not even a condom! As mentioned previously, black eyes, cut lips and bruised ribs were commonplace. Being kicked in the balls or the stomach was an occupational hazard. Beastings were administered with no quarter given or taken. There was no insurance. You didn't have water breaks and you didn't fucking whinge, no matter what happened to you. Also, you didn't question Sifu. This would have been sacrilege. If he told you to jump off the roof, you did it.

I am not saying this was right or wrong. I am just telling you that this was the way it was back then. In this day and age, you can't touch another person without a lawsuit being thrown at you. You didn't train in these places for a bit of a laugh. You either knuckled down and took it serious or you were told to fuck off, or words to that effect.

How times have changed. Now I see people strolling onto mats late or wearing baseball caps or beanies on their heads and addressing their instructor as 'mate' or 'pal'. There is no fucking way you would have done that back in those days. Personally, I still don't have it now! You would have been told to get out of the club, or you would have had the shit beaten out of you.

Martial arts discipline was akin to army discipline. After all, they were originally arts of warfare. This type of training as a young man did me no harm. It forged my character and I believe that there should be more of it today.

The kung fu class stayed open for around two years until, unbelievably, the numbers dwindled from around seventy members to a dozen. The would-be Bruce Lees had gradually fallen by the wayside as the training got tougher. It just wasn't profitable for Sifu Taylor to travel all the way from the Midlands any more. He did give us plenty of notice, but it was still a big disappointment when he left. I had reached orange sash, which was the third grade, and I felt that I was really beginning to get the hang of things. I was fifteen years old now, and school was ending. I still had no direction in what I wanted to do for a living. Those Friday night training sessions were all I cared about.

I can recall a funny incident around this time. Every week, I would get a bus back home after training, and I would usually end up with the same driver. He was a nice black guy, who always spoke to me and had a bit of a laugh. One night, he asked me where I went every week with my training bag. I told him, "Kung fu classes." He replied that he didn't rate all that oriental stuff, he liked boxing. But I, of course, begged to differ. He wanted to prove his point, and as if from 'Enter the Dragon', he uttered the famous line, "Show me some!" So here we are facing each other in the aisle of the bus. Being the first stop, the bus was empty, except for a couple of 'old dears'. He came at me like a boxer, and I lashed out a series of roundhouse and hook kicks, the last one catching him lightly on the face. "Whoa! That's enough, man. You've proven your point," he said, and we laughed and shook hands. I don't know what the old ladies thought of our impromptu sparring session, and now I look back and laugh. I can't believe we did this on a bus!

When Sifu finally left the club, about eight of us decided to stick together and hire the training hall and just carry on practising until something else showed up.

So, we started pooling ideas. The Davies' brothers had been doing some judo, so by digging out a few old mats, we started to combine a few throws and a bit of groundwork. It was genuine fun and kept us training.

I was beginning to get stronger in the last six months, and had also taken an interest in wanting to use weights. A few of us at school, with the help of Rob, had persuaded the PE teacher to let us go to the 'Empire' club in our games period. Now, we were too young to body build, so we had to learn weightlifting instead. This didn't work out how I thought it would and I ran into more problems.

"Slow progress is better than no progress at all"

Another Direction

As I mentioned in the previous chapter, when I went to the 'Empire', I really wanted to build my body up and increase my strength to aid my martial arts training. Dennis Welch, the owner, told me that I had to be sixteen years old to enter the bodybuilding gym, but learning to weightlift would be fine. At the time, I thought if I was working out with weights, it would be all right. So, each PE period I went to train.

Dennis wanted me to compete in competition, but it was not what I wanted to do. He had seen Rob begin to do well and thought I might be interested too. Instead of speaking up and telling him what I thought, I just got roped along.

The weight rooms were separate to the main gyms. I remember going down an alleyway and downstairs to a basement where the gym was situated. One senior lifter commented that this gym was separate so that your screams couldn't be heard by the rest! At first, I thought that it was a joke. I was in for a shock!

Training consisted of strict lifts with a barbell. Clean and press, squats, dead lifts. Then, you had to practise the two competitive Olympic lifts. These were the Snatch and the Clean and Jerk. I found out straight away how weak my right leg was, and I struggled terribly with my balance.

Competitive weightlifting requires great technique and balance, and I had major problems. Try as I might, I just couldn't get the lifts right, and a part of me was saying, "I don't really want to be doing this anyway". The sessions became a nightmare, particularly if any of the seniors were training in the gym. They would deride sadistic pleasure from putting us youngsters through torturous routines. For example, making you squat with a barbell until your legs were like jelly and you couldn't stand up properly. Even then, they would make you carry on until you collapsed under the weight and they would just about snatch the bar off you. Also, if you couldn't do a proper lift without dropping the bar, they would put a heavy metal collar from the end of another bar behind you on the mat. You were then informed that if you fell backwards with the weight, you would crush your spine on the collar. Wonderful! This, of course, spurred you on out of pure fear. As you made your lift, unknown to you, they would kick the collar away at the last moment, but we naïve boys didn't realise this.

Dennis entered me for a competition in Newport about twelve weeks into my training. I told him that I was nowhere near ready, but he said that it would be valuable experience. That coming week, I had many sleepless nights and come the weekend of the event, I was a nervous wreck. The walk to the pick-up point for the competition seemed one of the longest in my young life, and when I arrived I saw the coach there waiting, I bottled it. I turned and walked back home. I told my parents the event was cancelled. Secretly I hated myself for lying to them, but I hated myself more for bottling it out. I felt a fucking failure.

I decided there and then to tell Dennis that I did not want to competitively weightlift, but when I was sixteen years old in a few months, I would like to return to body build. I shit myself having to tell him but, surprisingly, he understood. He realised my commitment to martial arts and said that it would be okay for me to do this.

As mentioned previously, the 'Empire' housed some weird and wonderful characters. Situated in a tough part of town, most of the guys who went there were hardcore trainers and fighters. When I returned and was able to work out in the main gym, I loved it. There were so many great people to give you help and advice, especially the old-timers that would tell you many 'secrets' of their trade and recommend a few 'special supplements' if you wanted them! This was all a big learning curve for me, good and bad.

The gym could sometimes carry a lot of racial tension. Many an argument or brawl would break out in there, as well as constant piss-taking. Problems such as non-payment of fees, sneaking into the saunas without paying, selling or indulging in illegal substances and thieving were so say dealt with not by police intervention, but a quick trip to the back room, accompanied by a few of the biggest lads in the club for a little attitude correction, so to speak. It was an educational experience for a young sixteen-year-old!

Here is an incident I recall. It illustrated to me back then that you can't judge a book by its cover.

In the gym was a rest area with tables and chairs and a TV on the wall. There was also a bar that served fruit juices, energy drinks and protein shakes, etc. A lot of the guys would hang around here after their workouts. The guy employed to work behind the bar could be described as nerdy, was not!

He was small and slight, wearing thick-rimmed glasses and sporting a classic 'teddy boy' hairstyle. He was always the butt of some joke or piss-take.

Sitting at one of the tables and had been taking the piss out of this little guy for some while. Again, they were confident in the knowledge that he was no threat and began pounding him. The bodybuilder was so shocked. He didn't know what had hit him! He fell from the chair that he was sitting on and hit the floor with 'Wally' clinging to him like a leech. 'Wally' continued the beating until two other big guys pulled him off the battered bodybuilder.

Everyone else stood silent in shock. Then, 'Wally', still breathing hard from his exertions, looked around at everybody present and announced, "Well, he just pissed me off!"

As illustrated here, sometimes, the false sense of confidence you can have believing your size is enough to handle situations can be sorely proved wrong.

Fitness training started to go hand and hand with my martial arts practice even to this present day. In the current age of hi-tech expensive health clubs, clubs like the 'Empire' still survive, and I think that anybody like me who took up fitness training in the seventies in Bristol, certainly trained there at one time or another.

As well as going to the 'Empire', I was still practising kung fu with the same group of lads. I now had a job so I could afford to visit the gym twice a week and train in kung fu.

So, as I earned my weekly wage, I went training. Life was simple at that stage. Incidentally, I got my first job after being sent out of a class for fooling around. Whilst standing outside, I decided to follow some lads on the way to the headmaster's office to meet a guy interviewing for some job vacancies. Ironically, from this episode, I got a job set up before leaving school. What a stroke of luck!

Just before I left school, the kung fu lads said that they had heard of a taekwondo class opening in a part of Bristol called Clifton. They were going to check it out and see what it was like.

Taekwondo was beginning to emerge then in '76/'77 as the next big art. I had seen some demos of it on television and was impressed by its powerful and flashy kicks. Again, I was a young man with stars in his eyes! The guys reported back. The class was good, and the instructor said that he would honour our present belt grades. His name was Thomas (Kin Man) Yau of the British Taekwondo Association. He was Chinese and had also, ironically, trained in the Pak Mei system as well.

Martial arts class. Thomas Yau was very good, and I can still remember his ambitious standards all these years on. Once again, I was lucky to have found a genuine instructor. Although he had accepted our grades, we felt that the others in the class resented the

42

fact that we had just waltzed in. We were to find out later that we were going to have to fight for respect.

Taekwondo was very different in its approach to what we see now. It was very traditional. Basics, Hyuns (katas), 3, 2, 1 step sparring and then free sparring. This was tough. No pads. No protection. Just get in and start fighting. We also had to endure loads of brutal exercises for leg strength and power. We would have to do lap after lap around this gymnasium with bunny hops and duck walks, interspersed with leapfrogs and jumps over a partner's back. When you completed this, it was on to kick drills one after another. Front, side, round hook, spinning, jumping, crescent, etc., etc., over and over.

Each class ended with free sparring. You would do this in lines. You face an opponent spar, and then when called, go back to your place in the line and move up on to the next opponent and so on.

As I mentioned, some of these taekwondo boys were out for blood and often drew it! But our previous training held up well, and we used to bring in a few unorthodox moves from our kung fu to favourable effect!

I regularly came up against my nemesis in the sparring. He was a big black lad who hardly ever spoke a word. He would impassively wait in line to spar. Every time that I closed in on him, he would spear me on the end of a wicked front kick with the biggest foot imaginable. This always reminded me of the scene in Bruce Lee's 'Game of Death' film where he fights Kareem Abdul Jabbar, the huge basketball player. Kareem hits Bruce with a front kick in the chest when he approaches him, leaving a large footprint on his yellow tracksuit.

Each week, he would catch and hurt me, and I would go away with sore ribs, planning revenge for the next time. What really pissed me off was that each time he caught me, I saw the glimmer of a smile on his lips and I didn't like that.

I must admit that I struggled with the high kicks in taekwondo. One reason was, as usual, the right leg. Balance and power were still a problem, and I mainly supported my weight on the left leg all the time. The second reason was that I began to question in my mind if I could really pull some of these flashy kicks off in real life. I was only five feet seven inches sparring six plus feet guys. The question for the moment was left unanswered.

One of my best kicks at the time though, was a spinning back kick. I could deliver this one hard and fast. I decided that this was my weapon to beat 'Big Foot'.

Next time we sparred, I deliberately let him catch me with his trademark front kick to drop his guard. As I moved in again, I saw him cocking the kick and that's when I dropped in my spinning back kick. It landed fast and hard and my nemesis fell to the floor faster than a premiership footballer being tackled! He lay there with a look of pain and surprise on his face. I must admit that I thought he was going to get up and go berserk. But no, he did regain his feet and congratulated me. Afterwards, we shook hands.

I had earned his respect and we became friends. In fact, after about three months of hard fighting at the end of the classes, all the kung fu lads had been accepted.

We were in, and I stayed with the class for twelve months before something else began to beckon me and grab my attention… No, not another martial art, but the dangerous combination of girls and alcohol!

"Real strength is internal, not external."

The Aikido Years

I finally left the taekwondo class, as my misgivings about the system came to a head. I was slightly sad about leaving behind some good mates, but I felt that there was so much more out there in the martial arts world and I needed to discover it. This was going to turn out to be a theme for me until I found my answers.

Again, I was without any club, but I carried on training myself and avidly read any material I could get my hands on concerning martial arts.

I still went to the 'Empire' and I also attended a local youth club. Remember those? At the club, I played many sports from football to table-tennis. I also did a small bit of boxing. It was nothing formal. There was a cardboard box full of old lace-up boxing gloves in a cupboard at the club, and my mates and I persuaded the youth leader to let us use them.

Each week, he would monitor boxing matches in a backroom between us. It was all very crude and normally ended up with a free-for-all and everybody being wrestled onto the floor. It was all a bit of a 'blood and snot' fun affair.

I can remember when the youth leader himself boxed with my mate, Rob, and Rob was taking a bit of a beating, so by an unspoken signal, the rest of us jumped the youth leader and gave it to him! For all the messing around, I did enjoy boxing and it would play a bigger part in my training later in life.

The youth club was church-run and we would travel and play football or table tennis against other youth clubs. It was at one of these I met a priest that was a good judo player. When he knew my interest in martial arts he shared on occasions his knowledge of throws and locks. His grip was incredibly strong and he had a handshake like a vice. This only whetted my appetite to know more about the grappling side of the arts. I don't recall his name but my mates and I secretly called him the 'flying vicar'.

I could imagine him in the confessional box saying, "Now for your penance you will say three Our Fathers, two Hail Marys and practise that osotogari more often!"

Obviously, at that age, you have a big interest in the opposite sex and looking for a girlfriend did encroach on my training time. Although I liked a beer, I wasn't massively sold on it as I knew I wanted to keep fit, so I didn't end up getting into the pub culture that a lot of my friends did. Deep down, the knowledge that I wanted to be a martial artist did keep me from not straying too far off the path.

When I started work, I befriended a guy called Alan who, at the time, was in his mid-twenties. He looked after me and became a mentor in various matters in my life. He had been a bit of a tearaway in his younger years and had been part of a motorcycle gang. When I met him, he was a lot calmer after getting engaged to a girl who worked in the office above the warehouse where we worked.

I used to talk about martial arts and Alan always said that it wasn't real fighting. We used to argue and it always ended up with a bit of a light-hearted scrap. Nearly every day, we'd end up rolling about but it was usually pretty much in good humour. He introduced me to the art of 'dirty fighting' and how to use a few weapons which really opened my eyes.

One day, I remember whilst working, Alan grabbed me from behind in a bear hug over pinning my arms. He was a lot bigger and stronger than I was, and I struggled to break out as he lifted me off the floor. In a desperate bid to break free, I got the soles of my feet up against the wall and pushed back hard. He flew back quickly, losing his balance and crashed hard to the stone floor with me on top of him. I immediately spun free as his grip loosened and went to pin him down when I noticed that he wasn't moving. He was spark out! Shit, I panicked. Suddenly, he woke up with a start and I was so glad to see him awake. What a relief. You think we would have learnt our lesson, but the next day, we were at it again.

Alan was a great friend. He helped me with work and gave me sound advice on life. Outside of work, I also had become friends with an ex-school colleague. Our history was a strange one together. We first met in primary school and for the first four or five weeks of meeting up, we beat ten bells out of each other every playtime! Don't ask me why! He took an instant dislike to me (amazing, I know) and I just fought back.

I never told my parents about this. I kept it bottled up. You didn't tell the teachers either. You just got on with things.

He was also of Irish parentage but from the south. It got so bad that our parents had to intervene in the end when Shaun's mother came knocking on our front door and the truth emerged. We were instructed to try and make peace, which we did and that was the end of the matter.

We grew up through primary and then secondary school together. We weren't really mates but reasonably friendly towards each other. Then, in one of the last school terms, a bunch of us were fooling around together and totally by accident, I threw a stone over a wall which hit Shaun on the head. He was on the other side and I didn't realise it. He did have a bad temper at times and he just went ballistic! I really was sorry and attempted to apologise as he came storming around from behind the wall. He piled in and started swinging punches at my head. I just froze with shock and he hit me in the head unanswered a dozen times or more until some other lads pulled him away. I tell you, I had more lumps on my head than a Picnic bar! I began to know how Humpty Dumpty felt! I had a job to rest my head on the pillow to sleep for a week! Again, I told nobody about this. I knew that I genuinely didn't want to fight him and had wanted him to accept my apology, but the other thing that bothered me was that I didn't bring any of the fighting skills that I had learnt into play. I had just frozen. I couldn't understand why and because I never confided in anybody at the martial arts club, nobody gave me any sage advice or help on this problem.

When we left school, the incident had been forgotten and not long after this, his mother suddenly died. Living so near, my own mother suggested that I go around to his house as he might need some company. I really didn't want to do this, but in the end, I made my way there. When I went into his house, we both felt awkward. But once we broke the ice, things got better. We started going out and about and within three months, we were the best of buddies.

It was on his suggestion that we tried a local martial arts club called the 'Bristol Budokan' and investigated a martial art called aikido. This was early 1977. Aikido was still pretty much an obscure art in most circles and not too much was known about it, particularly from my point of view.

Aikido focuses not on punching or kicking opponents, but rather on using their own energy to gain control of them or to throw them away from you. It is not a static art, but places great emphasis on motion and the dynamics of movement. Many years later, film action hero Steven Seagal would bring aikido to the public's attention in his films such as 'Nico' and 'Out for Justice' to name but a few.

The 'Bristol Budokan' was a legendary dojo in our town. I hadn't really noticed it before, yet it was only fifteen minutes' walk from my house. It was a large, odd-shaped, red brick building, three storeys high. The building itself was quite old. Originally, it was the humble base of the then fledging company 'Kleeneze'. Then, it became the Bristol Boys Five Club before a Mr. Ray Jenkins bought the building in the early seventies. Ray was a good judo man and so was his whole family. Various members of his family, I believe, are still practising and teaching judo today.

The building was purely for martial arts. Judo, Karate and Aikido. It had three matted floors. Also, it had a small rest area with toilets and showers. In the seventies, it was heaving with people training every night. Again, nearly everybody who practised martial arts in Bristol one time or another trained at the Budokan. Little did I know but the 'Budokan' would become on and off my spiritual home for many years to come. Today, it sadly no longer exists. It is now student flats. I pass by now and again and wonder if the students going in and out of the building know about its past rich martial arts history. I can almost hear the shouts and the thumping of bodies on the mats even now as I walk by.

The first day that Shaun and I walked in to the dojo, it was quiet. It was a Saturday morning. The place smelt of sweat and feet. A typical dojo. It was basic. Spartan, but an ideal place to train.

The first floor was empty. On climbing the second floor, we saw a children's judo class in operation. We asked the instructor if the Aikido class was on and he pointed upstairs. We turned to climb the stairs to the top floor. Shades of Bruce Lee's unfinished film, 'Game of Death', again.

When we reached the top floor, we saw half a dozen guys training. A small ginger-haired man broke away from the class and came and introduced himself as John Bennett. He told us that he was looking after the class while the chief instructor was in the States. He went on to explain about Aikido and invited us onto the mats to give it a try. Leaving our shoes and socks at the mats' edge, we went for our first taster of aikido. God, It was a disaster! It all felt so strange and different to what I had been used to before. I felt like I had two left feet and two right arms! We were shown classic Aikido techniques, which any seasoned practitioner out there will know with their eyes shut. Shihonage, Kotegeishi, Nikkyo, etc., etc. I struggled to get to grips with the subtle balance breaking, leverage and locks. At the end of the session, my brain had gone into overload and I am sure that John, the instructor, thought that we would never return. I was all for leaving it, but Shaun, again, convinced me to give it a month and see how I felt. There was another full class on the Tuesday and we agreed to go again. The Tuesday class was busier, and I was glad to note that we weren't the only novices. Alan Drysdale, the chief instructor, was back and John assisted him. We got on better. Not an overnight success, mind you, but then again, anybody who has trained in Aikido will know that it's not the easiest of arts to pick up straight away.

The small ginger-haired man, John, gave us great encouragement. John was a straight talker. A man's man. He was then in his mid-thirties. He was an ex-judo man who had also done his stint of national service. John became a massive influence on my life, a good friend and ended up my best man at my wedding years later.

Around this time, I will admit that my training became a little erratic. The urges to go out, chase girls and have a few beers were strong. It did disrupt my training and although I never gave it up totally, my mind was on another type of 'grappling'.

If Shaun and I had missed training in the week, we would go to the 'Budokan' on a Saturday morning and work out on an empty mat. Going through the aikido moves, bits of kung fu and taekwondo and now and again learning a bit of judo from a guy called Bob who was one of Ray Jenkins' black belts. We were all gung ho and thought we were 'the bollocks'.

One morning, I asked Shaun for a sparring match. The last time we had fought was in that one-sided fight in the school playground. I guess I hadn't really got over it and knew I now had the confidence and skill to get revenge! Yes, I battered him a bit, mercilessly until he said he had enough. Suddenly, I was overcome with guilt, looking at my mate in a heap on the floor and I picked him up. From that day on, we never seriously fought again. It was just young 'bucks' marking their territory.

We went back and did our month's training, and then we did another month. Although I kept up my punching and kicking, I was beginning to enjoy the close quarter techniques of aikido, and a few things were now beginning to make sense.

By this time, John had inherited the class as Alan had left to live in the States. This was good for me as I loved John's approach to teaching. He enjoyed the whole art of Aikido, but he did like to emphasise the more practical applications, and that was right up my street. Another John, who was of Polish descent, also assisted the class. I am afraid I don't recall his surname, but he went on in years to be a well-known figure in the Aikido world. Sadly, he has now passed away. He preferred the more flowing and Ki energy aspects of aikido, so the two Johns were really chalk and cheese, but at least you got to experience the complete art.

The classes were quite small, and soon, Shaun and I became regulars. It was nice to be part of a smaller group rather than just a face in a crowd, which I felt I had been in previous clubs.

I can recall now my very first demonstration. It was held in the Holiday Inn hotel, which is now the Marriott at the bottom of Bristol's famous Old Market Street/Castle Green. This must have been near the end of 1977. It was a big occasion and the cream of Bristol's martial arts scene was there. I recall a great demo by Bristol's Higashi Wado Ryu club and Bristol Lau Gar amongst others. I took part in the Bristol Budokan's aikido demonstration team. I was just sixteen years of age and I was shitting myself but in the same instance I wanted to do it.

We had to wait to near the end but it went well and I loved every minute of it. It's funny how you can remember these things so clearly years later and dozens and dozens of demonstrations down the line. Little did I realise in those early years the bigger stages that I would demo and teach on. Great memories.

Around this time, Shaun and I were both asked to help run a local youth club in the area. Earlier I mentioned that I had been part of one for some years. This club was for younger children and the two young ladies that ran it needed help with the boys. Some were getting out of hand and bored and needed some direction. We were asked if we could help. I immediately accepted the offer as I fancied one of the young ladies who ran the club. Her name was Tina and through time, with a little bit of messing about here and there, I finally plucked up the courage to ask her out. Doing this was harder than any sparring match I had been in, I can tell you! She was older than me by nearly three years and, at first, I didn't think she'd be interested. But when she said yes, I was gobsmacked. This was the start of a great relationship. We weren't just girlfriend and boyfriend; we were soul mates, kindred spirits and good friends. The relationship would blossom into marriage and we are still together, still great mates after nearly thirty-six years to date. Wow, that's some time. When we were going out together, I was training three to four times a week, and as our relationship became more serious, Tina decided if she wanted to see more of me, she would have to join the Aikido class.

So, she did join. Initially, she admitted that it was just to see me for another night but, in the end, she became hooked on martial arts too and became a very competent exponent herself.

Being the only woman in the class, she learnt to look after herself quickly and having been a bit of a tomboy in her childhood, she adapted well. Soon, she was just treated like one of the lads and she could give as good as she got. I can testify to this first-hand!

So, I was a happy lad. I was training now harder and more dedicated than ever before. I had a girlfriend who also trained and understood my passion for martial arts. What more could you want?

Around 1980, John told us that we were going to join the club to the British Aikido Federation. This federation was run by the Japanese; it was the Ueshiba style of aikido. Morihei Ueshiba as I mentioned earlier was the founder of aikido and although he had passed away some years previously, his son had taken over the mantle. The BAF had direct lineage back to him at the Honbu HQ in Japan.

When we joined, we were exposed to some of the best Aikidoists in the world. I was honoured over the years to train with many, many great instructors, Japanese, American and European, and learnt much.

Also, in time, I was fortunate to travel and train in Japan, the spiritual home of martial arts.

The BAF was very traditional. The syllabus was in Japanese and you had to learn to decipher it and speak it as well as practising the techniques. In our class, the only time you spoke English was 'hello' at the start and 'goodbye' at the end. It was extremely difficult and now seems in some ways so unnecessary. The belt system was also traditional. White belt until you obtained black and the ceremonial hakama (split Japanese skirt).

When you went on a seminar, there would be loads of white belts on the mat. Some could have been practising months; others maybe years. You had a job to initially know.

In Aikido, your first techniques are learnt from wrist grabs. This, we were told, was because you could detect a person's experience by their grip. If it was weak or tentative, they were a beginner. If it was strong and confident, the person was an advanced practitioner. Also, it came from its origins of Samurai ju jutsu, where the attacker was trying to stop a sword being drawn from the scabbard by holding the wrist. I found this a good method, although I also found many black belts would treat you like a five-year-old child if you weren't wearing a black belt as well.

We trained hard in this system, eager to be accepted and recognised. The leader of the BAF in England was Kanetsuka Sensei. He was a superb Aikido man. I first encountered him on a weekend seminar in Leicester in 1980 and was amazed by his speed, power and grace of technique. Up to this point, I hadn't seen aikido at this level and I knew I had much to learn. Over the next three years, I learnt plenty.

I was training week in week out religiously and going away on seminars nearly every other weekend. I travelled the length and breadth of Britain training. I trained in Oxford at Kanetsuka's private dojo; I attended National and International courses and experienced the best in the Aikido world.

Any of you reading this book that has practised Aikido will know the names of the following and recognise them as great Aikido men. William Smith, Gordon Jones, Terry Ezra, Tony Cassells, Arthur Lockyear, Mike Narey and so many more whose names I can't recall. I also was fortunate to train under dozens of Japanese instructors on some memorable seminars and with some greats such as Kisshomaru Ueshiba (founders first son) Koichi Tohei, Chiba, Saito, Tamura, Shibata, Kanetsuka – all absolute monsters of the Aikido world.

Those who know me personally will have heard me speak about Chiba Sensei. This man was/is a martial arts phenomenon, a true Budo

Master and a Samurai placed in the modern world. Just as karate has its legendary and revered Senseis such as Suzuki, Enoeda and Kanazawa, Chiba was one of Aikido's legendary masters. Sadly, as I write this book, I have learnt he has passed away at the age of seventy-five on June 5th 2015. A tragic loss of a true 'Samurai Warrior'.

Anybody who is anybody in the Aikido world will have known Chiba Sensei. Normally people's faces drain of blood when he was mentioned, and then there will be a story to tell. I managed to train under this legend on only a couple of occasions as he had moved from the UK to the USA. He was also recovering from a back injury from which doctors had said he would never train again. He did and he would visit Britain a few times a year. When I saw him in action, John, my instructor, informed me that he wasn't as fast as he used to be. Bloody hell! He looked a blur to me. If you can visualise Steven Seagal's Aikido in his early films and crank it up tenfold, we might be getting near! He was awesome for such a little man. When he arrived on the mats, he seemed to grow in stature and send a shockwave through the crowds.

When he first came to Britain, he had a fearsome reputation. In his classes, broken bones and blood on the mats were not unusual. On most large seminars, the Dan grades would proudly kneel at the front of the rows, waiting to be picked by the instructor to be their uke (a receiver of technique). When Chiba was the guest instructor, they visibly shrank inside and tried to make themselves invisible! When Chiba pointed to one of them and grunted a command, you could see them inwardly groan, as they knew they were in for a tough time.

I had heard countless tales about this man. About the time that two muggers decided to attack him as he came out of a railway station and steal his briefcase. He left them both rolling on the floor with broken bones. Or the occasion when giving a demonstration, he turned to speak to the crowd and his young and foolish uke decided to tap him on the head with his bokken (wooden practise sword). Chiba instantly spun around outraged and knocked him out. Also, I recall a humorous tale about the time when he sat in kneeling posture waiting over an hour for his class members to arrive. When they eventually strolled in late, he couldn't understand why they weren't hurrying. He angrily confronted the instructor and was informed that the clocks had gone back an hour the previous evening. Being relatively new to England, he hadn't known of this custom. The tales go on and on. I witnessed first-hand on a seminar how he made Kanetsuka Sensei look like a novice when he practised drills and techniques with him. It was a hugely humbling experience.

Although he had a reputation as being hard and harsh on his black belts, he was immensely gentle and controlled with the lower grades. I appreciated that at the time! This is the sign of a true master. I only wish that I had been able to learn more under him, but the chances were few and far between. His Aikido to me was the *real* aikido. He had learnt directly from the founder, Ueshiba.

Although people's images of Ueshiba may be as an old man with a white flowing beard, in his younger years his own aikido was extremely powerful and rigorous. Obviously in his eighties, he had to adapt and soften the practice.

One of Chiba's British instructors was William Smith. This man also had a tremendous influence on my training. He came from the West Midlands and was the head instructor for that area. He was an extremely powerful and dynamic Aikido man and a true gentleman. He even apologised when he hit you, which was quite often!

He, again, was everything that I believed a true martial artist should be and more. On the mat, he was very powerful but as a teacher, caring and always had time to help or talk to you. The same could be said when he was off the mats. I graded to my green belt under him and I owe him so much. Although I lost touch over the years, Tina and I think and speak of him fondly with upmost respect. I was shocked and saddened to learn some time later that he had passed away in 2006. He was an Aikido legend who was honoured by Her Majesty the Queen in 2001 with an MBE for his services to Aikido. The only person to date I believe that has got this award. I am honoured to have shared the mats with him and received his instruction.

I had personally progressed immensely in the couple of years that I had now been training in Aikido. I had not only experienced Ueshiba style but also Tomiki, which is a sporting version of Aikido that includes randori (free sparring) against knife attacks. I can remember training in a class and competing as a young buck with testosterone flowing and beating everybody in sight. I loved it, but I'm not so sure about my opponents!

I also trained in Yoshinkan style, which was used by the Japanese Police for control and restraint. This style is very direct and practical. At that time, I had so many experiences that sitting here now and writing this, I have a job to recall them all. I do know I was going through a 'proving' stage of my career and would go anywhere to train and mix with just about anybody. I did become a bit of a bully and I didn't have time for whingers or wasters. My motto was 'If you are on the mats and you've got the belt, then you take what's coming'. Mind you, I never dished out anything I couldn't or wouldn't handle myself.

I recall an incident that showed me how effective my training was becoming. One evening I was walking back from Shaun's house to mine. At the top of my street was a flight of steps that led down to my road. As I have mentioned it wasn't the best of areas to walk around in at night.

As I neared the end of the steps, two lads stepped out from the shadows. A streetlamp that normally burnt brightly at this spot was not working, therefore I didn't see them.

"All right, mate," said one of them. "Been out to the pub?" I guessed he wasn't really interested where I had been, he was just trying to get me to stop and converse. No doubt when I did, both would jump me. I carried on walking and replied I had been around to a mate's house.

"Hey, hold up a minute, I want to ask you something," he said. I kept on walking, my house wasn't far.

Then both ran up in front of me and stopped me. It was then I knew this wasn't going to end pleasantly. I felt the surge of adrenaline in my belly. I felt sick. I looked at the lad who was doing all the talking, and I then noticed the glint of a knife in his hand. They both moved forward. I knew I was going to have to react instantly and take the knife carrier out fucking fast.

Memories momentarily flashed back some years to when I was stopped in the same street by another bully with the knife who wanted my pocket money. This time it was going to be different.

"Give us your fucking wallet, cunt," he snarled. He pushed the knife towards my face. Although frightened, my training took over. It was like I was having an out-of-body experience. I felt strangely calm as I moved into action.

I applied *kotegeishi* (inner wrist crush) to his knife hand. I heard his wrist crack as he fell to his knees. I blasted the other guy with a reverse knifehand to the neck and he went down as well.

I didn't wait to admire my handiwork. I just ran like the wind for my house. My hands shook uncontrollably as I tried to fit my key in the lock. Eventually I managed it. Before I shut the door, I glanced up the street but all was quiet.

My parents were in bed, so I slipped up to my bedroom and laid in bed shivering. The aftermath of adrenaline was crippling but at the time I had no idea what I was going through. When I eventually calmed down, I did afford myself a smile. This stuff really works!

This incident helped me thrive in my training and I loved it. I just wanted to be on the mats.

I was used as uke and bounced all over the place by many top instructors and I thrived on it. Some of the Japanese Senseis really twisted your joints and threw you over with ferocious power, but I would always bounce back like the proverbial rubber ball. I was lighter and leaner in those days and very quick, so I just took what was coming. For me, this was my apprenticeship. I loved training and learning from these masters.

Sometimes I was told off or admonished for fighting on the mats or being excessive, but I was only looking after myself. If anybody came to train at our class at the 'Budokan' and I thought that they were a bit cocky, I was over there and ready to prove a point.

In Aikido, you trained not only in open-hand technique but Jo staff and Bokken, and I enjoyed them all. I had some great battles and knocked people down and out with all the weapons. I played no favourites. Looking back, it was just youth and you can't change what you have done. It was just the way it was at that period of my training, but I may have been a bit tough on some of my partners. But let me emphasise in my defence, not against beginners or lower grades than myself.

I also hated politics in martial arts and how it controlled certain aspects of training. For example, if you showed your face at the right seminar or summer school training camp, you were almost guaranteed your belt promotion, whether you were worthy of it or not. I also despised the idea of honorary Dan grades. Individuals who were awarded their black belt because they were of some financial importance to the Association, or they were Goffers with brown tongues that happened to be in the right place at the right time. Fuck 'em.

I couldn't get my head around the fact that other people, me included, were training long and hard through the grades, and these people were just given them. If I was on a seminar and spotted one of these said people, I would home in on them, and if they were training (which was a rarity), I would start sharing some of my pain with them. I just couldn't help myself! I saw the grading system clearly in black and white with no shades of grey whatsoever.

Other pet hates were some Dan grades treating lower grades like they were imbeciles. I would sometimes partner one who would presume that I was a complete novice and start explaining a technique in language a young child would understand, and then show me how wonderful they were by cranking the technique on me! I would wait patiently for the immortal words, "You try it now," and then I would go into turbo drive, smashing the technique on hard and fast. I loved to see the smug expression on their face change to one of horror and pain! A Dan grade is a measurement of your skills and certainly to be respected, but respect is like a girdle, it stretches both ways, and as a high grade, you shouldn't assume that you are God and everyone else is inferior physically or mentally. That is a bad mistake and one I have seen made umpteen times by instructors that are so wrapped up in their self-importance that they have disappeared up their own asses! Hey, don't get me started on this subject.

Anyway, by this time in my training, my mate Shaun had left the club but Tina was there with me and going strong, in more ways than one. We were engaged to be married, and on August 14th 1982, we tied the knot. As mentioned, John Bennett, my instructor, was my best man. He had become a valued friend and mentor, kept me on the straight and narrow path and gave me sound advice.

You can tell how fanatical I was about training. The Friday night before the wedding on the Saturday, which back then was the groom's stag night, I went training! Another instructor, Mike Narey, who had come down from the Midlands, was taking the class and was under strict instructions not to use me as an uke, as nobody wanted me turning up at the altar the next day with a black eye or an arm in plaster! I, of course, didn't know this and was progressively getting more frustrated throughout the evening, as he hadn't called me up for our ritual bashing around. Five minutes from the end of the class, he did call me up and gently showed a few throws. I was miffed. Only after class did he tell me what had been going on and we laughed. I was so young at the time that I didn't see any dangers whatsoever.

Anyway, I made it to the altar in one piece. Some people say that I got married young, and maybe I did, but I was happy with the way my life was heading and I had a girl who not only loved me but understood me and could have a bit of a scrap. I was in heaven. Why spoil it? I missed out on nothing and I don't regret a thing. I had two or three years of fooling about before meeting Tina and it wasn't anything special. I can take it or leave it. Because of my training, I wasn't into partying or clubbing. I'm glad I chose the path I did.

It taught me, at an early age, to be responsible. I had an obligation to look after my wife and work to pay off a mortgage. It made me set standards about how I wanted to live and this, in turn, ingrained my belief system and the ethics and code I thought I should be living by. Martial arts training only reinforced this belief.

It made me take responsibility for myself and my actions. It taught me to make no excuses and blame nobody else or anything else for my shortcomings. Basically, it made me stand up on my own two feet and take the good and bad that life can throw at you. I was happy to do that. It forged my character and self-belief. Trying to live a life of a warrior isn't all about being able to have a fight. It is about being a strong and caring character as well. Somebody people will look up to and respect. I wanted to be that person.

So many of my friends didn't take this option and ended up in trouble or just wasting their lives away. Also, now at fifty-four years old, I have done most things in life but a lot earlier, so I am reaping the benefits.

I am not up to my neck in a mortgage, bills or nappies, and Tina and I are getting our own lives back. Plus, I am young enough and 'handsome enough' to enjoy it! I am also a grandad and enjoying the experience.

If I'm asked how I like to unwind, then I have no better pleasure than, after a hard week of training, teaching and working, sitting at home with my feet up with my wife or family around and a cold bottle of beer in my hand, watching TV, reading or listening to music. Simple pleasures, yes, but priceless. As my friend Geoff Thompson once said, "When you train and work hard, a simple cup of tea can taste like sweet nectar."

I have many mixed memories about my later Aikido training. The good things were the comradeship that was built up in our small club and the support we gave each other; the not so good things were dreaded politics, internal bickering and power struggle.

A lot of special training sessions stick out in my mind. Going over to Cardiff to train on a blazing hot Saturday with Shibata Sensei, who was over in the UK visiting from Japan. I went alone and eventually tracked down the club by asking a policeman for directions. Now there's a novelty! A 'Bobby' on the beat! The club was in a disused warehouse in a decidedly dodgy area! We trained upstairs on a matted floor space and the session was going to be videoed. Along with the outside temperature being about eighty-five degrees and the sun beating relentlessly on the corrugated iron roof of the building, there were two large powerful lights focused on the mat for filming. Boy, did I sweat in that session. Shibata was a powerful Aikido man and we trained hard and fast. The canvas mat area was soaked with our sweat. You could have wrung a pint of water out of my heavy judo gi, but what a memorable session!

Travelling back to Bristol by train, I sat slumped in my seat, gulping bottled water as if it was going out of fashion to pacify my thirst. I was severely dehydrated and aching all over, but what a fantastic day! I sweated off about five pounds, and at that time, I couldn't afford to lose it.

Another session that stays in my memory was the other end of the scale from scorching hot to absolutely freezing. Occasionally, we would travel to a club in the Forest of Dean. This dojo was a long prefab type of building on the edge of the forest itself. We always seemed to visit in the winter when the forest was picturesque with the woodland covered in snow or frost. The dojo, though, was absolutely sub-zero. You had to train excessively hard just to melt the frost on the windows and soften the mats up. Eventually, your body warmed up but your fingers and toes stayed as cold as icebergs. Not ideal if you jarred them or if they got trampled on! As the steam from our bodies warmed the atmosphere, the doors would be opened and the watery winter sun would filter in, giving a golden hue to the mat. It was still bloody cold and those Welsh boys were tough buggers. Happy days!

As mentioned earlier, I trained under Kanetsuka Sensei on many occasions, but his training changed drastically over the years. When I first met him, he showed fantastic technique, but gradually, he changed and showed less and less. Instead, he made you do endless cuts with a suburi bokken (heavy wooden sword for developing grips and forearm strength) repeatedly in kneeling or low squatting postures until you lost all feeling in your lower legs and you would keel over. Sometimes, he would check your balance and posture by whacking you relentlessly on the back with a bamboo kendo shinai.

Also, we did loads of suwariwaza (traditional Japanese kneeling techniques). Sometimes, we did two-hour sessions without getting to your feet. This was bad enough on the canvas mats where you would burn layer after layer of skin off your feet and knees, but I also did this more than once with him on a wooden floor. Extremely painful!

We found out later that he had been diagnosed with cancer, and I think that it just changed his whole concept of Aikido practice. Thankfully, he got over this illness and is, as far as I know, still training and teaching.

But although the latter type of training developed tremendous character and spirit, it didn't do anything for my technique or progression. In the end, these relentless sessions just became survival and mental strength. This type of training would eventually lead to my dis-enchantment with the whole Aikido scene. After nearly five years training, because of political red tape, I was still only graded to green belt. Because I could not afford to pay the money to go on the Summer schools or Easter courses, I was getting overlooked. Kanetsuka played his favourites and if your face didn't fit, you weren't going to progress. Don't get me wrong, I wasn't the best of Aikidoists but after training as long and hard as I did for those five years, I certainly deserved to have progressed further. I know some people who have achieved a black belt within two years! Although gradings weren't the be-all and end-all for me, when I was on seminars, I saw people around me with high grades that didn't have half my ability.

I remember once doing my orange belt grading in front of Sensei Kanetsuka. It took nearly an hour. This was after doing a two-hour class with him beforehand and him throwing me around like a rag doll. He failed me and I was absolutely devastated.

Afterwards, he suggested that I come up to Oxford to practise in his special invite class. I told him that I thought you had to be green belt or above to do them, and he replied that I had his permission. I couldn't understand the logic.

Maybe because I didn't bow down to political pressure, I stayed where I was. But that's me. I've been like that in many areas of my life and probably held myself back because of it.

One hilarious memory, which didn't seem quite so funny at the time, was when I went to do a demonstration of Aikido with Sensei Mike Narey. I loved working with Mike. I would throw the attacks in hard and he would bounce me around. A perfect combination, I thought.

I toured around my home city of Bristol and over into Wales with him on and off over six months, with Mike using me to promote and demonstrate Aikido. I saw this as part of my apprenticeship, just as many martial artists have done when they were young men. It was part of the traditional Budo culture.

This night, we went to an evening class centre to give a demo. Mike had contacted them earlier in the day and asked if they had mats, to which they replied, "Yes." So, we were all set.

Entering the room, we found that they had plenty of mats. The only problem being that they were the type of mat you put down in front of the fireside at home! I protested to Mike that I wasn't falling on them, but somehow, he persuaded me. We overlapped as many as we could and he did the demo. I was thrown from pillar to post, sometimes landing on the mats, sometimes not. The watching group must have thought I was crazy. Perhaps I was! Afterwards, I was black and blue and Mike said, "Well, I think that went off okay." Fucking unbelievable! Mike is still around now teaching in Bristol. I liked and respected him very much. We had some fun times together.

These are just a handful of incidents from these years. I did so many training sessions, courses and demonstrations I just can't recall them all. But I had gathered a wealth of experience and knowledge. My training in Aikido really came to a head when we invited Kanetsuka Sensei down to Bristol for a weekend training course and grading.

I had been training for my second kyu blue belt now after achieving my third kyu green finally from Sensei William Smith. At the end of the second day's training, John brought forward to Sensei our licences and he looked at them to see who had passed us on our previous grades. It had been mainly graded by William Smith who, at that time, he didn't see eye to eye with.

He then looked up and told us that we were all going for high grades within Aikido, and this weekend he thought we couldn't do our basics, let alone attempt anything advanced. He asked us to think seriously about whether we were ready for this grade, and he called for a fifteen-minute timeout. Again, frustration set in for us. Every time we seemed to be making progress, we just got knocked back. It had been this way for every grading. I, personally, was at the end of my patience and told John that I thought we were being treated badly and it wasn't right. Tina voiced the same opinion, as did many others waiting to grade. John knew that things had come to a head. We returned to the mat and Sensei called, John first up to grade. I must say here that John Bennett was an absolute stalwart for aikido and as my instructor, first class. He had trained so hard and was only going for his first brown belt grading after having relinquished all past grades on joining the BAF and wanting to start with us from the bottom.

When John stood up on this seminar in front of about seventy people, I had no idea what he was going to do. He rose and said, "Sensei, I have thought long and hard about what you have said and I have decided not to grade." Kanetsuka was shocked and implored John to grade. But he was adamant and walked forward to retrieve his licence. This spurred me and others to follow and claim our licence back as well. We just lined up and took them. Kanetsuka was speechless. Only 'Polish John' decided to grade and successfully passed his brown belt. Maybe we would have as well. Who knows? We all left the mat and I, personally, never trained with Kanetsuka or the BAF again.

I knew now that our club would be splintered, and it would never be the same as it had been. I felt great loyalty to John, but I also knew it was time to move on and explore pastures new. The grading incident had been the straw that broke the camel's back, but there had been other issues as well.

I'm a practical man and loved the combat side of training but in the past year this was missing. I was young, eager, fit and wanted to test myself, so I had to leave.

Telling John this was one of the toughest things I ever had to do, and I agonised over it. He had become such a good friend and the club was like a close-knit family. I was about to lose that identity and comfort zone and go out on my own. It was scary but also exciting.

John understood. He didn't want me to go, but he couldn't hold me back. It was a sad day for Tina and I. John respected me for coming and telling him to his face instead of just disappearing. I wouldn't have done it any other way. I had too much respect for him, and that's why now I like people to speak face-to-face with me if they have any problems in my classes.

The Aikido journey was over. I had invested five full and totally committed years. It took some guts to drop five years training and start afresh, but I had been taught much and was no longer a raw beginner.

As I write this chapter, I find it hard to believe that I am the same person now. Those days are somewhat hazy, but, God, did I train. Everywhere and anywhere I would go. I just wanted to learn. Martial arts were now becoming more than just a hobby. They were becoming a passion. It began to consume more and more of my time.

I look back fondly on those days on the top floor mats of the Budokan. I really got a first-hand insight to what Japanese Martial arts were about and I am thankful for this.

The best things I personally took from my Aikido experience were great self-discipline, respect and spirit. The training had developed a decent work ethic in me and helped me also focus on other aspects of my life. It also gave me a deep understanding of the Japanese Budo culture and their warrior code and mindset. I loved training under the Japanese. I trained with so many, learning not only open hand Aikido/Aikijutsu but stick, bokken and Iaido (a weapons art associated with the smooth, controlled movements of drawing a sword from its scabbard or saya, striking or cutting an opponent, removing blood from the blade, and then replacing it back into the scabbard). I learnt a warrior's mindset and work ethic from these men.

Training was very hard. You practised one technique over and over, seeking perfection. Crunching wrist and armlocks were the order of the day. If you were thrown by the Japanese Sensei, you had better be good at falling; otherwise, something was going to break. Some of them showed no mercy. Training was repetition, repetition and more repetition. You never questioned it, you just did it. I witnessed many broken bones and was responsible for a few in a very tough era.

I loved the discipline and finding out just what the body and mind could take. The more you did the more you wanted to push on and on to the next level. It's a mindset that most will never reach.

Before I left school, I had toyed with the idea of joining HMS forces, but my parents weren't keen and persuaded me against it. I guess I was looking for the focus and discipline that comes with being a soldier.

I now think martial arts gave me that same type of focus. I loved to be drilled and pushed beyond what you thought you were capable of and my Japanese Sensei were good at that.

To learn directly from the main source, so to speak, gives you a sense of their proud history and traditions. You felt you were getting the authentic art, which only enhanced your whole experience of the Japanese Martial arts.

I have never lost these lessons and I would go on to need them all for the next leg of my journey.

"Traditional martial arts has given me discipline and respect, two admiral qualities that can in some cases be sadly lacking these days on the mats."

Hunting Down Ju Jutsu

As I have already mentioned, I loved the practical aspect of martial arts and as a young man, it was extremely important to feel that I could handle myself if the need arose.

I had begun to have reservations about the effectiveness of my aikido training on many occasions before I finally left training.

I recall a conversation that I once overheard in the pub between my instructor John and a guy that had recently started training. He was a good lad, but he also had had some real street fighting experiences. He asked John how he thought his aikido may hold up against a boxer in a fight. John replied that he thought a good boxer would probably be too much for the aikido man, as he didn't practise against boxing punches. I was gutted. Here I was training hard with belief in what I did, and then I heard this. I thought to myself, well, this isn't good enough. You need to know how to handle a boxer. Your chosen art should have the answers. I have always had an open mind to martial arts and had accumulated a great number of books on the subject, exploring all avenues. I knew there was much more to discover.

Also, I had concerns over the effectiveness of some of the techniques in the street. Over the years, I had witnessed many fights kick off and none, and I mean none, had the ritualised movements of martial artists. It was all fast, explosive and scrappy, ending up usually with both participants rolling on the floor. Aikido was a good martial art but it wasn't giving me all the answers I needed.

On reflection now, I realise that I had got caught up in the whole spectrum of the aikido world and had forgotten my basic interest, which was effective fighting technique.

During the aikido years, I still kept my interest in the punching and kicking arts. I was keen as ever on boxing and watched avidly some of the best fighters of that time on TV. Big names like Hearns, Hagler, Leonard, Duran, Holmes, Arguello, Pryor, McCallum and Chavez. I not only watched but also studied their technique. This was an era of champions, which I believe will never come around again in the boxing world.

I also had an interest in ju jutsu, one that had been with me on and off for some years. I first saw ju jutsu techniques in a magazine in the late 70s. Each month, this magazine (unfortunately, I don't recall its name) would have colour step-by-step photo strips of ju jutsu techniques demonstrated by the late Robert Clark and other giants in this art such as Richard Morris, John Steadman, Charles Allmark and Eric Marshall.

At that time, I had no idea who these famous jujutsu greats were. Then, I was more interested in kung fu. But later, when I got into aikido, I went back and studied these magazines with a different eye and saw some similarities in the arts. The jujutsu techniques seemed much more complete, with each move starting with Atemi-waza (vital point striking), then a throw or takedown, followed by some amazing joint locks or strangles.

To me, in that moment I realised that this was the missing link that I had been looking for up to now. It was the missing skills of blending striking and grappling arts together.

This art although I had heard it mentioned and seen a few snippets of it in old black and white films such as *'Bad day at black rock'* starring Spencer Tracey and *'Blood under the Sun'* starring James Cagney but it was all new to me.

Crazy really seeing the first British man to actually practise the Samurai Budo arts was a William Adams (1564-1629) and the first British man to bring ju jutsu to the UK was Edward William Barton (1895). I suddenly began to realise my new-found art was some two thousand and five hundred years old.

I believe most martial arts out there now in this day and age will have a link to ju jutsu in its past. It truly is the Granddaddy of all martial arts and rightly so. More on the history of ju jutsu later.

I began to seek out more knowledge about these great masters who really had been responsible for ju jutsu's rebirth in the UK during the earlier seventies. I managed to find some good ju jutsu books, which just whetted my appetite for the art, and when I finally left aikido, I knew where I was heading. I needed to find a ju jutsu class as soon as possible.

For a few months, I was in limbo and found it strange not to be training, but I am not one for letting the grass grow! I sent off for a martial arts directory (similar to the Yellow Pages) so I could scan the area for a ju jutsu class. When the directory arrived and I read through it, I discovered that there were no clubs near Bristol. The nearest was a club in Taunton, which is about fifty miles away. Their classes were on an evening and it just made it impossible to get there after a day's work and fighting rush-hour traffic.

I then spotted a ju jutsu club in London run by a Sensei Del Connelly. I had never heard of this man before, but I decided to write him a letter and explain my situation. These were the days long before email or text!

A few days later, I received a reply. He said that I was welcome to visit his dojo on a weekend and train free of charge. Sensei Connelly informed me that if this helped me into the martial art of ju jutsu, then he was happy to do this for me.

This was great news and a very generous offer. So, the following weekend, Tina and myself, along with two other friends who had also decided to leave aikido, Brian Barker and Mark Fortune, headed by train to London. We got connecting tubes to East Ham and tracked down the dojo.

We were warmly greeted by Sensei Connelly and ushered into his dojo. It was a smashing place. It had a large matted area, rows of punch bags and a small rest area.

Over a welcome mug of tea, we chatted and he told us that the day was ours and he would show us whatever we liked.

Sensei Connelly was a third Dan in Juko Kai Jujutsu under Professor Richard Morris of the British Ju Jutsu Association, whom I had read a lot about. Sensei Connelly is now a ninth or tenth Dan, I believe, and still active on the mats.

We were taken through some of the BJJA syllabus. I loved the freedom of being able to use strikes and combine these with much closer body contact throws than I had been used to in aikido. Also ground work and floor pins were new territory.

There was a young lad training there who was a yellow belt. Sensei Connelly demonstrated techniques on him. This lad's standard was excellent and I was told that he had been practising for a couple of years. I mentally made a note that if I was as good as this lad in two years, then I would be happy. Later, some other guys arrived to train. There was one big guy who was a black belt in Kyokushindokai karate. This style of karate was very tough, and they had a sporting element called 'Knockdown Budo' which was an early barehanded format of full contact fighting. Its founder was the legendary Mas Oyama who was revered for knocking out bulls with his bare hands!

This black belt introduced me to low leg kicks, leg blocks and shin roundhouse kicks. My legs were black and blue after half an hour. We then moved on to the bags and went through kicking and striking drills. Later, we practised ground grappling. I was in heaven!

Coming from five years of very traditional training, this relaxed and open style was a breath of fresh air. Plus, it felt as if I had the leash let off me and I could explore whatever I wanted. I loved every minute.

At the end of the day, we thanked Sensei Connelly for a wonderful time. He had been true to his word. He had showed us a wide range of skills and hadn't charged us a penny. He was a first-class ju jutsu man and I haven't forgotten the generosity he showed me all those years ago in 1982. On that day, he was instrumental in starting my ju jutsu journey. I thank you so much for your time.

Travelling back on the train, although we were all tired, we couldn't stop talking about the day. My mind was absolutely racing with ideas. I was totally committed to developing the stuff we had learnt, and I knew my long-term goal was to open a ju jutsu class in Bristol and eventually teach this art. I was a man on a mission. But as they say, Rome wasn't built in a day!

Ju jutsu and its development in Bristol became an all-consuming passion for me. I lived and breathed it. I was totally committed to the cause. It was going to be a huge task ahead of me, but I was up to it. I was excited and fearful of the prospect, all at the same time.

When we returned home, we decided as a group to find somewhere to train as soon as possible. Brian came up with a room at a community centre in an area of Bristol called Stockwood. We clubbed together and bought some cheap mats, and we were off!

We could only get the room once a week, so every Tuesday from seven p.m. to ten p.m., the four of us trained, working on ju jutsu technique, boxing, grappling and basically pooling our knowledge together. It was a time of experimentation, and it was embryonic stages of the ju jutsu that I would eventually teach. I was like a sponge soaking up knowledge from all available sources. I was totally obsessed on developing ju jutsu in Bristol. This became my major goal and I was determined to succeed. Nothing was going to stop me. It was an incredibly exciting time and my energy and drive knew no bounds.

A few weeks after our London trip, I received a letter from another instructor that I had written to. A Sensei Mike Marshall who was based in Southampton. He asked if I wanted to come down to train with him and see what his system was about. We were all up for this, so we made the trip. I didn't realise at the time, but Sensei Marshall would figure highly in my martial arts career for the next few years and would become my first proper ju jutsu teacher.

"Who said ju jutsu was a gentle art?"

The Wild Bunch

Sensei Mike Marshall was, to say the least, a bit of a maverick. He was unconventional in what he did, but I enjoyed my time associated with him.

His ju jutsu was different to what I had previously experienced up to then. Most of it was basic and simple with the emphasis on being workable. The reason for this was that Mike had taught his ju jutsu and close-quarter combat to HM Special Forces. He had been a member of the famed SBS as well as having worked as a high-level bodyguard.

My association with him was my first venture into what I like to call 'Applied Combat Martial Arts.' This man had walked the walk and talked the talk.

I enjoyed my first day's training and I got on well with Mike and his people. We had gone through a lot of techniques, and my colleagues and I had given a good account of ourselves, so we were invited to join Mike's association, which we accepted.

Mike ran two associations. The first was the Japanese Ju Jutsu Association, which taught pure combat ju jutsu. Mike's father had trained in Japan after the war and learnt his ju jutsu there, and he, in turn, had passed down the association to his son.

The other was the Great Britain All Styles Self Defence Association (GBASSDA). This was an umbrella association where all styles of martial arts would come together to teach and train in the self-defence and combative elements of their chosen system. It was a big melting pot to exchange ideas and techniques, and it worked very well.

GBASSDA was an early pioneering association for later ones that came along, such as the British Combat Association and Self-Defence Federation. Although now currently, we have many multi-styled organisations, back then in the early eighties, this was something new and radical. I was glad to be part of all of it. I gained a lot of experience during my time with them.

GBASSDA was made up of some weird and wonderful characters. The good, the bad and the mad (all were ugly anyway!). You had to sort the wheat from the chaff, so to speak, until you came across some hidden jewels.

Mike Marshall was an off-the-wall character whose past and experiences were shrouded in a bit of a mystery. Then, there were 'Mad Dog' Dave Vincent and 'Mental' Micky Upham – two tough ju jutsu men from Merseyside. Typical Scousers. Hard-training, hard-living guys with a profound sense of humour. I went on to train with both men some years later. We also had Dave Turton, one of the most experienced and knowledgeable combat men in the UK today. Dave still remains a good and much-respected mate of mine. He is known for his no-nonsense approach to training and his hard edge. Back then, his edge was a lot harder and his training sessions were tough. He taught Goshinkwai Combat, not only unarmed skills but single and double sticks, Yawara Bo, fighting knives and a whole host of makeshift weaponry. Dave is a fountain of knowledge on all things combat and I am proud to have trained under one of the UK pioneers of real combat arts. He now holds the rank of tenth Dan.

Another good mate was John McCartney from Belfast, Northern Ireland. He was another enigma. His lads and he would travel over to England by boat for every national course and would be decked out in camouflage and black woolly hats! He was a doorman in Belfast, but in the past he had worked as a mercenary, fighting in the then-named Rhodesia in South Africa. His system of CQC was very hard and brutal.

Next up was John Sheridan and Mike Middleton of the Aikido Research Federation. Both were good aikido men schooled also in Aikijutsu and Hakka Ryu ju jutsu. They asked me on more than one occasion to grade for my black belt in aikido. But I turned it down as I felt that would be going back in time and not forward. My thoughts are if you wear the black belt, you must have one hundred percent belief in the art you achieved it in.

Finally, was my now good friend, Jamie O'Keefe. Back then, he was a young, lean and mean karate man from Essex. He was very confident and outspoken in what he did and quite rightly, as he did it well. Jamie, of course, went on to be a renowned doorman and self-protection instructor in the UK and author of numerous books on the subject. He also owned and ran the New Breed Publications, who published all my early books. Jamie is a very knowledgeable man on the self-protection scene after having worked in frontline security for many years. He is genuine, down to earth and old school. I have much respect for him.

There were others also in the association, but I just can't recall their names. It really was a band of mavericks, renegades and misfits. But hell, we had some fun! The original Dirty Dozen!

So, after joining up and receiving our memberships, we began to work hard on the syllabus, determined to get our grades. I wanted to open a class of my own as soon as possible, but I wanted the proper grades and official backing before I did this.

I would travel, whenever I could, down to Southampton to train with Mike and attend the national seminars in Birmingham. Between this, we just kept our private training going together.

The community centre where we trained had plans for expansion, so they wanted more space. The space they needed being the back room where we trained. That was not good news for us.

After some persuasion, they took half of our room and built a partition wall for us to train behind. It was weird – us one side belting the hell out of each other, and on the other side would be people sitting drinking or playing pool or darts in a pub environment.

We didn't care though. Nothing would get in the way of training. Not even when the cigarette smoke used to seep through the partition wall from the bar and the strains of Frank Sinatra could be heard on the jukebox. 'I Get a Kick out of you' seemed quite ironic!

In this era, only the chosen few had their own dojo. Most martial artists could be found training in church halls, community centres and somebody's garage and, on some occasions, in the back room of a Chinese takeaway's premises.

Regardless where we trained, the four of us worked hard and when we travelled up to the next national course, we were informed that we would be grading.

Tina, Brian, Mark and I went into a room in front of the grading panel and were tested. Sometime later we emerged. Tina and I with first Dan black belts and Brian and Mark with brown belts. What a result! We had all trained extremely hard for this, and we just didn't put a foot wrong. We turned it on and breezed through the grading. I believe that preparation is everything no matter what you are attempting to achieve. Our preparation had been first class. We were fit, strong, conditioned to last the pace and we had rigorously gone over and over the techniques until they were second nature. Nothing was left to chance and that's how we had succeeded.

I was over the moon with my grade but Tina's had been extra special. She was the first lady in GBASSDA to be awarded a Dan grade, and she had earned it the hard way. No quarter asked or given. Her performance had been faultless.

One classic moment sticks out in my mind on the grading. Tina and I still laugh about it today. It happened when we had to perform knife defences. Mike handed me a real knife in a leather sheath. As I went to take it out, I noticed how difficult it was to extract from this sheath. Finally, I pulled it free and thrust it towards Tina. Mike stood up in alarm and yelled out to stop, but by then, Tina had deflected my hand and had taken me over in a vicious wristlock and disarmed me! Mike and the panel looked ashen-faced. He said, "We normally keep the knife in the sheath for safety. We just wanted you to feel the weight of a real blade!" Tina and I just looked at each other puzzled. We had trained with 'live' weapons before, so you could appreciate distance and have a healthy respect for an edged weapon. This practice must always be done extremely carefully, and only when you have the skill to do so. On that day of the grading, we hadn't given it a second thought!

We travelled home that night tired but happy. I told the others that it was time to open up the club to the public. We were now ready. So around about 1984/85, the first class of what eventually became the Bristol Goshin Jutsu Combat Academy opened, although at this time we were called the Bristol Self Defence Academy.

We now had the main hall at the community centre with lots more room. We initially had about twelve to twenty people show up to train. Looking back now, the training and the teaching was a little raw, but I was learning my trade all the time.

I didn't have the luxury of a full-time Sensei living on my doorstep. I had to do a lot of things in trial-and-error fashion. I would travel most weekends to increase my knowledge, but for the most part, I developed my clubs in Bristol through my own tenacity and a burning will to succeed. Tina, Brian and Mark had given me great support, but at the end of the day, it was my name advertised as the instructor and I ultimately carried the responsibility.

The class now consisted of three hours. The first hour would solely be down to exercise and conditioning and I did 'beast' people. The training was without compromise. Last man standing sort of stuff.

I used to bring along to the class a large 'master blaster' (remember those!), and play a music cassette tape through both sides (remember that!) whilst we did the exercises. Star jumps, jump squats, burpees, squat thrusts, push-ups, sit-ups, leg raises, jumping squats, etc., etc., etc.

I remember one guy who had joined the class say to me after struggling through the Bruce Springsteen tape 'Born in the USA', "I love Springsteen but when I listen to that fucking tape next time, it won't ever be the same to me again!"

After the warm-up, two hours of ju jutsu, self-defence and sparring methods would be practised. Students came and went, but gradually I built up a little hardcore following.

I had some lean times at the class with three or four people turning up; sometimes, on other occasions, the hall was full! The training was hard and it didn't allow for different ages or fitness levels. It was very much take-it or leave-it sort of stuff. I was still developing myself and following a certain path and those who wanted to come along for the ride could.

A year or so later, I graded for my second Dan under Mike Marshall and Dave Turton. Brian also gained his first Dan. Mark had unfortunately left us and Tina's training had been cut short because she was expecting our first child.

Motherhood takes up a lot of your time and it certainly changes your life forever. We have three children all told. Now presently, they are aged as follows: Thomas, thirty-one, Jacob, twenty-eight and Lauren, twenty-six. They are all great children and all successful.

Tina never really got back into training after the births of our children. She did help me with numerous ladies' self-defence courses and she keeps fit now by going to the gym, hitting pads and swimming. She still can handle herself, mind you, but back then, she was a very, very capable martial artist. She has an incredible steely resolve and gives up on nothing. Her discipline is phenomenal and when she puts her mind to something she will not let go until she sees it through. People these days may view her as that likeable 'mother hen' figure, but underneath that soft, caring exterior is one tough lady.

Brian went on to be a very loyal and trusted instructor with me. He never let me down. He was always there with help and advice. Brian supported every class, travelled with me on seminars and was my uke for demonstrations and so much more. He was thirty-five years old when he started martial arts and was in his early forties when the classes were really taking off. He had a catalogue of injuries during his training. A double hernia op, broken collar bone and chronic rheumatoid arthritis in his wrist joints. These were just a few of his problems. His doctor had told him on more than one occasion to give up ju jutsu, but he kept on training until the pain in his joints got too much. Now, I didn't realise how hard it must have been for him to keep training the way he did. I was in my twenties and training like a lunatic. It's not until these days that I can appreciate the calibre of the man to keep up with being my training partner through some very, very hard sessions. He finally retired from the martial arts and the last I heard was living a life of 'luxury' touring around and staying in Europe. Good for him. He was a very close friend and a strong and trustworthy man. I owe him much.

From the hardcore group of students came other guys who would go on to become my first generation of black belts. They were Martin Williams, Neil Bartlett and Mike Griffin. All were good martial artists but different in their approach and techniques. These guys emerged at a time along with other tough lads worthy of mention such as Scott Hurse, Bob Kingdon and Andy Loxley.

The word was getting around about my ju jutsu and the profile of the club was getting bigger. Bristol was really a stronghold for Wado Ryu Karate, taekwondo and Lau Gar Kung Fu. Ju jutsu was a 'new kid' on the block. I was proud to be the man establishing it in my home city. I was on a crusade.

I was now becoming 'battle hardened'. The days of my insecurities were gradually fading. I was developing balls and confident to step up to the plate.

I recall I was training avidly, and one weekend I went to a local fair. They had a travelling boxing and wrestling booth there. I was fascinated by this as I had read about these booths and how some great champions and tough men had started their fighting careers working them. The booths date back some two hundred years and, sadly, they are no longer with us.

I paid to go in and watch the show. I watched a wrestling bout where this gnarled old wrestler with a big bushy beard issued a challenge to the assembled crowd for anybody to step in the ring and last a round with him. I remember this young guy jumping in. He was a big lad and he gave this old wrestler a tough time and just narrowly missed out on going the distance. Looking back now, his guy was a 'ringer'. He was a plant in the crowd to drum up interest so some poor, unsuspecting mug would think he could have a go. Yes, you guessed it. I was the mug next up for a crack at the prize. I was young and fit and thought I could get the better of this old boy.

Whipping off my t-shirt and shoes, I was ushered in the ring and introduced. The crowd gave me a hearty reception. I was up for it and feeling good. Boy, was I in for a shock.

The old guy that had been battered around a bit by the previous challenger suddenly shed about twenty years off his demeanour and came at me like a fucking wolverine. He took me by surprise and to the canvas with a single leg and processed to twist the living daylights out of my ankle. I thought it was going to snap. I grabbed hold of his beard and twisted it, this only made him twist my ankle more, so I did the only honourable thing a man could do bar cry, and I submitted. It was all over. My brief forage into the wrestling ring.

The old guy was a gentleman. He shook my hand saying, "Well done, lad." Those men that worked the booths were no mugs, and they were tough as nails taking on all comers no matter their weight or reputation. I have nothing but utter respect of them.

The experience made me realise that no one is bulletproof. Also, it reinforced my belief in cross training and learning all ranges of combat. Something that my hero, Bruce Lee, had been preaching since the mid-sixties. Funny how it would take another thirty years for a huge section of the martial arts community to take this idea on board.

I decided now that it was time to open another class and returned to the Bristol Budokan. It was inevitable that I would return to my old club. I started back on a Thursday evening, and that night became a special class especially for all our senior grades. There was nothing better in years to come than seeing a mat full of blue, brown and black belts having a hard training session. It was great to witness, and I was proud to have taught these guys. They were all warriors back then. They trained hard, took the knocks and came back for more. No fuss and no moaning.

I was around twenty-three years old when these two clubs were running. Things were busy, what with a job working from eight to five in a timber yard/saw mill down at the Bristol Docks, helping bring up a young family, sleepless nights and trying to keep my training going! Tina was very understanding and knew my passions for the clubs. She supported me and gave me no hassle when I went out to teach or train. She unconditionally looked after the children and never complained. This helped me immensely. She is a wonderful wife and mother.

I was still regularly travelling to train with Mike Marshall and by then, I had also joined his Japanese Ju Jutsu Association. Over the next few years, I was also graded to first Dan in Japanese ju jutsu and Atemi Jutsu (the art of striking vital points on the human body). It was a great honour to receive black belts in both of these arts. I also received a certificate for proficiency in the use of the Yawara-bo (a small hand-held stick).

I had come so far so fast and I had learnt so much. Mike also schooled me in CQB techniques that he taught the Special Forces. Unarmed dirty fighting and stick, knife fighting, improvised weapons and firearms handling and disarms. Also, as mentioned previously, the Yawara-bo. It was the original forerunner of the kubotan (its literal translation is 'Ju Jutsu stick'). It can be used to strike, lock, restrain and manipulate pressure points. Back then, instructors would graphically show you its effectiveness by striking you without reserve and crushing your bones. I have been hit on the arms, legs and body to collapse and have had bruises on my bruises. I once did a five-hour instructors' course with this weapon and had a job to move the next day. I recall a certain Mr. Turton being particularly vicious with the Yawara-bo. All these weapons are part of my Combat Ju Jutsu syllabus still today.

By 1988, the GBASSDA began to fall apart. Major players were leaving like Upham, Turton and O'Keefe. The great originals were now disbanding. I just think we all came as far as we could with the Association and it was time to move on.

I stayed another while but decided I had reached a learning curve and I needed to expand my horizons again. So, at the end of 1988, I left as well. Mike wasn't so happy originally, but in the end, he relented and let me go.

I think that not long after that, GBASSDA came to its natural end. I lost track of Mike and never spoke to him again. In recent times, through email, his son, also named Mike, contacted me to break the sad news that his dad had passed away. I was shocked and saddened, as I always had a picture in my mind of how I remembered him. Again, this man was a major influence in my ju jutsu career. He was a mentor and friend to me. He held nothing back in his teaching and gave me it all. We finally just outgrew each other. As mentioned earlier I view him as my first ju jutsu instructor. His incredible 'war' stories were always the source of a good 'campfire' tale. It is a sad loss. I hope he rests in peace. I got a feeling though: whether he went 'upstairs' or 'downstairs', he will be twisting some unfortunate souls' joints or choking them!

After leaving GBASSDA, I still liked to go on different seminars and keep an open mind. I enjoyed great training sessions under Professor Brian Dossett of Spirit Combat International. He is another martial arts maverick that burnt his fifth Dan black belt in front of the WJJA panel, and left to form his own association – Spirit Combat International. They said that he wouldn't last. Oh, how he proved them wrong.

Professor Dossett had his many critics, but I enjoyed every training session with him. His down-to-earth cockney approach is unique and for a man of notable talent, he has no edge or ego. He has done everything in the martial arts world, and put himself on the line many times. He has stepped in the ring to box and kickbox as well as teach his Spirit Combat system all over the world. Now in his seventies, he is still active on the mats. They don't make them like Brian any more.

I attended many of his B and D combat courses in his Middlesex dojo. These courses were open to martial artists, bouncers, bodyguards and fighters of every ilk. The course advert read 'No cry-babies please', so you knew you weren't in for a picnic.

I recall two other instructors, the mighty Tom Baldwin, an extremely powerful ju jutsu man, and ex-forces CQC expert, Gary Stringer. Along with Professor Dossett, we trained in hard street combat techniques, grappling and no-holds-barred type fights where everything was all in and you just had a good tear-up.

It was rough and ready, and I suppose you had to be slightly mad to participate. Again, I met some crazy people and would-be Bruce Lees! They were soon exposed though when the training began in earnest. I was just a face in a crowd and Brian Dossett probably would not remember me being on his mat.

I remember one incident when I was training with a guy who dropped me on my spine across his knee. This fucking hurt, and the first time he did it, I gave him the benefit of the doubt. Perhaps it had been an accident. When he did it a second time, I saw red. When I got hold of him, I lifted him high and dropped him hard onto my knee. He shrieked like a banshee and rolled and writhed around the floor. Brian was walking past me as this happened and I caught his eye. I thought that I was in for a bollocking for using excessive force but, instead, a small smile played on his lips and he walked on. The guy was carried off the mat and didn't participate again in the session. Well, it did say no cry-babies!

I look back with mixed memories of fondness and fear at those great sessions. Driving up to London from Bristol was long and arduous when you knew what was waiting for you, and you had plenty of time to talk yourself out of it. But part of the training was learning to deal with your fears and still carry on and do it. I now had made a promise to myself that I would do all in my power never to back down from any hardship in my life ever again.

If you didn't walk away from one of these crazy classes without a bloodied nose, thick lip or bruised ribs, then you had escaped a minor miracle. I can remember waiting on the mat's edge with a mixture of fear and excitement and my stomach churning in knots. It was a bit like queuing up for a wild rollercoaster ride: part of you wants to experience it and part of you doesn't. I suppose that it has to be done!

These were incredibly exciting times for me, and I loved every minute with a passion. There was so much more to come.

"I could see further by standing on the shoulders of giants."

Ju Jutsu's Unsung Warrior

On a few of the GBASSDA's national courses, I had witnessed the skills of Micky Upham. Mike Marshall had always told me if I ever had the opportunity, I should train with this man. So, when I left GBASSDA, I decided to see if I could track him down. Was he elusive or what? This guy was harder to trace than Lord Lucan!

I enquired about him through some of the instructors who were in GBASSDA, but with no luck. Then one month, I was flicking through 'Fighters' magazine when I saw an advert for Mick's Goshin Ryu International Association. Bingo! There was an address. So, I wrote a letter to him, explaining who I was and that I would like to join his association and train under him.

Now I believe that this was the one and only time that Mick ever advertised in a martial arts magazine, and I just happened to read that issue. I do believe in fate, and this certainly was a case of it.

I had heard much about Mick Upham. That he was an elusive character and that he didn't take in outsiders to his clubs. He ran a tight ship with a small group of clubs in his native Liverpool area. He referred to them as his 'warriors' or 'army'. I had also heard some pretty hairy things about Mick and that he sailed a 'little close to the breeze'. But this still wouldn't put me off. I was desperate to learn from this guy.

Micky is a unique man. He is a crazy Scouser with a profound sense of humour, a little seen gentleness and balls so big that they come in a dumper truck! On the mats, he is a perpetual motion!

Micky and his then uke, 'Little Mike', were a great double act together. Their demonstrations of Combat ju jutsu were fantastic with sound effects and crazy antics thrown in. I loved it. Mick was a demon martial artist. He had the hand speed of a pro boxer, the kicking ability of a top taekwondo performer, backed up with the grappling and throwing skills of ju jutsu. He was something special. I have never seen a better Combat ju jutsu man, and that is with no disrespect to those I have learnt from over the years. Mick is a one-off and when I first met him, I realised that I had contacted somebody who would again influence my martial arts training greatly.

At the time, Mick was a fifth Dan in Goshin Ryu and Kodai Ryu Ju Jutsu, and also held a black belt in Oikura Ryu Kempo Jutsu from the legendary Soke Rod Sacharnoski of the Juko Kai Ju Jutsu.

Sacharnoski had seen and done it all in the world of combat as a US marine and cop. He was also known across the globe for his displays of 'kai' or inner energy. It was witnessed on many occasions in demonstrations and filmed. An incredible feat of the demo consisted of the taking of a one-thousand-and-one-hundred-pound per square inch testicle kick delivered by a six-feet-eight-inches, two-hundred-and-ninety-pound martial artist who kicked with the shin instead of the foot. The demo also consisted of the taking of a full-power knifehand strike to the 'relaxed' Adam's apple which was measured at more than six hundred pounds per square inch. This man was a unique martial artist.

Mickey also held a black belt in 'Mugendo' – a very progressive system of kickboxing pioneered by the Irish man, George Canning, another very gifted martial artist. So, Mickey had a great pedigree, and I wanted to train with him. I wasn't going to be put off without a fight.

Mick had also done a lot of high-level security work. He was one of a team that took care of Michael Jackson's security when he come to the UK in the 80s.

If Mike Marshall's 'war stories' were entertaining, then Micky's were worst. I found it all fascinating and soaked it all up.

I received a reply to my letter and at first, Mick didn't want to entertain the idea. But I wrote again, pleading to give me a chance. If he didn't rate me, so be it, but let me come up to train.

I received another reply from him informing me that I could come up to Liverpool to train and he would assess my skills. If they were up to his criteria, he would accept my club into his Association.

In the letter, I also asked if Brian and I could come up to Liverpool to grade under him. Mick agreed to have us up and look at what we could do.

We drove to Seaforth just outside Liverpool and waited in a designated pub car park for Mick to arrive. Finally, he did arrive in a battered white transit van. With a quick handshake and a few words, he asked us to follow him and we drove to his dojo.

When we arrived, Mick explained about his style and philosophy on the fighting arts. His outlook was one hundred percent practical. He said that he could show us all the classical and fancy ju jutsu or could show us the 'real stuff'. We settled for the latter!

First, he took us through a grading. He fired technique after technique at us: throws, locks, chokes, self-defence, ground grappling and weapons. We just kept going at a terrific pace for a couple of hours. Then, he showed us some of his methods of ju jutsu.

The 'Goshin' system that he taught was stripped to the bone of any unnecessary movements or overcomplicated techniques. It was short, sharp and powerful ju jutsu at its best. Brian and I trained hard in the new methods and at the end of the day, I was awarded my third Dan black belt and Brian his second Dan.

Mick organised the certification and he even had them countersigned by Soke Brian Walsh, tenth Dan – another of his old instructors. I believe that Soke Walsh is the highest graded ju jutsu man in the UK. He is also based in Liverpool.

Returning to Bristol, we worked hard on modifying our ju jutsu and began to streamline it so it became sharper. Both the clubs were doing well, and I felt at long last that I was reaching some of the long-term goals that I had set myself.

My relationship with Mick Upham was a strange one. I couldn't really refer to him as my Sensei because he used to seemingly disappear off the face of the earth for months and then reappear. I also got Mick down to the 'Budokan' here in Bristol two or three times. But once again, I would have to piece the training together myself from whatever I had been given and just carried on. Even under Mick, I carried on my open-minded practice and went to train on other seminars.

I travelled to Stoke to train and to teach on the Bushi Kempo Ju Jutsu Association national courses. Here, I met and got to know Sensei David Hand, who was a gentleman on and off the mat and acquainted Shihan Peter Browne. Both these men ran this association. I enjoyed the freedom of just being able to train and have a good bunch of lads with me. For me, the beauty of ju jutsu was whoever you went to learn from, they all had something a little different to show you.

I laugh now when I recall us all clambering into a Venture Scout mini bus that we would hire cheap to go on seminars! How the thing got us to the venues I'll never know. It coughed and spluttered its way along, and I wonder what people thought when it pulled up outside a seminar venue and we all climbed out! It was just like Del Boy's three-wheeler! They were good days and learning ones.

I also managed to train on large seminars under Robert Clark and Richard Morris – two of the most senior ju jutsu men in the country. I even attended a Ninjutsu seminar under Brian McCarthy, the very well-known and respected exponent of this art.

I remember this seminar well as we were the only group outside of Ninjutsu that showed up to train, and I think some of their lads thought they could have a bit of fun with us. Wrong! We certainly held our own and dished a bit out. On this seminar was supposedly the cream of the UK Ninjutsu world, but we weren't phased by that. Guys like Martin Williams, Neil Bartlett, Mike Griffin, Andy Loxley, Scott

Hurse and Bob Kingdon were my hardcore students and they would go anywhere and give me one hundred percent, no questions asked.

I recall that I had broken my big toe a week prior to that seminar and to say it was sore was putting it mildly. At the start of this seminar, we had to do lots of partner drills, very gymnastic based. One drill was to make a human pyramid. You started this with four men on the bottom standing, and then three would climb up on their shoulders, then two on to theirs and finally, one little guy at the top. I'm not a great one for heights and had to climb to the top! I usually get a nosebleed changing a light bulb! I tell you, I was all over the place and ended up jumping down. Then, I was on the bottom row of a decidedly shaky foundation. All was going okay until the guy next to me stood on my broken toe and I jumped a mile, causing the whole pyramid to collapse in a heap! It was a weird and wonderful day. McCarthy was very good at what he did, but I personally didn't rate anybody else.

My third Dan was achieved in 1988. This gave me the authority to grade students up to first Dan. Martin Williams, Neil Bartlett and Mike Griffin became my first generation of black belts behind the original founder members. None of them, unfortunately, train today.

Martin was a tall and powerful lad with enormous potential to become a very good instructor. He had been with me since he was seventeen years old. He gave up training for the love of a woman (poor lad!) and I lost track of him until he turned up at my fortieth birthday party. At first, I didn't recognise him because he was bald as a coot! In fact, I've seen more hair on a piece of bacon but hey, who am I to speak about baldness! Alas, that's what the love of a good woman does for you. He did come back for a short while to try and resume training but unfortunately, ill health prevented him continuing. I have bumped into him in recent years and I am glad to learn he is now happy and in good health.

Neil Bartlett was a superb martial artist. He stood about five feet three inches, but what a pocket dynamo! He was skilled in ju jutsu, Kempo and Muay Thai. A chronic injury to his back vertebrae put pay to his training and he later moved to New Zealand. Recently, I hooked up with him on Facebook and he now resides in Australia. I had many an adventure with Neil. He was an unpredictable and funny guy.

'Mad' Mike Griffin came to me as a ju jutsu blue belt, but got a bit of a culture shock when he saw how we trained. However, he took to it like a duck to water. Mike was one of the toughest men I ever trained with. He was a PTI in the prison service and had had his share of real-life drama. He had handled some dangerous inmates in his time including the Krays, Peter Sutcliffe and Charles Bronson.

He loved to train hard and him and I would have some infamous tear-ups at the Thursday night 'Budokan' sessions. We would be training and sparring in all-out bouts back then, well before NHB events came into force. He was relentless and really pushed me hard. At his peak, he was around fifteen stone and was six feet two inches. He was a bit of a monster and not many people liked training with him.

I have so many tales to tell about my times with him that I could write a chapter just on this. Here are a few of the best ones.

When he was taking his brown belt grading, he was giving a torrid time. At the end, he had to grapple two of us at once. This ended with him crashing into a group of other students who were kneeling on the mats also waiting to grade. Neil and I dived on Mike, and we gave him another battering. He was doing his best to escape but couldn't. Then I noticed that three of the lads waiting for grading were also pinning him down so he had no chance! He never realised this and after, he couldn't figure out how he didn't escape.

On his first Dan grading, surprisingly nobody turned up to be his uke so 'Muggins' was left to do it. Mike was hyped up for it. His adrenaline was running wild, and I had to tell him on numerous occasions to control it. When we came to weapon defences, I was on red alert as at black belt level, we trained with live weapons. I can remember Mike disarming me of a small knife and pinning me to the floor, holding the blade under my chin to finish. With his adrenaline flowing like crazy, his hand shook and he stuck the tip of the blade into the fleshy underside of my chin. First blood had been drawn!

We also drilled gun disarms against a replica blank-firing pistol. Mike disarmed me of the gun and had once again pinned me to the floor with it pressed to the side of my head. Yes, he forgot it was loaded with blanks and pulled the trigger. I was deaf in one ear for days after. What a crazy man and a crazy grading! He did pass it, though.

Mike also had a habit of jumping out on people and surprising them, very much like Peter Sellers and Cato in the 'Pink Panther' films. One day, I was in Bristol town centre with Tina, and I spotted him in a shop in Bristol's well-known Galleries shopping complex. I told Tina to let me know when he was coming out of the shop and I waited outside.

Bear in mind that this is a Saturday afternoon and the place is crawling with shoppers and security. Mike came out of the shop and I jump on him. He thinks that he's being mugged and starts fighting back hard before he realises it is me.

"You bastard," he panted. "I was ready for you."

"Yeah right," I replied.

I'm surprised that we weren't nabbed by security.

On another occasion, we were coming back from a seminar. Mike was driving in one car and I was in another. We both pulled in to get some petrol at a motorway garage. I was waiting in the passenger seat of the car while Martin, who drove, filled it up. I suddenly looked up and saw Mike running across the forecourt with a police baton in his hand. He yanked open the door to get me out. I kicked out at him and grappled the baton away. He broke into hysterical laughter as he ran back to his car. God knows what the poor woman cashier thought who was watching the scene unfold from behind her till.

Mike and I did many seminars together over the years, and he was a loyal friend and instructor. His job moved him around the country quite a bit which put pay to him training with me. He was a great character and we had some wild times together.

In 1992, I asked Mick Upham if I could grade for my fourth Dan. He informed me that nobody under him had ever received that grade and if I wanted to come up and try for it, I could, but he warned me that it would be fucking hard.

I felt that over the years, I had to prove myself to Mick. I'm sure he thought we were all southern softies down here in Bristol and didn't have the balls for real training. Well, I attempted to prove at every given opportunity that I did have the balls, spirit and resolve.

I knew the grade was going to be hard, so I started on a severe training regime of fitness to get myself in top shape. I was running, lifting weights, doing loads of callisthenics and ju jutsu training. At my work, I was using shifting loads of timber, boards, doors, bags of cement and sand as part of my fitness training. I was lifting heavy and carrying loads various distances as well as up flights of stairs, punishing my body at every opportunity. In my dinner hours, I would disappear upstairs in a quiet part of the warehouse and bang out half an hour of press-ups, squats and sit-ups, followed by going through all my strikes and kicks. To practise gi chokes, I would put an old gi on a bag of sand or cement and tie it with a belt to get something that would resemble a body. I would always find a way to train. No excuses. I was like a man possessed. I was totally focused on achieving this grade and proving myself beyond a doubt.

When the day arrived, a minibus full of my students and I met Mick again just outside Liverpool, and then followed him to an outdoor venue, which would be where the day's training would take place.

This was to be one of Mick Upham's infamous 'In the Woods' seminar, and it wasn't going to be a fucking teddy bear's picnic. I had been told about these before where a bunch of unexpecting trainees would be brought out in the woods, beasted and left to make their own

81

way home or have their train or coach tickets ripped up and made to run home. I had been warned that they weren't for the faint of heart and to be prepared for anything.

As our minibus pulled up behind Mick's car at the designated venue, I told all my people to pull out all the stops and give me one hundred percent. They and I were on trial and we couldn't afford to fail. I looked around and saw looks of nervous apprehension on their faces. It resembled a scene from one of those old black and white war films just as the battalion was getting ready to go over the top!

We followed Mick into the woods and walked along the trail. Although I was talking to him, my eyes were peeled on the bushes and trees waiting for a mad ambush.

Finally, we came to a semi-clearing. A fine mist was rising off the grass and light drizzle was coming down. There, in the clearing, were Mick's 'warriors', all warming up, decked out in full camouflage gear and army boots. We all acknowledged each other and after a basic introduction, Mick told me that I was going to be assessed throughout the whole day's training. This meant that for five hours, I was going to be under the microscope. I would have to have total concentration throughout and couldn't afford to lapse. After a brief warm-up, we started with Kempo strike combinations and Kotsu-ho-Jutsu (joint breaking and locking). We went through umpteen variations and then continued those with sweeps and takedowns.

All the while, the rain came down getting heavier. The woods were situated by the coast of Seaforth and it was damp and cold.

Mick was having fun by going around and setting off firecrackers and thunder flashes whilst we trained. It was like a bad day in Vietnam. Next up was the marathon throwing session. The ground was a mixture of sand, mud and bracken, and it had become very wet and boggy. We began one-for-one throws, hip throws, hip wheels, body drops, sweeping loins, half shoulders, full shoulders, winding throws, leg throws, head throws, etc., etc. Over and over, we just kept banging them out, Mick making sure that he gave me more and more throws to execute. Every time you hit the floor, you were getting wetter and wetter, and the odd combat boot kicking your ribs or stamping your ear didn't exactly cheer up the proceedings! After a solid hour of throws, we stopped for some lunch and a well-needed drink. These sessions were spartan and nobody stopped for fluid unless instructed to do so.

When the break was over, we started back with weapon defences and using the short baton, Yawara-bo and flashlight as weapons. This was followed by groundwork, combat-style. Grappling around in mud might make a great night's entertainment for some, but when you are doing it yourself, it is very tiring. I do admire those lady mud wrestlers. They must be fit.

You would fight an opponent, then stay in as a fresh person took their place over and over until in the end, about six or more opponents would pile in on you all together. This was all done barehanded and sporting combat boots. I can still feel the pain now!

Micky also had a unique way of testing you on your knowledge of anatomy and pressure points. His methods made sure you remembered. For example, he would shin roundhouse kick you on the outside of your thigh and while you were on the ground clutching your leg in agony, he would ask you the name of the pressure point he just kicked. If you didn't name it, you were going to get it on the other leg next.

Another of his favourites was to throw you to the ground with a hip throw and then knee or stand on your ear and ask you how many bones were in the ear. As you yelled triumphantly, "There are three bones, Sensei," he would then ask you to name them! Whether you want to call them anvil, stirrup and hammer or malleus, incus and stapes, it still hurt like hell trying to splutter the names out when it felt like your head was going to explode. You also didn't ever need a chiropractor. Mickey could click and crunch your neck and spine in some weird and wonderful ways, all free of charge.

He was also fond of backhanding you in the balls to see if you were wearing a groin guard. If you were wearing one, he would take the piss calling you a 'southern softie', and if you decided not to wear one, you would drop to your knees in pain. It was a no-win situation.

Tough and harsh maybe but you soon recalled your pressure points. Amazing what a bit of pain does for the memory!

Next, I was taken with my partner, Martin Williams, to another area with a stretch of clearing between the trees a couple of hundred feet long. A dozen or so of Mick's boys accompanied us. We separated and faced our partners at either end of this course. Mick then announced that it was stamina training time. He warned that anyone who flagged or quit would have a long walk home. I looked up the course at Martin and knew as a young and fit black belt, he would be with me all the way. Then, we were off and running, literally. I first sprinted the course to Martin, he then threw me with five hip throws, we both hit the floor and did ten press-ups and then sprinted back to the other end of the course where I threw him and we again did the press-ups, and so we went on and on, circuit after circuit. At one stage, we were doing ten throws each and then twenty press-ups. Next came wheelbarrows on your knuckles, your partner guiding you down the course. You had to plough through whatever was on the floor. No questions asked. When you reached the end, ten push-ups and then bring your partner back. This went on for what seemed like eternity. Then, it changed to worse torture! Piggybacks down the course, ten squats at the end with your partner on your back, five hip throws and then, your partner did it. This was excruciating. At this stage, we had been going for an hour non-stop.

I vividly remember as I was carrying Martin's six-feet one-inch and thirteen-stone frame down the track, Mick was sitting at the other end, sipping on a can of Coca Cola and asking if I wanted to stop for a drink. I knew that this was one of his devious ploys and I would shout out, "No, Sensei. I'm fine".

"Are you sure?" he would reply. "It's beautiful. Ice cold."

"No, Sensei," I would again shout, and go back up the course.

I must admit, the inside of my mouth felt like a Russian wrestler's jockstrap!

Next, he would be jogging down next to you with a cup of warm tea, telling you how wonderful it tasted and did I want a sip. This was all mind games. He would then start telling me how tired I looked and that he didn't think I was going to make it. I just shut him out and gritted my teeth and inwardly thought, "You bastard".

Around this time, everybody else joined the circuit for moral support, and I must say that my students, both male and female, did me proud. We were now into body crawls, jump squats and duck walks up the course. At the end, one person would lie down and execute fifty sit-ups, then lift their legs off the floor six inches whilst their partner would punch and palm slap them in the abdominals. Lovely stuff!

Near the end of this torturous ninety-minute marathon, some of Mick's men were flagging, a few falling to the floor totally exhausted and dehydrated. Mick was screaming, "Get up, you lazy bastards. You'll never train with me again." He was pulling guys up by their hair and pushing them back onto the course.

Within all this, there were still some moments of humour which I always love. At one stage, I jumped up onto Martin's back and Mick was playing psychological games, telling him he looked finished. This spurred Martin on into a new lease of life and he shot off down the course. Mick, with a look of surprise on his face, shouted out, "Bloody hell, lad. What are you? A fucking gazelle?"

Another one of my students said that at one stage after a wheelbarrow walk, he was doing push-ups and was on the verge of collapse. As he was sinking down towards the grass, he spied a dog's turd directly in his eyeline and this spurred him on to complete the rest of the exercises or get a faceful.

Finally, Mick shouted out to stop. At this stage, I had gone beyond fatigue and was badly dehydrated. Mick came up to me and said, "You know, if you had stopped for a drink, I would have failed you." I just nodded. He then shook my hand and said, "Well done, lad. You've passed. You are the first fourth Dan ever under me. You put some of my lads to shame. It was good." This was big praise coming from a man not known for giving much out.

I was elated but very tired. I remember being led back to the minibus between two others. Dehydration had claimed my sense of balance and my legs had disowned me, but I was grinning inanely. I was dragged to the bus. I was like Bambi on ice with half a dozen shots of JD inside him!

For the first half hour of the journey I sat in a trance and then I suddenly got diarrhoea of the mouth and babbled a load of shit before finally going quiet again. It was the aftermath of adrenaline.

We now had the long journey back to Bristol, and Martin, who had been my right-hand man all day, had to drive back. The bus was awash with excited chatter and congratulations. I just sat in the front passenger seat and soaked it all up. About an hour into the journey, it had gone strangely quiet and I peered back over my shoulder to see that everybody was crashed out, asleep.

I smiled to myself. They had earned it and done me proud. Although I could have slept as well, I kept my mate, Martin company all the way home to Bristol.

That day, I felt that I had really come of age and had proven much, not just to Mick, but to myself. My physical and mental fitness had been tested and I had come through.

The type of training I was receiving under Micky was exactly what I had been looking for, and I was so glad that I had found it. Yes, he could be a frustrating guy, only ever drip feeding you little snippets of what he could really do. But I was glad that I stuck with it until I earned his respect and trust.

Mick was another person who left an incredible impression on me. He had stepped out of the box now and was showing some very forward-thinking techniques way beyond the standard fare. I was excited by what I saw and considered myself lucky to be privy to his technique. I am so glad that I didn't give up on training with him the first time that I got knocked back. It just goes to show that if you want something bad enough, you have got to keep getting up no matter how many times you are knocked down. This is easy to say but extremely hard to do in practice.

Currently, many people are guilty of waxing lyrical about great Japanese, Thai, Filipino, Brazilian or American instructors; Micky was one of the best of British that gets on with it under the radar. He was a terrific exponent of the martial arts and a tough man. But the hands that I witnessed executing brutal strikes, chokes and locks also gently held my first son, Tom, only a few months after he was born.

I still, occasionally, get the odd email from guys that have trained with him or mention that he is still around and still teaching. That is good to know. I was really fortunate to train with this man and to become not only one of his instructors, but to also become a friend.

You google this man and you will not find him. He should have graced the front covers of every martial arts magazine and taught on the world stage, but he was happy to stay in his 'back yard' and do what he did best, all low-key.

He was one of a kind. I thank him for his guidance and help in my ju jutsu journey.

"Our greatest glory is in never falling, but in rising every time we fall."

Extreme Training and Breaking New Horizons

Between the years of 1988 and 1992, although I associated and trained with Micky Upham on many occasions, I still went to other seminars and met new people, one of these being Shihan Alan Tattersall, ninth Dan of the then United Kingdom Ju Jutsu Association.

Allan was a very experienced ju jutsu man, originally gaining all his grades from the late ju jutsu great, Professor Robert Clark. He went on to form the UKJJA which was based in Rochdale.

UKJJA ran some great seminars, which I attended regularly over the years and got to meet and train with the likes of the legendary Wally Jay of small circle ju jutsu fame and his son Leon. There was Kirby Watson and Ian Griffiths of the Daito Ryu Aikijutsu, Peter Browne of Kempo Ju Jutsu and also Trevor Roberts, 'The Bolton Ironman'. Trevor is a prolific grappler and Combat ju jutsu man as well as a veteran doorman. I believe that comedian Peter Kay based his doorman character, Max from 'Phoenix Nights', on Trevor. A wealth of experience, talent and varied training was on display in these seminars.

On one such weekend seminar in Sheffield, 1989, I encountered one of the toughest training sessions that I have ever experienced. This was with one of the visiting instructors from the Israeli Anti-Terrorist Squad. He brought along with him his two sons, also instructors of CQC.

There were various mat areas with different instructors on each. All third Dans and above were told to head for the Israelis' mat. So, people like myself, Upham, Roberts, Browne and others were all together.

This Israeli instructor, without a doubt, was a combat veteran. He had fought in the conflict of war and had killed. He was an expert in unarmed combat, knives and firearms as well as sentry removal skills and garrotting. He had a presence about him that I hadn't felt on the mats since my training with Chiba Sensei.

I think that his sole aim for the day was to not only educate us in his real-world combat methods, but also see what us British were made from and how tough we were.

Israel has been a country in conflict throughout history and these guys' skills were being put to the test on a regular basis. Now, it was our turn to be put to the test.

The instruction started with a brief demo of their combat skills and a lecture in broken English about what techniques work and those that don't under extreme pressure.

We ran through some of the moves: low kicks, palm heel strikes, elbows, knees, sharp chokes and takedowns. Then, we had to put these techniques into live sparring practice.

We just kept swapping partners, facing a new one and sparring. No pads and no rules. I tell you, it was unnerving and frightening. This was an extreme test of your bottle. I don't mind admitting that I was scared. A lot of the more classical ju jutsu stylists struggled with this type of training. They were not used to the pressure of it all, and I could clearly see that some didn't like or agree with it.

The one thing that I instantly noticed was that a lot of the fights ended up on the ground. Old news now to the initiated but way back then in 1989, it was an eye-opener. I got to have a bit of a 'play' with Mick Upham's right-hand man', 'little Mike', and we had a hard-little scrap. I also went up against Mick himself and gave as good as I got. His kicking was fantastic though, and my ears rang with a few good roundhouse kicks. Some people were getting lumps knocked off them and were visibly flagging.

You could palm heel to the face but not punch it, but then everything else was allowed. This included knees, kicks, body punching including groin shots, and all grappling holds. You fought until you were stopped, and then swapped and went again. There were no weight categories, so whoever you came up against, you fought. No questions asked.

I dished it out and took it. I was soaked in sweat and my lungs felt like they were on fire.

I remember taking a palm heel blow to the nose from one guy, and it made my eyes water like Niagara Falls. Blood and snot were everywhere. He was a big lad and through the blur of tears, I saw him move in for the kill, so I managed a front kick into his balls. As he stopped short in his tracks, his eyes bulged out of his head like a shrimp. I dropped a finishing shin round kick into his thigh, and he was down. As soon as this happened, another person was in your face and you were at it again.

Finally, I ended up out in front of the whole assembled group fighting one of the Israeli instructor's sons. It was all in. No quarter was asked or given. This was as real as you could get, and I had to hold on to my bottle. I must admit that my ass was twitching. But this is why I had a black belt around my waist. There was no place to hide. I had to honour that and get stuck in.

We exchanged blows, palms, punches and kicks. No pads, no gum shield, no protection. I got a few early palm heels into my opponent's face, but received a few hard knees in return to the body. We clinched and I got caught in a standing guillotine choke. This guy kindly whispered in my ear that if I struggled, he would break my neck. Nice lad! Deciding that this might spoil my day, I seized his testicles and squeezed hard for a release. As this happened, he raked and gouged at my eye and opened a cut up underneath it. I felt blood trickle down my face, and I saw a small grin playing on his lips. That did piss me off. We went at it again, ending up in the assembled crowd. Once more, we were separated. I took a few more knees to the body which I felt, but returned with another palm heel to the face and a few body shots to the ribs. We clashed again, headbutting each other into the grapple, looking for openings. Eye gouging and pressure point attacks were exchanged. Finally, we were separated but not before the cut under my eye was ripped at again. I must admit that I had lost it slightly and fired a 'Judas punch' at the back of my opponent's head as I dived on him. It was broken up for a final time, and it was over. Fuck, that was intense. No semi-contact back fists here. My heart was beating so hard that I thought it would burst.

Not long after this, we broke for dinner. I remember sitting in a toilet cubicle drenched in sweat, blood seeping from my eye and my forearms and shins bruised, thinking what the hell was I doing here. It was the aftermath-effect of adrenaline and I felt bad. I was shaking like a shitting dog. I just had to sit there until they passed.

I didn't understand this at the time. A big part of me wanted to go home. Later in life, as I gained a deep understanding of fear and the effects of adrenaline, I realised what I had been experiencing. I have gone on to coach and lecture on this fascinating topic many times. It is now a vital part of my current 'Winning Minds' training programme.

When I joined the others for lunch, many were complaining that the training was too severe and dangerous. Some were not going back on the mat after the break. A few of these were big names in the martial arts world today, but I shall let them remain anonymous. Mind you, part of me wanted to go back to Bristol too, but I convinced myself that it couldn't get any harder. What a fool I was!

After the break, the sparring started again, but this time, two people would fight. Then, on a signal, one would drop out and be replaced by a fresh opponent. These were two-minute bouts. Now that doesn't seem long until you experience all-out no-holds-barred combat for that length of time over and over.

I remember that I came up against this lady aikidoist who had no punching or kicking skills. I was just keeping her at bay. She was a lovely girl and I was reluctant to engage with her. I was being urged to finish it, and the Israelis and the assembled crowd vocally made it known to do her no favours. They also shouted at her to attack me.

This must have fired her up, and she whizzed a sudden palm strike past my nose. Then, I went up a gear and fired a short roundhouse kick to her thigh and as her hands came down, I grabbed her in a headlock and drove her to the floor. No sooner had I done that, another guy launched himself on me from the crowd and we were having a furious grapple on the floor. I eventually managed to get over the back of him while he was on all fours and drove a downward elbow between his shoulder blades. This took the fight out of him as I went for a choke. Then I was out, and another took my place.

There were some brutal battles, none more than Mick Upham against Trevor Roberts. It was brilliant stuff. I can remember Mick reversing a position on Trevor. He was just getting off the floor when a change was called. Mick was off, and I was back on again.

Now, I was a young, up-and-coming instructor; Trevor Roberts was a ju jutsu legend and I don't expect for one minute that he will remember this. As I was called out, it was almost as if I was in a dream. There was Trevor 'The Bolton Ironman' on all fours just about to rise. I thought, there is no way I am letting this bloke get to his feet. So, I ran and launched myself into mid-air. It seemed to take an age. Then, I was on him. I gripped him in a side headlock, and I suppose that the scene resembled one of those Wild West rodeos with the cowboy hanging onto a wild steer (no offence meant, Trevor). I just gripped on for dear life and rode out the storm until another change was called. I was fucking glad this monster of a fighter didn't get hold of me. It is great to still see him active on the mats, still dishing out his uncompromising style of ju jutsu.

The finale to this part of the seminar were three people stood back to back in a triangle formation in the centre of the mat and the remaining thirty-odd people ran in and just attacked them as one mass. Guess who was one of the three? Yep, it was yours truly.

Well, the three of us went down under an avalanche of bodies and I thought that at one stage I was going to be crushed to death. Then, pure survival instincts took over. These guys were playing for real and weren't going to relent. I started butting, biting and gouging my way to freedom. There were screams and grunts as I went for it, but I was on autopilot. I recall, at one stage, a face looming above me and attempting to strangle me. I just clamped down on their little finger with my teeth and I was away. I managed to scramble to my feet, beaten but not bowed. It reminded me of surfacing from a prolonged period of time under water, gulping for air and flapping around all over the place. I was wide-eyed and panting like a train. I had a quick check to see if I was missing anything like an ear, finger or my testicles! No. All was intact.

The final part of training was specialised stuff. Prisoner restraint techniques, hog-tie-ups, sentry removal, knife combat, multiple opponents, firearm disarms, garrotting techniques and combat ground grappling. I strongly suggest never letting yourself be hog-tied and carried around. Not even in the privacy of your own bedroom! 'Fifty Shades of Grey' it wasn't! It's a highly unpleasant experience, especially whilst lying helplessly as your so-called mates stick the boot in!

What a finish to the weekend! This had been a seminar to put you fully to the test, and I felt that I had come through doing all right. I shook hands with the Israelis at the end and they all signed a certificate for me. No, it's not one for being criminally insane, in case you ask.

I saw respect in their eyes and it was mutual. It had been an extreme test. The free fighting was just as hard if not harder than any MMA fight I later had. Only back then some twenty-six years ago, it was not for sport; it had been for pure survival. I don't think that we would get away with seminars like this today, especially when the chief instructor showed you how to choke, knock out and disable an enemy with a real M16 machine gun, I kid you not. God knows how he got it through fucking customs. What would all the PC and human rights' brigade have to say about that? Those memories, I think, will stay with me forever.

I went home that day, feeling that I had really come of age and had experienced something that I would never forget.

As mentioned, the UKJJA hosted many great seminars. I tried to attend as many as I could and still kept in touch with Mick Upham, but our visits were getting fewer and fewer.

UKJJA were one of the first martial arts associations in 1992 to bring in NVQ coaching certification. Alan Tattersall was a leading light in trying to get all instructors to attend these special coaching courses.

Most sports, now, had taken on board NVQ coaching, but the martial arts were a grey area. Was it a sport? Some practised it as just self-defence or as a traditional art with no sporting application, so how could all the rules, regulations and guidelines apply to it?

It was a time of uncertainty. Instructors with ten, twenty or thirty years' experience were arguing the points, "What can I be taught?", "I have been running clubs successfully for years,", "I have official grade certification. What more do I need?", "I don't need some sports coach coming in and telling me how I should teach.". There was lots of unrest and bad feeling.

I attended an initial meeting at the UKJJA HQ in Rochdale and listened to the arguments for and against. I could understand both points of view but at the time, the bottom line was that eventually, all instructors would have to have NVQ coaching certification or they would find it hard to teach in any public building.

By this time, my original class had now moved to a new venue at a sports centre and I was concerned that if I didn't have the appropriate certification, I would be pushed out. I decided that I would attend the seminars and Brian agreed to also do this.

So, we went on weekend courses at the Rochdale HQ which a well-known and respected sports coach named Tony Gummerson took. The courses weren't about how to teach martial arts. We had all been in the game long enough to do this. Topics covered were how to set targets and plan training, working with children or disabled, counselling students over training setbacks and injuries, nutrition, fitness, managing a club, organising events, training safety, coaches' responsibility, how to deal with emergencies, first aid, etc., etc.

For all my misgivings, the courses were interesting and in the long run, they certainly made me a better coach and helped me run a more professional set-up. Exams were done in both written forms and practical demonstrations. You were also given workbooks to take away and implement certain principles and techniques into your classes and get feedback from the coaches who would monitor and assess your ability.

After about a year, I received NVQ level certification in the following: Assistant Coach, Club Coach, Coach Level and Senior Coach Level, all endorsed by the National Ju Jutsu Council and signed by Alan Tattersall and Tony Gummerson. This certification added a lot of weight to my other grade certification and certainly gave me more experience in the world of coaching martial arts.

I still kept my travels going around the UK and would bring my guys to train with anybody I felt I could learn from. Between 1992 and 1994, I travelled regularly and enjoyed some great and varied training.

Highlights that I particularly remember are training with Master Larry Tatum tenth degree black belt in the American Kenpo karate system. He lived in Hollywood, California, and was one of Ed Parker's (the founder of American Kenpo Karate) top instructors. Master Tatum's speed of hand was awesome and his combination strikes were blindly fast. He was a powerful martial artist but a true gent.

I also contacted Master Bob Rose, a then sixth Dan in Kenpo, about teaching a seminar in Bristol. I believe that he is now a master tenth Dan. This man was a great character. He was British but had a dual nationality passport for the States as well. Because of Native American blood in him, he fought in two tours of Vietnam, trained under Ed Parker and Larry Tatum and knew a host of stars who also trained in Kenpo such as Elvis Presley and film star Charles Bronson. Through the Kenpo scene, he had seen and done just about everything you could in the martial arts world. He was a very experienced instructor and a great storyteller. I liked Kenpo and thought it blended in well with the ju jutsu that I had learnt.

I also attended a seminar in 1993 in Coventry run by the International Martial Arts Federation and got a chance to train with the great Japanese ju jutsu Master, Shizuya Sato. He has recently been awarded his tenth Dan in Nihon ju jutsu. This gentleman was getting on in years, but he was technically brilliant and still powerful. He had a wealth of knowledge and experience. He chose me on a few occasions to demonstrate his techniques on and I felt those powers first-hand. It was an honour to be on his mat.

My first taste of Brazilian ju jutsu came in the same year on a seminar hosted by Peter Browne. Franco Vacirca, a Brazilian-based instructor in Switzerland, came to London. Along with his brother, Demetrius, he showed some amazing ground skills and first-class instruction. Franco is a fifth Dan under Reyson Gracie who is the third son of the founder of BJJ, Carlos Gracie. I don't think that the assembled crowd really appreciated what they were taught back then. I already had read some articles about Brazilian ju jutsu and the Gracie family. The two hours of first-class instruction and rolling were a wonderful experience. I got to 'roll' with both these gentlemen and they were great. Their technique was so relaxed and effortless. I fully enjoyed my first introduction into this fascinating art.

Once again, I got a taste of martial arts Israeli-style when Krav Maga-expert Eyal Yanilov came to Bristol. Ironically, the Bristol course was held at 'Lifestyles Fitness Centre' which in a few years to come would become one of my permanent and most popular class-training venues.

When I turned up for this course, there were only a handful of people there to train. How crazy. A world-renowned instructor on the doorstep and not for the first time, Bristol was sleeping. It was their loss and my gain. Krav Maga was initially a military-based system that was then taught to civilians for self-defence. The system is based on quick, sharp and straightforward techniques. Simple in nature and highly practical. Eyal is one of the highest graded instructors in Krav. His grades were awarded to him by the founder Imi Lichtenfeld. Eyal has brought Krav Maga to over fifty countries. This was a unique opportunity to train with somebody top of the tree in the then very little-known art. Today, Krav has gone global. For good or bad, everybody and their dog trains in Krav. It has in my opinion become the 'crossfit' of the martial arts. It has many imitators, but I am glad to have got my taste of it from one of the best.

We trained in multiple drills. Good practical stuff backed up by Eyal Yanilov's worldwide knowledge of his first-hand experience of self-defence, having worked in security in some of the most dangerous countries in the world. It was a highly enjoyable training session and a stone's throw from where I was then living.

I was also surprised and honoured that Eyal had heard of me, and we talked at length about our martial arts training. This would not be the last time that I would train under him in Krav Maga, and it was nice to know that this man had heard of my name in Britain and had gone out of his way to give me some personal instruction and advice.

The late, great Gary Spiers was another man that I got to train under on his special 'applied street' karate seminars. Gary was a native of New Zealand and a big man in many ways. His seminars were always lively with plenty of workable techniques and sage advice from a man, who was the godfather of front-line security for over thirty-five years. His stories of his real-world experience were without equal. To listen to his sage advice was worth the asking price of his seminars alone. Although I didn't personally know Gary, I was greatly shocked and saddened by his untimely death. He was a man who literally cheated death on many occasions and seemed virtually bulletproof. He faced down knives, guns, bottles, baseball bats, iron bars and mass gang attacks. He was a larger-than-life character, not just in physique. He will be sadly missed. I treasure some of the gems of wisdom he left from those seminars. He inspired me greatly. I hope his full life story will be told one day and made into a film, so he can be remembered for the great martial artist he truly was.

At this stage of my martial arts journey, I was relentless to train with the best from any style or system. I wasn't into politics. All I wanted to do was improve my knowledge from as many sources as possible in real-world combat.

More seminars and training were to come my way. As 1995 began to loom, I didn't realise that this year would change my life considerably and set me on my lifetime ambition to become a professional full-time martial arts instructor.

"The one thing we haven't got enough of is time, so don't waste it."

Beginning of a Lifetime Ambition

At the start of 1995, I was determined to try and expand my classes and my profile. I felt that there were a lot of people out there who would be interested in training in my Combat ju jutsu but weren't aware of the classes or myself. I set out to try and rectify this. But I found that being stuck in an eight a.m. to five p.m. job day in day out wasn't giving me the time to do what I really wanted to do with my life.

I had been working in timber yards and sawmills most of my life and although I was a qualified sawyer and a yard foreman, the job was beginning to get me down and I had lost all enthusiasm for it. There were many reasons for this but basically lack of staff, wage cuts and constant hassle from the management were all taking their toll. On top of this, having a young family and many responsibilities, plus my heavy training regimes. Also, I wanted to do something on a day-to-day basis which was fulfilling. I didn't want to end up one of those people sitting in the pub on a Friday night, moaning about missed opportunities and having regrets. Something had to change. I had set myself a massive work ethic, and I was in danger of being swallowed up by it all.

I had a bit of a shock when I went for a routine health check and the doctor found my blood pressure was a little too high. I went back the next week and it was still the same. Now for somebody who prided himself in being super fit, this really did trouble me. I knew I ate sensibly. I didn't smoke. I drank little and I didn't use salt or eat over-high quantities of fat. When I sat down and analysed my present lifestyle, it was stress that was the factor. It can creep up on you. No wonder it's called the 'Silent Killer'. Duties, responsibilities at work, home and training, plus lack of sleep due to my young kids and basically running around like a blue ass fly hadn't helped.

I knew something had to give. This had been a gradual build up and now, I had to re-address the balance. Once I was aware of the problem, I began to get it under control, but it took great discipline. Eventually, the blood pressure went back to being normal by itself.

This and my gradual dislike for the job prompted me to see if there was life beyond the gates of the timber yard. The stress was also making me become overly aggressive and confrontational with people. It was a tough job in a predominately male environment with some unsavoury characters who, if they saw a weakness in you, would walk right through it. This wasn't a time of political correctness. If somebody thought you were a cunt, they told you. If you didn't like it, then they weren't averse to throwing a punch your way. This was not tears and tantrums over the boardroom table. Life in a dockside timber yard is not a Boy Scout picnic. You sank or learnt to swim with the sharks. If they were bastards, sometimes you had to become a bigger one. I am not proud of some of the things that I got involved with at that time, but it was a dog-eat-dog scenario. Tempers would flair and emotions could run high. It was a bit of a dark time for me and I was worried that I wasn't using my training for the right causes. After more than a few 'hairy' incidents, I decided that I had to get out and change my lifestyle quickly. I was becoming a person that I didn't much like.

You must remember that working in the places I did back in the 80s are a world of difference from the workplace now. Some disputes were settled with fists, not a memo or a strongly worded email. These were tough environments. You had to learn to stand up for yourself. Rough and tumble skirmishes were an everyday occurrence. There was always somebody up for a piss-take or a bit of a fight.

If they thought you were an easy target, then you were done for. My training came in very useful, but sometimes it all went a bit overboard.

I recall an incident when this big lad that used to come into the timber yard found out that I practised martial arts. He used to try it on with me, always goading me and trying to get me to react. One day, we were out in a reasonably quiet part of the yard and he called me out. I didn't want any of it, but he wasn't going away. He suddenly lunged forward and grabbed me by my jacket lapels. My training instinctively took over. I double palm slapped him over the ears and brought my knee up fast into his balls. He hit the floor as if he had been shot and stayed there.

I rolled him onto his side and he gradually came around. I think he was in shock because he just got up and stumbled off in the direction of his van and drove off. My hands were shaking with the surge of adrenaline. I didn't feel great about what I did, but he had pushed me into a corner.

I saw him a few weeks later and he apologised and all was okay, but I was concerned that I could have done him some serious harm.

On another occasion a guy came into the yard and surprised me by grabbing me in a bearhug from behind. My training took over and I grabbed him by the balls and squeezed; as his grip loosened, I applied 'Sankyo' wristlock to his right arm and he hollered in pain as I took him to the floor. Job done. This ju jutsu stuff was good!

Working environments of builders' yards, timber yards and building sites were no place for cry-babies or sensitive souls. They were places of non-stop banter, piss-taking, arguments and fights. Nobody complained; that was the way it was. There was no hiding behind authority then. I witnessed supervisors, foremen and managers hit the deck for mouthing it. There were no favourites.

There has been more than one occasion where I have had to put my skills to the test on the streets. I don't particularly want to glorify them either. But I can say that whenever I have been forced to use a strike or a choke, I have always had the fear that the person on the end was not going to get back up. I had one such incident where I thought that this was going to happen and it scared me enough to really respect my skills and try to avoid conflict like the plague.

I realised that the skills I was learning were not 'tip tap' sparring. They were proper combat techniques that could result in permanent injury or worse. (More on this subject later.)

I had always dreamt of teaching martial arts for a living and I decided that this was the best time. I had the necessary qualifications and experience and I felt the need to stretch myself. I was thirty-three years old and I was nearing my peak and didn't want to leave it another five years and then regret it.

The decision to make the change was a frightening one but also exciting. It was a big step and a gamble. I had a comfortable monthly wage coming in, but now I was ready to sacrifice this security for ambition and to chase my dreams. There is a saying by Winston Churchill that goes something like this, "Many men go to their grave with their best song still inside them." I didn't want to be one of them. When you break out of any comfort zone, you will feel fear, but I was beginning to understand that fear could be your friend and not your enemy. My burning desire to do something worthwhile in my life overrode my fear.

I didn't want to be one of those individuals who spend their every waking hour moaning about their job, their boss and their life. We only get one shot on this planet. Why waste it? Why let fear get a grip on you so tightly that it snuffs out your ambition like the flame of a candle in the wind?

I set the wheels in motion by contacting some of the local sports centres and asking if they would be interested in a ju jutsu coach and a self-protection instructor. I met with the managers and brought my CV, trying to convince them that what I taught was different to the multitude of classes teaching kickboxing or taekwondo.

A few months earlier, with the help of a contact, I had made my first training video of my grading syllabus. My good friend and fellow black belt, Andy Wintle transferred a short montage of this onto another tape and I brought this with me and asked each manager to view it and then make their decision. It took many months to arrange meetings and sort out details, but in the end, after numerous refusals and doors being shut in my face, I secured work at three Bristol-based sports centres and was employed by the Bristol City Council as a martial arts/self-protection coach.

It was a start, but it wasn't going to give me a massive income to support my family, so I devised a plan to ask my manager at the timber yard if I could step down from my job as foreman and take a part-time post. The only reason I thought he might go for this was because he used to practise karate and often spoke about martial arts to me and he knew my passion for them.

After consulting head office, he went for the idea and I was on a three-day week, giving me two days off to promote and expand my martial arts business.

At first, it was hard, and Tina and I struggled for money, having to cut back on a lot of things and tread water for many months. I'm sure our parents would have helped us out financially, but we were too proud to ask. It was my decision to pursue my dream, so I had to live with the good and the tough times. No moaning and no self-pity. My father was a great believer in your standing on your own two feet and getting on with it.

You learn to 'grow a pair' fast or you will sink. To establish myself, I was going to have to bust a gut and try everything and anything to succeed, and when I had exhausted those options, do it all over again and again.

Some people don't realise that to obtain even a hint of success, you have got to be in it for the long haul and not bail out at the first failure. There is no quick fix and if there is, it is only short-lived!

Tina supported me every inch of the way and never once doubted me, even when I began to doubt myself. She would encourage me and fire me up and never let me become down for long. What a lady. Now, most people will live above their means on credit cards or loans but, back then, that wasn't the way it was done. You cut back or went without. At one stage, I even had to sell my car. Tina budgeted incredibly to keep the family going.

I was last in the pecking order. My wife and kids came first. I must admit that there were many dark nights when I lay in bed wondering if I could make it. The only luxuries that we were experiencing at this stage was putting food on the table and ensuring the kids had school uniforms. Week by week, we lived waiting for any change for the better.

Each class would have me nervously looking at the clock and then at the door, hoping students would come onto my mat. This became a mainstay feature for many years. I learnt that just when you thought you had cracked it, you would get a nasty surprise as your numbers would drop and you would have to start the entire process again. All you instructors and coaches out there will know what I mean.

I gradually got the three new clubs up and running from scratch. I would travel and turn up to teach two or three people for weeks until it became five and six and so on. Once again, all you instructors out there will know how hard that can be. The work and planning that needs to go into this area to make it be successful is immense. Also, the long and worrying times where you are trying to make it pay.

Self-employment makes you aware of the fact that you carry all the weight of expectation on your shoulders. You can't pass the buck onto somebody else, nor can you blame your failures on them. You can't go missing in action. You have got to stand up and be counted. There are no paid holidays or sick leave. No having a crafty Monday on the 'sick' after a weekend of overindulging. Your incentive is to produce a wage to live on this month and hope you get one the following month and so on. Yes, it is nice to be your own boss, but for me, "the buck stopped here."

In the meantime, I was writing letter after letter or phoning different associations, groups, etc., asking if they wanted self-defence training during the day. This was a time well before emails and text messages. It was a time-consuming and laborious process, but it had to be done. It was no good sitting on your hands waiting for somebody to magically open the door to success for you. I had more knockbacks than I care to remember. It can be soul-destroying. I used to wait for the post to drop through the letterbox only to open half a dozen rejection letters, and that was just a few of those who bothered to write back to me. The hard part of any business is getting your foot in the door. Once that is achieved, I feel the best advertisement is word of mouth and a testimony from somebody.

This is how it went month after month, gradually building and relentlessly never taking my foot off the pedal. I absolutely refused to be put down. Tenacity can eventually move mountains and I was beginning to develop it by the bucketload. I was determined never to go back to the timber yards. Fear of failure was keeping me going as much as hunger for success was.

Now, I also began to develop my writing interest. As a young boy, I used to enjoy writing stories for fun and always kept an interest in this subject. I thought if I could get a few articles in some magazines, it might raise my profile. So, I started by writing articles and sending them off to mainstream martial arts publications. In the beginning, I had little success and then gradually one or two were published.

The now long gone 'Steve Grayston's Martial Arts' was the first publication to give me regular space. I am extremely grateful to Steve for his help on setting me off on the road to exploring bigger and better writing projects. Getting established is challenging work and you must have dogged persistence and belief that somebody out there will want to read your stuff.

You must get the publishers and editors to know your work and know your credentials as they receive shedloads of articles every day. You must be able to rise above the mainstream.

Paul Clifton of 'Combat Magazine', Bob Sykes of 'Martial Arts Illustrated' and the legendary Terry O'Neil of 'Fighting Arts International' all gave me space in their publications. But Tim Ayling of 'Fighters' magazine was an incredibly loyal supporter of my burgeoning writing for many years and did me proud.

I wasn't being paid for any of my articles in the martial arts publications but it was like a free advertisement for the system, club or products that I sold and this helped me immensely in raising my profile and developing my business.

Also, at this point, I must mention Geoff Thompson, self-protection pioneer and prolific author, film and playwright who unselfishly gave me so much advice, help and guidance and used his influence to help open a few doors for me. More will be coming soon about how I first met Geoff and why I'm proud to call him a valued friend.

I also started to make more training videos on different aspects of my art. These were not BBC broadcast quality but good enough and reasonably priced for people to learn from. Hey, the 'Blair Witch Project' did okay on a dodgy handheld camera! They have all been very successful, particularly the 'Impact Ju Jutsu Series' which has sold really well.

I have had positive and complimentary comments from people who have purchased them, including many high-graded martial artists, which is always nice. Since then, I have produced many DVDs on a variety of subjects. There might be another one or two in the pipeline. I always enjoy making them but they are demanding work.

Firstly, you must plan it, write it, choreograph it, direct it and also be in it. No mean feat. Ridley Scott and Martin Scorsese, beware!

Later, I met and worked with top-class production companies who helped me with these processes. Back then, it was very much a 'Do It Yourself' project. I would also like to thank all my students and fellow instructors who have appeared in the videos/DVDs with me, and endured the pain and suffering I dished out whilst demonstrating techniques.

Next up, I began to plan a book. I had been an avid reader of martial arts books for years and had built up a vast library. With the help of two brilliant specialists in rare and interesting books, Mr. John Sparkes and my old pal Mr. Tony Downing, I have managed, over the years, to purchase many diverse and out-of-print publications. These guys are simply the best at what they do and nine times out of ten, they will come up trumps for me if I am looking for a book that is obscure. Tony became a lifelong friend of mine and still lets me know if he tracks down anything of interest.

I had an idea to write a book on self-defence for the smaller person because there were no texts solely addressed to this problem. Being below average height myself, I had trained with taller and bigger people all my life. I had developed techniques and strategies to combat a large assailant, and I felt that this would be a different type of book that hadn't been covered before.

I spoke with Tony Downing about the idea and he assured me that nothing had been written on the subject and I should go for it before somebody else took it.

I began the project and worked whenever possible to get my ideas down on paper. Sometimes, I would sit up to the small hours of the morning writing and in the long run, it all paid off.

Now, writing a book can be a problem in itself but trying to get somebody to publish it is an even bigger headache. Believe me, it can deflate your ego and self-belief in seconds.

I wrote countless letters to every publisher under the sun. I used to go into Waterstone's bookstore and spend hours writing down the addresses of every martial arts publication house. I bought the 'Writers' Handbook' to find more addresses and editors' actual names so I could address my letters personally to them. No whipping onto the worldwide web then.

Rejection! Rejection! Rejection! No one wanted to know, or wanted to take a risk on it. I really didn't think I would get any interest. After so much rejection, you start questioning the book and wondering, is it any good in the first place and what made you think you could get a book published anyway. I was no Stephen King or Dan Brown. I had no university degree or writing qualifications. Who the fuck did I think I was! I knew nothing about writing a book. I was kidding myself, wasn't I? These thoughts all sailed through my mind on a regular basis. It became a big psychological battle and it was very difficult to keep upbeat about the whole thing. It really knocked my confidence.

I had first toyed with the book and began to write notes around 1992. It was now speeding towards the end of 1995, and I was still having no luck with publication. Looking back, I had been a little naïve thinking somebody would just instantly take this book on which, in retrospect, wasn't exactly fucking 'War and Peace'. Once again, I put the idea on the backburner whilst I pursued other things. Then, out of the blue, I got a break!

I was reading through one of the latest martial arts magazines when I came across yet another advert that would change my life for the better. The advert was for a new book release. The title intrigued me. It was called 'Dogs Don't Know Kung-Fu.' Looking closer, I saw that the author was Jamie O' Keefe. Now, there was a name from the past.

I ordered the book and enclosed a letter explaining who I was and our connection in the early 80s with GBASSDA. Jamie returned my letter, saying that he remembered my name and he asked me what I thought of his book.

I phoned him up and we chatted and he told me how he had just started up his own publishing company. It was called New Breed Publications. I seized the opportunity to ask him if he would look over my manuscript for my proposed book. Jamie agreed and I immediately sent it off to him.

Within a week or so, Jamie rang me and told me he thought the manuscript would make a terrific book. I was gobsmacked. After so many negative responses, I couldn't quite believe it. I could have kissed him. You will appreciate how happy I was when you see what Jamie looks like in the photos section of this book!

So that was that. The wheels were beginning to turn for my ambition of getting my first book published. Okay, New Breed were a burgeoning publishing company, not one of the big boys, but that didn't matter to me. Somebody had given me a chance after receiving more rejection letters than you could build a house with.

I sorted out a business arrangement with Jamie and he set about getting the book entitled 'I Thought You'd Be Bigger' into print. I really enjoyed this period and learnt so much about the book publishing business and the work entailed to get it to the finished article. Jamie worked professionally and tirelessly to give me help and advice and slowly the project came together.

Just before Christmas 1995, the book was ready. Jamie, who was travelling down to the South West, took a detour to Bristol and delivered the first print personally to my door. It was great to see the first copy and also my old friend in person. I will cherish that moment forever.

Although Jamie had done the entire computer work, scanning and printing, I was proud of the fact that everything in the book had been written by me. All the text, all the illustrations and the entire photography arrangements and photo placement had been my work. There is a real feeling of achievement when you see a project go through from a bundle of handwritten notes to emerge as a complete book with your name on it. Remember, all of this was achieved with no computers.

I had left school at fifteen years of age with no O or A levels. I was, by my own admissions, an underachiever and destined initially for a life of manual labouring. But somewhere along the line, the little spark that was still flickering inside me began to burn ever brighter as I pulled myself up the ladder of life and reached a little higher. For me, writing a book and having it published was a dream come true. Holding that book in your hand for the first time was like cradling your new-born baby. After all, you had helped to create that too.

I was so proud that I wanted to walk around with a copy in my hand all the time. Shit, I even had one under my pillow! Only kidding… honest!

This started a long and continuing partnership with New Breed and Jamie. He has helped publish my other books as well: 'In Your Face,' 'Grappling with Reality' and by the end of 2001, 'Bad to the Bone.' Later would come 'In the Face of Violence' and 'Unleash the Beast.'

From 1995 to 2001, I had written four books. More than I could have hoped for. They have all sold reasonably well enough and I am pleased with my achievements. It had always been one of my main ambitions and I had fulfilled it. Not too many people get to do this in their lifetime.

I try to write each day. It is the same as any skill: you must practise to get better. I look back on some of my early writing these days and cringe. But I then try and remember I was on a new journey, a journey I am still working hard at. When I read some other writer's books, I marvel at their words and hope to, someday, aspire to their level. That said, I don't expect some of them know a hip throw from a roundhouse kick. I must put it all in perspective.

New Breed went on in the coming years to greater success, publishing many more books on the cutting edge of self-protection and martial arts. Jamie did a first-class job. Writing is not easy. You learn and develop as you go along, and you have got to be prepared to spend many hours planning. You must develop much self-discipline to motivate yourself to get on with it. In my early writing career, I did all my work without the aid of any computer software. I handwrote the manuscript and Tina typed it on a typewriter! Old-fashioned in this day and age maybe, but it goes to show that with the will and determination to succeed, you can achieve anything you want. I truly believe the discipline and confidence that martial arts had given me also gave me the belief to write.

"The man who won't read is no better than the man who can't read."

Relentless

Along with the first book in 1995, I was also still keen to further my abilities as a martial artist and keep making a success of my ever-expanding clubs.

I now had a new hardcore section of people training, and they were to become my third generation of black belts. Great guys like Rob Cannon, Matt Sperring, Paul Flett, Andy Wintle and Phil Davies were all going to be heading for black belts in the next few years to come and became extremely good martial artists and highly valued members of my then 'Bristol Goshin Ju Jutsu Combat Academy'.

These guys all trained so hard. They were incredibly dedicated. I find currently many people just flit in and out of training with no purpose or goal, and many are soft, not just physically but mentally. They are not equipped to go the distance. How times change.

On a personal level, I was again seeking new instruction. I hadn't heard from Micky Upham for some time, so I thought I would seek out his old partner, Dave Vincent. Dave had been a close pal of Mick's and had helped develop the Goshin Ryu-style of ju jutsu in the Merseyside area, but in recent years, their partnership had split up. Dave now had his own association called the British Kempo Ju Jutsu Union.

I contacted Dave and explained once again who I was and that I wanted to do some training with him. As luck had it, Dave had a few clubs over in Wales, not too far from me. Just a quick trip over the Severn Bridge. So, whenever Dave visited Wales, I went over and reacquainted myself with him.

Dave was a superb martial artist who, unfortunately, lost a great deal of his mobility due to a hip injury. I remembered him in earlier years as a fantastic kicker. Now, he was unable to use these skills but he still had fast and sharp hand speed. What I also liked about Dave was the fact that on his seminars, he gave me many opportunities to teach. He wasn't just going to hog all the limelight himself. He was generous like this and I thank him for giving me the opportunity to show my stuff.

He informed me that he would very soon like to give me the chance to grade for my fifth Dan. This was a fantastic opportunity for me, and I was determined as always that when the time came, I would be ready!

Also, at this extremely busy time, I encountered another person that would have a massive influence on my future and that person was

Geoff Thompson. I first really became aware of Geoff when I read his cult book 'Watch My Back' in its first printing. I was totally absorbed by the book and Geoff's story of his journey from a young, bullied and frightened kid to becoming a nightclub doorman and world-famous martial artist. The first time you read it, you just see an extremely violent character. But if you take time to read it again, you will see the underlining story of a bullied boy who totally changed himself, conquered and controlled his fears and became a better person in the long run because of this. Geoff has gone on to incredible success from these early days.

The book was, and still is, inspirational for me. It also intrigued me when Geoff spoke about subjects like the fence, action triggers, adrenaline switches and fear control. His philosophy of self-protection was quite radical then. Not many people in the UK were approaching these topics like Geoff, and I liked what I read.

In search of valuable information on self-protection, I had been reading books by top US experts like Bradley Steiner, Marc Mac Young, Tony Bluer and Peyton Quinn.

As I was becoming a bit of an expert on all books on close-quarter combat from way back, I became an avid collector of texts by the greats such as Charles Nelson, Fairbairn, Biddle, Applegate, Styers, etc.

I scanned bookshops far and wide. Remember that there was no Amazon online back then. These books were hard to find and like gold dust outside the UK. If you sent off a 'fistful of dollars' in a letter to the USA, you were never sure if you would see the return of a book or your money. It was all a bit hit-and-miss really.

The 'Outdoorsman' bookstore in Brecon was excellent for these unusual titles, and I used them so much over the years as were 'Mona Books'. I was relentless in my thirst for knowledge and invested a lot of money and time building a grand collection of unusual martial arts texts. Many had been out of print for decades.

Bradley Steiner's work was excellent and in the 80s, again, quite controversial. His system of self-defence called Combato was based on World War II close-quarter, ju jutsu and Kempo. His books such as 'No Second Chance,' 'Subway Survival' and 'Below the Belt' were excellent. I corresponded with Mr. Steiner on a few occasions by letter, and he gave me sage advice on combat training and we discussed many aspects of real-world self-defence.

Geoff Thompson's work and approach was similar, and to have somebody in the UK teaching these principles was enlightening and I knew I just had to meet and train with him.

Geoff had just set up the British Combat Association with UK martial arts legend Peter Consterdine. The association was designed to practise pure self-protection and both men were embarking on a seminar tour. When I saw that they were coming to Bristol, I knew that come hell or high water, I was going to be there.

The venue was one of my old training homes – Whitchurch sports centre. On the day, the centre was already booked for a large karate tournament, so Geoff was relegated to the indoor bowling green for his seminar!

Peter couldn't be there that day, but Geoff arrived with his wife, Sharon, his brother-in-law and, at this stage, his top student, Alan Peasland (Al has since gone on to be a very accomplished instructor in his own right and is an excellent martial artist) and another then up-and-coming self-protection instructor, Dave Briggs.

The day was top-class. Geoff started with his theories and experiences of violent situations, and then we went on to practise pre-emptive shots on the pads, power punching, knock-out techniques, power kicking, line-ups and fence work. Later, we drilled kick defences and ground-grappling techniques before finishing with the customary ground grappling, no rules, 'all in' against various opponents. The green baize of the bowling green wasn't the best of places for this. I ended up with lots of skin burns and I was coughing up bits of green fluff for days after, as well as finding bits of it in many a strange place. But the experience had been brilliant.

I kept in touch with Geoff and trained again some months later when he and Peter came back to Bristol. Also, I visited Pete Miller's dojo (another very good martial artist and fighter) in Backwell near Bristol when Geoff came to do a seminar there. I recently reacquainted myself with Pete and, for a time, he was training and teaching out of my gym. Also, Geoff travelled to my old mate Darren Richardson's dojo in Gosport. I just tried to get on as many of the seminars as I could to learn and absorb information from two first-class pioneers of self-protection. The training was real and demanding. Every seminar tested your mettle and made you confront your fears. These days, 'reality self-defence' is bandied around all over the place, but I felt privileged back then to have been in at the dawn of it with the British Combat Association. I had some tough but memorable times with them. I am still with the BCA today. I joined the British Combat Association in June 1995 and was determined to establish myself in its ranks. The BCA opened up many new doors to train with some of the best combat instructors, not only in the UK but indeed the world. I also got to meet, train, grapple and spar with many new friends, colleagues and acquaintances. Below are a few of the top-class people that I have met over the years.

There was Alan Charlton who ran the then Self Protection Association. He is a giant of a man, an accomplished martial artist and a gentleman. Also, Russian Sambo specialist Darren Richardson; Vale Tudo champions and instructors of Geoff's real combat system, Matty Evans, Tony Somers and Justin Gray; Sambo champion Vadim Kolganov; Dave Briggs, self-protection specialist; Maurice Teague, an extremely experienced combat veteran; Jim Burns; Glenn Smith and Alan Peasland – all boxing coaches. There are bound to be more and I apologise if I have missed you out.

I got the opportunity to go on instructor's courses in Coventry and train with the best. Peter Consterdine's impact and power striking is totally awesome. It must be felt to be believed. He is also an incredibly fit man who trains fanatically. His 'Fit to Fight' training sessions are legendary. Also, his knowledge of self-protection, security and bodyguarding are second to none. He is really one of the premier experts in the world, and we should be proud that he is British. Peter and Geoff have supplied some hard and truly memorable instructor's courses.

Others I have trained under are ex-world champion and Olympic judo silver medallist, Neil Adam, OBE. He is a true gent and a fantastic judo man. I have witnessed and experienced Neil grappling on the mats against all corners, one after the other and going through them without breaking sweat, arm-barring them for fun. We all rave about the ground skills of Brazilian ju jutsu but here is a British guy who is top drawer in all aspects of grappling and is truly world class. The same can be said for the powerful and flawless judo of then British champion, Wayne Lakin. These guys can throw you around like rag dolls.

I also trained with ex European featherweight boxing champion Jim MacDonald and his then heavyweight fighter Scot Welch who appeared in the film 'Snatch' fighting Brad Pitt at the film's climax. Jim's fight stories and marathon pad work sessions were worth their weight in gold.

A few years down the line, I was fortunate to have former British light welterweight boxing champion, Bristol's own Ross 'The Rooster' Hale come to train in my Mixed Martial Arts classes. Ross wanted to learn grappling skills, which he picked up extremely well, but he also imparted some of his boxing knowledge on to me. A pro-boxer has the best hands in the world of combat sport, without a doubt. They can hit you hard and fast before you know it, even when you think you are covered up. If you get a chance to train, be sure to use the mitts and spar with one. Ross is a superb boxer and a true gentleman. I learnt so much from the many rounds we sparred together, and I thank him for not knocking me out, although I did take many a stiff dig.

Once more, I trained with Krav Maga expert Eyal Yanilov. Also, the brilliant Rick Young and I reacquainted myself with one of my old instructors, Dave Turton of Goshinkwai Combat.

I hadn't seen or heard of Dave from our GBASSDA days, but I did know that he was a member of the BCA.

I recall finishing the end of a seminar, hosted by Neil Adams, by competing in some back-to-back grappling. I was leaving the mat after about six continuous fights and the last one being a bit of a war with then European Vale Tudo champ, Justin Gray. I was knackered and spitting out blood when I heard a broad Yorkshire accent say, "All right, Kev?" I looked around and there was Dave. It was great to see him. We chatted and promised to keep in touch and do a seminar together. Dave would figure again in my life in later years.

Also, in this year, the great grappling explosion hit the martial arts world. Gracie Ju Jutsu and the Ultimate Fighting Championships hit the scene and all this would change the way martial arts would be practised forever.

I had read some years earlier about the Gracie family and their Brazilian ju jutsu in the iconic American martial arts magazine such as 'Black Belt'. I read how it was a fantastic ground grappling art and how they were unbeaten in challenge matches. Also, that the system was going to become massive and that Mel Gibson had learnt it for a fight scene in his then latest film 'Lethal Weapon'. Brazilian ju jutsu appeared then to be the next big martial art, and it certainly did become just that along with other grappling systems.

When all of this was occurring, my own ju jutsu classes began to get several new people joining on the strength of watching Royce Gracie's victories in the UFC. Although my system wasn't Brazilian, this didn't seem to matter as long as we had some form of grappling. This was fine with me and I wanted to make the most of this opportunity.

I sensed this whole thing was going to be huge and I wanted to be part of it. I certainly didn't want to miss the boat. Reality training and grappling were the buzzwords, and I decided to expand this side of things and develop specific sessions for those who wanted to test their skills in a high-pressure environment and maybe go on to compete.

Geoff had also been pushing his infamous 'Animal Day' sessions and these were getting good but controversial publicity, and I knew I would also incorporate all this into my own training. Over the coming years, this would all develop in a big way and open many more doors.

I really admired all the guys who went up to Coventry to do this stuff. It took incredible 'bottle'. To know you were going to be facing another person that was essentially a stranger and then having to go at it 'hammer and tongs' took big balls.

Those days were a massive learning curve for all who thought their martial art was indestructible.

Some held up under fire, others fell apart like a cheap suit.

Many didn't agree with 'Animal day' and what Geoff was doing but for others, myself included, it was revolutionary. I take my hat off to him.

This was all a forerunner to the massive storm that was to come when mixed martial arts and cage fighting appeared on the horizon a little while later.

The world of martial arts was never going to be the same again. Some were ready for it and many more weren't.

I knew that I was and couldn't wait for the next chapter of my journey to unfold.

I'm a great believer in seizing opportunities if they come along and not letting them pass you by. Too many people sit and moan about what they could have done given the chance or 'if only they had done such a thing' and 'if only they got that break'.

I believe that you make your own luck. Nobody will hand things to you on a plate. You must have initiative, drive, get-up-and-go. You must be prepared to work hard and make sacrifices, but at the end of the day, the rewards will come. But it isn't going to happen overnight.

In 1995, I seized a lot of opportunities and with tenacity and a will to succeed, I had achieved much. This year was, once more, a massive learning curve for me. I felt that I had grown again, not only as a martial artist but as a person. I was relentless in my pursuit to train with the best and to strive to be the best. When I attended these seminars, I wasn't there for the photo and the t-shirt at the end of the day (although that was always nice). I learnt the lessons and brought that knowledge back with me and drilled it inside out until it became mine. Then, I would teach it. I took vast amounts of notes and still have, to this day, loads of old notepads crammed full of my scribbles from many seminars and courses.

There just didn't seem to be enough hours in the day to do what I wanted to do. I had achieved a fair few of my ambitions, yet more was to come!

"A man's destiny knows that beyond this hill lie another and another. The journey is never complete."

Turning Professional

At the close of 1995, I received the final push to try and make a full-time living by becoming a professional martial arts instructor. I had nearly completed a year on my part-time working arrangements and the firm was now looking for redundancies. Being part-time, I was obviously in the firing line. So when the news came, it was no great surprise. But it still gave me that tingle of adrenaline in my belly which told me that this was it. I would finally have to cut loose the metaphoric 'lifeboat' that I had been clinging on to in times of emergency and now go it alone and start swimming by myself.

It felt strange saying my final goodbyes and knowing that I wasn't going to turn up as usual for work the next week. The three-day week had been a good weaning period for me and although it was the end of an episode in my life, I sensed new doors were opening. I felt I had something more to offer than just being stuck in a mundane job with no satisfaction from it at the end of a week.

I had reached a crossroads in my life and I was ready for a change. My children were getting older and settled into their school. Tina had secured some part-time work at the school, as she was an ex-nursery nurse with teaching skills. I felt the time was now right to go for it.

I realised that the martial arts work alone at that present moment wasn't enough to keep us financially afloat, so I began to work on another idea that I had been keen on for some time. I wanted to become a qualified fitness coach. I had been in and out of gyms all of my life. I had avidly followed loads of fitness regimes and weight training programmes and along with my martial arts training, had built up a good knowledge of the body's functioning and how best to get it into shape.

My local sports centre where I had started a ju jutsu class were looking for part-time coaches, but I needed some form of qualification to secure the work. So, they got me on a BAWLA course. This is the British Amateur Weightlifting Association. I completed a series of weekend workshops and an exam to get my leaders certificate so that I could start teaching weight training to rank beginners.

Within a few months, the gym was updated and new equipment was shipped in from an American firm, Life Fitness. Also, there was a wide range of cardio machines, steppers, cross trainers, treadmills and rowers, etc. Once more, remember that back then, this was all ground-breaking stuff.

I went on another series of courses to learn all about this new equipment and the theory behind exercise, the muscles' workings, anatomy, proper programme organising and teaching methods.

I passed these exams and acquired NVQ level coaching certificates. I was now doing full gym inductions, personal programmes and working with and supervising schools whilst they used the facilities. This work grew and I was employed at other Bristol City Council sports centres and my schedule got busier.

Sometime later, I did another intense week's course with Fit to Perform Ltd. This course went into the finer points of exercise, nutrition, physiology and personal fitness programmes. Once again, I passed the oral, written and physical skills exams and felt now that I really could make a go of things in the fitness industry as well. Over the years since, I have worked with all types of people and advised and helped them with their fitness from school children, the elderly, physically and mentally challenged, clients referred from their GPs with serious health problems and sports-specific groups and individuals. I have met some wonderful people, some very ill people who have shown great courage to even come to the gym and also some oddball characters.

The job has given me a better understanding and tolerance of people's various levels of fitness. Because I was fit and came from a background of hard physical pursuit, I had to re-educate myself with the average person's fitness needs compared to the serious competitor or athlete. It was a great learning curve for me and made me realise that you can't take your own fitness for granted.

Between my martial arts and fitness work, I was eventually beginning to earn a decent income at long last.

People over the years have said how lucky I am to be doing a job that I love. Well, luck doesn't come into it. Hard fucking work and an unshakable belief that you can cut it is what it takes. Yes, I loved the job but at no time was it ever easy.

The year 1996 started with me pushing on to establish myself as a professional full-time coach shared between my two pursuits. Also, I kept my magazine articles going and writing my books. I was building up a demanding but rewarding schedule. When people thank you for your work, your guidance or help and show genuine appreciation, it makes everything worthwhile. It was something that I hadn't experienced very often in my past, regular eight-to-five jobs. You do get a deep sense of fulfilment and it boosts your confidence to try harder and reach further.

In March of this year, Dave Vincent came to Bristol for a seminar and to grade me for my fifth Dan black belt. I knew that this would undoubtedly be another challenge. But I had been meeting so many recently that I was ready for anything. Plus, I felt at my peak physically, not only in my fitness, but also my technique.

I remember this seminar for one of those massive throwing marathons that Dave and Micky seemed to favour. This one was a 'throwing pyramid' where you started off throwing each other five times each with a hip throw followed by five push-ups, then move on to ten throws and ten push-ups, then fifteen, twenty, twenty-five, thirty, forty and fifty and when you reached the top of this pyramid, you started coming back down again to five. This is a massive throwing regime. It took nearly an hour to complete and many people afterwards were badly dehydrated, physically sick or just collapsed in a heap on the floor.

I honestly gave it my all. I stayed focused, gave and received the throws and did not falter. I had learned to dig deep and I knew what I was capable of those days. I was on turbo boost and nothing was going to stop me from achieving my goal. After the throws, we went through many Goshin Kai close-quarter combat drills, incorporating strikes, joint locks, chokes and takedowns, which took another hour.

After a lunch break, I was taken to one side by Dave and put through a whole regime of ju jutsu techniques. I demonstrated twenty-five different throws, twenty-five different joint locks, twenty-five strangles or chokes, defences against frontal and rear grabs, defence against punches, kicks, knives, basketball bats, coshes, bottles and firearms. Then, it was standing to floor pad work. Next up, techniques using the baton, Yawara-bo, fighting knives and makeshift weapons, finishing off with ground grappling/sparring and anatomy and physiology questions.

It was a full and demanding grading but by the end, I had achieved the grade of fifth Dan. It had been a long, tiring but hugely successful day, and Dave had been great, giving me every opportunity to show what I could do. Plus, once more, my 'lads' didn't let me down and gave an exceptional performance.

Fifth Dan was a high rank to hold and I realised just how far I had come from those early days, dreaming of achieving my black belt. If I wanted to, I could now wear the famed red and white belt that I had seen other high-ranked instructors wear when I was younger.

I knew how much work I had put in to get this far. The same as anything that you want to achieve in life, you won't get it by half-heartedly having a go. You have got to want it one hundred percent and pursue it one hundred percent.

I had read enough autobiographies of famous sports people to know that they didn't get to where they are in life without relentless drive, ambition and belief. I had to do the same. It's not easy, but then if it was, everybody would be walking around with a black belt or whatever it was they wanted to aspire to.

Other avenues were also beginning to open for me teaching self-defence. I was putting my skills to use with varied groups. I taught over-fifties groups, specific ladies' groups, schools and most challenging, wheelchair-bound disabled people.

I got involved in the latter project through another local council who rang me up and asked if I could teach physically disabled people self-defence. I said, "Yes," and immediately took up the challenge. With the support of the local authorities and police, I taught a six-week course. I did a lot of thinking on my feet and ad-libbing as I went along.

A lot of these people had lost the use of their legs or had multiple sclerosis, but their upper body strength was good. I got them hitting the focus pads with palm heel strikes that carried enough impact to put the most determined of attackers on their back. They also learnt basic self-defence against holds or people blocking their wheelchairs. This all went down well along with advice on security and awareness. The highlight of the course, for me, was getting one of the male participants out of his chair to practise simple techniques from a lying position which he performed wonderfully. This group of people were great. They gave everything a go and I found the whole thing hugely inspiring and rewarding. We also got coverage on local BBC television and Radio Bristol where I was interviewed. It was the first time that I had been involved with the media. It was an enjoyable experience and not to be my last!

I had now decided it was time to branch out and start a children's ju jutsu class – something that I hadn't considered before. Through my coaching certifications, I had learnt the correct way to coach kids and was prepared to put this theory into practice. I was to teach a very different method of ju jutsu, eliminating the more dangerous and combat elements of the art. No chokes or strangles, no joint locks (as young bones are still developing) and no dangerous strikes were some of the techniques to be excluded. Also, you must remember that children haven't developed the explosive short-term endurance of adults, so they are better suited to longer endurance-type fitness. But you must also never forget that some will have a short concentration span, so training must be varied and constantly moving. These points and many others must be considered to run a safe and professional class. Also, because of the close contact nature of ju jutsu, you must be careful how you teach children, especially the girls. Good, safe and thoughtful methods will put them at ease and you will be trouble free.

I had seen some terrible teaching over the years at children's classes on my travels and I wasn't about to make the same mistakes.

My three children joined the class at various times and have all developed into good martial artists. I have never pushed them to train. They have just grown up with it and took to it all naturally. It gave them all good fitness and self-confidence. Also, it has honed their discipline and respect which in modern times, can be lacking in many youngsters. Martial arts have been good for them, and I am happy that they have wanted to carry on training and come into the industry with me in one shape or form. Both my sons, Tom and Jake, are now very accomplished martial artists and fitness coaches as well as fighters.

The children's class started off slowly. For months, it was just my sons and two children of a friend. We trained in a small upstairs room at a sports centre, so I had to hump the mats up two flights of stairs and put them down on the floor of the room before even starting. Who said that martial arts was glamorous?

But gradually, through word of mouth, things began to pick up quickly. I was learning all the time but enjoying it, as it was a totally different challenge to teaching adults.

The class became well-established over time with forty or more children training from the ages of six to fifteen. I was now teaching in the main sports hall. It had a good atmosphere. All ages mixed without bullying or ego. Plus, we had a nice blend of girls and boys. Also, we encouraged parent interest and backing which was also nice.

Children, as they say, are the future, and I am glad to have guided many onto the path I followed and gave them focus and purpose in their life and hopefully in some small way influenced it.

Over the years, I have had various people help me coach the large numbers but have then moved on to other things. I had a few different coaches help me teach this class, but I would like to take this opportunity to thank Dave Tanner for all his help. I am most grateful for his contribution to teaching and his work behind the scenes.

The children's class gave me another television opportunity in August '96 when a children's weekend programme called 'No Naked Flames' asked if they could film my class as they covered different sports or recreations each week. The programme went out on ITV.

We filmed outdoors on the grass as the weather was glorious. The kids were brilliant, demonstrating lots of different aspects of ju jutsu. I did an interview and then I had to teach the young lady presenter some basic self-defence moves which she then performed on me. It was all good fun and an interesting experience.

One part that I do recall was when the TV host had to perform a full shoulder throw on me as a counter to a rear choke. Now, when she completed the move, she had to say a short closing sentence. But every time that she did it, she made a mistake in the dialogue. I tell you, being dumped continuously from a shoulder throw onto some sparsely grassed area was beginning to get bloody painful, to say the least. I was glad when she finally got it right! The things you do for a spot of TV coverage!

I appeared numerous times on television and radio, mainly to give advice and instruction on self-defence. I appeared on a local Bristol daytime show called BLT hosted by well-known Radio Bristol show host Dave Barrett. I gave self-protection advice for women after a series of attacks on females in Bristol. My wife, Tina, demonstrated some simple self-defence techniques.

Also, again for the same reason, GWR, a then local Bristol radio station, contacted me about coming in to train their staff after one of their employees had been assaulted after leaving work one evening.

I went to meet some of the staff at their workplace. I was going to give a short demonstration of the sort of things I could teach them. As always, I found the women were really interested and receptive. The males mostly get insecure and start acting up.

I recall being in the lift with a lovely lady who showed me around the building and spoke excitedly about what I was going to do. Just then the lift stopped and the doors opened and in came a guy. He was introduced to me and I knew him as one part of a popular GWR breakfast show duo. I liked the show but within twenty seconds of this guy speaking to me I realised he was a complete dick. He spouted on about how he didn't need self-defence training and made jokes about it, whilst the young lady with me looked embarrassed.

I hoped and prayed that this asshole would be in the group I was going to train – I wanted to 'bend' him a little bit and hear him squeal!

The group I met were at first sceptical of any training, but once I started showing some 'real' stuff with one of my fellow instructors, they began to warm to it.

I have found most TV and radio people to be a bit 'luvvie-like' with not a violent bone in their bodies. It was a bit of a culture shock to them.

My 'funny friend' was there in the room briefly, but when I suggested I might demonstrate a technique on him, he soon made a lame excuse and left.

It had been a wonderful experience, and as I was leaving the studios I bumped into *'Steps'*. (No, I didn't fall down the stairs. It was the pop group!) They were there for an interview. The look on the grinning face of 'H', one of the male singers, was enough to make me want to show him one of my favourite moves, but I resisted the temptation.

Another funny story I recall was when the *Western Daily Press*, a local newspaper, came to my class to do a piece on a seminar I was teaching on makeshift weapons. I was going to show how you could use everyday articles that you might carry on you for a weapon in an emergency.

In came a cameraman and a cocky newspaper reporter who immediately after a brief introduction handed me a copy of the newspaper he worked for and said sarcastically, "So show me what you can do with that."

"OK," I replied. I grabbed one of my instructors and told him to attack me, and then, with the newspaper rolled up tightly, I processed to smash him in the balls, throat, eyes and temples with it at blinding speed.

When I finished, I turned to the guy and said, "Is that enough or would you like to experience it?"

He had a total attitude change on the spot, and after the colour came back to his cheeks and his jaw had returned from the floor, we got on splendidly. I do love working with these people.

A great guy who interviewed me on Radio Bristol when I released my first fictional book (more later) was Graham Torrington. The tag line to introduce me was *'from the cage to the page'*. I thought he might try to belittle the subject matter or again poke fun at it but he didn't, he was a gentleman and gave me great coverage.

I also did some work on a late-night TV (the name escapes me now) show with James 'the Colossus Thompson' when I was training and preparing him for one of his up-and-coming fights. I held pads for him and we had a 'roll' together. It was great footage and James gave a top-drawer interview; the piece went down well.

I feel martial arts always manage to capture the public's imagination, and the television companies know it is a good topic to cover.

I am grateful to have had the opportunity to promote myself and my art numerous times for TV and radio.

This year forged on. Along with ju jutsu training, I was regularly attending the BCA courses and bringing more and more of their principles into my art. The Sunday morning sessions at the 'Budokan' were taking off and the impact/sparring training was flourishing, plus a lot of my students were progressing nicely in the full combat side of things and the reality pressure testing. These sessions were becoming quite notorious but, although they were hard, I constantly made sure that they were run correctly and that everybody progressed and didn't just come along to be battered.

They really were the forerunners to MMA classes. We did lots of conditioning, pad work and then sparring. Boxing, kickboxing, ju jutsu, ground fighting with and without the gi and all in street grappling.

It was a big learning curve for us all. The sessions were tough. Blood and snot stuff. We had people from all backgrounds attend. There was some tough full-on sparring. Many came and went, only a dedicated few stayed.

I recall a guy who trained with me for some time that worked the doors. He had a reputation for being a hardman, and he certainly had seen his fair share of violence on the street and in clubland.

He often asked me how I rated boxing over ju jutsu, and I replied they both have their merits. Both have their strengths and weaknesses. This conversation came up on more than one occasion. I began to get the feeling there was a subliminal challenge there.

He attended one of my Sunday morning classes, and in this one we were doing some all-in sparring. One guy would stay in and fight two different opponents, then another would come in and we would keep going until all the lads present had a go.

You would start at boxing range, and if you wanted to take it to the floor, that was fine.

I thought I would start it off. I asked for a volunteer to spar with me. This guy's hand was straight up. I saw it in his eyes as he pulled on the gloves, he meant business, he wanted to test me and see what I was made of. Well, he was about to find out. I knew when I asked for an opponent it would be him. I needed to face this challenge and put it to bed.

I already pre-empted the fact that he was going to come out swinging. He was a big guy. Six feet plus, fifteen stone or more compared to my five feet seven and a half inches and twelve stone at the time.

I bit down on my gumshield and steeled myself. He came in as predicted like a wild man, swinging big bombs. If one of them had landed, it would have taken my head off my shoulders. He could hit a bit.

But I was ready for him. I came under the swings and landed a huge left hook to his head. He wobbled and was stopped in his tracks. I moved in for the finish. Left to the body, straight right, left hook to the head and he was down and he wasn't getting up.

He learnt a tough lesson and he took it. We went on to be good friends. When he left the doors, he left the violence behind with him and became a born-again Christian.

It was an amazing transformation. When I first knew him, he had been a very aggressive man and a fighter of repute.

What I had going for me that Sunday morning was that I was a professional martial artist and fighter. My skill made the difference. Strength and size on this occasion didn't.

What most people don't realise is that a properly trained martial artist is a different breed. These guys fight for a living. They can punch and kick like a fucking machine, they can twist you into a pretzel, break your bones and choke you to sleep faster than any lullaby. They are dangerous. When you get into an argument on the street, be sure you are not facing one of these dudes!

I was still regularly reviewing videotapes, reading, researching and attending seminars to bring the latest and best techniques to my classes. I always felt Bristol was a little isolated from the main sources of martial arts training, but I was determined to put it on the map and kept pushing the profile. It took a lot of hard and single-minded work, but a day didn't go by when I didn't take another step forward.

I had many ideas and projects, but a lot fell through or didn't materialise. Sometimes, you meet people who promise you wonderful things and then let you down. I have found that because of this, I trust very few people and have built most of what I have achieved by myself with the help or guidance of a small group of trusted friends and colleagues. These people are true to their word and will not let you down. You people know who you are and many thanks.

At this stage of my career, I began to feel that I could make a living at full-time coaching. Up to that period, I did subconsciously wonder if I could keep it all going. This is not because I didn't believe in my abilities, but because I didn't know if I could get the breaks needed to further myself. Plus, you had to stay fit and in good health. As mentioned previously, when you are self-employed, there is no sick pay or five weeks' holiday a year.

During the year of 1996, I worked tirelessly to get my name around, to try to get on the seminars that mattered, and to meet the right people that could open more doors for me.

By doing this, I was invited to teach on many seminars. My good mates, Darren Richardson in Gosport and Alan Charlton in London and Dave Peterson in Surrey, invited me to hold seminars at their dojos or national courses. I also organised a multi-styled course down here in Bristol with other local martial artists joining in and training together. I had Martyn Hurd of then Muay Thai, John Bennett, my old aikido instructor, Simon Evans of taekwondo and myself teaching ju jutsu. It was an effective way to break down barriers and get people of various arts to mix.

Sometime earlier, I had taught on another mixed course in Bristol which reunited me with Andy and Chris Davies, who I hadn't seen since my early kung fu and taekwondo days. We had all come a long way since those times.

I regularly held a shared seminar with Martyn Hurd. Martyn is a former British middleweight Muay Thai champion and a top-class instructor here in the South West, along with John Munden. Martyn has since moved on to become a very accomplished Brazilian ju jutsu practitioner and coach. He is 'old school' like myself. We taught what we called 'standing to floor' seminars mixing Muay Thai and ju jutsu together for MMA fighting. We have had good success with the idea, which back then was quite innovative.

As this year ended, I had completed twelve months as a professional full-time coach in martial arts and fitness training. I had totally changed my life around. I had met new friends, new contacts and new colleagues, and was getting satisfaction from my work. I felt good about this and I aimed to keep working to expand in the coming year. It is an amazing feeling when you are living your dreams. Each day is an exciting prospect. One where you can't get out of bed fast enough to explore new challenges. Pursuing your dreams isn't without fear and trepidation, but the flip side is a sense of fulfilment and excitement.

I had also begun to change as a person. In the last few years of my employment in the timber yards, as mentioned early, I had grown to be very aggressive and short-tempered. This really wasn't me, but pressure and a dislike for the job was weighing heavy on me. Plus, I had been doing some hard and heavy contact training, sparring and fighting, and I had begun to enjoy the violent nature of the martial arts a little too much.

I had cultivated a bit of a morbid fascination with darker subjects of combat. I was seeking out and reading books entitled 'Killer Elite,' 'Death Dealers Manual', 'Bare Kills' and 'Black Medicine' amongst many more jolly little titles. All these books and their like explained the more nefarious nature of close-quarter combat. I became a little obsessive and dangerous to know, but I didn't realise it at the time, and I don't suppose anybody wanted to tell me! I was living in a tough inner-city multicultural environment. Being a husband and father, I felt the need to protect my family. The area where I lived wasn't the best, so I wanted to be trained and be ready if the need arose.

Through martial arts, I had found myself as a person and squashed a lot of my fears and bad memories of childhood confrontations, ridicule and bullying. I no longer wanted or needed to carry this aggressive approach around with me.

By changing my life and setting out on new paths, I had become mentally stronger and had disciplined myself greatly and taken on more than I had ever dreamt I could handle. I also began to realise that real strength came from the inside, not the cosmetic show of muscle on the outside. I do not obsess with violence these days but I am also no longer afraid of it. I have lived with it inside out and understand it and myself.

The inner monster is firmly shut in the glass bottle labelled 'Break Open in Case of Emergencies.' I am glad that he is, but I had to work every day to achieve this and control it. Remember that if you can't control yourself, you cannot hope to control somebody else.

My advice to anybody who feels aggressive and violent is to go and seek out a good full contact combat art. You will have no shortage of challengers and you can fight to your heart's content and rid yourself of your violent tendencies in the controlled arena and not out on the streets. Many would be 'hard men'; when given this option they suddenly don't want it.

I recall a time when I was constantly being subliminally challenged by individuals. They were always asking how good I was and trying to push my buttons. Eventually, I gave them the ultimatum. I informed them of where I would be training that evening and at what time. I told them to meet me there and get on the mats and we could settle our little dispute 'mano a mano'. They never showed.

I can honestly say I fought many in one shape or form, won some and lost some, but the main thing was I always turned up.

I have never been afraid to step up to the plate when needed. But there is a time when you just instinctively know if you tangle with a certain individual, win or lose, you are going to come out of the encounter with a piece of you missing!

Most of the time if you afford that person the respect they deserve and they you, you can both go about your business unscathed.

I liken it to the uneasy but mutually respectful attitude the US and Russia reserve for each other.

Martial arts don't make you bulletproof, nor do they give you magical powers. You should always know your limitations.

At my time of life now I am not into playing the 'My dick is bigger than your dick' games.

If others want to trade insults and challenges about who is harder or which martial art is better, then, fine, but I won't be involved in what Rory Miller calls the 'Monkey Dance'. It's all bullshit. Normally a gun settles most fucking arguments quickly and finally no matter how hard you think you might be!

"Change is not made without inconvenience, even from worse to better."

My Personal Training Methods Through the Years

Those that know me know that I pride myself on my fitness. Since my early training days, I have discovered many ways and means of always exercising, no matter where I am.

I have found that over the years, people make excuses about the fact that they haven't got time to exercise or that their gym hasn't got the right equipment or they haven't got the room, space or necessary apparatus. These are all lame excuses. I believe that you can train anywhere with next to nothing if you have desire, hunger and spirit. I have never let circumstances defeat me from not training. I have just rigged something up and gone for it.

I can recall at fourteen years of age getting my dad to rig me up a punch bag in the garden. We didn't have much money to go out to buy the proper kind, so my old man put some sand into an old polythene bag and we sewed part of an eiderdown (a forerunner of the duvet) around it. This was hung by a rope onto part of an old door frame upright, driven into the grass. I used that 'bag' relentlessly every day when I came home from school. If it had been raining or frosty the previous night, the sand went nearly solid but I still worked away on it in all winds and weather.

Dad also made me my first pair of wooden nunchakus which I thought were brilliant and which I still have somewhere. I practised with them all the time, knocking lumps out of myself, but through the pain, I still persevered.

At Christmas, I used to receive as presents some of the latest fitness fads like the 'Bullworker', push-up bars, doorway chinning bars and that steel springy thing you bent in half (remember that?), wrist grips, wrist and ankle weights, finger strengtheners, etc. You name it, each year I would ask for something different and then spend hours working with these things. Later, as I got older, I could afford my own weights, bar and bench and used these for years in the confines of my house.

As my children were born, the equipment kept getting relegated to a different part of the house and although sometimes it was a pain to set up and be quite awkward to use, it didn't deter me. When I didn't have equipment, I improvised. Dips between chairs, doorway chins, calf raises on the stairs, inclined push-ups off the steps, squats with a sandbag across my shoulders or just go out with a pair of army boots on and a loaded rucksack and run five miles up my local cycle track. I ran in baking heat, rain, gales and snow. It never stopped me; it just built my spirit and resolve.

I hate running. It hurts my bad ankle and leg. Sometimes, after I ran, I would have a job to put weight on my right ankle for days. I have made myself do it and gradually increased my distances. I've run on all surfaces and done loads of sprint and hill work using many drills from Peter Consterdine's classic 'Fit to Fight' book. I have pushed myself to many extremes running. One regular weekly training routine that I did for a year was running five miles up the local cycle track. At around the two-and-a-half-mile mark was a steep incline, which brought you back up onto the main road. The incline was winding and demanding. It became my nemesis each week, as I would make myself sprint up and down it ten times before I would turn back to complete my other two and a half miles home. Each time, as I neared the spot of the incline, I had a feeling of complete dread through my body because I knew it was going to blow my legs and lungs away. It would have been so easy to pass it by, but I wouldn't and I didn't. I conquered it in the end and built up enough physical and mental muscle to get up and down the slope with more to spare.

I have done this sort of thing so many times in my training. Setting another physical challenge and seeing what I could do. It was this inner battle that I have fought all my life.

I remember when I got my first doorway chinning bar. I struggled to do a few pull-ups. This bugged me. Where I was working at the time was about a twenty-minute car journey back to my home, so each dinner hour for a few months, I drove home every day to work on those chin-ups/pull-ups and then drive back to carry on my working day. It was a big commitment but, boy, did it pay dividends. Even today, chin-ups and pull-ups are my favourite exercises.

If I read about somebody else's training and I hadn't tried their methods, I would be straight at it to test myself. Things like Ken Shamrock's '500 free standing squats routines', Geoff Thompson's '40x2min rounds on the bag', Peter Consterdine's 'hill work sprints and pad drills', Steve Redgrave's '2000 metres rowing routines' and so it goes on and on. I thrived on the challenge and would not let advancing age deter me.

I worked on my running to the stage where I was able to run four Bristol half marathons covering the thirteen-mile courses. For somebody who at one stage of his life had a job to walk properly and wouldn't cover any notable distance walking without moaning, I am pleased with what I have achieved. To do these runs, my ankle would have to be strapped up like a mummy to last the pounding it would take. The last two miles were always completed on pure mental strength, as my ankle by then was screaming with pain, but I have never stopped or walked the course.

Throughout the years, I loved to challenge myself. I was not born a natural athlete, but I had a great desire and appetite for new and innovative training.

I guess in the early years when I was self-conscious of my slight disability I shied away from exercise, falsely believing it wasn't for me. But, gradually, my mindset began to change and I thought, fuck it, I will do this, no matter what.

Outside of martial arts, as well as completing many running races, I have swum in a swimathon for charity where I swam two hundred lengths of an Olympic pool. Now, I don't hate swimming as much as running, but I am not the world's best swimmer either. I completed the whole two hundred lengths in breaststroke and was in the water two hours and twenty-five minutes. Obviously, because you are in the water, you don't realise you sweat but when I got out, I found that I was badly dehydrated and walking on extremely rubbery legs. Also, that amount of time in the water can play havoc with your bladder as it fills up. At one point, I was so desperate that I felt the weight of its fullness dragging me under. I tell you, peeing and swimming at the same time are an art form not to be trivialised!

I have competed in fitness challenges in gyms, 'Fit to Fight' nights at my classes where we would relentlessly complete two hours of hard exercises and endurance drills, as well as many outdoor challenges such as assault courses, commando challenges, circuits, etc.

Many years back, I even did a trial for the 'Gladiators' show. I travelled to Bournemouth to go through a regime of time trials on different fitness exercises and did some duelling with the pugil sticks. Unfortunately, I didn't make it through as the second time up a thirty-feet rope climb, my arms just seized and I slid back down to the bottom, taking many layers of skin from my palms. I needed a bucket of water to cool them down. Fucking hell, it hurt. I was desperately disappointed but what a wonderful experience.

It wouldn't be the last of my challenges on a television fitness show.

A few years later, I did get to compete with a Gladiator champ. One of the ladies' champions, Janet Allen, was from Bristol. At the local sports centre where I worked, we had a 'Gladiator Day' for the children. There were different events like the real game. At the end, I got to fight on 'Duel' with the pugil sticks against Janet. She beat the crap out of me and knocked me off the platform. She was very good though and I was, in my opinion, a bit off balance when she hit me! Well, that's my story and I'm sticking to it!

When I was training for my fourth and fifth Dan black belts, I trained every day for months in my dinner hour when I worked in the timber yard. This training supplemented to nightly workouts.

I rigged a makeshift gym upstairs in one of the warehouses with the help of my work colleague and black belt instructor, Andy Wintle. We hung up a six-foot punch bag, a ceiling to floor speed ball, chin up bar from wood, a fourteen-foot rope climb, straddle jump bench, sand bags for lifting, skipping ropes and some old rusty weights.

Every day, I would do a fifty-minute workout like a man possessed. I trained up there under the corrugated roof in one hundred degrees in the summer and sub-zero temperatures in the winter when the icicles hung from the roof and the chill winds blasted up the docks. None of this stopped me. Whatever the weather conditions, I was drenched in sweat and would use a hosepipe attached to a water tap at the back of the building to wash myself down. Looking back, it was extreme and sometimes, I was totally wasted.

I know there are a lot of tough lads about now, but my era still bred toughness. Somewhere in the 90s and onwards, society became soft and we became a 'Nanny Nation'.

I grew up in a house with an outdoor toilet and no central heating, fridge, freezer, telephone, colour TV or car.

I loved my home life but it wasn't a fucking bowl of cherries. There was no mollycoddling. You fucking just got on with it. I remember every morning from when I was about seven to fifteen years of age, waking up in my box-size bedroom and sticking my head out of the blankets and breathing out freezing air in a mist where my room was so cold. Ice was on the inside of the windows as well as the outside. I thought nothing of it. Currently, too many kids and young adults don't realise how 'cushy' they have it.

In my time, growing up you could count the fat kids on one hand. They didn't exist. We didn't eat shit. You ate at meal times what you were given and there were no McDonald's, Burger King or KFC. If you didn't eat your dinner you got fuck all else.

Plus, there were no computer games. We played outside. We ran, jumped, climbed, kicked a ball around and walked miles. We were no strangers to exercise.

I recall standing freezing in a vest, shorts and a pair of plimsoles with my school mates in the dead of winter ready to do a cross country run. There were no excuses. If you didn't do it, the P.E. teacher would kick you up the ass or clip you around the ear. Also, if you were late back you would have missed your bus home!

Getting a belt around the ear from your parents or the cane from the headmaster didn't do me any long-lasting damage. You took it all in your stride. Now you can't so much as look at somebody and then cry human rights, racism, etc., etc.

Anyway, I have digressed slightly again. But it was all relevant on how I viewed the world and my training at the time.

Once or twice a week, Andy would come up and train with me and we would go through pad work, boxing, kickboxing, weapon sparring, ground grappling and Vale Tudo (all-in sparring) without fail. I must congratulate Andy on his resolve in those days, because I was at my vicious best and took no prisoners, but he kept coming back for more.

Then, on my own, I would set up different circuits to punish myself. Here is an example workout: twenty minutes bag work, three sets of ten long arm chins, three times up the rope, fifty push-ups, fifty jump squats with a barbell on my back, ten sandbags lifts, fifty squats thrust, two hundred sit-ups and leg raises, two times three rounds of skipping and a ten-minute round on the standing to floor ball. Usually, this took about fifty minutes or so. I then went back to work. I did these routines religiously for nearly two years. I had everybody up there from the yard and the office to spar with me that wanted to give it a go. I sparred with them all including one of my managers. He was a young guy, a big lad and a bit of a rugby player. I slap boxed him (this was a crude form of boxing using open hand slaps to the head and body. It may sound easy but getting a heavy slap upside your ear isn't pleasant.) and knocked ten bells out of him before putting him on his ass and he called it a day. How many jobs could you be in where you get to hit the manager? Fucking great!

I went through a phase of body conditioning and seeing that I worked in a timber yard, I used all the materials available to assist me in my quest. I had a bucket of wet sand for conditioning my hands (this old standby really works). I could break one-inch thick wood with my fist, edge of hands and fingertips (no mean feat). But my party piece was to punch holes through doors. This would come in handy in another big challenge I will outline later!

I would have lumps of chipboard 'packers' broken over my forearms, legs, stomach and back. I found this all genuine fun at the time! I learnt to break blocks and bricks with my bare hands and smash lengths of wood with my shins. This used to make some of my mates watching quite nauseous.

Looking back, I really abused my hands, and I am lucky that I can still move them after the pounding I gave them. I always punched bare-handed on the bag and used the traditional makiwara boards until my knuckles would bleed through the effort. Body conditioning is fine if you are sensible and don't go to extremes. When I started breaking boards with my head, I realised that it was getting silly and stopped these extreme methods. All arts have their own body conditioning from karate and kung fu to Muay Thai. Care and a good instructor is the key to safe progress.

I was fanatical now for training and I was really at my fittest. I was doing a lot of competitive grappling, MMA sparring and 'Animal Day' sessions. I was very aggressive and uncompromising. I hurt quite a few people and looking back, some certainly didn't deserve some of the stick I gave them. But having said that, it was a two-way thing. I also took what they dished out. That was the name of the game. When I left to start full-time coaching, I took a leaf out of Geoff Thompson's book and trained just as if I was doing an eight-hour working day.

The training sessions were mammoth ones. I would get up and run, go up to the 'Budokan', work through twenty or thirty rounds of bag work, run through conditioning exercises, makiwara board toughening drills and then do three or four private one-to-one lessons with various people. I would then come home, read, write or watch videos on martial arts and then in the evening teach classes. Some days would be broken up with my gym work, but I always found time to get in a workout. I did this six days a week. At one stage, I was teaching ten classes a week of martial arts and four classes in the gym, teaching personal clients and training myself. My workload was massive. In between this, I would be writing magazine articles and my books as well as researching new training tapes for more techniques.

On top of this, I never had a car. I hadn't driven for years. I just got fed up with the expense and found I could spend the money I saved on better things. So, I would pack all my kit in a big hiker's rucksack and walk or catch the bus everywhere. God, I was fit!

I never missed an opportunity to train if I could. No matter where I worked, I found time to train or use my work as a training tool. From my days in the timber yard working in all weathers, I built up a mental toughness and strong will to get on with things.

I can remember going in to work at seven thirty a.m., half an hour before the rest of the staff would arrive, and locking myself away in an old brick building that I used as an office. This place had no heating or lights and at seven thirty a.m. in the winter, it was pitch black. There, in the darkness, I would practise my weapon training for gradings with real nunchakus and butterfly knives. I became so good that I didn't need the light and I just developed a feel for these weapons. Fantastic times.

Once, after a particularly insane workout with a pair of Filipino butterfly knives, I was unaware, in the darkness, that I had cut my knuckles on both hands. When I came out into the daylight, I then noticed this and treated the wounds and plastered them up. Later along, with my manager, I had to go into the old building that had become my training home. It was now daylight and all we could both see in the back room where I had been twirling the knives like a maniac was blood splashed here, there and everywhere up the walls! It was like a scene out of the film 'The Texas Chainsaw Massacre.' He looked shocked and asked if I knew where it had come from. I hastily replied, "No," and dug my plastered hands into my coat pockets!

For around twelve months or so, in our dinner hour, a workmate and I practised knife throwing. Being in a timber yard, we had no shortage of materials. We would use a damaged door and draw a life-size figure on it with certain vital points shaded in. We would then spend an hour using proper throwing knives to hone our skills. I tell you, we got so good that we could have pinned the wings of a fly. It was frightening how accurate we became.

I learnt the original skills from Micky Upham, but 'Fred' (my workmate) and I took this to another level. We became obsessed with throwing knives. Not only could we throw a proper throwing knife, we could also throw penknives, sheath knives and even a dinner knife. Fred's party piece was to get hold of ten little disposable 'Stanley-type' blades and bang the whole ten in unison into a target. Over arm and under arm, we could make them stick. We even moved on to a hatchet. Crazy stuff!

I can remember getting a young work experience lad to stand against a large stack of polystyrene blocks, and Fred and I fired half a dozen knives in to the polystyrene around him. It was just like a scene out of a circus. The kid didn't flinch. I don't know whether it was because he had faith in us or was just plain scared. I just loved to be doing something and improving my skills. I couldn't stand still.

Another crazy stunt I did was when we were changing a large saw blade from a circular band saw. The new one was lying on the concrete floor, teeth up like the huge round jaws of a great white shark. I bet that I could breakfall and roll over the entire length of the saw blade. Bearing in mind that if I missed, I would be ripped up badly. My colleagues took the bet and I not only cleared it once, I did it twice to show it wasn't a fluke!

On another occasion, I was discussing martial arts with a work colleague who told me if he picked up a crowbar and attempted to hit me with it, my martial arts wouldn't be worth a light. I was very gung-ho at the time and told him I would take him out. This developed into an argument and I told him that we would resolve it. We went upstairs and amongst a pile of tools, I found a crowbar. I threw it to him and I told him to get on with it. He informed me that he was really going to let fly and he wasn't holding back. Yes, it had got to that stupid stage. He went for it and within a second, he found himself on his back, my hand around his windpipe and the crowbar safely 'disarmed'. He was dumbstruck and we never had the conversation again!

I had to treat my work as a fitness challenge to get through the days. I used to work with some young lads and I put them through hell. We would carry hundreds of doors up two flights of stairs. I would start off with two doors, then raise the challenge to three or four and so on, charging up and down the stairs. Christ, did we sweat. I used to get some sadistic pleasure out of it all. I did the same with massive loads of timber, going like a train in all winds and weathers. Hard graft but it kept you fit. I tailored my training to suit my needs. I found that as I got older, I couldn't do what I did when I was twenty but I can and will still train hard but smarter.

When I was involved in MMA in my forties, I still had the fitness and experience to spar, grapple and fight all comers and last the pace. Recovery time gets a little longer and aches and pains come and go, but my constant training meant that I could still compete at the highest level in submission wrestling and MMA when many others had long retired.

I believe that by looking after your body, being careful what you put into it and by getting enough rest between training, you can be capable of many remarkable things, even in advancing years.

I have never been a 'watching' instructor; I have always been a 'doing' one. I haven't gone soft through lack of training or lost my edge through body redundancy. Even these days on a seminar, I will dome the white belt and get out and train with whoever is hosting that course. I am not worried about belts, status or ego. My respect has been earned by getting in there and doing it and continuing to do it.

I have put myself through some wild and crazy training over the years. I have pushed myself beyond what I thought I can do and found great new inner strength. When all physical power has been drained away, you survive on the mental side of your training. Some people may not believe that I have done this amount of training and worked a job afterwards, but I was fanatical and became a man totally obsessed with fitness to the point of illness. There is a fine line between both, and I have cruised it many times. Some never push themselves to that limit and never realise their potential. You must be careful though; there is a definitive mark between training hard and training excessively. The latter can make you ill and leave you badly fatigued and susceptible to injury and illness. Plus, later on in life you may suffer because of it. I know myself that some of the things that I put myself through were excessive, but I know that if I had my time back to do it all again I would do the same. That is the type of personality I have. In training for the MMA competition, I put myself through a personal hell. I started seriously fighting in this arena when I was thirty-six years of age. My training partners left me many evenings in a heap on the floor after pushing me to my physical and mental limits. Many a time I lay there and thought, "Why am I doing this? Do I need this at my age?" Then, the next session I was back again and putting myself through it once more.

This was a gruelling routine for somebody half my age. I was also teaching my classes in between these sessions. I suppose it is the nature of the beast and it will stay in your blood in one shape or form for life.

"There are no gains without pain, wisdom without adversity."

Old Faces and New Faces

It was now 1997 – the year that saw the grappling arts expanding and becoming huge. Many top instructors were coming to our shores to give expert tuition. The whole scene of the martial arts was changing. At this period, it was buzzing. It was exciting and I was glad to be part of it all. I wasn't going to let this bandwagon go riding on by. I wanted very much to be firmly on it and heading wherever it was going!

Sessions designed for grappling, hard sparring and pressure testing were getting more and more popular. At the 'Budokan', Sunday mornings and Thursday nights were two noted classes, and some great training was done and much blood, sweat and tears spilt. My top students and instructors would all come together at these sessions, and there was no better sight for me than to see them all drilling and working out, showing immense spirit, skill and technique. All those years of teaching were beginning to bear fruit.

I had found some long-time students would reach blue or brown belt and then 'drop out' of class. They just couldn't seem to go that extra mile in pursuit of their black belt. For me, it was incredibly disappointing and frustrating. That was a lot of demanding work down the drain, and although a few had made it all the way to first Dan, I should have had more. If the journey was easy, everybody would be on it. The journey and reward are for the chosen few.

However, in 1997, a real hardcore group established themselves and they went on to much success, led by excellent black belts: Rob Cannon, Matt Sperring, Phil Davis, Tony Watt and Paul Flett. Below this, I also had some great up-and-coming people. Ross MacKenzie, Steve Thomas, Pete Dunn, Paul Hirst and Ismail Kadi were but a few of the lads that would also go on to bigger and better things as the years went by. This was all very promising for my clubs and their future.

One of my black belts, Paul Flett, who originally came down to Bristol from Durham had been a good amateur boxer in his younger days. He was keen to expand his ground grappling so in exchange, I got him to improve my boxing skills. When I had first dabbled in boxing seriously, my two training partners had been six feet-plus and I found it extremely difficult at five feet seven inches to get past their long arms. I taught myself to 'bob and weave' and move my head by studying videos of Joe Frazer and the then-young Mike Tyson fighting. I became decent at this and used it to great effect in sparring.

With Paul, though, I wanted to improve my long-range game and he was excellent at this. He got me to spar round after round with him at long distance using the jab, cross and lead hook. No close-quarter stuff at all. I found this extremely hard going and he 'peppered' me with his great jab. But through persistence, I got better. I was a southpaw naturally, but Paul made me fight orthodox and use that left hand for jab and lead hook. I was amazed that I could box this way and it gave me more options. Every week, we would put on the ten-ounce gloves and gum shields and box all-out six to ten three-minute rounds. No quarter was asked or given. This was tough and I take my hat off to any professional boxer who climbs in the ring and does a dozen rounds. The stamina and toughness of body and mind for this is extreme. So, next time any of you are at home, sitting in the armchair slagging a boxer off while watching him on the television, take time out and think, could I really do that and if you think you can, give it a try. It's a whole different world when you have a real 'tear-up' instead of standing hitting a punch-bag.

For the boxing knowledge Paul gave me, I worked on his ground grappling with him and shared any new technique I had found. He became a firm training partner of mine and we worked hard together. He went on to compete in many different grappling-based tournaments and did brilliantly well. His particular field was gi grappling and he has captured gold and silver medals at the European Brazilian Ju Jutsu Championships amongst others.

I recall in an inter club grappling tournament I fought him for charity in a grappling match. We went thirty minutes nonstop and the fight was declared a draw.

During this period, I was leaning more heavily towards 'reality' training, but I did realise that not everybody who came to me wanted that extreme test. This profession was my living and I had to cater for everybody. I wasn't going to water my art down, so I separated sessions so that everybody could train in the aspect they wanted to. This worked well for me.

I was still attending seminars. In this year, I travelled to Birmingham to train on a weekend seminar taught by Carley Gracie who is the eleventh son of the founder of Brazilian ju jutsu, Carlos. Carley is today a ninth Dan red belt. He is a highly experienced teacher. Back in 1997, this was his first visit to the UK and the first official BJJ seminar to be held on our shores. It was a wonderful experience to be on the mats with this man and learn from his level of knowledge and skills.

Also, now I was being asked to teach on more seminars myself, which was great. I taught on Peter Browne's famous BKJJU self-defence seminar in London. That day, I taught alongside the great Professor David James, tenth Dan, in Vee Amis Jutsu who had travelled over from the USA. What a charismatic and dynamic character he was! It was good to share the same mat as him. My teaching went down well, which made it all worthwhile.

I also taught on Alan Charlton's Self Protection Association annual seminar with another guest instructor, Bob Spour of Muay Thai. That was another good day. I also travelled to many traditional or sport-orientated karate clubs who wanted to learn grappling or CQC techniques and I was always well received.

In this year, I also invited Soke Bryan Cheek of Jukoshin Ryu Ju Jutsu down to Bristol for a seminar which my good friend Neil Bartlett helped arrange.

Brian is a true stalwart for ju jutsu in the UK. He has also travelled the world, teaching and promoting his art. He is another tenth Dan master. It was an honour to have this man come to train.

Although our ju jutsu was slightly different, he didn't care. We had a great day's training. What I also liked about Brian was that for such a high-graded martial artist, he didn't take himself too seriously. He was down to earth, shared a joke and had time for everybody, young or old. I admire him for this. I have all the time in the world for this sort of person.

I have met so many instructors that are the total opposite. They are wrapped up in their own self-importance and are legends in their own mind. I have found these people to be rude, arrogant and egotistic. They spend a lifetime slagging off others, their art and their methods and try to impress on you how wonderful they are.

I have no time for this. My theory is that the martial arts world is a vast one and there is room for everybody. If we all were the same, the place would be boring. If somebody sees something in a different way or teaches in a different manner to me, then that is fine. I am not the least bit concerned.

I don't care what an instructor is doing in their classes in Glasgow, London, Manchester, Cardiff or even up the road. That is their business. Let them get on with it. I afford them that respect and I hope they afford me the same.

Instructors who go around continually slagging off others are insecure of their own abilities and jealous of what others have achieved. As I said before, opportunities are out there for everybody. You have got to be prepared to stop moaning and get up and grab them.

Martial arts are the same as any other business. You are always going to have competitors, some better than you. That's life. You have just got to do your best and that's all you can do. If I worried about every new club that opened in my area, I would have given it all up a long time ago.

The people I admire most in martial arts are those who have achieved greatly but when you meet them, they always ask first what you have been doing and how you are getting on. I have met too many of the other sort who will impress upon me, in the first five minutes of meeting, their life history and how deadly their system is and how much better it is than anyone else's. Who are they trying to convince? Themselves or me? Do I give a damn either way? Anyway, back to my travels!

I was also going over to Wales on a regular basis. I had met two guys from Newport who had come over to Bristol and trained with me privately for some time, and now they had opened small classes and asked if I would go over to Newport once a month to teach and monitor their progress.

One of these guys was Ian East, a very good judo man. Ian was a giant of a guy. He was around six feet four inches tall and seventeen-plus stone. When I grappled with him, it was like rolling with a grizzly bear! I learned much from these sessions though and it improved my gi work no end, as he was a very competent Newaza man.

The other man was the incredible John Wetter. He was in his early sixties when I met him and he was an exponent of Chinese Kempo. For his age, he had incredible stamina and was as tough as old boots. His passion and desire to learn was massive, and I trained him in every aspect of my combat ju jutsu. He could hold his own with any youngster. John's son had been a pro-boxer and had fought the likes of Terry Marsh and Nick Wiltshire amongst others in the 80s. He was a super lad and he also would come over and train with his dad. Occasionally, it would all end up with us putting the gloves on and having a spar. They were good times and I enjoyed my visits to Wales. They had a bunch of great lads over there training, and they gave their all each time I visited.

Another great guy that I must mention who I trained with on Geoff Thompson and Gary Spiers' seminars was judo man, Aaron De Le Pledge. He was a local West Country man from Bridgwater and we had some great scraps whenever we met. He was a very strong guy with great pinning skills. I haven't seen him for years, but do remember him and wish him well.

Rupert Bancroft was another good judo lad who trained with me for a while. He also had a wide variety of skills. He travelled around quite a bit and had trained with many top people in boxing, Muay Thai and JKD. He had also participated in one of Geoff Thompson's first 'Animal Days'. He became a good mate of mine over a period of a few years and we had some cracking grappling matches. He was considerably heavier than me and had a great judo base. We had some marathon sessions with and without the gi and I hope he took as much away from them as I did. One last time that I spoke to him before he left Bristol, he had just returned from the States after a week's training with Dan Inosanto, Machado Bros, Eric Paulson and Chris Hauer! What a lucky guy! I believe these days that he is a bodyguard.

I have been fortunate to meet and encounter many, many good people in my time as an instructor and practitioner of martial arts. So many that I couldn't possibly list them all. They're all there in the memory banks but they are just not registering at present. I have covered some ground so far, so you will know who you are if I have forgotten you. I could honestly fill a book with just the names of the many great people I have met on my journey.

I just loved martial arts and each one of them excited me. Ju jutsu had become my base art, but I wanted to learn from as many sources as possible. I could see good things in all of them from an Aikijutsu wristlock and Muay Thai leg kick to a blinding American Kenpo strike combination and a BJJ armlock.

As I mentioned earlier on, the grappling explosion had really hit the UK and many forms of new competition had surfaced, giving particularly the ju jutsu-based stylist a chance to test their skills. One of the forerunners was the Ju Jutsu Kumite founded by Ross Iannoccaro. The format was founded by this Midland-based ju jutsu man and it has become a massive sporting competition in the UK. It also spawned the professional 'Strike and Grapple' format.

I wanted some of my lads to test their skills in this format but decided I had better try it out first and see what it was all about. Plus, at thirty-six years old, I knew that my competing days were numbered!

Paul and I entered their International Ju Jutsu Kumite Championships held in Worcester. The format dictated that you wore a gi, gumshield, groin guard and a pair of karate-type open hand mitts, and the object of the fighting was to win by submission, knockout or points. Rules dictated backfist and hammerfist to the head, but no straight face shots. Punching and knees to the body were permitted. All kicks were allowed anywhere above the waist. Throws, takedowns, pins and submission were also all allowed. You were given points for different techniques, so at the end of a five-minute round, if nobody had won outright, the person in front on points would win.

I competed in the middleweight veteran category. I won my three fights to reach the final (two by chokes, one by points). The only drawback was that I had to wait nearly two hours to fight again. As you get older, you don't relish this. I started thinking of being home with my feet up drinking a nice cup of tea, so I had to do my best to keep mentally focused. I did have the distraction of cheering Paul on, who did extremely well to reach the semi-finals of the highly competitive middleweight group. He narrowly lost to then three-times champion Trevor Cunningham, another excellent ju jutsu/martial artist.

My final fight was even until I caught my opponent with a good backfist on the temple, which stunned him badly and almost knocked him out. Because of a bad cut, he had time out to get first aid. If he didn't return after five minutes, the bout was mine. I was only glad that I didn't get disqualified for excessive contact! To his credit, my opponent returned but was still groggy and I held on for the win and took first place in my category as middleweight vets seventy-five kilo open champion. I returned the following year to grab the runners-up second position, losing narrowly to a man that I had beaten in the championships the previous year, Steve Kilmer. I enjoyed the experience of this type of competition and brought some of my students to compete in the following months.

From these, Paul and I went to Nottingham to check out the 'Knockdown' sport budo circuit run by Paul Davies and found this to also be a very good and, at that time, well-established format. We went back a few times and trained on their fighter's courses with good fighters like Shane Rigby (catch wrestler) and Mike Gregory (BJJ, submission wrestling) and Paul himself.

Just like Ross, Paul Davies worked tirelessly in the UK to bring these exciting forms of competition to the martial arts world and well done to them both. They were certainly the forerunners of MMA. Many MMA fighters cut their teeth in these formats before entering the cage, including top British MMA and UFC fighter, Michael Bisping.

Once more, this year had ended on a good note and new and exciting territory had been broken. My journey was getting more and more exciting.

"The only place where success comes before work is in a dictionary."

Memorable Training at the End of the Century

When you get the chance to train with some of the best, it really puts you on a high. Around the period of '99, I managed to do this and have lasting memories of many occasions.

Brazilian ju jutsu had now settled into the UK. In Birmingham, the world-famous Gracie Barra was formed by Mauricio Gomez. Mauricio was one of the 'famous five' who achieved his black belt from the legendary Rolls Gracie before his untimely death. Mauricio is now a seventh Dan and teaches regularly at Roger Gracie's academy in London. He is Roger's father. In Lewisham, London, the 'Anaconda' club was also run by Chen Morales' members of the UK BJJ association. Both were becoming the first established venues for this art in Britain.

In 2000, Renzo Gracie, the nephew of Mauricio and cousin of the legendary UFC veteran Royce, came to Birmingham for a weekend seminar, and Paul and I secured a place on it. Renzo is a top-class ju jutsu exponent, but was also a world-rated MMA fighter. To be in this guy's presence and have him instruct and fine-tune your technique was a great moment.

All his techniques were executed very smoothly and technically with power but also grace. He was a very approachable man and spent time with everybody on the course and gave them all photo opportunities at the end.

On the first day, Renzo demonstrated his MMA techniques and strategies, showing takedowns, avoiding strikes and ground submissions. The next day was gi workout. Throwing, takedowns and ground grappling were all covered in good detail. He also spoke at length about his training regimes, fitness and diet and passed on good advice for those wishing to compete. It was a truly excellent weekend and a memorable experience to get a chance to 'roll' with this man.

At this time, I was trying to make a transition into grappling competitions but was still struggling with the crossover from my combat ju jutsu. On this seminar, I grappled with a few BJJ blue, purple belts and black belts. I recall that one of these guys got me in a leg triangle and rolled me under him into mount where he began to squeeze my neck and verbally tell me to 'tap out' as there was no escape. Now, I had trained all my life for real combat and my mindset was not programmed for sport. So, as I felt myself beginning to go dizzy from the hold he had on me, I somehow created a little space to turn my head and proceeded to bite him three or four times on the inner thigh! This poor guy yelped like an injured puppy and instantly let me go. He shouted that I couldn't do that and it wasn't allowed. Looking back, he was right, but I wasn't yet conditioned to rules. So, it wasn't very sporting of me but on the other hand, it fucking worked a treat! As a note, biting can fuck up the best of grappler's day. I remember that afterwards, this guy was going around the changing rooms, showing these bite marks to anyone who cared to listen to him. I dressed quietly and beat a hasty exit with a small grin on my face.

Sometime later, I got an invite to Bob Breen's Academy in London. Bob, who is one of the UK's stalwart JKD instructors, was hosting a seminar with John Machado. John Machado is a member of the famous Machado brothers – cousins of the Gracie family who also include two of the world's greatest gi grapplers, Reagan and Jean Jacques. John himself has a reputation as a master technician on the floor.

On this occasion, John had literally stepped off the plane from the States and come to the seminar venue, but he still put on a tremendous performance, showing little sign of jet lag.

The seminar had a select number attending and some very good ground grapplers indeed were amongst them. The day started with entry techniques to throws and takedowns, then ground drills from open and closed guard, and then submission work. After a break, John said that he needed waking up a bit and proceeded to ground grapple with a dozen or so opponents, one after the other.

This was a great part of the seminar to see his smoothness and power in action. He reminded me of a big cat playing with its litter. Sweeps, reversals, chokes and arm bars were applied to hapless opponents. At one stage, he achieved the mounted position on an opponent and whilst this lad struggled to escape frantically, John held the mount, readjusted his gi top and retied his belt.

I took a turn to 'roll' with him and I gave it my best shot. I don't really know what percentage of effort he was working at, but I survived without being 'tapped', although he did control the situation. I was proud and pleased to have had the opportunity to take to the mats with the great man.

Later, the class split down into two groups and the seniors could do some back-to-back grappling bouts. We did four or five each with John Machado supervising. Paul and I had some cracking fights with some talented and skilful BJJ opponents. I certainly knew that I had been in a good workout when time was eventually called. I recall a young John Kavanagh on the mat. John has gone on to be one of Ireland's and indeed, the UK's, premier MMA fighters.

I found now trying to pass some of these guys' legs nearly impossible but they were vulnerable to leglocks which worked really well.

To end the day, we had a question-and-answer time with John, and he candidly answered many varied questions and talked about Brazilian ju jutsu in his home country, the States, and the UK. It was another superb training experience.

As I became more versed in the BJJ rules, I entered myself and a few of my lads into the Brazilian European Open championships in the year 2000 in London. The tournament was organised by Mauricio Gomez and Chen Morales.

Chen Morales invited me in at blue belt level (I am not graded in BJJ by the way), and I won a silver medal at the middleweight veteran's category. It was a great experience to compete in what I believe was the first major BJJ tournament to be held in the UK. The guys that came with me won bronze, silver and gold medals. Not bad, seeing that we were the only club there outside of the BJJ circles. I was proud of them all and their ground skills. We proved to some people in certain quarters we had more to us than just 'ground and pound' tactics.

All the lads were either MMA fighters or combat ju jutsu, so they did extremely well to go into somebody else's 'back garden' so to speak, compete with their rules and do okay.

I have always been of this mindset. I don't mind going back to white belt and mixing on anybody's mat and any style. I have no ego. It doesn't worry me to put it on the line. It is the only way to learn rather than hide from it. I have sparred with boxers, kickboxers, taekwondo exponents, Muay Thai fighters, wrestlers, judoka, BJJ, etc., etc. I have learnt from all my experiences and am a better martial artist because of it. Yes, there were times when I was scared, but I made myself step up to the plate. Yes, I have taken a battering, bled a bit and had my ego well and truly kicked up the ass, but I have also dished a few out. That is the name of the game. I have ducked nothing and nobody in my quest to be a true warrior.

I didn't expect to go into some of these guys' arenas and win but at least I can say I experienced it first-hand rather than talking about it on Facebook!

Another great seminar that sticks in my mind from that period was one organised by my good pal Alan Charlton. This was one of his SPA's annual seminars, and he had my good friend Dave Turton teaching his brand of Goshinkwai Combat on it. It was good to hook up again with Dave, and everybody gave it their all, training in some brutal and painful street combat techniques.

Dave is a fountain of knowledge and wisdom on the practical side of martial arts, and just listening to him speak about the combat is enlightening on its own. It is great to still see Dave out there teaching. But that day, Alan had also captured a special guest speaker and I mean special. It was none other than the late Roy Shaw. Roy was a legendary ex-bare knuckle fighter, pro-boxer unlicensed boxer, legendary street fighter and hard man. The Kray brothers had once dubbed Roy as the most dangerous man in Britain.

Roy came to speak and promote his bestselling autobiography 'Pretty Boy'. This man has really seen and done it all and lived to tell the tale. He spent a large part of his life in some of the worst prisons in the UK, including a spell in Broadmoor. He had come through this dark side of life and was now a successful and respected businessman. But he still had a big reputation and nobody messed with Roy Shaw.

Roy spoke openly about his life, his fighting career and some of the brutality he had faced. He spoke and demonstrated his fighting technique and took a question-and-answer period. Obviously, he wasn't used to this sort of scene, but he handled it magnificently.

My highlight was to get a copy of his book personally signed and a photograph with the man. I also got to speak personally with him and ask him about his famous encounters with Lenny 'The Guv'nor' McLean. What struck me about Roy was that to him, fighting held no mystery. It was something that he had done naturally just like eating, talking or sleeping. There was no ego or boasting about what he had achieved. It was just a part of his long and lively career. I must say that even then in his sixties, Roy looked in tremendous shape and when you looked into those piercing blue eyes, you knew he was still capable of looking after himself. On the day, Roy mentioned how hard we as martial artists had trained. I think he found it a little comical how we strive so hard to learn fighting techniques. This man was a natural-born fighter. If you ever get an opportunity to see any tapes of his fights or read his book, I highly recommend them.

At the end of 1999, I attended the end of the year instructor's course held by the BCA in Coventry. Geoff Thompson and Peter Consterdine were taking this one. The course sticks in my mind particularly for a display of pure power, aggression and endurance fitness from the great Peter Consterdine. This man's level of fitness and skill has to be greatly admired. He is constantly pushing himself to new goals and I find him extremely inspirational as he is also not a man in his youth!

I witnessed him perform these ninety-second all-out power punching drills on a large kick shield held by a brave partner. The idea is to punch completely all-out and as hard as possible with every shot over this ninety-second period until you are totally spent. Take a short twenty-second break and then do sixty seconds in the same manner. Take another short break and then thirty seconds in the same manner. These drills are absolutely exhausting and must be tried to be believed.

Peter totally punched himself to collapse. He bent the shield with awesome power and nearly bent the guy in half that was holding it. Not much in the martial arts world these days really makes me stand in awe but this display did!

Later, he demonstrated his conditioning and mental toughness by letting Geoff who was gloved up throw punch after punch into his midsection and ribs without flinching. In the end, Geoff was exhausted from punching him. It was a truly tremendous display.

The whole 'Fit to Fight' workout which we did was great and pushed you towards your limits and beyond. It was no wonder why this man is highly regarded in his field. He is premier class.

I have been on many, many seminars, some good and some bad. I have become choosier on which ones I now attend. I suppose that after nearly forty years in the martial arts world, there isn't much that's going to get you excited any more.

We in the UK have been lucky enough over the years to have had some top-class martial artists visit our shores, but we shouldn't forget that we have got plenty of unsung heroes here in the UK too. Time to stand up and be counted, guys, and don't hide those lights under a bushel!

The one thing that I have always done is when I am on a seminar, I strive to learn and bring back with me new ideas, different approaches or compatible techniques to add to my repertoire. I have trained on pre-emptive strikes with Geoff Thompson and power strikes with Peter Consterdine, brought these drills to my club and drilled them for months to get a proper understanding. I have attended seminars with great grapplers and come back inspired to spend longer on the floor trying to perfect the techniques. I have wasted nothing. My philosophy is: why spend fifty pounds, sixty pounds or more to come back to your own clubs and forget or never practise what you have learnt and paid for. Yet many do. Telling everybody you have trained with Royce Gracie, George St Pierre, Neil Adams or Eric Paulson isn't enough. It's what have you learnt and developed off these masters that really counts.

I have gone to seminars and learnt one or two new or different things but if they were good, they were worth it. I would privately drill and drill the moves to get a good feel for them and introduce them to the class. When I perform a certain technique, I can remember from whom, where and when I learnt it and I will also credit that person for it.

In the early 2000s, I got the opportunity to train under legendary UFC champion Dan 'The Beast' Severn who had come over to the UK to fight in Ultimate Combat IV. You just can't miss the opportunity to train with someone of his calibre, particularly when it is on your own doorstep.

I was amazed at how few people had made the effort to attend the day, but it was their loss, as Dan proved to be an excellent instructor as well as fighter. The power of the 'Beast' was unmistakable, especially his awesome takedowns and ground and pound style. A superb day!

I have been blessed with a pretty good memory and a photographic mind when it comes to martial arts. I can go on a course or watch a video/DVD and remember a big percentage of it. If you can't do these things, I suggest that you write down notes as soon as possible while the information is fresh in your mind and then make use of it. Don't just become a seminar 'groupie', turning up at all the big seminars, showing your face and learning nothing. I can honestly say that I have never travelled to a seminar to watch. What is the point? Especially if you are fit enough to still get on the mat. My advice is to get in there and experience.

I am amazed at the amount of martial artists who have a bad opinion of a fellow instructor and slag them off without ever training on one of their seminars, visiting their clubs or giving themselves enough time to find out what really makes them tick. Anything I have written about or spoken about has been gleaned from first-hand experience or knowledge, not hearsay. There is too much badmouthing and disrespect in the arts. Don't contribute to it.

"Success is not a destination; it's a journey, and it is the direction in which you are travelling."

No Holds Barred Fighting

The new millennium was here. No, the world hadn't come to an end and there was no big meltdown of all the computers as predicted. I was heading into the year 2000 at full steam, looking for new experiences and testing myself in yet another arena.

The first part of the year saw the publishing of my third book 'Grappling with Reality' which was received well. Also, my website that was originally put together by my good friend and personal student Mark Pieterse was up and running.

Now, I still kept close contact with Geoff Thompson. I continually followed his work and was constantly inspired by what he achieved.

Geoff did a three-part interview with me for 'Fighters' magazine at the end of the 90s and in this year, I returned the favour and interviewed him for the same martial arts publication. He also sent me an original unpublished copy of his hardback bestseller 'Watch my Back'. He asked me if I would read it and review it again for 'Fighters' magazine. I was honoured as Geoff obviously knew many people in the martial arts world, and he had chosen me to do the review. It proved that he felt my opinion mattered and carried some weight. I was only too pleased to oblige. Again, I'm sure as a way of thanks, in the final original release in the book's centre which contained many coloured photos, he included one of me and him taken together at his book signing in Bristol. My name was also printed under it. It was a very nice gesture and typical of this great man.

Every time that Geoff has visited Bristol on his book signing tours I have attended and made sure that I have brought plenty of support for him. They have been great evenings and Geoff is an extremely articulate and charismatic speaker.

I believe that if you give your time to others, they will give their time to you. I have lived by this principle for some time now and I have found that it always pays in dividends. Currently, there is too much selfishness and people only think of looking after number one. That is not the way to succeed or be successful. You may well reach the top, but when you get there, it will be a lonely place because you will have nobody with you!

Around August of this year, a young man called Dale Adams visited my club and asked to train. He was heavily into Mixed Martial Arts and submission fighting. He told me that he was working for ML Sports UK and was setting up the Combat Sport trials MMA

Competition in Bath and wondered if any of my guys would be interested in taking part.

I hadn't formally fought in this format before in the competitive arena. In the past I had, with Micky Upham, experienced 'behind closed doors unofficial bouts'. Basically, we just put bag gloves on and had a go, just to test ourselves by mixing up the fighting ranges and trying out our techniques. Up until the recent Kumite bouts, I had experienced ju jutsu but never really had any formal competition, so a lot of groups did their own unofficial versions. These were mostly scrappy affairs, practically unsupervised. If you were knocked out or choked out, water would be flung over you and you would be dragged to the mats' edge to recover. There was no insurance or rules. Scary stuff. MMA may be the new extreme sport on the block in the millennium but slightly more hybrid versions have been around since the 70s, but more 'underground' so to speak. Many traditional martial artists and clubs frowned upon this type of stuff. I was fortunate (if that's the term) to meet some open-minded and progressive instructors. A lot of these bouts were fought with no safety equipment or gloves. Bloody noses and black eyes were a common occurrence. Being kicked in the balls or poked in the eye was often on the agenda. Even back then, I was aware of the need to train upright and floor skills, and I also realised how physically demanding this type of format could be. Being in decent shape was essential and something I have carried with me since.

People may be interested to know that the first show to feature what would be coined MMA in the UK was 'Night of the Samurai' in 1998.

Being given the opportunity to possibly have a go in the MMA arena at this stage of my career was a dream come true. Ever since the early Ultimate Fighting Championships, I had become hooked on this new and exciting sport and was an avid fan of the format and the fighters. Whilst watching these UFC tournaments, part of me longed to have a go but deep down, I really thought that I had missed the boat. Now, here was a chance to give it a try and I was always up for a challenge!

I asked around and there was good interest, especially from the lads who had been doing my Sunday morning 'Impact' and 'No Holds Barred' style classes. The first trials were scheduled for November, so my lads signed up and guess what... So, did I! Well, I thought to myself, if I'm going to be training them for these competitions, I might as well have a go myself and experience the format. So, at thirty-nine years of age, I was back in the competing arena. At the sharp end, so to speak. We all did reasonably well in the first trials. There were some top-class lads here from all over the UK.

Many had been doing this type of competition for some time. The fights were hard. Full contact. Strikes, kicks, punches, knees and grappling were all allowed. My first fight team were Rob Cannon, Matt Sperring, Ross MacKenzie, Mark Clemmings, Steve Thomas, Phil Davis and myself.

My two fights went the distance and both were draws. I had two good and spirited opponents. My first opponent was a lad named Lee Gibson. As I said, I was still in the transition period to MMA. The rules here dictated that a fighter could wear a rash guard or a vest, but you couldn't use said items of clothing to choke them with. Under pressure, I forgot and promptly ripped one of the poor guy's vest straps, then looped it around his neck and choked him. I was lucky not to be disqualified. My next opponent, Gareth Roberts, would go on to much success in the MMA arena and we would meet again. This was a tough but evenly matched fight. It was a learning curve for all of us who entered and we met many new friends and contacts.

From my first foray into the MMA arena, I found it very difficult to adapt to the rules. It just wasn't natural. My combat ju jutsu training certainly included a lot of MMA techniques, but also all the stuff that was banned from it. I knew that if I wanted to seriously fight in this format, I was going to have to change my training somewhat. It was a big ask after so many years of training in one system, but I was determined to give it a go. I was going to have to reinvent myself. It wasn't going to be easy, but I wanted to compete in this new and exciting sport, so I was going to have to bite the bullet.

In the same month, Rob, Matt, Paul and I travelled to Huddersfield for the British Demonstration Team Championships. This was run through Bob Sykes of 'Martial Arts Illustrated' magazine in conjunction with the 'Clash of the Titans Kickboxing' event. Again, this was a big moment for us to be in a big arena with many well-known martial artists and personalities in that crowd. There were six teams in the demonstration competing for the Millennium Sword. We had trained extremely hard for this at a time when we had also been heavily focused on the combat sports trials. Much training had been done and a lot of sweat lost in the pursuit of both things. Initially, you had to put a ten-minute video together, send it to the magazine and wait and see if you would be picked for the finals.

Our ten-minute demo was a non-stop blitz illustrating the many facets of a combat ju jutsu system. Only the four of us participated and we showed standing to floor ju jutsu throwing and submissions, multiple unarmed self-defence, pad work combined with ju jutsu and multiple weapon defences, all done high speed, high powered and with one hundred percent intent to a montage of music by rock legends Thin

Lizzy. We booked our place in the championships and trained every week, running through the demo three or four times in a row to get it right. This was a massive cardiovascular workout. But we were all as fit as a butcher's dog and as hungry for success. By the time the November date arrived, we were raring to go.

We arrived at the venue early and watched from the balcony overlooking the arena. It gradually began to fill up and the tension started to mount as the adrenaline started to flow. We were in good company with some good demonstration teams, noticeably last year's winners, Dave O'Donnell's 'Elite Fighting Academy' from London. They were very experienced demonstration players and I felt that they were the ones to beat.

We were first to come out and demonstrate. As we waited behind the scenes listening to the build-up and the announcement on the PA system, the nerves kicked in. I shook hands with my guys and fired them up for the last time. I saw in their eyes a mixture of fear, excitement and anticipation. Then, we were on. The music started and we were away. We gave maximum effort and performance. The demo was demanding enough on its own but with the crowd and the atmosphere, the adrenaline really hit the cardio system and we were glad when we came to the end. The following demos were entertaining but I didn't feel they touched ours. It was down to the 'Elite'. Their demo was a blend of martial arts, slapstick, comedy and combat techniques, all very cleverly put together. The crowd seemed to enjoy it, but I felt that we were still in with a shout.

The judges called out the results in reverse order. I don't recall who was third. We waited for the second place and the Bristol Goshin Jutsu Academy (the then-name of my club) was called. 'Elite' once more took first place. We were disappointed but accepted defeat graciously. I know that the lads were gutted, especially Rob who still thought we had done enough to pip it.

In retrospect, I suppose you have to look at what the crowd wanted. I was under the impression that you had to give an honest demonstration of your system, which we did, without all the props, slapstick and razzmatazz. Maybe I got it wrong and people didn't want to see this. They would rather go for the fantasy element of the arts. Never mind. We went there and did it. I do feel as a last word on this type of event that it may be more of a who you know and not what you know. Maybe they weren't ready for a bunch of West Country mavericks (although out of the four of us, one was a Scouser, one a Geordie, me part Irish and one an Englishman. What a combination!).

For the best part of this year, MMA training and competing took priority over other things, although I still managed to attend a seminar

147

in Worcester which was one of the first in the UK for the Russian CQC style 'The Systema'. This combat art has some very clever and unique techniques within it. A lot of it is built around leverage and balance breaking. It deals primarily with unarmed combat, knife fighting and firearms training. The chief instructor, Vladimir Vasiliev, very good indeed, but those under him didn't impress me.

I was also asked to join a special association put together to promote and teach grappling. It was arranged by the Kansen Ryu Jutsu and it was called 'Grappling Styles International'. I was part of a senior panel that encouraged and promoted all styles of grappling in the UK. I taught for them on a few occasions and it was a great honour to be asked to be part of the set-up.

My name was beginning to reach far and wide, and I was enjoying some international interest.

American author, Ned Beaumont, who wrote 'The Savage Science of Street Fighting' for Paladin Press in 2001 generously sung my praises in its pages.

This is what he wrote:

"I have provided a short course in close-quarter combat here. If you want to learn more, I recommend that you read 'In your Face' (New Breed Publishing, 1998) by Kevin O'Hagan. Kevin is a British Martial Artist and instructor whose primary 'style' is Ju Jutsu, but also is a good puncher with boxing experience. His techniques are for real street fighting and I think most of my readers can benefit from Kevin's book and even more from his attitude of aggression tempered with good sense."

I was very surprised and humbled to see this, and Ned and I corresponded regularly, sharing our knowledge over a period.

I also went over to Wales again to teach on an annual 'Goshin Ju Jutsu' seminar for Shihan Billy Doak, eighth Dan. Billy was a very well-known and experienced ju jutsu man who had amazing power in his techniques. It's fair to say that we may not have seen eye to eye on all things, as Billy had a big personality and had a different approach to ju jutsu than me, but I had no animosity against Billy. Sadly, he passed away in 2009 and leaves a big void in the Japanese ju jutsu world.

Ju jutsu is a vast art and it can have many interpretations of how it should be trained. I have met and trained with a variety of instructors in my time and they all stressed and emphasised different things in their ju jutsu art. My thoughts on this is, great! Wouldn't it be boring if we were all the same or clones of our instructors? The martial arts world is a big one. There is room for everybody. I don't care what style, system or art others are training in, if they are enjoying it, brilliant! Carry on!

Cross training has taken the martial arts by storm. Nearly everybody, unless they have been on planet Mars for the last decade or more, now realises the importance of having a balanced fighting system, allowing you to be competent at all fighting ranges, i.e. kicking, punching, upright grappling and floor grappling. Many hybrid systems have evolved catering for this, and it seems martial arts are heading in this direction for good.

I have trained in martial arts for some forty years now and have at one time or another experienced most arts and still actively train in any system or with anybody who I feel has something worthwhile to offer. For all this, my base system has been ju jutsu since 1984. When I first got introduced into ju jutsu, it seemed a much more complete martial art than any other I had experienced up to that point. It also dealt with certain attacks and techniques which I sought the answers to. This art is probably one of the oldest in existence, at least two thousand and five hundred years old. It has admirably stood the test of time. From being a warrior art for the Samurai on the battlefields, to law enforcement when the feudal era of Japan died, to being taught to the forces in World Wars I and II, to being taught to many of the security forces of the world, to BJJ today which has fared so well in the 'no holds barred' arena. My ju jutsu is a hybrid art and since its birth, it has had to be adapted with the times to incorporate short stances, boxing like foot and handwork, rapid fire strikes and very close-quarter joint breaks, strangles, sweeps and throws. Also, it includes pre-emptive strikes and takedowns to combat the enemy of today. Impact training on pads, bags, shields, etc. is essential, as is grappling and glove sparring for realism.

Although many ju jutsu systems still take a traditional approach to training, all have stressed an all-round knowledge of standing and floor arts for a very long time. If you look at classic CQB texts like Fairbairn's 'Get Tough', Applegate's 'Kill or be Killed' and 'Cold Steel' by John Styers, they all based their training around ju jutsu techniques. Even today, HMS forces, such as the Royal Marines, still use ju jutsu techniques as their unarmed training.

My personal feelings are that most grappling and multi-faceted arts owe something to ju jutsu at one time or the other.

Ju jutsu today is still a strong self-defence art that has now made its name in the sporting arena through various associations set up solely for this purpose. Cross training may be a new buzz word for some, but for the ju jutsu practitioner, it has always been a part of their repertoire. The chameleon of the martial arts can adapt to anything.

So, is ju jutsu the best system to train in over other martial arts? The answer is no. All arts have their strengths and weaknesses and at the end of the day, it's the man in the art, not the art in the man. But if you want a good form of all-round training with a good pedigree, ju jutsu could be the art for you. Since I first started training in the martial arts way back, people have been searching for that one elusive fighting art that answers all the questions, the ultimate one, the best, the one and only. That is like searching for the Holy Grail. You would think with the coming of mixed martial arts that the myth of the one perfect system of fighting would be dispelled forever. But no, even now I come across individuals raving about the 'new kid on the block' in martial arts terms and how this latest art is the best ever, and the instructor is out of this world. If I had a pound for every time that I have heard this over my forty years in the martial arts, I would now be living in the Caribbean, a rich man and retired.

I have seen the clamour before and no doubt I will see the clamour again. As they say, "the grass is always greener." That is until the initial sparkle wears off and the daily week-to-week grind of training sets in, and then they will begin their quest again for the 'grail'. Wasn't Brazilian ju jutsu the best and the ultimate in some people's eyes a few years back? People were flocking to the BJJ gyms. Wow, when the dust has settled, most of the time it is the diehards that are seriously training. The part-time trainers and 'grail' hunters have fallen by the wayside when the shine wore off of working the guard continually and training that arm bar or triangle, drilling those solid basics. Just the same as any other martial art. The ironic thing about this is that judo had these techniques in its arsenal of groundwork for years, but most people didn't give a monkey's about it. It wasn't fashionable to train judo. So while BJJ flourished, many judo clubs went to the wall!

I was around for the kung fu craze of the 70s, the taekwondo and then ninjutsu of the 80s. Somewhere in there were Muay Thai, Hapkido and Tang Soo Do. The 90s brought the rebirth of ju jutsu, and wrestling and grappling arts in general. Suddenly, thousands of grappling experts appeared out of the woodwork. If grappling had been so effective, where the hell were they before? Then, MMA got massive, but we also had Krav Maga and Russian Sambo and military CQ combat and so on and so on. There is nothing new. It has just been repackaged and sold again. I have trained in ju jutsu since 1984, and it was a complete art which included all manner of strikes, throws, locks, chokes, pressure points, etc. I was sparring and fighting with all-in techniques back then as were many others of the same mind.

150

This is a concept that has been around as long as man himself. It's not new.

Ju jutsu is a misunderstood art these days. People will say, "Oh, that's that ground grappling stuff." They are basing this assumption on Brazilian ju jutsu and not realising that ju jutsu is a much more complete system than most martial arts. Samurai warriors were using rear naked choke and arm bars some two thousand years ago. Nothing new there then. The bottom line is that you can spend your life's savings on travelling to train with the top martial artist/fighters in the world, but it doesn't guarantee that you will become world class or a master. Remember there are no ultimate systems. It is the man in the art, not the art in the man. Dedication, blood, sweat and tears are the key success. There are no magic solutions. The latest flavour might seem the answer at the present, but there will always be a new latest flavour waiting in the wings. We can be a fickle lot. Loyalty to one's own instructor doesn't cut it these days.

Take and don't give back is a sad part of today's martial arts culture. Don't forget that it is like the footballer who makes his dream move to the top European club. He will forget where he started and who gave him that start and showed belief in him in the first place. Without this start, he would be nowhere. Yet, every week, somebody is heading off to the latest and greatest. I have run and taught classes since the early 1980s, and I have seen fads come and go and the ultimate art give way to a new, improved ultimate art. If I had worried about every new club or system that had opened a class in my area, I would have gone under years ago. My belief is that no one art has all the answers, which is why I have always been open-minded and trained on many mats in many arts with many instructors, but still maintained my base art. I am not afraid to leave my ego at the door and just get on with it. There is plenty of room and choice for everybody to do what they want and train in what they want. If they honestly believe that it's the best they are training in, more power to them. If they are still training in it in ten years' time and that club is flourishing, great, but don't forget that many instructors are out there to make a quick 'buck' and a quick name for themselves and disappear into the night. Week in, week out, instruction requires great staying power and loads of selfless patience. Not many have that quality. I have had many people leave my clubs for pastures new, only to return sometime later with their tail between their legs. Do I tell them to fuck off? No. Not even if I feel like it. If they come back to me, I will treat it as a compliment. I am still here doing what I do best, and I think if I am still around after all this time, then I must be doing something right. It takes great tenacity, dedication and hard work to stay the distance, most don't. The same goes for the fickle trainer who will probably move on and still be seeking the 'Holy Grail' years down the line. As Winston Churchill once said, "Men stumble upon the truth, get up and walk away." Sometimes, we can't see the wood for the trees and the bloody obvious is staring you in the face. Instead of spending time flitting from one 'new' art to the next, spending quality time in one for a while might be better.

"It takes a brave man to step out of his comfort zone and seek pastures new."

Evolving and Climbing in MMA

February 2001 saw the fight team go back to the second 'Combat' sports trial in Bath. Again, we made a good showing against some even better class fighters this time around.

My fight was against Paul Jenkins from Wales. Paul has a pedigree of contact fighting from boxing, knockdown karate and Thai boxing to strike and grapple events and MMA.

To say the fight was tough would be an understatement. Paul was a big puncher and kicker and my conditioning and experience kept me in the fight. We did have what could be called a bit of a 'tear up' and it went the allotted distance and finished a draw. Paul went on to be a big name on the British MMA scene, fighting out of the 'Dogs of War' camp from Wales. He has had nearly one hundred MMA fights. I was his first one. A little bit of history there.

I damaged my hand in that fight and although part of me wanted to fight again, my whole living relies on me being fit and well and able to function effectively, so I withdrew my fight card for the day.

The hand injury was on the base of the thumb and it originated from the twisting the thumb in a gi collar some twelve months earlier when I was grappling. It can be fine for a while and then it will suddenly flare up if caught wrong. It is something that has become reoccurring.

A month or so later, I received official notice that on my trial results, I had captured a place in the National Championships at middleweight. Also, two of my students, Ross MacKenzie and Mark Clemmings, had also gained places in the same middleweight group. Unfortunately, only one member from a club can compete in the same weight category.

I thought this over and realised that at thirty-nine years of age, this would probably be my last chance to compete at this level, so I asked Ross and Mark if they would step down and allow me the chance to enter. They agreed, and as both were young men, I knew their chance would come again.

The Nationals were set for June and this date would be two weeks short of my fortieth birthday. I knew I had a task ahead of me, but as always, I was ready to give it a shot!

I trained hard for six weeks in preparation for this championship. My schedule was tough, fitting it around my normal teaching.

I can tell you that I was sore and had to mentally lift myself to keep the routine going. My training partners pushed me to my physical and mental limits and got that bit extra out of me.

Before I knew I had a place in the Nationals, I had signed up to fight in a submission wrestling tournament also arranged by ML sports and Dale Adams. This was to take place in May and in retrospect, I should have pulled out of this event and kept focused on the MMA. But I decided to enter and have a few fights for experience.

When it came to the weigh-in, I had a shock. I had been training hard on my stamina and I was down in weight to seventy-five kilos. This was lightweight and not at the middleweight category that I was due to fight in at the Nationals. I was a little worried. It mentally threw me out. Back then in my early days of competing, it was all trial and error. I didn't have the knowledge or experience. I was coaching myself, so you did what you thought was right. In its early and burgeoning years, fighters and trainers really had to learn this way. We had nothing to compare to. It was literally style against style. Just turning up and having a go. MMA was not the giant it now is. In fact, back then, the name MMA hadn't even been coined. It was still called 'No Holds Barred' fighting or the Portuguese name 'Vale Tudo', translated as 'anything goes'. We really were the trailblazers and early pioneers of this sport around the UK. The big names from this time were Ian 'the Machine' Freeman, Leigh Remedios, Mark Weir and Lee Hasdell. These men forged a path for many others to follow. It was exciting and heady days and I am privileged to have played some small part in this in the South West of England.

I competed in the submission wrestling tournament at lightweight but my mind wasn't right. I dominated my first fight against a very flexible and rubbery opponent who I managed to keep subdued with my scarf hold, but I couldn't get the finish. In my second bout, I was up against a good up-and-coming fighter, Roger Woodward. I got careless when trying to choke him out with his own belt. He slipped into a very neat armbar and I was forced to tap out. I couldn't afford an injury. You live to fight another day.

After that tournament, I was concerned about making the middleweight bracket, so I had to change my training. I cut back on the cardio work and began lifting heavy weights. Basis lifts, strict and slow and at the same time, I started eating for England.

Over the six-week period, I touched no fatty or sugary food and drank no alcohol whatsoever. I disciplined myself to a strict and healthy eating regime with plenty of protein. Some of it was darn right boring and repetitive, but I stuck religiously to it. On the day of the

154

fight, I tipped the scales at eighty-one kilos. I was at my heaviest and I felt strong and solid.

The Nationals was an enjoyable day. A good crowd was there and I had plenty of support. There were championship belts and trophies for all that participated and Dale Adams ran a very professional tournament.

I was drawn to fight Richard Stopgate. He was another excellent young fighter from Wales with good MMA and NHB experience. The finals were a sudden-death format. If you won your fight, you were going through; lose, you were on your way home. From the trials, I knew that he was a very hard leg kicker and I had to get my game plan right to survive this one. It was a four-man tournament at middleweight and no disrespect to the other lads involved, but I felt that I had drawn the best guy there. I knew that this was going to really push me.

The fight proved every bit as hard as I expected. Richard got some big hard kicks in earlier on, and I knew I had to close the gap to survive. I did this and took the fight to the floor. Richard is no slouch there either, and we had a tough battle up to the end of round one.

Round two, I was fairing a bit better. My timing was getting better as I warmed up and the 'old body' began to respond. At one stage, I drove my opponent across the area with a flurry of punches, then got a headlock on him and jumped up to the guard, bringing him down with me.

I felt comfortable in the guard and punches and attempted submissions were working. Richard attempted a bar choke, but I felt okay and defended this with no problem. Then he very quickly altered his position and slapped on a Figure 8 choke. At first, I felt no danger and then very quickly as he leant his weight in, I felt the blood rushing in my ears and I knew I was on my way to 'Sleepsville'. I tapped the mat, but it felt like slow motion. Then, it was lights out.

I came around to the voice of Rob, my corner man, and Paul, who assisted him, asking if I was all right. Yes, I seemed fine after the briefest of sleeps. I was helped to my feet and shook hands with the waiting Richard Stopgate. It was all over for me, but I had given it my best shot. My opponent's youth just made him faster and stronger than me on the day.

After reviewing the fight, I had felt that my opponent just had that extra edge in speed which came with his age, and I was just a second behind him in doing what I wanted. You can't stop the sands of time trickling away, and I suppose it proved to be on this occasion.

After this busy schedule, I was glad of a break and was looking forward to a holiday, which I felt was well earned. I enjoyed the break and had a chance to recharge the batteries. I find that these days, unless I actually get away for a break, I end up falling into the trap of working in some shape or form every day. When you work for yourself, you always end up picking up the ringing phone and doing some business or ending up arranging a private lesson or get involved in some project. This is great and I love what an unexpected phone call or email might bring in the shape of a new opportunity, but this is infuriating to the family who want some quality time together. I have learnt with experience when to work and when to take a break from it. You need to do this from time to time so you can unwind and take things a bit easier. I treasure quality time with my family, and I will not miss out on this when the opportunity arises. Anybody that works for themselves will know that their business doesn't just revolve around a nine-to-five schedule. You find that sometimes work will eat into your free time and you must be careful to get a balance. I have tried to do this and have allotted time schedules for my training, teaching, clerical work, writing and research and my family; otherwise, they all overlap and you fall out of balance.

When I returned from holiday, the combat trials were starting again at the end of August. One of my top students, Ross MacKenzie, was going to compete in the lightweight division, so I started helping him with his training. As the training progressed, I began to get an itch to compete once again. I think the summer weather had eased away any aches and pains and I was feeling good, so I decided to send my entry and give it another shot.

I remember that the day of the event was very warm indeed and it was extremely hot in the competition area. I was first up to fight again at middleweight against a veteran kickboxer, Mark Woodall. Mark had many years of experience in the kickboxing field and had travelled extensively in the UK and around the world competing and coaching. Mark had some great fighters in his then 'Roughhouse' stable, notably MMA competitor Paul Sutherland. Since these times, Mark has made his name as a top MMA referee and Paul runs the very successful 'Trojan Free' fighters.

Mark and I were speaking before the event and he commented that he thought he would end up fighting against me. We had a laugh about this. When I was called out to fight, whose name was called as my opponent but Mark's! Although he wasn't greatly experienced in the MMA competition, I knew he was a wily opponent with first-class kickboxing skills, so I had decided from the off that I would attempt to grapple him.

After an initial exchange of kicks and punches, I secured a front guillotine choke on Mark. As I worked it, I jumped up to bring him down in my guard, but he held his balance and didn't fall. I put my feet back on the ground, manoeuvred around a bit and put it on again but much tighter. I arched my back and squeezed, and I felt my opponent's breath labour. He struggled to escape. I had the choke sunk in tight and then, he was tapping out. It had been a quick victory and I was glad of that. Mark told me after that it was the tightest choke he had felt, and I feel his lack of grappling experience prevented him from attempting to counter. Much respect to him. He is a first-class martial artist and good friend.

My second bout was against a young fighter from Weston-Super-Mare Ju Jutsu Club run by another old friend, Ian Rossiter. This lad was a good amateur boxer and came out firing on all cylinders with punches. I covered, closed and dropped a good left hook to his body and took him over with a body drop throw. I fell into scarf hold position and settled in. I had managed to work two of my favourite techniques: the left hook to the body and the scarf hold. I have won many matches with these techniques.

Once I had the scarf hold locked in, I hooked his arm with my leg into an elbow lock and then cranked up his neck and got an instant submission. It was another quick win and a good one. I was well pleased with the performance.

I had a third fight against a heavyweight, Charles Halliwell from Bob Sykes' Huddersfield gym. This lad had come down to fight, but there were no heavyweight fighters signed up on the day, so I agreed to have a go.

He came up with some big bombs, kicks, punches and knees. So again, I decided to take him down. On my first double leg attempt, I got caught with a big knee strike squarely in the breast bone, which did knock some of the steam out of me. I went in again though, and this time he sprawled back and got me in a guillotine choke. I went to sit through to counter this, but in a blank moment, I went the wrong way, the choke became a powerful neck crank and I was forced to tap out whilst my head was still intact on my shoulders! The weight difference was just too much for me on this day.

It had been another good outing and although I had decided to enter these trials at the last minute, they had worked out to be the best yet for me.

The next trials were at the end of September and I decided to enter once more as I could see a possible opportunity of reaching the Nationals for the second year running, which a few months previously I hadn't envisaged happening again. Matt and Ross, two of my top fighters, also went to fight in the heavyweight and lightweight division.

At this event, the standard was even higher than before and many competitors didn't even get a chance to fight as so many had entered.

I fought against a guy called Suley Mahmoud, a very good fighter from the London 'Shootfighters' gym. It was a fast and explosive affair straight from the off, but that's the only way I can go. I was looking for another quick victory.

This fight again was quite even. I felt stronger standing up this time whilst my opponent wanted to go to the floor. The fight ended a hard-fought draw, and both of us had felt the pace.

I knew that, with this result, I had done enough to make the championships.

Matt and Ross both turned in good performances to also book themselves places in the Nationals. For the second year running, the Bristol Goshin Jutsu Combat Academy was represented.

Between these championships, for a short while, I was ranked as number one middleweight in the combat sports rankings, which I was very proud of at the age of forty. Before the finals, I had two seminars to teach. Both promised to be good days.

The first was for my old friend Dave Turton at his newly formed association 'The Self-Defence Federation'. This federation, again, was dedicated to the more combat-orientated arts and street-applied technique. Their annual major seminar was held in Batley, Yorkshire at Neil Hall's 'Fighting Chance' Academy. Many top-named martial artists in the combat field attended that day, and I taught combat ju jutsu techniques for self-defence, which went down very well.

A couple of weeks later, I was in Dudley in the West Midlands to teach an MMA seminar for 'Grappling Styles International', the organisation I mentioned earlier, set up by Paul Dunne through 'Combat Sport Worldwide' for the practice and promotion of MMA and NHB competition. I am also proud to have been a senior instructor within this newly formed group. I enjoy the seminar scene and this side of my teaching. It's nice to meet up with people that know you through your writing or videos and that have travelled to train under you. On seminars, you can meet many new friends and contacts.

I have done many varied types of seminars in the last few years from street self-defence, combat ju jutsu to MMA. I have also taught CQC for the reserve Parachute Regiment organised by an ex-student John Banfield. I have taught on numerous occasions for TA and army reserve. I have also taught ex-members of the Special Forces and bodyguard world. I have always been well received and enjoyed experiencing what some of these guys have got to offer in the world

158

of real combat. I recently taught a parachute reserve team hand-to-hand combat as they were going in on the ground as peacekeepers in Afghanistan and Iraq.

The end of 2001 was the National Championships once more in Bath. The fight card had an impressive line-up, and I drew to fight the reigning middleweight champion, Gareth Roberts. We had met before and had drawn our fight. I must admit that I fancied my chances of pulling off a victory.

Ross, fighting in the highly competitive lightweight division, fought a cracking fight, but was caught in a triangle headlock in the dying seconds. Matt, once again, made it through to the heavyweight final to fight his old nemesis and reigning champion, Nick Jones. The fight was a thriller going the complete distance and an overtime period with no submissions. Nick took the judge's decision, but Matt had pushed him all the way and I was proud of his performance.

As for me, my bout with Gareth Roberts was a close call. We had matched each other move for move and there had been nothing in it. Close to the end of the first round, Gareth received a 'yellow card' for an illegal move, which instantly put him behind on the judge's card.

As the second round wore on, I sensed his frustration as he couldn't get a position or submission on me. Gareth was a leglock specialist, and in the dying seconds, he tried to submit me with an Achilles lock, but I blocked it and stopped the submission. He was moaning to the referee in desperation as I just had to hold on to win the match.

He went for a double leg takedown but left his head exposed and I face-barred him viciously, opening a nasty nose bleed. It was becoming a war of attrition. In the closing minute, he took me down and I pulled guard. I thought that I had the fight in the bag, but he showed that he was a true champion by suddenly pulling a spinning knee bar out of nowhere. I just couldn't fight it as I felt my knee straining to snapping point. I had to tap literally seconds from the end of the fight.

I was disappointed. Gareth was elated. It had been a very close call, but I couldn't have done any more. When the knee bar is set in, you can't do much about it if you want to walk the next day.

I look back to those times and I realise that I just didn't have all the knowledge I needed to really excel in this arena. At that point, I didn't have a counter to a kneebar. MMA was in its fledgling state. Now, there are unending techniques and information on the web and answers to every fighting position you could hope to find yourself in, but not then. You can only go in equipped with what you had at your disposal. I learnt, though, from each fight and constantly went back in again armed with some new knowledge.

I must state here that the trials were a great arena to gain MMA experience before stepping into the cage. ML sports spawned many future champions and there were some talented guys back then. Here are just a few of the guys that fought in the trials: Jeff Lawson, Mick Broster, Alex Owen, Paul Sutherland, Oliver Ellis, Mark Spencer, Ross Pettifer, Mark Chen, Paul Jenkins, Matt Bowen, Jon Williams, Ian Pratt, Kasan Hipkiss, Gaz Roriston, Glen Brown, Sol Gilbert, Paul Daley and Paul Reed. There were many more. They were heady days for this new and exciting sport.

In 2002, 'Ultimate Combat' was launched. It was one of the very first professional MMA shows in the UK. Dale Adams, who had organised the amateur trials I had been involved with, was the brainchild behind this event. In the coming years, 'Ultimate Combat' became one of the biggest and best shows in the country, showcasing some of the UK's and Europe's best MMA fighters.

I was lucky enough to have a cage side table at the first event, and I told my good friend and sparring partner, Rob Cannon, that I would watch the show and at the end if I thought I could get in the cage and have another fight, I would find Dale immediately after and sign up for the next one. The show was excellent. Veteran Ultimate Fighting Championships' announcer, Bruce Buffer, was flown in from the States to open the show and the top of the bill was a cracking fight between Leigh Remedios and John Kavanagh. The atmosphere was electric. I loved every minute of it. Up to then, I had only watched professional MMA shows on video tape and now I was ringside (UC fights were all in a ring, not a cage) soaking up the action live.

I was buzzing at the end of the night and went and found Dale Adams and asked him to consider me for the 'Ultimate Combat II'. He said he would. True to his word, a few weeks later, I had a fight contract through and I was in the next show.

Sunday June 9th 2002, I was back into the competitive arena for a fight on the 'Ultimate Combat 2 – The World Warriors', held at Chippenham leisure centre, Wiltshire. The fight card was promoted by ML Sports and sanctioned by the British Association of Mixed Martial Arts.

I decided to fight at welterweight this time, not middle, so I was going to have to drop about five kilos of body weight. I wanted to get some more speed and movement that I felt I lacked in previous fights. So, I started an eight-week programme of intense training to hit my target.

I started running, wind sprints and hill work to begin to burn the calories. Cycling and rowing were also thrown in for cardio and endurance.

Once more, back then many of us didn't really know the principles of weight cutting and re-dehydration, etc. Most people were fighting the weight they walked around at.

I feel if fighters today did this, it would save them all the agony of getting down to a lighter weight and then trying to put it all back on after weigh-in. If the other guy is also doing that it becomes pretty pointless.

I knew that if I was going to have a chance of winning this time, I had to somehow cut back on my workload and devote more time to MMA training. So, some of my other training had to take a back seat.

My good friend and sparring partner, Rob Cannon, for whom I owe so much, trained with me constantly on upright and floor skills, conditioning and speed training.

We also went regularly to the 'Spaniorum Home Farm' near Bristol, which is run by Tex Woodward, a top boxing coach, and home to many great boxers over the years. We used the ring to work our mixed martial arts skills and get a feel for it. Back then, the lads training there wondered what we were doing as they were all boxers. They hadn't seen MMA trained before. Now, it is common knowledge in most gyms.

This hard training, combined with a strict diet, got me to 74.9 kilos on the day of the weigh-in.

My opponent was a Commonwealth wrestling champion from Scotland named Andy Proctor. A good lad and a seasoned fighter. My game plan was to try and stay on my feet and use my striking skills and if he 'shot' for my legs, I would sprawl and remain in the top position and keep punching.

I was two weeks shy of my fortieth birthday when I stepped into the ring that evening. I had massive support in the crowd, and I felt good. I knew that I was in decent shape, and I was ready to give it my all. With Rob's ringside guidance, it all went to plan and I won the bout by unanimous decision. I kept the fight up on my feet for some time but also dominated the floor work by maintaining top position and using relentless 'ground and pound'. I didn't allow my opponent into the fight. My continued work rate was down to my conditioning. All the hours of training had paid off. I had felt strong and knew I had the edge throughout the fight. It was a more disciplined performance. I was gradually making the transition from street/combatives fighting into the combat sports arena.

As the result went up, I received a great ovation from the crowd. The support of my club members, friends and the Bristol crowd in general was phenomenal and I would like to thank you all here in writing. It was much appreciated.

I must also note that on this bill, Ross MacKenzie fought one of the first ever BJJ fighters to come to the UK. His name was Pedro Martins. He was a purple belt in BJJ and a Pan American silver medallist. It was a great moment for Ross and me. It was a good fight, although Ross eventually lost to submission. It was a learning experience way back then. Pedro lived in England for a short while and became friends with us whilst he stayed here. I recently looked up Pedro who is now a black belt and back living in Caxias, Maranhao, Brazil. He recently won gold at the European Ju Jutsu Championship. Good to see him still training.

The whole evening was a marvellous way to bring me up to my birthday. To have got a chance to fight in probably the world's toughest extreme sport on one of the UK's biggest shows was an honour and a pleasure. I took the fight for my own personal challenge, and I was one hundred percent up for it. I had peaked at the right time, and I knew that losing was not an option. It was important for me and a test of my fitness, skill and dedication to MMA Combat. I must take this opportunity also to thank organiser Dale Adams who put on a first-class show. 'Ultimate Combat' was off and running. It was going to be big. Dale and his wife, Laura, knew their stuff. So much so that Dale had a big hand in bringing the 'Ultimate Fighting Championships' to the Albert Hall, London, in this year for the very first time. I was proud to have had a ticket to watch this unique occasion and see the British lads fighting on the show, proudly smash it with some great performances, particularly Mark Weir's incredible knockout win and Ian Freeman's emotionally charged battle that he dominated in one of, in my opinion, his best performance in the cage.

You may ask why I would have put myself through all that training at my time of life when many my age are content with a game of golf and a pint down the pub and a talk about the 'good old days'. Well, I suppose that there's your answer. I wanted to feel alive and still have the desire and passion to achieve. Life would be dull without a challenge and it makes the quieter moments sweeter. When you have spent the best part of your life involved in the martial arts and training for goals, it is extremely hard to bring the curtain down or take a back seat.

Now I had the bit between my teeth, I wanted to fight again and come November of that year, I was now going into the cage at the Winter Gardens in Weston-super-Mare to fight on a show named 'Ground and Pound 1'. I had been asked to initially judge on this show.

Two of my lads, Matt and Steve, would be appearing on this fight card. The promoter, Justin Dodd, rang me about two weeks before the show's start date, informing me that a welterweight fighter had just pulled out of a bout and they were looking for a last-minute replacement. Did I know any decent seventy-five-kilo fighters? Well, let me think. Seventy-five kilos. Welterweight. Mmm, that's my weight. I felt the tingle of adrenaline course through my body. I was fit and I was still training hard. I suppose I could give it a bash!

I took the fight, but looking back now, maybe I shouldn't have. I had a lot going on in my life at that time, and maybe I wasn't as focused as I had been for the previous one. Nevertheless, it's not an excuse and you can't have regrets.

I fought a very good fighter from Rob Locke's gym named Kasan Hipkiss. The fight was fast and furious. His last opponent he had keyed with a head kick: that broke his jaw. Call me a 'softy' if you like but I didn't fancy that. So, from the bell, I closed the gap to punching range and drove my opponent to the cage wall and threw some big shots. We clinched and wrestled before hitting the floor. We both went to the floor and secured leglocks on each other. I made a costly mistake of wearing wrestling boots for this fight and as Kasan changed from an Achilles lock to an outside heel hook, I couldn't get my foot out as the boot gave him good purchase. The lock went on fast and I felt the bones in my foot begin to crack. I had to tap out. I was disappointed, but fair shout to my opponent. Again, I had learnt a valuable lesson and never wore wrestling boots in a fight again.

After this fight, I did a bit of soul searching, wondering if I was too old to compete with these young guys coming through the ranks. I decided that I had achieved my goal of reaching a decent level to fight in the cage and it may be a smart move now to move on and call it a day.

I knew I wasn't going to make a career out of MMA. Firstly, I was too old and secondly, I knew that I wasn't going to be able to put the time and sacrifice in that you have to if you want to reach the top of the tree. You have to be a realist and know that what you put in to something is what you get out and that will be the level you will attain.

I entered MMA for my own personal challenge as part of my martial arts journey. That was my motivation. I had wanted to see if I could step into that arena and hold my own and I did.

I remember watching the first UFC and I never dreamt then that I would get the chance to step into the MMA arena myself. But I did and I am proud to have done so.

"There is little you can learn from doing nothing."

Early picture of me practising Aikido with Simon Webb around 1978.

My first Jujustsu instructor, Mike Marshall and John McCartney.

The one and only Micky Upham. One of the best martial artists I ever met.

Jamie O'Keefe my good mate and fellow Martial artist who helped me so much with publishing my early books.

Striking a pose with my friend and mentor, Geoff Thompson.

Legend, Peter Consterdine.

Early MMA fight against Paul 'hands of stone' Jenkins.

Training in London with Canadian self-protection expert, Richard Dimetri.

Shaking hands with the legendary, Roy 'pretty boy' Shaw.

Pictured with John Machado and my fellow combat jujutsu instructor, Paul Flett.

Rolling with John Machado.

My ultimate
combat fight
with Sami Berik.

One of the bravest
MMA fighters I
ever trained, Ross
Mould. He had the
heart of a lion.

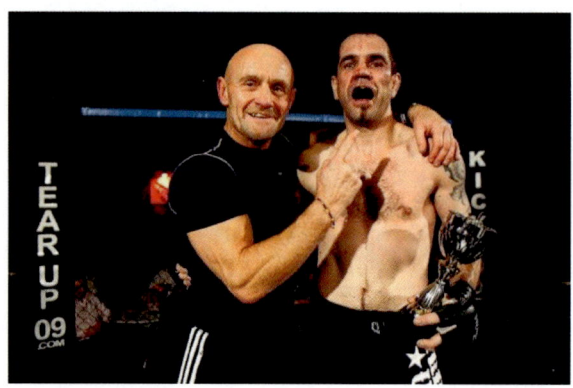

'Facing off'
with UFC
legend Chuck
'the iceman'
Liddell.

Heading to the cage with another Impact fighter.

One of the best MMA fight teams ever.

The 'Colossus' James Thompson and 'Rampage' Jackson. Pride, Tokyo.

Having breakfast
in Japan with
Alistair Overeem.

Pride, Japan with
Bas Rutten.

Meeting 'the
axe murderer'
himself,
Wanderlai
Silva.

Don Henderson, Pride and UFC champion.

The man a 1000 submissions. The great Erik Paulson.

Grading my good mate and fellow jujutsu and MMA coach Richard 'Shaky' Shore to 2nd Dan.

Conflict management
with PPs and my good
friend, Mark Hewitt.

My sons, Tom and Jake,
with me after a tough
bootcamp.

My two present
Combat jujutsu
coaches, Jay
Newton and Lea
Welsford.

Renovation of Impact gym. A truly massive project.

Finished work on Impact gym, ready to open.

At the M.A.I hall of fame awards with my old instructor, Dave Turton.

My good buddy Paul Bush and me commentating on a 'Zero to Hero' fight night. We look like 'Right said Fred'.

My alter ego 'Diablo the masked assassin' in the ring.

Down amongst
the Zombies.

Hosting a seminar at Impact
gym with Nino Schenbri and
Salvador Pace of BJJ.

My rock and my soulmate, Tina, my wife.

Proud moment with my lovely daughter, Lauren, at her graduation in Paris.

Winning a silver medal at Naga 2015 at the age of 54.

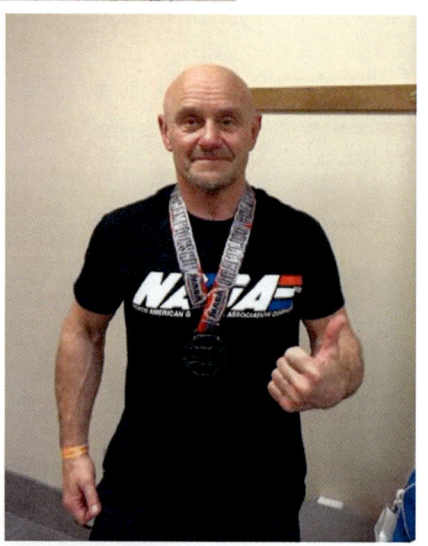

Just doing my job.

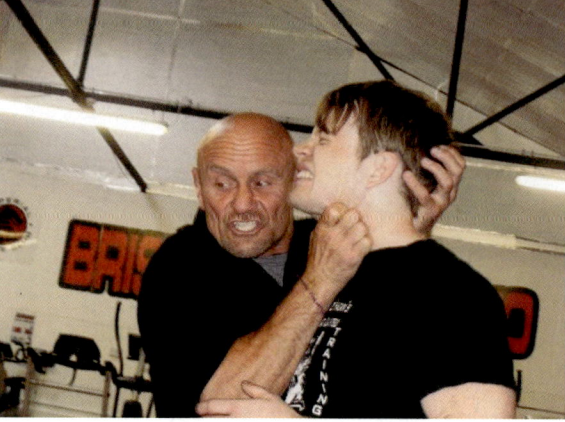

Muscling In

I have trained many door supervisors and security personnel over the years. My combat ju jutsu has a host of restraining holds, locks and pressure point attacks that are all useful for individuals in this line of work. People in the world of security these days are under the microscope from many new legislations and laws. Plus, CCTV is everywhere. It is not like the 'good old days' when bouncers could merrily punch somebody's lights out or chuck them down a flight of stairs with no comeback for misbehaving or excessive force claims.

They seek me out because their basic training isn't always enough. I respect these guys and don't come in as a 'know it all'. I ask them where they feel their training is lacking or can improve, and I help them out. I have also stood on doors with some of these men to observe what they must deal with. Many of my students were also door staff, and they all used ju jutsu techniques at times when they were needed with remarkable success.

I have also worked off the record with the police force where they want to beef their training up a bit. I have done a few seminars for the 'bobby on the beat' and the CID. I have made some good friends from both the police and security world. This was all good news for me, as the latter has allowed me access into many venues free of charge if I wanted, which is always nice. But in truth, I am not a party animal-type. Also, it is nice to have a few friendly faces in the Police.

In my younger years, I had done a little bit of door and security work in a few pubs, but I didn't really enjoy it. Plus, the money wasn't good enough to warrant some asshole trying to stick a glass in your face. The 70s and early 80s' club scene was extremely violent. I left it quickly. I knew I didn't want to make a career from it.

I was approached some years back by one of my then-students, Mike Hockett, and asked if I would like a small part in an up-and-coming 'fly on the wall' documentary called 'Muscle'. The six-part BBC 1 programme was planning to follow a firm of door security staff for a six-month period to see how they operated in the clubs and pubs around Bristol.

Mike was one of these doormen and had trained with me on and off for several years. Part of the programme would cover how they trained for fitness and fighting skills and this is where I came in.

I was only too glad to get another opportunity to showcase my skills on television. This time, it would be national TV and peak viewing hours. It couldn't do me any harm and hopefully, it would send some business my way.

The BBC camera crew filmed my bit with Mike at the old Bristol 'Budokan'. We went through an hour of filming. We did pad work, weapon disarming, locks, restraints, pressure points, strangles, defence against holds and grabs, pre-emptive strikes and combat ground grappling.

I think that the producer and camera crew were suitably stunned when we had finished. I don't think they had any idea what to expect, and I turned it on for the camera, which you must do to sell yourself, and they loved it.

Because the programme was going out after the watershed, we could be a bit more explicit with dialogue and techniques. It was great fun. Although I don't know if Mike agreed, he was on the end of a hell of a lot of technique.

Sadly, when the programme went out, a lot of my stuff had been cut or edited down into just a few brief moments. But having said that, it was well put together and hopefully had the right impact on the viewer.

The power of television is amazing. Just from those brief clips, I had phone calls of congratulations and praise from colleagues in the martial arts world and also interest about my art and classes. So, it was a worthwhile experience.

I must admit that I do harbour an ambition to do some serious stuff for TV or film. I love the whole package of filming and being in front of the camera. I feel happy and natural there! So, if there's any film directors or producers out there, just give me a call now while I still have a bit of life left in me!

Initially, the programme came in for a lot of stick, primarily because of the way a situation was handled at the end of the first episode. This was when a mass fight broke out over what seemed a pretty innocuous opening scenario. The lads were slaughtered for it from many quarters. I think, in hindsight, that they even felt they got it wrong, but they couldn't change the situation as the cameras rolled. In my opinion, I feel it was handled incorrectly, but in their defence, you can only react to how you perceive the situation in that instance. We all get things wrong in our own job on occasions. Fortunately, we haven't got a camera crew breathing down our necks, and the outcome of our mistakes won't result in a 'kick in' or worse. We can't be right all the time.

It was unfortunate that the whole thing was filmed for everybody and their dog to give an opinion on. I think that as the series went on, it managed to give a more balanced view of the job, and the guys came out of it all in a good light.

You must remember that you are always going to be open for criticism as soon as you do something like the 'Muscle' programme. Also, the public must remember that it is meant to also have a degree of entertainment value for you to watch. Controversy always gathers viewers. It is good TV. You shouldn't take it all to heart.

From the point of view of the job of a door supervisor, as it is known these days, the majority do a great job. They see that the average man and woman can enjoy a safe night out without any hassle or trouble.

I have trained door staff/security for a long time and have had many come to train in my classes, and they have all been smashing people and not what you may expect. As I have often told their critics, somebody must do the job. The police haven't got the resources or manpower, so these people put themselves on the line, week in, week out.

You get good and bad in every line of work. Door work is no different. You also have different scales of experience and expertise. Some people have vast experience and are true 'pros'. They are top of their tree and are extremely good at what they do and nine times out of ten will diffuse any situation without the need for violence. Massive names in the martial arts world all worked the doors at one time or another, such as Dennis Martin, Terry O'Neil, Gary Spiers, Peter Consterdine, Geoff Thompson, Jamie O'Keefe and Lee Morrison, to name but a few. I have been fortunate over the years to call these people my friends and colleagues. These guys were at the top of their game and highly experienced.

Obviously, you get some 'young bucks' go on the door to prove themselves or because they are in love with the glamorous image. Also, they do it to pull the pretty girls or peddle drugs. These are all the wrong reasons and a recipe for disaster. If you land a job in a student wine bar, the likelihood of serious trouble kicking off is slim, and you can get complacent and think you are a top dog. Work in the city centre in a large night club or pub venue and it can be a totally different ball game. You need to be switched on always and have three hundred and sixty-degree vision.

You can face some potentially life-threatening situations, and you have got to ask yourself, do I want to do this? Some can stand the heat; others can't. My advice to anybody thinking of going into the door security world would be: think long and hard about the reasons why you want to do it.

When it comes down to physical skills, I would say that a fair percentage of doormen are average or below average fighters when in a one-to-one situation. I am talking from the viewpoint of a professional martial artist. I have trained lads that have had great spirit, heart and more front than Blackpool, but do not have particularly good fighting skills. There are other door staff that are already skilled fighters and have brought that expertise into their work.

Again, there are many young lads working the doors who believe that they are bulletproof and they may be in for a shock when the real deal shows up and wants to kick off. A few months of Muay Thai, karate or wrestling isn't going to stand you in good stead for the reality of a brutal street attack.

For most part, a doorman's job will involve tact, diplomacy, good conversational skills and the knack of de-escalation, but when it gets down to the crunch, you need to be able to efficiently look after yourself. Normally you will be working as a team so one-to-one confrontation is not on the agenda too often. But you still need to watch your back, particularly at the end of a shift.

Many are all front. Buff and talk with very little else. The 'cream' is in their minority. Sporting a shaven head, tattoos and every orifice pierced doesn't make you a hard man, neither does heaving a few heavy weights about. Some believe that this is enough. These are superficial barriers put up to warn people off. A suit of armour, so to speak, and it may work well until a professional or a psychopath sees through them. Looking the part isn't the same as being the part. Luckily, the average punter doesn't know the difference, but there is always someone who will, and they will take you right up to the doorway of violence to find out. You have got to be prepared for this moment and be trained appropriately. Many aren't.

Some are living on reputation or past glories. As I stated earlier, as you get older, there is always some young gun looking for a scalp. Make sure it isn't yours!

Door life is a hard life. You don't get many thanks for it and inevitably, you can't win. One minute you are a good guy; then, you are a bad guy. A crowd in a pub or club can be a fickle lot. A group of lads can come in a club all smiles and greetings, and come out at the end of the night baying for your blood with hate in their eyes. Currently, with more and more drugs on the streets and mega-strong alcohol, people can be dangerous and unpredictable.

For those of you who watched 'Muscle', you witnessed this for yourself. I think that the lads in the show did a decent job over all. It's easy for somebody sitting in the comfort of their armchair to give their opinion, but it's not the same as being out there doing it.

I take my hat off to the 'pros' that do and do it well. The night club culture is a safer place with you guys in it. Much respect to you, unsung heroes.

"Door security staff are a bit like the police. Everybody hates them until they need their help."

Britain's Hardest

It's late August 2003 and I have just returned from a holiday. I am rested, tanned and ready to get back to work.

An avalanche of post awaits me when I return home, and when I'm ready, I begin to sift through it. I open one letter and it immediately intrigues me. At the same time, it gives me an instant shot of adrenaline in my belly.

The letter reads that a Sky TV company is putting together a TV show entitled 'Britain's Hardest'. It briefly outlines that the show is a series of mental and physical challenges. It also says that they are looking for certain types of individuals who are up for the challenge, and they think that I might be a suitable candidate.

After reading this, I put the letter on my desk and try to forget about it for a while but my thoughts keep slipping back to it.

I ask myself the question whether at forty-three years of age, do I want to be bothered to put myself through this again? All the training? The discipline? The sacrifice?

I had achieved so much in recent years, but any success always comes with a price.

My body had been put 'through the mill' a fair few times and I was carrying a few niggling little injuries. I didn't know if I really wanted the challenge anymore.

I went to bed that night and could not sleep. I battled with all the previous questions. I chewed over the positive and negatives. When the morning light filtered through the bedroom curtains and I pulled my weary body out of bed, I knew that I was going to ring the contact number on the letter and find out what it was all about.

I rang later that morning and got directly through to the producer. He was still very cagey about the programme and the types of challenges involved. He said that he was looking for martial artists, ex-forces, fighters and fitness freaks. Anybody in that sort of mould. He said that he had seen my profile on my website and thought that I would be ideal. But firstly, there was to be a series of UK auditions and fitness tests to see if I came up to scratch. He told me that in two weeks' time, they would be coming to my home town of Bristol to hold these auditions and gave me details on how to sign up for them. I thanked him and put down the phone. The adrenaline had really kicked in now, and I knew I was going to go for it.

I tried to be positive. I was in decent shape for my age, and I knew if I got myself mentally right, I could step it up a gear.

I also knew that it was one of those opportunities that come around maybe once in a lifetime and I didn't want to be watching the show in six months' time from the comfort of my armchair, wishing that I had given it a go.

What did I have to fear? Well, maybe looking an idiot in front of God knows how many viewers. Having a reputation to uphold. Knowing probably that all my friends and family would be tuning in with high expectations. Not knowing the best sort of training for the show and what to expect. I hoped that there was nothing involving heights. I fucking hate heights. Well, apart from all those things, it will be a walk in the park! For all my fears, I was determined to face them and conquer them. I had learnt much about facing fear in recent years, and I knew I wouldn't let it get the better of me.

I started training towards the audition. I just stepped up my usual cross-training schedule. Cardio, strength, endurance and flexibility. I worked in the gym on cardio and weights, increased my bag and pad work, added outdoor hill runs and sprints and stepped up my body weight exercises. I wanted to be as prepared as I could.

When I auditioned many years back for the 'Gladiators' show in the 90s, I didn't prepare right and suffered for that. I had learnt my lesson from this and I knew that I had to get it right. The only problem was that I didn't really know what I was preparing for. In hindsight, I couldn't have totally prepared for the diversity of challenge waiting.

The two weeks shot by and I found myself sitting in a corridor of a Bristol hotel, waiting my turn to go into the audition room. The details sent to me had said to also bring along a motivator/trainer who you wanted to be with you on the show.

I had chosen my then right-hand man at my martial arts clubs and my sparring partner and close friend Rob Cannon. Unfortunately, he was away with his work and couldn't make the audition, so I sat there alone. I could have done with his company and words of encouragement.

Suddenly, I heard voices and two guys appeared in the corridor, also here for the auditions.

I recognised them both straight away and grinned. It didn't surprise me that they were there. One was ex-British and Commonwealth light welterweight boxing champion Ross Hale, and with him was Paul Moylett, ex-boxer and Thai fighter and now a BJJ black belt who owned 'Mowers Gym' – a favourite hardcore haunt for fitness fanatics and fighters in Bristol. These were two truly tough men, but also incredibly humble guys.

We all shook hands and sat down and chatted. Although we were there for the same thing, there was no animosity. Ross and I had trained together many times and all three of us had immense respect for each other.

The door of the audition room then opened and two huge bodybuilder-type guys walked out. They had done their auditions. They looked at us as if to say, "You've got no fucking hope." After all, in their eyes, they saw three smallish guys well past their first flush of youth sitting before them.

We smiled back at them. I had seen it all before. As the old saying goes, "Don't judge a book by its cover." It really is a profound statement and one that I have found true many times.

A guy suddenly appeared in the doorway, introduced himself and told us to come in.

He explained that the idea was to do a screen test in front of the camera. Talk a bit about yourself, your background and why you thought you should be on the show. Then, we would do a few physical and mental tests.

Ross was auditioning for the show and Paul was going to be his motivator. Ross and I were going to have to go up against each other in the tests with the motivators giving instruction and encouragement. Great! I didn't have my motivator here!

After the screen tests, which I was quite comfortable about, we got set for the physical tests. I recall a few of the exercises we had to do, but some of it is a blank. It has been a while now. One test was to get down and do as many proper push-ups as possible. We both went head to head with one of the TV guys counting us. As we banged out a continuous fifty and were heading on, he brought it to a halt. He said that it was great and that nobody the previous day or up to now in these Bristol auditions had managed that many. Oh well. So much for our bodybuilding chums!

Another test was to stand facing each other with two carrier bags holding two bags of flour in each. We had to raise the bags to horizontal shoulder height and hold them there as long as you possibly could. The first man to lower his arms lost the challenge. So, we went for it. I can't remember the exact time that we held them, but it seemed like a lifetime. Both of us were staring the other down. Then, I saw a slight wobble of Ross's arms. The wobble rapidly became a shake. His face began to betray the discomfort he was in, and I knew that I was going to outlast him. Twenty seconds or so later, he dropped his arms. I carried on holding and eventually clocked up the best time of all the auditions so far. I was mightily chuffed.

After a few mental games involving instructions from the motivator and you reacting to those commands, the auditions were over.

The TV guys on the day said that we would get a letter in the post in a week to let us know if we had made it. I think a hundred or so people auditioned in Bristol that weekend.

I headed for home quietly confident that I had done okay. I just had to wait now to see if that confirmation dropped through the letterbox for me.

The following week when I returned from the gym, I noticed a handful of letters on my desk. One had a red stamp on the back reading 'Zeal TV'. I instantly knew this was the TV company for 'Britain's Hardest'.

I tore open the envelope, my heart rate increasing. I unfolded the letter and scanned down it. I was in! I had passed the auditions. Details would be sent later when and where the show would be filmed.

I now put my training into full swing. Another letter a week down the line informed me that filming would start in mid-October up in London.

Rob Cannon, my motivator, and I travelled to Finsbury, London, on October 7th to hopefully compete for the full two days. The show was to be filmed in a disused timber yard in Mount Pleasant, Clapham.

Throughout the month, fifty-four contestants would do battle. The show's tagline would be, "54 hard men over 10 shows, but only one can be Britain's hardest." The winner would scoop a cool ten grand.

The show was not going to be 'Gladiators'. It was 'dark' and uncompromising. We weren't going to have any cheesy grinning game show host. The man in charge was none other than the 'Daddy' of the UK cage fighting arena – Ian 'the Machine' Freeman.

The overall show would be introduced by 'EastEnders' 'hard man'', Phil Mitchell, otherwise known as the actor, Steve McFadden.

The filming kept things raw and stark. It looked scary and intimidating, and in reality it was!

When we reached the timber yard on the first morning, we were shown to a room that had been set up for us and we were told to wait for the producer. All eight of us were in this room together with our motivators. It was crammed and you could cut the atmosphere with a knife. I recognised a few faces. One of them was Sol 'Zero Tolerance' Gilbert. He was a very skilled professional cage fighter from Brighton.

Sol had come down to Bristol earlier in the year to train for a fight and came to me for some private tuition. We had a few 'rolls' on the mat, and he is an extremely strong guy. I liked him a lot. I knew that I would have my work cut out with Sol, let alone some of the other boys.

I tried to switch off any negative thoughts and just tried to enjoy the moment. But with a room full of heaving testosterone, it was difficult. The word was that there were also some ex-SAS boys in this, but nobody had a clue who they might be.

After about half an hour, the producer of the show, Stephen Lovelock, came in. Now, it was all going to get a little bit clearer.

The idea was that all eight of us would go head to head on the first challenge. The last man to finish went home. It was as simple as that. No second chance. No chance to try all the events. No pat on the back. No money and no 'bendy bully' or any other trophy or trinket. Harsh? Yes, but that's the name of the game. It was 'Britain's Hardest' after all, not 'Countdown'. No use crying to your mum afterwards.

The format went on the same way until one man was left. He would then go into the final later in the year. I knew now that this was going to be one of the toughest things I had taken on in my career. As the oldest man there, in my heart, I knew that the odds weren't stacked in my favour.

I was going to have to rely on my mental strength as much as my physical. There were some big boys here. Rob talked with me after Stephen had left. He tried to instil the right mental attitude in me and keep me positive. I was glad that he was with me there. I will admit that my ass was twitching, but I also knew that so was everyone else's as well. You had to play the game and not give anything away. Poker faces all round was the order of the day.

A little while later, we were called to a trailer. There, we had to change into our training gear. No Lycra and spandex here! It was t-shirts, sweatshirts, combat trousers and heavy boots.

It was a freezing October's day and a fine drizzle made it damp. Given that I had spent a great deal of my younger working days in a timber yard by the Bristol docks, the environment didn't unduly worry me. But it was bleak.

We next went to a disused warehouse where three of us were told that we each had to go in front of the camera and perform something. You could stare down the camera, say something or throw a few punches or kicks. This was for the opening credits of the show.

We all watched from a portacabin as each of us was called, one at a time, to perform our piece. When this was done, we all sat in the portacabin waiting for the start. It seemed like an eternity and I just wanted to get on with it regardless of the outcome.

The adrenaline which kept rising and falling was beginning to get to me and I began to feel lethargic. I realised that I had to snap out of it. I got up and walked around a little outside and took in some fresh air. But you weren't allowed to stray too far. Anyway, there wasn't much to see in an abandoned warehouse. There was just debris and the odd rat or two. It was not exactly inspiring stuff.

I practised a breathing technique that I had learnt years previously from one of the Japanese Sensei that I had trained under. It always helped keep a rein on the adrenaline and kept me focused. I was grateful that I knew this.

We were eventually called out and we were led across the yard to a huge warehouse. Outside, we were told to wait by the door. The plan was for each of us to be led into the warehouse and in front of the cameras for the start of the show where we would be introduced.

There was going to be no fanfare or glitzy entrance. No. We were going to have a hood put over our heads and blindly led in by a tough-looking doorman. Well, that's showbiz.

We would be shown into a makeshift cage to be used as the holding area. We could stand in there or sit on the timber planks balanced between a few oil drums. The Hilton Hotel it was not.

My adrenaline kicked in again. I took deep breaths and watched as the first three went in, one by one. Then, I was being roughly shoved forward and a sack was put over my head and tied. I was totally reliant on the 'security' guy to lead me through. I heard a door open and I was guided through and then I knew I was in the cage. The hood was pulled from my head, and I was staring down the lens of a huge camera. This was the point where a voiceover was introducing me. With that done, I sat down and waited for the remainder of the contestants to enter.

Next, Ian Freeman entered the cage and told us what was going to happen. Our motivators would be taken away and shown our first task. When we eventually were brought to the task, our motivators had sixty seconds to explain what was required of us, and then we had to do the challenge. It was going to be fast and final.

Rob was led away with the other motivators. We waited. I warily eyed the other guys and they eyed me. We were all doing an excellent job of hiding any fear. We were all experienced men and knew how to play the game.

Ian Freeman returned and told us that the task would be done in two heats of four men. The slowest person out of the complete eight would be on their way home very shortly. I was one hundred percent determined not to go home first, no matter what happened. I hadn't trained this hard for nothing.

I was in the first four to go, and I knew the other lads with me were all big, strong boys. It had been a long, hard journey to arrive at this point. Nobody wanted to be first to go. The pressure was well and truly on. We all filed into the arena and were presented with the first task.

Now at this point, we didn't have a clue what task we would face. Going into the unknown is hard. Would it be a task of strength? Endurance? Agility? Nerve?

Once the show went out on television, we knew what all the tasks were, but not until then.

The events challenged our strength, but were also quite tactical, so that often the strongest man would fail by poor strategy. Here are a few of the events we all participated in:

Pull a heavy ship's chain along the floor a marked distance.

Stop a car from rolling down a slowly steepening slope by pushing against it.

Smash up a car until it can be pushed under a parking barrier.

Sit with your head in a box that slowly fills up with water until you quit.

Sit with your head in a box that slowly fills up with sand until you quit.

Dangle upside down while you are dunked in water until you quit.

Smash your way through ten doors to the finish line with your bare hands.

The first challenge I faced and one of the toughest was the 'Door' challenge. Set in steel frames were ten individual doors. They were all in a row. All we had to do was to smash our way through them, one by one, and run over the finish line. Straight forward then! The only thing was that we had to smash our way through them with our fists and feet.

I did inwardly smile to myself that years previously in the timber yard I had worked in, one of my party pieces was to punch a hole in a door. It seemed ironic that I had to do this now. But I didn't just have to punch a hole in these doors; I had to make a hole big enough to get through. That was slightly different. We were all issued with MMA gloves. Rob gave me last-minute instructions. I focused and waited. My adrenaline was at fever pitch. At that moment, I felt so strong and fired up like I could walk straight through the doors!

Ian Freeman instructed that when the glass bottle he was holding smashed on the floor, you were in his words to "get knocking." The adrenaline was pumping big time and I yearned for a release.

The bottle smashed and we were off. I drove a fist into the first door and dented it. Another six punches broke it, but I knew that I couldn't keep up the punching as I felt sure that I would break bones in my hands. I changed to plan B and started kicking. I wore a pair of army boots. They were hard-wearing but not steel toe-capped as some had on. Maybe they had been privy to a little previous knowledge from a source about the challenge? I toe punted my way through and smashed through to the next and did the same. I could hear Rob shouting to keep going and not stop. I was vaguely aware of the others around me, but I just tried to keep kicking. I blasted through the fifth but by then; my left kicking leg had lost all muscular working action. It felt like it didn't belong to me. I just kept going. My lungs were bursting. As I came through door nine, in my mind I thought that it was the final door. When I got up off my knees and saw another one, I could have cried. I was aware now that a couple of people had finished. I steamed in and started kicking with every ounce of energy I had. The hole was made, but it wasn't any bigger than a cat flap. I just couldn't kick any more. I thought, fuck it. I dropped to my hands and knees and blasted head first through the hole. Wood, hardboard and splinters flew in all directions. I ripped open a nasty gash on my shin crawling through. But I was up and over the line. I made it and I wasn't the last!

Rob said to me sometime later that when he saw me drop to my knees to go through the hole, he had thought, what is he doing? He'll never get through there. The next instance I was fucking through. Amazing!

We were all led back to the cage and sat down to await our fate. I cannot explain the intensity of the challenge. The combination of adrenal release and fear of losing was immense. Add on top the physical exertion of going from zero to a hundred miles an hour in a blink of an eye. The heart and lungs had gone into overdrive. The test had been massively anaerobic, putting incredible stress on the body. Although it hadn't been long, we all had felt the strain and we were all fit lads.

I knew that I hadn't been last through the doors, so I was reasonably relaxed. The last two guys from each heat were sweating it big time. Ian Freeman entered the cage and delivered the verdict in no particular order. When your name was called out, you had to stand up and be told whether you were in or out. Ian was a cruel man, insulting and goading you all the time. This was his persona for the show.

He addressed me as 'old man' who, as it happens, I was, against these other boys. He told me, "Well done on getting through." I sat back down glad that I was still in. I forget now the name of the competitor that left. I believe that he was one of Dave O'Donnell's ('Cage Rage' fame) then instructors.

When you left, there was no fanfare, backslapping or well done. You were humiliated by some cutting comments from Mr. Freeman and led to a back door of the warehouse and shown out. That was it. Over and out!

I was really pleased that I got through this. I was the lightest guy in my heat. I know that in future heats, some big lads didn't even get through the first door, and one knocked himself out cold from desperately trying to headbutt his way through a door!

The next task was a tough one for me. A car was driven onto a flat lorry bed. You had to lie on the lorry bed with your legs strapped to the bed itself. You then had to reach back and above your head to grab a bar that was welded to the front grill of the car. You gripped the bar and held on for grim death. Slowly, the flat bed would rise and the car would roll away from you. Your job was to hold the car as long as possible. I knew that this would favour the big guys. I just hoped that I could hold on long enough to get through to the next heat. It was going to be a tough order, but I was ready to give it my all.

When my time came, I was strapped in and ready to go. Ian Freeman was to come up to the lorry and ask me a question. Something like, "So you think you're strong enough?" I was to answer and then lie down ready to go.

This ended up having two takes and two false starts (nothing to do with me, I might add), which doesn't help the adrenaline or your focus. But this is the world of TV and nothing is as it seems in the final edit. On the third attempt, we went for it. Rob was close by, encouraging me as I took the strain. At first, it felt all right. But as the flat bed dips and the car begins to run away, it is only your arms and essentially grip strength preventing it from going anywhere. I held on as long as I could. It felt like my body was going to rip in two pieces and my grip began to give. Eventually, I had to release.

I was reasonably pleased with my effort, even if my arms were now two inches longer! I was concerned that there were some bigger and stronger lads yet to have their turn. Every second would count. You begin to question could you have hung on just a little longer? There was a technique to this task, but I didn't know it. I just hung on for grim death and hoped that I had done enough. Nobody was told their time, so we were all in the dark.

Back in the cage, we awaited the result. This was more nerve wracking as it had very much been an individual task. There had been no-one to compete against but yourself and that sizable chunk of machinery. Ian Freeman came in to deliver the result. But the producer decided to break for lunch. We would have to wait to hear our fate.

Dinner was served in an old converted double-decker bus. We, the contestants, were not allowed to speak to our motivators. We had to stay separated in case the result was leaked. I spent a nervous hour not eating much, but I managed to sit down with Ian Freeman and listen to some interesting stories from his UFC experiences. Ian is a fearsome fighter in the cage but a gentleman outside. He is a credit to the UK MMA scene.

After lunch, we returned to the cage for the result. As I suspected, some of the bigger guys were through. It came down to another small guy and me. We waited as Ian glared from one of us to the other, building the tension and toying with us. He then pointed to the other lad.

"You are in, but only by the skin of your teeth. There was one second in it. You, old man," Ian regarded me, "gave it your best shot, but it wasn't enough." That was it. I was led from the cage to the back door. I was gutted. I honestly thought that I had done enough. One second's difference. What a bastard! But that was it. I couldn't do anything about it.

As I said, you were out. You couldn't go back in to see the rest of the filming. That was it. As there was no audience watching the making of the show, it was deadly silent when you left. It felt such an anti-climax.

I met Rob outside and told him the bad news. He was as gutted as me. There would be no second day's filming for us.

We had to go to another area and film a bit of a profile and me doing some training/martial arts for the show. I didn't really feel like doing this, but it was part of the deal. After this, we were thanked for our time and that was it. We were heading back to Bristol.

In hindsight, I realised that my technique was wrong for holding the car. As I later watched the shows, I saw where I had gone wrong. But as they say, hindsight is a wonderful thing. At the time, I had done what I thought was right. You just didn't have the time when doing the task to fully analyse it. But that was part of the plan for the show.

I was also disappointed that I didn't get the chance to do some of the other challenges. There were some interesting ones. Having your head in a glass tank and water gradually poured in until you were submerged looked a challenge, so too was the same kind of thing but with sand. Hanging tough off a bar would have been up my street and I would have loved to have got to the end to fight on the podium. Trying to stay in a cell as 'prison warders' attempted to drag you out would also have been fun. Being immersed in water upside down and having to hold your breath too.

Some tests were pure strength; others endurance; others mental strength. It really was the luck of the draw how they came out and what you got.

There were many well-known names from the world of UK martial arts in the show. Mark Weir, Matt Unwin, Sol Gilbert and Rob Lock amongst many more. There were also some weird and wonderful characters. The eventual winner was from my home city of Bristol. His name was Leighton Morgan and he boxed out of the famous 'Spaniorum Gym' under the wise old hand of Tex Woodward, who was his motivator throughout the show. He was a worthy winner, although he was pushed all the way by runner-up, James Swindles, a fireman who had won my heat.

Across the board, Leighton was, without doubt, the most well-rounded competitor and a true gent. I take my hat off to him for getting past some tough opposition and some gruelling events. Also, I give massive respect to Rob Locke. He was a man in his forties, just like me. He reached the finals. It was truly a brilliant achievement. 'Britain's Hardest' was certainly something different. Many of us competing didn't like the name of the show, but you can't do anything about that.

In retrospect, I was pleased that I had been picked through the auditions to reach the show and to get a chance to perform on a tough stage again.

But I have watched back the tape of my show many times and wonder what would have happened if I had just held on to that fucking car a few seconds longer! I know after all this time I should let it go... but that was the problem in the first place!

"Winning isn't everything but wanting to win is." – Vince Lombardi

Ultimate Combat 9 – Rebellion

After the disappointment of 'Britain's Hardest', I felt that I had trained so hard and had a lot more to give. I felt cheated in the fact that I didn't get to push myself any further and that my challenge had come to an abrupt halt. I was restless for weeks and kept up my training schedule relentlessly as if I predicted that something might be just around the corner.

My MMA classes were doing fine, and I had a good group of talented lads training under me at that time. The biggest in more ways than one was James 'the Colossus' Thompson. James has since gone on to bigger and better things and is one of the best known MMA fighters in the world today.

I liked James the minute that he came to me, and I would like to think that he saw me as a 'father figure'. I really wanted him to succeed. James was/is a fighter. He has immense courage and heart and will step up to fight anybody.

I think James would not mind me saying that he is not the most naturally adept person at picking up new techniques, but nobody can deny his tenaciousness and work rate to learn. James has put in many hours of serious work to become the fighter and person he is at present.

Even though he is no longer under my training guidance, I always watch his fights with a trainer's critical eye and a friend's love. I wish him every success for the future.

Back in 2004, James was just beginning to send a few shock waves through the UK heavyweight scene. He had just had a series of very fast and ferocious finishes in the cage and already good things were being said about him. James is a huge physical specimen. He has a great personality. Camera friendly and a gentleman outside the day job of cage fighting, he is a media and television person's dream.

James was up to fight on the MMA show 'Ultimate Combat'. At that time, 'Ultimate Combat' was up there with 'Cage Rage' as the best two MMA shows in the country. Dale Adams and his lovely wife, Laura, were the brains behind 'Ultimate Combat' and put on top-class and very professional shows.

The show had many of the UK's and the world's top MMA fighters on it; and also, gave a start to some promising fighters of the future.

As outlined earlier, I fought on their show 'World Warriors UC2' and this up-and-coming show 'Rebellion UC 9' was going to be held in Bristol. James and another solid MMA fighter with me at the time,

Wes Murch, (who now successfully runs 'Olympians Gym' in Bristol and is also a seasoned professional fighter) were both on the bill.

One day, as I was on the phone with Dale Adams discussing their fights, he said, "Of course, it would be great if you also wanted to fight!" Bang. The adrenaline immediately kicked in. Dale enlarged on the fact that it was my home town; a big crowd would be present, etc., etc.

I found myself being swayed towards entering the cage again after I had faithfully promised my wife, Tina, that I had retired from fighting after my last outing. I knew that I should call it a day. It wasn't the smartest move I ever made but maybe, just maybe, going out on that loss was niggling at me. I don't really know why. But, by the time I came off the phone, I knew that I was going to do it. Dale had said that he would ring me back with a possible opponent as soon as he could.

My major and immediate concern was how to break the news to Tina. I would have to pick my moment carefully. Here I was ready to do battle in a cage, but I was more worried about telling my wife!

Just to set the record straight, Tina has supported me wholeheartedly throughout all my martial arts and fighting career. I was worried because I felt that I was breaking a promise and letting her down. When I confided in my sons, Tom and Jake, they thought that it was a great idea, although at the time, they may have been a little too young to see all of the consequences. They just thought it was cool that Dad was fighting again!

They always said to me that they found it funny when children were asked at school what their dads did for a living. The standard replies were that they worked in an office, in a bank, IT worker, builder, etc. When it came to them, they had immense pleasure in saying that he is a martial arts instructor or a cage fighter.

A couple of days later, Dale rang again and said he had an opponent lined up for me. The guy was Sami 'the Hun' Berik. He was originally from Turkey and now resided in London. Sami had fought on the 'UC 6' bill and was a San Shou European Gold Medallist with a 10-5 record at that time. He had a very unorthodox style and was a slippery fighter. Sami has since gone on to have a good MMA career. Sami is known very much as a crowd pleaser and a guy that will step up for any fight. He has fought some of the top UK MMA fighters.

At this time, I thought it was a good opponent for me. I felt that I would have the edge in experience and strength, and I wanted to make that count. I took the fight.

After the call, I went and found Tina and gingerly mentioned that 'Ultimate Combat' was coming to Bristol soon. Before I could say it, she said, "You're going to fight on it, aren't you?" Well, there it was. Just like a young lad caught with his pants down in front of his girlfriend's parents. Yes, she had seen right through me. I told her, "Yes." and although she didn't like the idea of me stepping back into the cage at forty-three years of age, she accepted that it was something I had to do. So, I got her blessing.

Now I could begin my training in earnest. I spoke to Rob Cannon, my long-term sparring partner and fellow coach, and asked him to honestly tell me if I had taken a step too much or if I had it in me to win the fight. He told me, "If you want it bad enough, you'll win it." The question was, did I? Well, I was about to find out!

I asked him to coach me and get me ready. As a loyal friend, he stepped once more unselfishly up to the mark.

Speaking of unselfishness, it is hard to come by these days in the martial arts world. Everybody seems to be on the fast track to success, and loyalty and unselfish behaviour don't seem to come into it.

I applaud the modern-day martial arts revolution, but I feel that some of the traditional values of respect, integrity, loyalty and humbleness have fallen by the wayside. That is not a good thing. I have many people come to me wanting to learn, and they talk the talk but don't give much back. It is sad.

Although I am very much a modern-day martial artist, I still try to keep and preach the traditional values. Fighting is certainly a tough business, but it doesn't mean that we have to walk around dragging our knuckles and snarling at everybody. When I see, guys walking around the shopping mall on a Saturday afternoon clad in a 'Tap Out' or 'Rage' t-shirt, it makes me wonder. I even saw a guy walking along with a pair of Thai boxing shorts on. What the fuck is that all about? Is he convincing us all that he's a 'fighter' or is he convincing himself? I will talk more on this subject later. I digress a little.

Enough to say that a good fight team succeeds on comradeship, unselfishness and togetherness. As the saying goes, "Ask not what your team mate can do for you, but what you can do for your team mate."

I was once more fighting at welterweight which for 'UC' was less than seventy-five kilos. I was happy that I could easily make the weight. But, I wanted to come in bang on the limit at my strongest. I am one of these people that melt pounds off if I do a lot of cardiovascular exercise. I had to get the balance right.

I prepared with shorter, more intense bursts of cardio over twenty to thirty minutes rather than long plodding hour-plus routines. The short-term work seemed to keep my cardio up for fighting, but helped me maintain my muscle mass and burn body fat efficiently. At seventy-five kilos, I was very strong for my weight.

Many people over the years have made the mistake of thinking that because I am five feet seven inches and around twelve stone, I will be a pushover for them. What they need to remember is that I am twelve stone of lean muscle with very little body fat. Up against a person of pie-eating fifteen-stone proportions, there isn't much difference. I believe in training for functional muscle, not cosmetic.

Training in the gym like a bodybuilder is not the way to go if you are a fighter. I have massive respect for the professional bodybuilder, but it is a different world to mine. If you look at explosive athletes like sprinters, gymnastics, wrestlers and MMA fighters, they have what I call the perfect body physique. In my opinion, this is what you need to strive for.

I got my training spot on. Sparring went well. I was knocking over and tapping out good lads in my club. I felt fit and strong. The mental battles were the hardest to deal with. These were a constant war.

I remember back then that my Sunday morning class was very tough. It was conditioning and sparring-based. When it came to sparring, there were never any easy fights. All the guys there were seasoned fighters. There was no hiding place. It also certainly wasn't a place for egos. You got humbled very quickly if you strolled in thinking you were the dog's bollocks.

To fight professionally, I was training twice a day, six times a week. It took its toll on my forty-three-year-old body. Recovery time becomes harder as you get older. Post-training stiffness and soreness can be a bastard to shake off before your next session. I would get out of bed in the morning and walk to the bathroom like a ninety-year-old. I would question my sanity at this point on going back into the cage.

Now, I was carrying a painful injury of tendonitis in my left elbow. It got so painful after training sessions that I eventually went to have acupuncture on it in a last-ditch hope to ease the pain as I had tried every other possibility. I was worried that any elbow lock would force me to instantly tap out as I couldn't even touch it. The acupuncture seemed to help, but I wasn't sure if it had now become just mind over matter.

The mental side of things were also testing me. After a training session, I felt on top of the world, ready to take anybody on. When the endorphin-enhanced moment faded, the negatives would try to creep in. Over the years and with significant help from Geoff Thompson, I have understood fear and learnt how to handle it. When the negatives got into my head, I pushed them back out.

The negatives would be, "Are you too old?"; "What if you lose?"; "What if you get knocked out in the first ten seconds?"; "What if you turn in a crap performance?"; "What if you get really hurt?"; "There will be a massive home crowd watching you. Friends, family and fellow martial artists would all be watching. It is being filmed. What if you fail in front of them all?"; "What will they think?"; "What will your students think?"; "Will they want to train with you again?"

The list went on. There was a lot of pressure on me. I knew that there would be people present at the fight who would want to come up and shake my hand, willing me to win. But I also knew that there would be people there waiting for me to fall. So, they could knowingly nudge each other and say, "I knew he wasn't that good!" But my positive side said, "Nobody forced this fight on you. It was your choice. You choose it because you can win and you will win." I went to that fight knowing that I would win. There was no way that I would lose. I was prepared to give it my all and put everything on the line.

'Ultimate Combat 9 – Rebellion' was the 28th March 2004. I weighed in at 74.5 kilos. I was happy with this. As I posed in my fight gear for some official photos, I knew that I looked ripped. I felt good, and I knew that I belonged amongst all these other fighters.

As the day wore on, many people came up and shook my hand and wished me luck. I just wish that I could have looked beyond their eyes to see what they really thought.

Bob Willingham, a veteran judo player who was taking the official photographs for UC9, said that he thought I was too old for this and was worried I had taken a step too far. It didn't worry me. I appreciated his concern and no disrespect to him, but he didn't really know me and what I am. I didn't need that shit in my head. I zoned it out. I was ready.

I hate waiting to fight. It is the worst part of the day. You live with the adrenal build up on and off constantly and if you don't check it, it can tire you and make you negative. My answer is to pop my earphones in and get some music in my head and lie out or sleep. I never watch any of the previous fights leading up to mine. I just like to go out when the time has come. I like to stay totally focused on the job in hand. Mingling in the crowd before a fight is not for me.

At the medical, my blood pressure was sky-high and the medic told me to go away and chill for a while. He said that he couldn't let me fight with a BP that high. It is not uncommon for fighters to get a surge of high blood pressure at this stage, and it is not surprising really.

I went outside in the fresh air and sat on my own. For a moment, I thought that this was it. After all the challenging work, I was not going to be allowed to fight. I tried not to think about this and relaxed, but it was like a vicious circle. The more I tried to relax, the worse it got.

I sat outside for half an hour and composed myself eventually and walked back into the medical room. I had my blood pressure taken again and the medic allowed me to fight. I breathed a huge sigh of relief. I could have kissed the bastard. Now, I could fully focus on the job at hand.

On the bill that night, Wes Murch was fighting out of my club against a good solid fighter, Phil McCall from Len Bates' team. When his time came, I wished him luck. Rob and James Thompson went out to corner him. Wes won in an impressive 0.21 seconds with a stoppage. A great start for the Bristol team.

James was on in the last part of the show. He was competing in a European heavyweight super fight against Aaron Marsa from 'Shoot España', Spain. Marsa was, at the time, Spain's strongest man and was ranked tenth strongest man in the world. In my opinion, he was also ranked in the top ten of the world's bravest men. Although he was big, James at six feet four inches and twenty stone of pure muscle seemed to dwarf him.

The bell rang and James steamed in, knocking Marsa over like a child. James dived to crossbody and unleashed a blistering beverage of punches, forearms and elbows. It was all over in twenty-two seconds! Aaron Marsa was out of it. He, unfortunately, had to be administered oxygen before he finally got to his feet to huge applause and left the cage. It had been an awesome performance from James.

Backtracking to the second part of the show and I was fighting straight after the first interval. This fight was billed as a European welterweight title eliminator for the Ultimate Combat belt.

I warmed up well with Rob working the pads and grappling with me. I need to be warm to function at my best. Just like an old vintage car – great once it gets going but it takes a little longer to run smoother than a newer model.

When I was called to fight, I took the walk to the arena, sweating and focused. As I drew nearer, I could hear the crowd and my heart thumped. This was it. You cannot describe the feeling unless you have been there yourself. It's a mixture of nerves, excitement and expectation. It's a feeling of being alive. Part of you wants to walk the other way and seek out your mum while the other part of you wants to just get out there and release all the pent-up adrenaline that has reached its peak.

I waited until I heard my name being announced and my entrance music from Linkin Park start up. The music vibrated through my body. I was totally in the zone and ready to walk through walls. I was another person. I was Kevin O'Hagan, Fighter. At that moment, nothing else existed. It has got to be that way.

Rob tapped my shoulder and said, "Whenever you're ready." I breathed deeply and walked out into the flashing lights and deafening noise.

I walked to the cage to rapturous applause and cheers. I was fully focused. Sami was already in there when I entered. Rob, James Thompson and Matt Sperring were cornering me. I had a good solid corner team. We went through the introductions and then the cage closed. It is strange but when the cage gate is shut, it suddenly seems like the area has shrunk down. It is almost claustrophobic. Everything seems to fade to the background. The entire crowd, noise and voices. Everything became muted. Just as if you were submerged in water.

This is the time when you find out if you really are a fighter. It's okay on the lead-up to the fight getting kudos from your mates and family and being a local celebrity at work or on Facebook. But when the cage door shuts all that bollocks doesn't matter. Now you have got to fight. Many would-be fighters have already lost the fight at this stage before the bell even sounds.

I have had individuals say to me that they fancied a cage fight. I reply, "No, you fancy a good glass of red wine, you fancy sex, going to the cinema or eating fish and chips out of newspaper once in a while. You don't fucking fancy cage fighting." You have got to want it one hundred and ten percent. Nothing less; otherwise, in my opinion, you shouldn't be in there.

As I now looked across at my opponent, I knew that I was meant to be in here. A strange calmness descended on me. This is it!

The bell sounded and we moved out. Sami surprised me and came straight out with a jumping knee followed by a rapid-fire punch combination to my head and finished it with a round kick to the ribs. I covered up instinctively. We went to the clinch and we hit the floor.

I had envisaged working my stand-up game in this fight, but as anyone will know that has stepped into the cage, things don't always go as planned. It became an even battle on the floor. We both worked for positions and submissions. He was a very slippery opponent and hard to get hold of. I felt that I had the edge in strength, but it was just getting hold of him to exploit it.

I managed to bridge Sami from the mount position that he had on me at one stage and we went to all fours. I attacked his body with some hook punches and went for the guillotine. As I fell back for the guard finish, Sami flipped over me to escape. We scrambled again for position. The fight was going at a terrific pace.

Sometimes, it is really hard to think clearly about what you are doing. You can hear your corner team shouting advice, but you can't seem to implement their instructions. It is easy to fight from the comfort of your ringside seat or sofa at home. The real thing is a million miles away.

I, then, took Sami's back and tried for a stranglehold, but he defended well. He rolled me off his back and came into my guard and landed a big elbow to my head. With the adrenaline flowing to the maximum, I didn't feel the shot at the time. Also, the endorphins were masking any pain in my own elbow. The pace was still very fast and frantic. I was breathing heavily.

I managed once more to reverse Sami and gain the mount right in the corner of the cage where Rob and my team were. I unloaded some big punches to his face. This eventually forced him to turn to his belly. Once more, I went for the stranglehold and this time, sunk it in better. I squeezed with all I had. I knew that we had to be near the end of the round and I wanted to finish there and then. After all, a man of my advancing years should be in bed by ten p.m. and it was quarter to now! If I could finish this, it would be another great milestone in a martial arts career that has spanned many decades. Hey, let's put this in perspective. It was going to be a big fucking achievement. I lock in the choke and begin to squeeze... The clock is ticking... I must make him tap out... Time seems to stand still... The roar of the crowd becomes muffled as if I am fighting underwater... Keep squeezing.

My opponent is still struggling; attempting to get me off his back... I must hang on and keep squeezing. My arms burn with lactic acid build up, but I have to ignore it... Squeeze!

Since a fourteen-year-old boy, I have trained in the combat arts and fought my many fears. I have faced many challenges and put my body through the extremes in my quest to learn the 'Way of the Warrior'. This is the ultimate test for me at this stage of a lengthy career.

It's been a hell of a journey to me being in the cage this night. I want to win this fight with every fibre of my being. I know I may never get the chance again. I also know I might never want the chance again. This is the time. It's now or never as the Elvis Presley song goes.

Now all I need to do is squeeze tighter and beat that damn clock. Squeeze...

I saw Sami's hand tap the canvas and that was it! I had won. I was ecstatic. I jumped up and took the full applause of the crowd. Only then did I recognise the familiar faces sitting out there. Up to that point, they had all been a blur.

Rob ran in the cage and lifted me up. Then, James came and hoisted me so high that I thought I'd have a nose bleed. Receiving a winner's trophy and a nice kiss from the cage girl was a bonus!

I raised Sami's hand high. He had given me a good fight, and he had been a lot better than I had anticipated. He is a super fighter but also a humble lad, and I wish him every success for the future.

So, on the night, it had been a hat-trick of wins for Bristol. I couldn't have dreamt of a better way to finish.

When I got back to the warm-up area, I guess that everything caught up with me, and I sank to my knees. I felt completely drained. All the build-up and pressure had now been released and I felt a heavy burden lift from my shoulders. The toil of a full-on professional cage fight on a forty-three-year-old body had been very hard. I was no fool. It was now the right decision to call time on it.

I knew then that I had done what I had set out to do and that it was my last cage fight. I had nothing left to prove. I had won. Every dog has its day and this was mine. I had managed to get out with my handsome good looks intact (do I hear a chuckle?), and had satisfied myself in answering the question of 'could I fight in the cage at a top level?'

When the UFC and 'no holds barred' fighting, as it was coined back then in the mid-90s, had burst on the scene, I had avidly watched it and wondered if maybe I still had enough to give it a go. At thirty-seven years old, I embarked on that journey. Firstly, I had competed in the Ju Jutsu Kumite and knockdown sports budo. Next came Brazilian Ju Jutsu and submission wrestling competitions. Then, amateur MMA, Semi Pro MMA and finally, Pro MMA.

In six years, I transformed myself from a martial artist/street fighter into a combat athlete. I was proud of that transition. It had taken a massive amount of practice time. It was not easy. I was, by no means, the best or the finished article, but I had given it my all. The early days of MMA were very much still style against style. MMA was in its infancy. We guys went into the arena armed with whatever martial arts knowledge we had. Some were prepared; others not. Some styles held up well; others crashed and burned. I didn't really have a competitive background. I wasn't used to fighting under set rules and guidelines. It was a hard transition and a big learning curve. Also, it was a humbling experience as some techniques you relied on in other quarters fell short in the MMA arena. It takes guts to go back time and time again and lay yourself bare so to speak, but I am glad I did. Now, MMA classes have sprung up everywhere. You can join and learn the sport right away. Back then, this wasn't the case. It was all new to many of us. It has come a long way since those early days. For the period of years that I fought, I lived and breathed the world of a mixed martial arts fighter.

I had already built a reputation as a good ju jutsu man and self-protection instructor. I had written books, made DVDs and written many magazine articles. I was being mentioned in the same breath as many of the UK's top reality training instructors. When I made the decision to fight in MMA, I had it all to lose and all to gain. Lose and I knew there were people out there ready to say, "I knew he wasn't as good as he thought"; succeed and I could cement my name as somebody who had won and achieved in the new world of MMA.

Looking back to the early days, myself and my guys, along with MMA fighters like Paul Jenkins, Alex Owen, Ian Rossiter, Mark Woodard, Paul Sutherland and their like helped pioneer and establish MMA around the Bristol, South West and Wales area. It was good to be part of those early rough and tough competitions. I worked hard to make the transition and find out what worked and what didn't in this arena.

Along the way, I have met some super people. MMA may have the image of blood and guts, but the big percentage of people I have met, be it fighters, trainers or promoters, have all been good guys and were passionate about their sport.

Dale Adams did much to push MMA to the forefront in Bristol and the South West. Many more were to follow. Of course, Dave O'Donnell had also done absolute wonders in making 'Cage Rage' a massive show in the UK, as did Andy Jardine with the 'Millennium Brawl'. 'Cage Rage' went on to be televised. That was a first as well.

In recent years, my son, Jake has pioneered 'Tear Up' promotions in my home city of Bristol. It was a great showcase for my fighters and we had some amazing nights at those events.

My only criticism is that MMA needs a proper governing body to control it. There are too many would-be fighters pulling out of fights and letting promoters down with bullshit excuses and being totally unprofessional.

Also, some of the match-ups are very dodgy and one-sided. When I fought and the guys fighting with me at that time, all wanted to fight and were passionate about developing MMA. Now many just want a bit of 'back slapping', post pictures of themselves on the social media but don't really have the heart or passion for the sport. Make no mistake: it is a fucking tough sport and only the dedicated few will make it to the top.

I am still amazed that people now still say to me, "Are you still fighting?" I am fifty-four years of age! The average man in his mid-fifties is probably happy with a bit of gardening, most certainly not cage fighting. I let them know that I chose to stop fighting. That is the difference. Now, I haven't got the desire or fire in my belly that I had ten or fifteen years ago. Your testosterone level also begins to drop and with that goes your drive to want to fight daily. I have other things in my life that now take priority. I have been there and done it, and I am completely satisfied.

For the record, I did it to test myself, but I was never going to be a top fighter. I just didn't have the time or desire to sacrifice what it took plus age wasn't on my side. But I am glad I reached a level where I got in there and answered some questions about myself. I put my ass and reputation on the line and didn't hide. Win or lose, I took it on the chin without excuse.

I no longer feel the need to prove myself in that arena. If a young guy wants to make a name for himself on the back of trying to fight me, these days I say, "Send your dad down. What does he do for a living?"

Fighting doesn't personally interest me anymore. I would only fight if my life depended on it and only then would I release the 'inner monster'. These days, it's firmly leashed up.

I don't think you can ever lose that fighting instinct if it has been part of your life, but I don't feel the need to go dragging that shit around with me all the time. Yes, I will talk martial arts but I am not a martial arts bore.

Guys who are into MMA will always ask, "Did you see the latest UFC?" I will be honest, I don't watch them anymore. There are not too many thrilling fights of late, and it has become more like a boxing or kickboxing match. No longer do you see the great mix of all ranges of skills that you did years back. If I wanted to see a kickboxing match, I would watch K-1, the best in the world.

I have watched boxing from the late seventies and every other form of fighting, including UFC, Pride, King of the Cafe, World Vale Tudo Championships, Cage Rage... The list goes on. I have seen thousands of fights. It doesn't do it for me like it used to. I loved the era of fighters such as Royce Gracie, Coleman, Kerr, Silva, Kimo, Severn, Abbot, Cro Cop, etc. In my opinion, they will not be replaced.

I primarily watched these shows to develop my skills and be educated in no-holds-barred fighting. Also, I wanted to see if I could compete in that arena. Now that I have, I am not as bothered. When I coached my own fight team, I would tell them, "Watch UFC and its like, but don't watch it in awe of the fighters. Look at it and ask, can I beat that guy? Could I aspire to be in there one day?"

Set your sights high. If you want to forge a career as a cage fighter, you want to make money out of it. You won't get that from the little shows. There will also come a time where getting a broken nose, having your legs kicked black and blue and getting your joints cranked won't be so appealing for the pure accolade of it or for a few hundred quid.

I have seen some appalling match-ups in the cage, where both fighters should never have been in there in the first place. But some disillusioned view of themselves got them in there and some inept coach probably encouraged and helped them.

It takes a lot to be a champion. It takes incredible self-discipline and self-sacrifice. Most don't have it. As a coach, it is hard to find an individual who really wants to go the whole nine yards. I have guys train with me hell for leather for a few months and then fall by the wayside. They realise that they are not going to acquire the skills overnight so they quit. It can be a tough and thankless job sometimes being a coach or instructor. You can invest a lot of time and energy into an individual only to find out that the pull of the beer and 'birds' is too much temptation for them. They are always going to be their toughest opponents.

Personally, I feel that MMA has probably had its heyday. It will stay around no doubt, but I don't think that there is the hunger or ambition in people these days to want to risk it all in the cage. I may be wrong. We will have to wait and see.

"But when the blast of war blows in our ears, then imitate the action of the tiger. Stiffen the sinews. Summon up the blood." –
Shakespeare King Henry V

Enter the Colossus

After UC 9, I decided that I would like to spend more time training my fighters. When you are still actively fighting, you can't give your full time and attention to others. I knew that if I wanted others to succeed, I would have to take more of a back seat when it came to participation and become more of a coach.

I have had many promising fighters over the years. Some that have gone on to good success. Others have fallen by the wayside for assorted reasons. It is a hard job to keep a good team of fighters and sometimes, it is a thankless task.

I have had guys training for two, three or four years and then, they just give it up. It takes so long to get people to a good standard to fight, and then when you think you have cracked it, they leave. Some give up completely; others move to other clubs, hoping the 'grass will be greener'. But at the end of the day, it doesn't matter if you are training with a MMA world champion. It doesn't mean that you will become one. If you haven't the aptitude or the dedication; it won't count for a thing.

In my opinion, there is no substitute for a structured week-in-week-out training schedule. You must drill the basics until they are ingrained in your soul. When you are knocking out or tapping out everybody in your club, then you might think about a professional career.

Too many people want to run before they can walk. If a club opens down the road and the guy teaching is called Carlos and he is from Brazil, everybody is clambering there because they believe that he is the best of the best. It was the same in the 60s when the Japanese instructors flooded our shores. If you weren't practising karate under one of them, you were not practising karate. In the 70s, every Chinese takeaway was purposely owned by a kung fu master and many were happy to cash in on that myth.

It's like in football. Without a doubt, there are some world-class foreign footballers in the Premiership and there are also many 'duffers' as well. My advice is: be careful who you train with and, don't neglect 'Joe Bloggs Martial Arts School' that has been on your doorstep for twenty years. He might just know what he is doing if he has survived this long. Too many people are in martial arts to make a quick buck and then disappear after a few months. Even if they are shit hot, they haven't got the discipline to coach year in, year out. Look for an established club that has been about for some time. You probably won't go far wrong.

One man who did show great dedication to his MMA training was James 'the Colossus' Thompson. James was with me for a few years and boy, didn't we have a few adventures together! I feel sorry for the fact that everybody wants to have a gripe about James. It was not his fault that at a certain time there were no heavyweight fighters big enough to give him a fight. James will fight whoever you put in front of him, regardless of who they are. He has never declined anybody.

James rose quickly through the heavyweight ranks, not just because he could have a fight, but because of his 'Mr. Universe' physique and his personality. He is a promoter's dream.

Yes, there were other guys out there that thought they were due more recognition, but maybe they didn't have the personality and the whole media package to go with the fighting skills.

It is not always the best that succeeds in their field. It is the person with the tenacity and the drive to get out there and be seen. James had that in spades.

I hope James won't mind my saying that technically at the time when he started with me, he wasn't the best. But, he was a novice who got put on the fast track and grasped the opportunity with both hands.

If any other fighters were offered a British title shot or a chance to go to Japan to fight in the then-biggest MMA tournament in the world, 'Pride', who would have said, "No, thanks; I don't think I'll bother!" Would they hell. There was a lot of jealousy and sour grapes out there.

Those opportunities don't come along too often in life, so you take them. I was pleased and privileged to have been part of that.

In Ultimate Combat X, James was handed his first defeat and it was a bad one. His opponent was changed at short notice to Tengiz Tedoradze – a top-class wrestler turned MMA fighter.

It was a big step for James, but he felt that he needed to do this to prove he was the genuine article.

The fight ended up very one-sided. Tengiz's wrestling skills were too much for James, and I was criticised in some corners for letting James take too much punishment. Looking back, maybe that was true, but I know how much this fight meant to James, and he pleaded with me between rounds not to stop it. At the end of two five-minute rounds, James was bleeding badly from an array of facial cuts. He was coherent and wanted to fight on, believing in the overtime round that he could win and KO Tengiz. The ref let it be known that if Tengiz took James down again and got control, he would stop it. I knew that in my heart, James wasn't going to get that KO and I told him, no more. I said, "Come back and fight another day." It broke his heart. He still wanted to fight. It was a massively hard decision to make because I knew what it meant to him, but in the end, I had to do it.

I don't feel that I got it a hundred percent right on the night, but it was a very difficult call. We all learn. I was now making that transition from fighter to coach. It can be a rocky journey sometimes.

That fight had been in June 2004. Come September, James was offered a shot for the vacant Ultimate Combat World Heavyweight title.

Again, there was outrage in some circles about how, after that defeat, he could get a title shot. The upshot behind this was that James was going to be part of a four-man eliminator for the title. But two of the four didn't or couldn't, at that time, fight, including Tengiz. The two fighters left were James and UFC legend Dan 'The Beast' Severn.

Both were asked if they wanted to fight for the title and both agreed. That's how the fight was made. Again, James seized his chance. Who can blame him for it? But, there was still controversy to come later.

James fought for the Ultimate Combat Heavyweight championship belt in September on UC 11 'Wrath of the Beast' show. Those of you in the MMA world will instantly know James' opponent. The man is a living legend in the world of cage fighting. He was one of the early Ultimate Fighting Championship champions. He fought the best of the best of that era. Gracie, Shamrock, Abbott, Coleman, Kimo, Rizzo and many more were his onetime opponents.

At the time of his fight, Dan was well into his fifties and still fighting and winning. He had an astonishing one hundred and eight cage fights. Going into the fight with James, he was on a winning streak of five straight victories. James had been travelling to and from Holland and Thailand to get some more experience and train with a few big guys. He had also been doing some work at the 'Trojan Fight Gym' under Charlie Joseph, a highly-respected Thai boxing coach. His boy, Ronnie Mann, is an extremely talented MMA fighter at present.

I didn't have anybody in my club anywhere near James' size, so although we could work pads, fitness and speed, he needed to be grappling around heavyweights. When James came back for his final preparations for this fight, I worked hard on his cardio conditioning, and I believe that he went into the Severn fight as fit as he has ever been. We also worked strategy. We knew that although Severn was advancing in years, he was still an extremely good world-class wrestler and a highly-experienced MMA fighter. I didn't want James ending up as he had in the Tengiz fight. So, we worked his stand-up game and his sprawl. We did this religiously, and I never let him deviate from that plan.

The fight went the way we wanted it to. Yes, it wasn't a great spectacle for the crowd, but we were there to win at any cost. Severn was thrown off his game when James never came out with his trademark rush on the sound of the first bell. James picked away with his shots and stayed, for most of the fight, away from the clinch. On a few occasions, Severn shot in for the takedown, but James sprawled perfectly to avoid going under and punished Severn with some good punches.

This was a war of attrition over five five-minute championship rounds. It was a lot to ask of two big men. In the final round, Severn was getting tired and James pushed the pace. Managing to get Severn down in the corner of the cage, James unleashed some bombs, but Dan was a wily opponent and survived until the final bell. I knew that James had done enough to win and indeed, he got a unanimous decision. James was presented with the UC Heavyweight title belt. It was a proud moment for me and a great moment for James. After the fight, we met up with Dan Severn and talked and took some photographs. He was humble in defeat. It was great to share a moment with the legend.

Many internet computer warriors insinuated that the fight was a fix. What this verdict was based on, I don't know. Just because James hadn't steamed out like he had in previous fights and because it was a somewhat subdued approach, people thought that it was rigged. James' strategy definitely put off Severn, and I don't think that he had a game plan beyond taking James down. When this didn't materialise, he ran out of ideas. James won it fair and square. I saw or heard nothing to the contrary.

Anyway, I can't see why Severn would go to all the trouble of travelling across the Atlantic to throw a fight. If that was his plan, he could have done that in any of the one hundred and eight fights and probably a hell of a lot closer to home. Everybody is entitled to their opinions, even the 'keyboard warriors' who will never step into the arena in their lives.

Based on this win, there were a few rumours flying around that 'Pride Fighting Championships', then the biggest MMA show in the world, had seen James' fights and were interested in bringing him to Japan. There are always rumours being passed around in the fight game, and I didn't pay too much attention to the fact until a few weeks later, I received a phone call from Dale Adams, promoter and owner of 'Ultimate Combat'!

What follows below is an article that I wrote for my website and 'MMA Universe' magazine of the fight report from that night, as well as some of James' background.

'The Colossus' Tames 'The Beast'
By Kevin O' Hagan, Sept 2005

Within the world of MMA is a young man by the name of James 'the Colossus' Thompson. He has taken the Heavyweight division by storm over the last twelve months, and has just consolidated himself as the 'real deal' by defeating none other than legendary cage fighting champion Dan 'the Beast' Severn. No small feat, and this superb win has put him well and truly in the big time, where an offer has been made for James to fight in the biggest MMA event in the world, 'Pride', in Japan. This looks like it will happen sooner rather than later, and this will mean that he will be the first British fighter to enter 'Pride' in Mixed Martial Arts. Certainly, an achievement in itself for a young man still learning his trade. But let's rewind a minute and see where it all started.

"I want to be world champion!"

James hails from Rochdale and moved down to Bristol in the West Country a few years ago. He had a wrestling background, but was also used to real hands on action working in frontline Door Security and as a bailiff. He had a fair reputation for being a ferocious street fighter.

He came to my classes to channel his fighting spirit into Mixed Martial Arts. He wanted to fight in the cage and when we discussed this, he told me that he wanted to someday be world champion. I think that, at that moment in time, we both didn't realize how quickly this would happen.

When I first saw James, I thought, "How the hell can anybody be this big?" My second thought was, "What am I going to do with him?" But I needn't have worried; James took to the training fine and showed good discipline and respect.

He first fought in 'Ground and Pound 1' and was like a man possessed. His brave but hapless opponent didn't know what hit him. He then fought on the 'Ultimate Combat' events, and signed up as a 'Team Ultimate' member. He has had five bouts and became UC Super Fight Champion. All but one opponent he has KO'd or TKO'd, his quickest win being fifteen seconds. He has also fought abroad on cage fighting bills and has won his bouts in style.

In the cage, he is like the terminator; outside, he is a quietly spoken and charismatic gentleman. It is frightening to see that Jekyll and Hyde transformation. Because of his immense size (twenty stone of pure functional muscle) and his charisma, James has suddenly found himself on the fast track to success. He has a massive fanbase in the South West, and his reputation is growing, not only in the UK, but worldwide.

What a lot of people don't realize is that he is still learning his trade. He is working hard constantly to add technical skills to his raw ground and pound. He is not just a brawler as the Severn fight showed. But he has more to learn.

His cardio/conditioning has improved immensely due to tortuous workouts and a good diet. These days, he is training like a champion, showing great discipline. For a big man, he is extremely fit and fast.

He has travelled to Thailand and Holland to work on his kickboxing skills, and has trained, amongst others, with the great Pele Reid.

At my classes, he does everything he is asked and more. Training with James is like confronting a grizzly bear and it takes its toll on my forty-three-year-old, twelve-stone frame. Some mornings, after a session, I feel like I have been run over by a truck!

James is on a learning curve and has certainly learnt from his previous fight when he lost to top UK Heavyweight Tengiz, who is a world-class wrestler. The fight was taken at short notice, but as usual, James will fight anyone, anywhere, anytime. He fears no one.

We all learnt from the loss and have taken many new things on board. But in terms of experience, Tengiz was years ahead of James. James could have pulled out of the fight, but decided to take it for experience. You can always learn and always improve. The key is to come back again and answer your critics. He has done this by capturing the vacant Ultimate Combat belt. Whilst nobody else stepped up to challenge Dan Severn, James accepted, and why not? What an opportunity to redeem himself and show what he really could do.

The Fight

The venue is Whitchurch Sports Centre in my hometown of Bristol.

210

The date is September 12th. The show is 'Ultimate Combat II'. The fight is the main headliner. It is scheduled for 5 X 5 minute rounds for the vacant Heavyweight belt.

Dan 'the Beast' Severn has travelled over from the US, hungry to add this title to the amazing triumphs he has already achieved. Ultimate Fight Champion on three separate occasions, 'Ultimate Ultimate' champion, veteran of 'Pride', 'KOTC' and many other cage events. He also, now, boasted a record of sixty-plus fights in MMA. He is a living, breathing legend, even if he is now in the twilight of his career. He is still dangerous, highly experienced and a world-class wrestler.

This is a massive challenge for James, and many are not giving him a chance of winning. In the final weeks of training, I saw that James was capable of winning this title. We had a game plan that he had to stay disciplined to. No more charging out and looking for the big KO. Tonight, he was going to show a different side to his fighting and silence the critics that said he could only fight one way.

I felt that James came of age in this fight. He came out on the first bell and methodically worked his game plan. Short punches, short leg kicks, avoid the takedown, sprawl, get up and make Severn get back to his feet. In most parts he did this brilliantly, avoiding the takedown on more than one occasion and making Severn pay.

It was not a comfortable ride though. Both men punished each other with punches and both were rocked.

Coming into the last round, although both were tired, the older man looked more fatigued. He just couldn't keep James off him. As the bell rang, James went for the kill, landing good punches that rocked Severn, and he was thrown to the ground, then pounded. In the closing minutes, James gained the mount and chopped away with punches, foiling a Severn bridge out and ending the fight on top pounding away.

As the bell rang, I ran into the cage to congratulate the big man. I knew that in my heart he had done enough to win, and he had! A unanimous decision.

So, the mantle was handed over from the veteran legend to the Young Gun. It was a poignant moment to watch.

On a personal level, I had watched Dan Severn fighting in the earlier UFCs against Gracie, Shamrock, Coleman, Kimo and others. I was in awe of this guy and now some nine years down the line, a man I have helped train had beaten him. A surreal experience. The beast had been tamed.

Dan Severn was humble in defeat and showed why he is a true ambassador for this sport.

James was ecstatic. It was like a dream come true, but he never doubted that he would win. He was very relaxed coming into the fight, and it showed in his mature and controlled performance. Yes, I expect the critics and keyboard warriors will have something to pick fault in, but hey, who cares! Let the man enjoy his big moment. I feel that it won't be his last. Beware, Japan! The Colossus is on his way. When was the last time that they had an earthquake there?

"Champions are made in the gym. Champions are made from something they have deep inside them – a desire, a dream, and a vision." – Mohammed Ali

Japan Travelogue (The Road to 'Pride')

The home phone rings and I pick it up. On the other end of the line is Dale Adams. He informs me that 'Pride Fighting Championships' (then, the biggest MMA show in the world) had contacted him, and they wanted James to fight in their October fight card 'Pride – High Octane'. It was scheduled for Halloween. This was literally weeks away at the time. James wants me to corner him, and Dale is going to look after all other arrangements over there.

I had to do a double take on this. I thought that at first, it was a wind-up, but then I realised that Dale was deadly serious. It was going to happen!

'Pride' was talking about Dan 'the Bull' Bobish as an opponent. Bobish had been a 'King of the Cage' champion and was a good wrestler who could punch a bit, but had suspect fitness problems. I thought that he was an ideal opponent for James. I envisaged the same game plan as we had for Dan Severn. I felt confident James could win.

That night, I saw James at training, and he confirmed that it was all on, and we would be going to Tokyo, Japan, in a few weeks' time. Once we had got our heads around it, we started training. Really, James hadn't stopped training since the Severn fight, so we just carried on with the same routine.

Then, a few weeks before we travelled to Japan, 'Pride' decided to change the opponent. Maybe they thought Bobish was too experienced? I don't know. But, instead, James would now face Alexander Emelianenko, brother of feared 'Pride' heavyweight champion, the Russian, Fedor Emelianenko. I hadn't heard too much about Alexander, but being the brother of Fedor, I guessed that he was going to be a tougher test than Bobish.

On the back of some research, I found out that Alexander was on his way up the MMA ladder the same as James was. He had a few good wins under his belt and had the advantage of fighting on a 'Pride' show before. I must admit that I did have more reservations about this fight than if it had been Bobish, but again, you weren't going to turn 'Pride' down. When you get this chance, you grab it with both hands and feet and anything else you can manage. This is the time leading up to the fight that James coined the nickname 'Colossus'.

The guys going to Japan with him became 'Team Colossus'. The Japanese love larger-than-life characters and James fitted the bill in every way.

The 'Colossus' was born in Japan and the fans would love him. 'Pride' is all about image and fighters showing heart and spirit. The whole concept of 'Pride' was based on this. Yes, winning was important, of course it was, but putting up a good show and winning over 'Pride' and its audience was just as important if you wanted to come back again. They didn't like overcautious fighters. They wanted thrills and spills. Their top boys like Fedor, Wanderlei Silva and Mirko Cro Cop certainly provided this. They wanted some of the same from the first British MMA fighter to ever be in 'Pride'.

This is why, after much discussion, we decided that the 'old' James Thompson would have to reappear and take the fight straight to his opponent when the time arrived. Rightly or wrongly, it had to be done as James was fighting for the bigger picture and not just the one-off fight. He wanted a lucrative fight contract. He wanted to win over the powers-to-be in 'Pride' and secure a long-term contract. Again, this was something that the 'armchair critics' didn't realise when they started tapping on their keyboards about James not deserving to go to 'Pride', and why did he get the chance when 'more able' fighters didn't. Much later would also come the after-fight analysis and the debates about what tactics he should or shouldn't have used.

You have to remember that not everything in the world is black and white, and there is usually more to it than meets the eye. It's not until you step into this world that you begin to realise it and what really goes on behind the scenes. What most people ever get to see is what the television will want to show.

What follows is my travelogue account of my time in Japan and all that happened. I wrote it as it happened day by day. I felt that it gave a real feel to this great occasion as I experienced it first-hand.

For me, personally, to have coached the first-ever UK MMA fighter in 'Pride' and cornered him was beyond any of my wildest dreams. Yes, it may have been a bit early in James' career to fight in 'Pride' but who the hell would turn down the chance if it came along? All fighters dream of such an opportunity. Even now, as I am writing this, it all seems surreal. I am very proud and privileged to have been part of 'Team Colossus'. Also, to visit Japan was another of my lifetime ambitions fulfilled. As a young man, training directly under Japanese instruction, I always dreamt of going to the 'Mecca' of martial arts. It didn't disappoint. It was a fantastic place and the people were wonderful.

I have some great memories to cherish from the experience. To be part of the then-biggest MMA event in the world and to feel it, taste it and smell it first-hand is something you will never forget. When I first started MMA training back in 1996 and used to watch 'Pride', I would never have thought that I would be walking into that famous ring with a fighter of mine.

Below is the original travelogue as I wrote it day by day during my visit to Japan.

Japan Travelogue – The Road to Pride

Tuesday 26th October
I meet up with James at the flight desk at Birmingham International at nine a.m. Dale Adams and Laura Richards of MJ Sports/Ultimate Combat arrive soon after. We catch a short flight to Munich, Germany, before getting on board the long flight to Japan. On the flight, James sat next to me which made it a pretty squashed journey up against the window. To make matters worse, he fell asleep with his head forward and down on the pull-down food tray, making it impossible to get past to use the toilets. Yes, I could have woken him, but you just don't wake the 'Colossus' when he is sleeping. It would have been like rousing a hibernating grizzly bear. Not recommended. Anyway, a ten-gun salute wouldn't have woken him, so I had no chance!

Tuesday 26th/Wednesday 27th October
The flight to Tokyo is ten and a half hours. I settle in for the long haul. This time, I have a better seat on the end of the row, thank God. The Lufthansa flight crew are very good, as were the meals. Between eating, chatting, watching a film and reading, the time ticks away. We arrive in Tokyo at nine forty-five a.m. their time, Wednesday. They are nine hours ahead of us in Great Britain. We go through immigration smoothly. I think that the fight t-shirts helped as everybody was asking what we were there for. When we mentioned 'Pride', they nodded knowingly. Everybody in the airport was staring at James because he just stood head and shoulders above all around him. It was comical. Everybody knew what 'Pride' was all about. As mentioned before, they are fanatical for these types of events in Japan.

A 'Pride' rep met us and we got on a bus to take us to our hotel in the heart of Tokyo. The journey took ninety minutes. We are all tired when we reach the hotel. The hotel is fantastic. First-class, and we are treated well. Once the rooms were sorted out, we all retired to them to relax for a while. This is around two p.m. I managed to keep myself awake so that my body clock would function on proper time. If you fell asleep now at two o'clock in the afternoon, you would not sleep at night. Jetlag is a strange experience.

Later, I went out for a meal with Dale and Laura. We let James sleep. Well, we had no choice after banging on his door for ten minutes! After, we walked around the streets of Tokyo and took in the amazing sights. At eight thirty p.m., we returned to the hotel, and in the lobby, I just happened to run into Bas Rutten, slightly merry after a few drinks. At first, he mistakes me for somebody else and puts me in a headlock. Then, he is mortified to realise that I am not the person he thought. He man hugs me and apologises. Then, he asks me where I am from and starts into one of his long, comical rants. This guy is one of my MMA heroes. To be speaking to him face-to-face was a surreal experience. But then, this was the start of many more crazy moments. Dale and I have a photo with Bas. I then turn around, and there is Erik Paulson. We shake hands and talk. I rate Erik as one of the best and most knowledgeable submission fighters in the world today. I had followed his stuff for a long time, and to get an opportunity to talk with him was awesome. Just as I was thinking about going up to my room, into the lobby now walks Dan Henderson and **the** Josh Barnett. For those of you into MMA, you will know that these guys were two of the biggest stars of this arena.

Also, Quentin 'Rampage' Jackson is meant to be around, but I haven't seen him yet. He is topping this 'Pride' bill by challenging Wanderlei Silva for his middleweight belt.

Next, as I am waiting for the lift to come to go up to my room, the doors opened, and who should be standing inside? The 'Axe Man' himself, Wanderlei Silva. This man is a legend and another person I greatly admire. Yes, he does look as fearsome in the flesh as he does on the DVDs. For a moment, there was a brief silence as our eyes meet, and then we shake hands and he introduces himself. I get into the lift as he exits. On the way up to my room. I must laugh out loud that is this really happening! What a first day!

Earlier, the team booked in a training slot at the dojo for James at ten thirty a.m. tomorrow. The dojo is in downtown Tokyo, and it's the official training place for all 'Pride' fighters in the lead-up to the show. We have a schedule for the week, and we know what we are doing and what's required. Laura is our main organiser and has us all on the ball constantly. We need to put up a skilled professional show outside the ring as well as in it.

Thursday 28th October

James knocks on my door at eight a.m. With him, he has a DVD recorder and a DVD of his fight opponent, Alexander Emelianenko. We view him in action. He is a good fighter, and we know we will have to work hard. As ever, James is confident. We sit down and watch him fight a few times more and analyse it. At nine a.m., we all meet for breakfast. James consumed enough food to last me the week. We then are shown directions to the dojo and we get our kit. James, Dale and I walk there. It is booked for two hours. I put James through his paces for the two-hour session. Pad work and some light wrestling and submission. Plus, we work on a few things that we saw from watching his opponent on the DVD earlier. James is looking good. Wanderlei Silva is training next door and through the walls, you can hear the loud sounds of impact on Thai pads as he blasts them.

As we return to the hotel, I am given another video of Alexander, which we again study. He looks strong and durable. He has fought in 'Pride' four times. It will be a big test for James.

Later, I have a walk on my own around Tokyo. It is vast but very safe. People are so polite and friendly. It is alive with the bustle of colour and noise everywhere. It really does take your breath away.

I return later to the hotel to go with James for a set of interviews and photos. He does fine and looks in good shape. The Japanese cannot get over his size.

I later, again, meet Bas Rutten who sits down and talks to me like an old friend, and I get another photo with him.

He has so many 'war stories' to tell. One of the funniest I recall was from his days working as a bouncer. He told me how he used to choke out unruly punters and then as extra punishment pull down their trousers and insert a Tabasco sauce bottle into their rectum. This must have been a hell of a surprise to the person upon wakening, especially if the top had been taken off!

Later, 'Team Colossus' all go out for dinner, and then we return to the hotel. James and I have a swim in the pool which is located on the top floor of the hotel, looking out over the city. We look 'fetching' in the bathing caps that you must wear. We retire to our rooms at nine p.m. to chill out. It's been another good day.

Friday 29th October

James has some interviews and photo shoots. He must do an interview with Bas Rutten and Stephen Quadros. Both men would be commentating ringside and introducing the show later. They are a great double act, and there was a lot of clowning around. There was a particularly funny moment when they asked James to remove a chunky and expensive-looking watch that he was wearing for a camera shoot. Bas said that he would hang onto it for a moment, and when James handed it to him, he promptly ran out the door and down the corridor, shouting out that he was going to sell it!

James does fine at the interview. He looks relaxed in front of the cameras and comes over well. Even Bas cannot get over the size of him, and he loves the fact that James mentioned that he was a bailiff. Bas said that if he was coming for him for an unpaid debt, he would have to get a baseball bat ready, or better still, an Uzi!

Then, we head off for more interviews with Japanese television. Next up, was a photo shoot. Then, poster signing and another great moment when James had to record a mobile phone jingle in Japanese. I was laughing so hard that I nearly pissed myself. This is really top-class entertainment for the Japanese and huge business. You see how far advanced it is in comparison to the UK shows we were used to.

I am fascinated and so pleased to get an exclusive behind the doors to look at what it takes to put on a show like Pride.

We see Dan Bobish who would have been James' original opponent. He is huge and built like a tank. He was also doing a phone message and didn't look overly impressed with the proceedings.

There is a training session booked in at the dojo later this afternoon after the weigh-in and rules reading.

I decide to go for a walk on my own and do some shopping for presents for my family. On the way, out in the hotel lobby, I meet Dan Henderson and have a photo with him. Dan is in fight mode and not too friendly. I got my photo and at least, he didn't slam me!

Walking around Tokyo is wild. You could easily get lost. It is a mass of people, vibrant colours, great smells, sights and sounds. It is truly an amazing place. The people are lovely. It brings back many memories of my early days training under Japanese Senseis.

I get time to buy some presents and souvenirs to bring home.

Weigh-in and the rules reading are at two fifteen p.m. As we walk in, photographers are snapping shots of James. We find our seats. As the room fills up, I look around, and it is hard to believe the company we are in. Sitting in front of me is Heath Herring, the huge Texan fighter. Up ahead beyond him are the Emelianenko brothers. Both are giving us the evil eye. James is unfazed.

In the far right of the room is Rampage Jackson and far left, Wanderlei Silva. Both men are being kept well apart. Next door to us, Josh Barnett and Eric Paulson are seated. Next to them is Bobish.

218

On the other side of us is the Dutch fighter Alistair Overeem, whom James knew from training with in Holland a few times.

The 'Pride' committee sit out front and tell us about the show, what is expected and the rules. The famous Japanese fighter and at that time 'Pride' chairman Tanaka reads out all the information. Then, the photographers are free to take snaps of the fighters.

After, I, once again, talk to Eric Paulson and then, have a chat and photo with the giant Heath Herring. What a nice guy he was. He was so different from his ring persona.

We go and train at the dojo for two hours, running through drills after once more watching video footage of Alexander.

As we finish, who should pop his head around the door but Quentin 'Rampage' Jackson. He is next up to use the place, and apologises that he has interrupted us. We ask him in. We all chat and again, take photos. He is another sound guy. We get back to the hotel and spy Wanderlei Silva in the lobby. I go over for another photo opportunity. This is unreal.

Today, Dale told us that 'Pride' like James, and win or lose, they want him back.

I am back to my room at ten p.m. where I am writing this. Funny thing I just remembered. At the photo shoot this morning, they took a picture of 'Team Colossus' all together and gave it to us. James is looking at it in the corridor and Bas Rutten sneaks up behind him and pinches it and runs off. He did bring it back. The guy is crazy!

Saturday 30th October
Today is a free day. I have breakfast with James and Lucy. We are joined by Alistair Overeem, the Dutch Pride and K-1 fighter. Also, I have a brief talk and photo with Mario Sperry and Ricardo Arona. Sperry is great. A real gentleman. Arona is in fight mode and not very talkative. These guys are Brazilian ju jutsu and Vale Tudo legends.

I recognise a lot of the 'top team' fighters around the breakfast tables. The breakfast is a help-yourself buffet, and it is weird queuing up behind the likes of Rutten, Bobish and Overeem to get an omelette or some toast. The breakfast area is heaving with fighters. God knows what the other residents having breakfast make of it all. Breakfast goes on and on. These guys can eat!

After breakfast, I decide to go and have another look around Tokyo and take some photos as we have some spare time. In the hotel lobby, I, again, meet Mr. Rutten. I ask if he has any books or videos of his training with him but, unfortunately, he hasn't. We talk about training, and he is enthusiastic about putting me in a choke hold.

219

I finally went shopping with my head still intact on my shoulders. It is raining and grey today. Some of the apartment stores are huge with fourteen or fifteen floors. You need a map to get around them. Outside each store is a rack of umbrellas. You can use them to go between stores and then put them back in the racks. Nobody abuses this trust. Imagine that in the UK. Somebody would have them away and be selling them down the road somewhere. Japan is nearly crime free. Workers leave their bikes unchained at the roadsides and return at the end of the day to pick them up. It is a different world here. We could certainly learn from them. I visit a huge bookstore, and I am in there for a few hours. That was like paradise to me.

After, I am straight into Tower Records, a massive music and film store. It doesn't get much better for me than that. I also go to the railway station and see the world-famous bullet train pull out.

I return to the hotel about two p.m. I decide to use their gym and have a swim after.

As I am finishing my workout, Rampage Jackson comes in to the gym. He is looking to lose one pound before his weigh-in. I ask if I can take a few photos, and I chat with his trainers. 'Rampage' gets on a cross trainer and begins to work up a sweat. His corner team are great lads, and we get on well. Then, in comes Eric Paulson. I have a photo with him, and we chat for twenty minutes about fighting and training. He shows me a few new techniques that he is working on. He gives me a few tips and talks about his new DVDs. This guy is so down to earth. He gives me his business card and tells me that if I am ever in the States to come and train.

Then, I return to my room to rest. We all go out for a meal later. The portions of food in the Japanese restaurants are not as large as the UK, so James orders numerous dishes off the menu and has a procession of waiters carrying them out to his table in a line. The other diners found it highly amusing. Downtown Tokyo at night is an amazing place. I have experienced nightlife in London's Leicester Square, New York's Times Square and the 'Strip' in Las Vegas. In my opinion, Tokyo is up there with them.

A little later, back at the hotel in the reception, I spot the huge figure of Antonio Nogueira, the brilliant Brazilian ju jutsu champion. I have a photograph with him and have a short chat. He is big, and his face looks like it has seen a hundred wars. He speaks good English. This place is like a who's who of MMA.

I come back up to my room and flick on the TV. They are showing 'Pride' re-runs. Who is fighting? You guessed it. Nogueira. How spooky is that? Eleven thirty p.m. and it's time for bed. The big day looms tomorrow!

Sunday 31st October. Halloween. Fight day

We all ate breakfast at nine a.m. We have inadvertently crossed paths a few times in the breakfast room with James' opponent, Alexander Emelianenko. I decide to take the long route around to get my Corn Flakes. I don't want a fight breaking out over the eggs and bacon!

He doesn't look at James or speak. We nearly have the misfortune of sharing a lift, but we both diplomatically choose one either end of the row. Anyway, I didn't fancy being squashed in there with the three of them and trying to keep them apart!

Right on the time of 11:10 a.m, the bus picks us up to go to the stadium, which is an hour's drive away. I am nervous for James, but he seems his usual 'chilled' self. Our bus has all the blue-corner fighters and trainers on there, as well as other 'Pride' staff.

I look around and seated on the same bus as us are Bas Rutten, Mario Sperry, Dan Henderson, Josh Barnett, Rampage Jackson, Dan Bobish, Eric Paulson, Ricardo Arona, the huge 'Giant Silva' and many more. We eventually arrive at the Saitama stadium. It is huge; a state-of-the-art forty-five thousand-seater complex. It was used as one of the football stadiums in the last World Cup. The bus pulls into an underground garage, and we are ushered through to the waiting areas.

Three fighters share a waiting area. There are separate named areas with food, drink, blankets, towels and mats. Each waiting area has a TV showing a live feed of 'Pride' as it is being broadcasted. We can see the stadium as it fills up later, plus the fights as they happen.

The blue-corner fight teams can go and see the ring, plus get in it. We are walked through corridors to a door where we wait to enter the stadium. The security is all armed military. They bow and salute us wherever we go.

We enter the arena. It is awesome. Five tiers stretch up into the gods. It really takes your breath away at its vastness and huge capacity. We head to the ring and get in. It is brilliant white with the 'Pride' logo in the centre in distinctive red. Large TV film monitors are at each edge of the arena. We are actually in this famous ring that has held witness to some classic fights.

All fighters from the blue corner are in the ring now. They are testing it out with a bit of sparring. It's unbelievable that I am in the ring with Quentin Jackson, Josh Barnett, Heath Herring and Dan Bobish. They are all drilling takedowns, slams, etc. It is a dangerous place to be with a twenty-five stone Bobish bearing down on you. I see up close the patented Jackson slam. I would not like to be on the receiving end of that! James gets a feel for the ring. It is a strange feeling that later, we will be walking out to it in front of a crowd of forty-five thousand people.

We return to the waiting area. The show starts at four thirty p.m. Before that, the fighters do a parade down the ramps either side of the ring. We sneak a seat to see this. This is the first glimpse of the crowd. The arena is full. I haven't seen so many fans live before. The atmosphere is electric.

Music booms, laser lights circle the arena and the big screens show lighted images of each fighter. The walkway ramps lower down from above, and James takes his walk to the loud cheer from the crowd. It is incredibly emotional. I have a lump in my throat as we all applaud loudly. We return to the waiting area. With the medical done and gloves sorted, we wait. James' is the fourth fight of the show.

We watch the first two fights on TV, and then, we are called to have the gloves taped. Dale and I check all the equipment needed, and then, we are off.

Gloves get taped by three officials in a small-screened area in the corridor. They even have a TV in their small office. The atmosphere and tension is building to fever pitch. You begin to realise what these fighters go through at this prominent level.

Then, we go to the area outside the arena, and I warm James up. He looks confident and switches into the zone. Time for talk is over. I leave him to his own thoughts.

We have decided that the raging Colossus will return tonight, not the cautious one. We have been told by everyone that win or lose, the fans and 'Pride' like a good show and a fighter with heart.

The music thunders and we hear the introduction for our entry. My heart is pounding and my mouth is dry. God knows what James is feeling like! We are ushered in. I tell James that this is it, and then we are off. James will come down the ramp first and we will follow him.

The fighter is introduced. A union jack with James' name appears on the huge electronic screens, followed by a montage of his fights. This is superb. The crowd loves it. I feel incredible emotion well up again inside me and immense pride (no pun intended) to be walking now to the ring, all of us here representing Great Britain.

What a feeling walking down that ramp towards the 'Pride' ring with the crowd going wild. Laser lights flash, smoke rises and music booms. You cannot really put it into words. I had watched so many fighters and their teams walk to this ring on the tapes and DVDs. Now I was taking that walk. This is hard to believe that it is happening.

James enters the ring, and Dale and I follow. James stands in his menacing statue mode staring down his opponent, Emelianenko, from the moment he walks onto his ramp. A huge image of James' glaring face fills the screen, and the fans cheer. Fedor, the 'Pride' heavyweight champion, is cornering his brother tonight, as he is injured and not fighting on this show.

Both fighters are ready to rock. James punches his gloves together and lets out a huge roar. The bell goes and, bang, James runs across the ring, slamming Emelianenko to the floor. The Russian is stunned. James runs in for the kill, but the Russian is up quickly for a man of his size. They exchange a brutal series of punches. James moves in again but slips. As he regains his footing, Emelianenko lands a solid left hook. James fires back, but then eats a brutal straight right to the chin. He hits the floor but is not KO'd. The Russian dives in for the kill, raining down punches, and the referee jumps in and stops the fight. Presumably because he thought that James could not defend himself effectively.

James is not happy. I feel that it may have been stopped a little early. But, it is over and safety counts first. We shake hands with the Russian camp and graciously accept defeat and leave the ring. I tell a disappointed James to milk the applause and the moment. The fight may have been short and he may have lost, but I can see that the crowd love him as we take our leave. It had all been a blare. It had been fast and ferocious and again, almost surreal. You can always look back in retrospect and say could we have done it differently, but you can only go with the moment, and there isn't time for regrets. If James had survived the first round, there would have been time to talk tactics. But with an early knockout, you are powerless at that moment as a coach to do anything about it. This is the sport of MMA, and no matter whom you are, getting caught cold with a big punch from a four-ounce glove will stop the best of fighters.

Back at the waiting area, the doctor checks James. He is okay but has sprained his ankle. I don't know what the outcome would have been if James hadn't slipped at that vital moment when he had the Russian down. But I guess that's the way it goes. He is inconsolable, feeling he has let himself and everybody down. I do my best to reassure him that this is not the case. At the interval, James has his ankle bandaged, and he goes to the ringside seated area for the rest of the show. We have four tickets to sit in the arena and see the final fights.

I watch Dan Henderson beat his Japanese opponent quickly. Josh Barnett dislocates his shoulder in the first few minutes of his fight with Mirko Cro Cop. The fight of the night was Rampage Jackson and Wanderlei Silva for the middleweight belt.

What a fight! It ended in the second round with a vicious KO by Silva after battering Jackson with around about twenty knee strikes from the Thai head clinch. He retained the belt.

Jackson was left face down over the bottom rope. He looks in trouble but, thankfully, finally walks out of the ring. What a show and one of the best 'Pride' line-ups ever. I was honoured to be part of it.

After the show, I ran upstairs to where the 'Pride' merchandise was being sold. As I went through the door, coming out the other way was the legendary 'Pride' fighter, Sakuraba, and he was closely followed by Croatian, Mirko Cro Cop. I claimed my souvenir 'Pride' t-shirt and hurried back to find James.

We then made our way to the underground car park for the ride back to the hotel. Here is another classic moment. I initially got onto the wrong bus. It was the red-corner bus. Halfway up the aisle, I spied the Emelianenko brothers staring at me, and it suddenly registered. Fuck, I'm on the wrong bus! As I got off rather sheepishly, the rest of 'Team Colossus' found it highly amusing. As the red-corner bus pulled away, I remember the Emelianenko brothers waving and giving us the 'thumbs up'. They even broke into a smile. It was a treasured and rare moment.

We travelled back on the right bus. There was a mixture of feelings. This is the difference between winning and losing. James has just fought in the premier league of martial arts. There is nothing to be ashamed of, and he is the first Brit to do this. So, big respect to him. I was proud to corner him, and it is a moment I will never forget.

I found it hard to sleep that night. Everything was whirling around in my head. It had been a big day. It certainly was a unique way to spend Halloween.

To have been part of this experience will live with me forever. I am disappointed in the outcome of the fight and maybe 'Team Colossus' would have a few of their own ghosts to exorcise for a while. But that said, I regretted nothing.

Monday 1st November 7:00a.m.
We are down to breakfast and then on the bus for an-hour-and-a-bit journey back to Nakita airport.

Our flight is at one p.m. to Munich. We wait around and buy a few souvenirs. I have a go on a massage chair, which is great! We board the flight; it is a long haul back. We go through time zones to arrive in Munich at five thirty p.m.

We have a three-hour wait for the flight to Birmingham. We arrive at Birmingham airport at ten forty-five p.m. James is feeling better and we all felt that we did well as a team and had shared a special experience that comes along once in a lifetime. I have no regrets.

James has been offered a three-fight deal. Whatever happens, he will be going back to 'Pride'.

I am nearly home at the end of an epic journey. One I will never forget.

Footnote

Unfortunately, 'Team Colossus' split up after this for assorted reasons. I deeply regret this, but life goes on. James went on to become a hugely popular fighter. He has fought all over the world. At the time of writing, he has just had fight thirty-four and is on a winning streak. I trained James for his first eight fights of which he won six, all by KO or stoppage. In amongst those six fights, he won the Ultimate Combat heavyweight championship belt and fought in 'Pride', Japan. Not a bad record. Now, coaching and cornering fighters was a pretty new experience for me, and I learnt much along the way. I still see James from time to time and we remain good friends. I have immense respect for the man.

The whole Pride experience is something I will always cherish. I had watched these top fighters on tape at the dawn of their MMA careers and then suddenly was meeting them face-to-face. Talking and training with them and being part of Team Colossus fighting on one of the shows. An incredible and surreal time that I will never forget.

I was honoured to be asked to go there and consider myself very fortunate to have met, trained and coached James and helped him to get to this level.

Now in my life I was living and breathing MMA. I absolutely loved it. But to go from a small little room under a gym with no cage, ring, or equipment as such, training a handful of guys to Pride fighting championships in Japan was like a dream come true. I relished and soaked up every minute of the experience and learnt so much from it. I fell in love with Japan. It seemed only fitting that I would go to one of my 'spiritual homes' after training with so many of its masters over the years.

Sometimes, even now, I look back and ask myself, did I really do this?

"In life, sometimes an opportunity will come along that you must grab with both hands and not miss."

Dealing with Conflict

With my fight and then 'Pride' behind me, I knew that on a physical level, there wasn't much left to challenge me. I had achieved a lot of my goals. But, I wanted to mentally test myself more, and I soon found the opportunity to do this.

I had been getting more and more interested in the psychological side of violence. What made people violent? Why did they become violent? How did the body react to violence? How can we understand the verbal indicators of aggression, body language, etc.? I had studied this more and more and liked the idea of teaching how to diffuse potentially violent situations rather than just showing what to do when somebody initiated it.

I myself had made a big transition from being an angry young man and a very confrontational to a much calmer person. I had learnt many hard lessons along the way and done some things that I am not particularly proud of. But, I came through this a better person, and the subject fascinated me. When I was younger, I wanted the physical tools to win a fight. Now, I had become more interested in developing the mental tools to diffuse one.

I had first become interested in this subject when I joined the British Combat Association. Its founders, Peter Consterdine and Geoff Thompson, talked and taught a lot about the subject. It was an area that I knew I wanted to explore more, so I read and studied as much as I could on conflict management, conflict resolution and diffusing violence. I started analysing how I had done this in the past many times, but didn't really recognise it. I talked to many people that had used these skills. This eventually led me to link up with Mark Hewitt, founder of Personal Protection Training Services.

Mark had designed his own conflict management programme and had been delivering it to many corporate businesses, councils and funding associations for some time. We met on a few occasions, and Mark asked if I wanted to come on board and help deliver the courses. It was a wonderful opportunity to stretch myself and delve into a different area.

At first, I sat in on the courses and seminars and picked up on how they were structured and delivered. I read and studied all Mark's course material, plus lots of website links that he gave me. Gradually, I started taking on parts of the course and delivering it. Mark and I hit it off well, and in the end, we became more like partners. He realised

226

my input and my experience in the field of violent confrontation and gradually, I shared the workload and added new things to the courses.

We worked as a good team, and what one didn't know, the other did. I also worked over a period to pass a BTEC Advance Qualification in Conflict Management, of which I am personally very proud. I also became a registered NHS certificated Conflict Resolution Trainer, a panel and subject advisor for Conflict Management and Personal Safety for Open College Network, and a specialist advisor for the development of Conflict Management and Personal Safety Qualification for CIEH.

Mark and I delivered courses all over Wales, South West England and up to London, Midlands and beyond. In a five-year period, we worked professionally on delivering courses and studying and developing new material.

We did countless courses and workshops for the NHS, from doctors' surgeries, hospitals, A&E departments and health care services. We didn't only specialise in conflict management, but also offered training in personal safety and security issues. Again, this was a massive learning curve for me and an interesting time.

Once, I was standing up, suited and booted, in the plush surroundings of a conference room in a beautiful country hotel, ready to address seventy-plus doctors on conflict resolution and personal safety issues. For one moment, the reality of the situation dawned on me. Here I was, a kid from Bristol. I left school with little or no formal qualifications and worked in tough manual jobs all my life. Now, I was in a room of professional people waiting on me to speak! Shit. I could have panicked. But no, I knew my subject inside out. I had prepared it as meticulously as I had prepared for any fight or black-belt grading. I was confident because I spoke from experience. It went down well. I had great feedback and many questions over a nice cup of tea and a slice of cake afterwards. Lovely.

The business grew. Not only were we delivering conflict management, we also started working with security and bodyguards, working on personal safety, aspects of the law, security issues and unarmed combat and weapons. We did some fantastic courses. We played out live scenarios, dealing with gun threats, edged weapons and weapon retention. We passed an accredited Tactical Flashlight course in 2014 and became instructors in tactical flashlight use for self-defence. We also taught the use of the torch to security personnel, along with handcuffing and restraint methods. I did a lot of unarmed self-defence. I covered all topics from control and restraint, to striking and weapon defence, multi-opponents and combat ground work. I owe the diverse nature of my combat ju jutsu for giving me these many varied skills to call upon.

Many of these men had been around the block a bit when it came to the physical. I worked with ex-SAS, paras, marines, police and hardened door personnel, but when I slapped on some of my favourite moves, they went down in pain and appreciation! They loved it, and we built up a great respect and comradeship. I have many a great memory of these types of courses. We worked for some top-notch security teams who were looking after some pretty important people. I am afraid I can't reveal who these people were. Sorry. I have been signed to secrecy, literally! This is the truth.

When I worked with men and ladies of this league, I wasn't there to teach them to 'suck eggs'. They already knew their stuff. I would ask what area of their training they felt was lacking and if it was an area I could help with, I did.

Mark and I also delivered many control and restraint courses for college/universities and mental health organisations. This area is a minefield of human rights, European laws and red tape.

At first glance, the criteria guidelines you had to work in, you thought that it would be easier to decline the task, but I knew that it would challenge us, so we worked hard on discussing a course material that would work. It was a major challenge but, again, we passed it with flying colours. The experience, knowledge and confidence I had built up in this field really inspired me. I felt that I had grown as a person again, but much of what I had done had been delivered in a suit, shirt and tie rather than a gi or MMA shorts and gloves. I knew that this was an area that I wanted to work more in. For the future, it seemed a natural progression away from constantly being on the mats 24/7.

On the back of my experience in the conflict management field, I wrote the book, 'In the Face of Violence'. It was a book I had wanted to write for some time. It was not a book on physical technique (although some was covered), but more about diffusing and avoiding conflict and all the pitfalls and hurdles that went with it. This book also stretched me. I had absolutely hundreds of random notes on many topics that I had to somehow put in order and then make a book out of. It was a huge project that required a lot of patience and time, but I wanted to produce a defining book on the subject of self-protection. One that covered most of the basics, and a book I could offer at the end of conflict management or self-protection courses. I wanted the book to include topics that were taught in the seminars, but also enlarged upon them.

On completion, I was extremely pleased with the end product. It was a flagship book for me, and I knew that it was the best written piece of work I had done to date at that time. I love to read other people's works that are renowned in the self-protection field to help inspire me, and I owe much to writers such as my good friends, Peter Consterdine and Geoff Thompson. Also, to people such as Gavin De Becker, Sami Franco, Richard Dimitri, Tony Blauer, Marc MacYoung, Peyton Quinn, Bill Kipp and Rory Miller for their great insights. Also, I thank my old buddy Jamie O'Keefe for his sage advice and for publishing 'In the Face of Violence' under his New Breed Publishing.

New Breed rapidly expanded in the late 90s to be *the* UK company for self-protection and reality training-based books. My book was released in November 2003.

Later, I also produced a series of manuals which can still be purchased straight from my website www.kevinohagan.com. The first one was called 'The Students' Guide to Personal Safety', which outlines sound advice for young people living away from home for the first time or travelling abroad. I was prompted to do this when my eldest son, Tom, went off to UWIC and lived in Wales for three years. In those situations when you are used to having your children around you, it prompts you to think about their safety. I hope the manual can be of help to parents and their children when this time arrives.

The manual, 'Are you looking at me?' It addresses the issue of anger in us and others. It also explores why this anger progresses to violence. It then gives you loads of tactics and strategies on how to control anger and diffuse other people's anger. I really enjoyed writing this manual. It has some great advice in there.

Ten years previously, I was *the* angry person that I was now writing about. Much of what I wrote was from personal experience. I was glad that I was now at a stage in my life where anger and violence didn't consume my every waking thought. I had found another way, and I was grateful for that.

Through writing this manual, I wanted to help others. I have been asked by certain groups and associations to go and talk to individuals about anger and violence management, and I was pleased and privileged to do so. I hope my advice helped.

The next manual I felt the need to write was concerning the subject of edged weapon attacks. This, again, was inspired by a spate of reported incidences in the media. I wanted to write something on how to teach people more awareness on the subject and have a greater understanding.

In the martial arts world, much had been written on how to defend against knife attacks but very little had been written on how to avoid them. The manual was set out to give the reader a better understanding of knife crime and the implications of it. Then, a safeguard of tactics was built upon to do everything to avoid being a victim of an edged weapons attack. Lastly, there was some sensible and practical work on defending against a blade. It was entitled 'Surviving Edged Weapons Attacks: A No Bullshit Guide.'

I felt that it was a good blueprint for an instructor to teach on this seriously underestimated subject, which is normally taught in a very blasé manner by so-called experts.

I, then, completed a fourth manual entitled 'Manstoppers'. This work was a no-nonsense guide to the techniques that I felt after my forty years' experience in the combat arts really worked under the most extreme pressure when your life was on the line. This work was my no-bones account of where and how to attack the most vital points on the body to stop a fight instantly in a self-defence situation.

Much has been written on this subject. A lot of stuff good; other stuff more like fairy tales. I wanted to write something for the average 'man in the street' with no formal training or no inclination to spend years in a martial arts class to help defend themselves when the 'shit hit the fan' and their lives depended on a response. In all my considerable years in the combat arts, I can safely say that in my opinion, there are no magical pressure points or Dr Spock death touches. I have endured the hardest of combat, and no one has ever stopped me with a touch on the arm or a pinch on the neck.

If there are such incredible techniques out there, then why hasn't one of these people entered the cage and shown us how they work in a real fight?

If I am switched off, sitting on the sofa with a beer in my hand watching 24 (Jack Bauer is God!), and my wife pinched me on the leg or prodded me in the ribs, yeah, it would hurt, but if I was in full fighting mode, I wouldn't be troubled.

Anything can hurt if you don't expect it. When the body is in fighting mode, it can take untold punishment. When it's not in fighting mode, anything is possible.

The manual looked at the three major ways to stop a person in full fighting frame of mind. A person who is hell-bent on hurting you. It used my ABC principle (airway, breathing, consciousness). Nothing but the most extreme reactions will do. Anything less and you are going to lose. Don't let anyone convince you otherwise.

More manuals followed as my writing flowed. 'Fear: Friend or Foe?' This one went into great depth about fear management and the effects of adrenaline on the body under extreme stress.

Next up was 'The Anatomy of a Street Attack.' This manual explored the blueprint of how a street thug worked, right the way up to physical violence.

Presently, my current manual is the tongue in cheek, '50 Shades of S**t Kicked Out of You: The World's 50 Deadliest Combat Moves'. The title was a play on the success of the 'Fifty Shades' books.

Back at that time, I also picked up writing again for 'Combat' magazine. Paul Clifton, the editor, rang me some time ago, and asked if I would be interested in writing a few articles again for him. I admit that it had been some time, as most of my articles are written for my website these days. But, now in the days of the internet and email, you can send your written pearls of wisdom through the air space at a great rate of knots along with colour images in no time. So, it wasn't so bad to get my magazine writing head on again.

I think back to the first time I sent Paul an article for 'Combat'. We could be talking fifteen years ago now or maybe more. It was first handwritten by me, and then my lovely wife typed it up on a typewriter (remember those?). Then, I took some black and white photos; got them developed and sent it all off in an envelope, hoping it would be published. I did this for years for all the magazines I wrote for. You must not forget that I came from an 'analogue' era. No computers, internet, tablets or iPhones. It was a time of getting up off your ass and doing things and making them happen by knocking on doors, posting letters and making phone calls. Knowledge had to be found in the library or bookshop. It was hard-found knowledge.

A lot of my writing over those years came as a direct result of working with Mark Hewitt and PPTS. I would like to personally take time here to thank him for giving me the opportunity to break into the field of conflict management and open new and exciting doors for myself.

"In a confrontation, we must have more options at our disposal than punching a person on the nose."

Gladiator Total Body Workout

Whilst working in the gym as a fitness coach, I had played around with an idea that I had in mind for some while. I thought the idea was good, but with my other work and teaching schedules, it was finding the time to get it off the ground. This was around the year 2006.

In earnest, I started putting the plan together and getting the structure right. It was something that I hadn't really tried in this format before, but I was ready to give it a go. Hence, my 'Gladiator Total Body Workout' was invented.

I wanted an exercise class in the mainstream sports centre that was different from Aerobics, Spin, Zumba or Circuits. I wanted to educate people into their fitness, how hard a combat athlete trains and how high their level of fitness was to do what they do.

I was used to training martial artists and fighters. I wanted to see how people outside of those circles would react to what I was about to show them and the manner I was about to teach it in. It was not going to be the 'softly, softly, nicely, nicely' approach. I wanted to take them right out of their comfort zones and push them hard.

Either, it was going to work, or it was going to die on its ass. But as you might have gathered by now, I enjoy a challenge!

In the many years that I have been involved in martial arts, fitness has always gone hand in hand with my training, and I believe that it is a totally essential element if you wish to excel at what you do. Make no mistake. You neglect fitness at your peril.

Those that know me will know that I have been a fanatical fitness trainer and that I have taught and coached my fitness regimes to martial artists, cage fighters, boxers, wrestlers and military forces.

I decided to construct a workout of bodyweight exercises that I have taught to the above-mentioned people and deliver it to the public. I took the core bodyweight exercises and built them into a class routine.

I have been a massive fan of 'old school' training methods for as long as I can remember, particularly body weight exercises. I am not a big advocate of machine training.

I loved reading about the 'old-time strongmen' such as 'Farmer' Burns, Arthur Saxon, Eugen Sandow, Charles Atlas and Steve Reeves. I avidly studied their training and exercises. They all supported body weight training as part of their routines.

I also read about the Japanese wrestlers and their torturous body weight workouts.

I knew that my local sports centre must have some hardcore gym users and fitness fanatics that wanted to challenge themselves with a different sort of exercise workout than the mainstream offerings. So, I pitched the idea to the sports centre and was given the green light to set it up.

I worked out a routine of exercises that required no equipment, and which was going to blast the aerobic, anaerobic and muscular endurance systems big time!

It was going to be a continuous workout with little or no rest, working to the sounds of heavy metal and punk music. It was going to be diverse, challenging and different!

The first class brought around about eighteen people. It was hardcore but fun, and everyone there expressed that they 'enjoyed' it! My only worry was how many would return next week.

As I had suspected though, these people had been looking for this kind of workout and wanted to break out of the 'comfort zone' and push themselves to new limits.

Now, this type of workout is no longer new with similar things such as HIIT and Insanity, etc. But back then, it really was ground-breaking, and I didn't realise how big and popular this workout would become.

I ran the class for about seven years. I had a cross mix of martial artists, tri-athletes, roadrunners, rugby players, skiers, ex-forces and hardcore gym users, to name but a few, that really enjoyed the workout. It developed a bit of a cult status.

I could only fit one of these classes into my weekly schedule, as my martial arts teaching and training took priority, but looking back now, I could have probably franchised 'Gladiator' and made it as big as say the 'Insanity' workout is today. I am not boasting or being big-headed, but it really did *rock*. I was getting fifty people regularly in the class, and that is no mean feat. Plus, there was always a waiting list. Along with the exercise, I like to think that I introduced the younger element of the class to the classic sounds of Motörhead, Iron Maiden, AC/DC, the Ramones and many more 'real' bands! I am also pleased that I fronted the class and did the entire workout up to fifty-three years of age.

The class structure was sixty minutes long and broken into three sections. The first five to eight minutes was a pre-stretch mobilisation of joints and muscles. The second part and core of the class is the thirty to thirty-five minutes combat conditioning with a non-stop variety of sprawls, tucks, plyometric jumps, Hindu squats, Hindu push-ups,

233

jump squats, mountain climbers, squat thrusts, press-ups, animal movements, neck bridging, abs workout, etc. The final part is ten minutes of full, slow stretching and deep breathing exercises.

Much has been publicised about combat conditioning exercises in recent times. But these exercises aren't new; it is just that their effectiveness has been forgotten currently of high-tech equipment.

Like Matt Furey (US combat conditioning teacher), I wanted to preserve these time-proven methods and give them to people who may not have seen them before or may have dismissed their effectiveness. The Gladiator Total Body Workout may not have been for everyone, but a hell of a lot of people did like this type of workout. It was a massive success for me, all borne out of a random thought and idea. I love it when a small seed planted grows into fruition. It makes the challenging work all worthwhile.

The format was simple and that is what I find people want when it comes to exercise classes. Anything too complex or specialised needs to be trained one-to-one. People like routine. We are all sticklers in one way or another for routine and are creatures of habit. That is why Gladiator 'did what it said on the tin', and I believe that was one of the major reasons for its success.

But as they say: all good things come to an end, and eventually I felt I had taken it as far as I could, and it was time to bring the curtain down on another episode of my life.

Since then, my son Jake's wife, Soeli, went on to devise, initially with my guidance, a body weight exercise class called the 'Amazon Total Body Workout'. Soeli trained with me for some years and is one of only a handful of ladies that I have taught that I really rate.

She is a tough trainer and a super fit girl. She can punch as hard as anyone I have known for her weight. She can do long arm hanging pull-ups and push-ups and throw weights around like a veteran. Also, she can grapple a bit. I am very proud of what she has achieved and the hard road she's had to travel in her personal and training life to where she is now. Her classes 'Amazon' are going great guns at our 'Impact Gym' and all over Bristol these days.

"You don't need fancy equipment to get a good workout, just a little space and a lot of heart and will to succeed."

'Old Guys' rule in the gym

I have worked in many gyms all around my home city of Bristol. In that time, I have seen a lot of changes in the fitness industry. Some of the changes have been for the good and some for the bad. I have also seen lots of fitness fads come and go.

I myself have had to adapt and change with the industry; otherwise, you can get left behind. I always think of myself as an old-school fitness trainer. I believe in solid graft and sweat.

The fitness champions of yesteryear didn't have the luxury of hi-tech treadmills, stair masters, cross trainers, etc., etc. But, they still built incredible physiques and developed great stamina and strength. The bottom line is that there is no substitute for arduous work, whether you are training out of your garage with only a punch bag and a pair of dumbbells for company, or whether you are knee-deep in the plush surroundings of the latest health club. Fitness is a way of life. There is no quick-deal solution. It must be worked at the same as any other attribute in this world. As they say, 'there is no such thing as a free lunch!'

I have talked much about my training routines. I have trained everywhere and anywhere. From a spare bedroom in my home to my garage to the timber yard where I used to work. I have been in dozens of gyms from my home city's legendary 'Empire Club' to the even more legendary 'Gold's Gym' in Venice Beach, California. If you have the drive and determination, you can train anywhere. Do not make excuses about your training environment. It doesn't matter a jot.

As I mentioned, although I see myself as 'old school', I have taken on new skills and enjoyed them. I have done things a few years back that I would never have thought about.

It isn't easy establishing yourself in a new gym when many of the gym coaches are young enough to be your son or daughter. I know many I have worked with probably thought, 'What's this old boy going to show us?' Well, the 'old boy' might have had a few miles on the clock, but he wasn't ready for the scrapheap just yet!

Some years ago, I became a qualified spin instructor. Spinning is a massively popular workout in leisure centres everywhere. It is a stationary cycling class, where the instructor will take a group of individuals through a virtual bike ride over a terrain of their choice. This is all done to their selected music. As I mentioned, I never would have seen myself doing this, but I passed the course and taught two regular classes and really enjoyed it. It was a two-fingered salute to my course instructor who said that I would never become a spin instructor in a million years. It was such a diverse skill to coaching martial arts! I did draw the line at wearing any spandex or Lycra though. Well, a man has his image to think about, plus, you don't want to highlight your shortcomings!

Some people will only know me from those spin classes. They knew nothing of my martial arts background.

I also worked to qualify to be able to teach special populations in the gym. These are people referred to the gym by their GP. They may have heart or blood pressure problems, diabetes or osteoporosis. They may be clinically obese or have lung disease. The list goes on. As a coach, you will design them a specialised programme and work with them to help them achieve their results. Again, this is very fulfilling. I also trained a group of people with COPD (Chronic Obstructive Pulmonary Disease). This illness is responsible for the highest number of health-related deaths in the UK. It is right up there with both cancer and heart disease. COPD cannot be cured, but it can be kept at bay.

I trained this group through a circuit and gym-based routine. They loved the exercise (although they moaned). Their improvement gave me a great sense of satisfaction. It's so much more enriching than my days lumping timber around in the cold and wet on the docks.

It is a million miles away from that life, which I am grateful for. On days when I feel tired or a bit below par, I remind myself and it 'bucks me up' immediately.

I have received some superb training from many great lecturers and trainers from the fitness industry, and it has dramatically changed a lot of my points of view. I realise that we can't harp on about the past all the time. We need to look to the future and keep developing. The fitness industry is well known for promoting the latest and greatest weight loss fast schemes or the newest piece of training kit to get you in awesome shape. Many of these things are as useless as a chocolate fireguard.

Things such as fitballs and Bosus certainly have a function in martial arts training, but being able to stand one-footed on a Bosu or kneel on a fitball won't help you win a fight.

My advice is not to get too fixated with the 'latest and greatest' equipment out there.

Two other pieces of equipment that are not so new, but have found their way back into modern gyms are the medicine ball and kettle bells. I am glad they have. I have been a big fan of them both for years and, again, they provide many functional exercises and drills for the martial artist or combat athlete. My son Tom devised and teaches an awesome medicine ball class called 'Orbfit' out of his 'Apex Fitness' personal training business.

As you know, I love functional training, and that holds true for when I work out with weights. I have found that in my experience, too many guys that want to improve their combat skills are lifting weights like a body builder. This is not the route to go. Believe me, I've been there and done it. If you veer off down that road, you will get lost. If you are using weights to enhance your MMA skills, for instance, then think of the movements you would like to recreate. Sitting down on a shoulder press or lat pull-down machine isn't going to do anything to improve your functional combat skills.

I am going to give you my view on the subject. I have found these methods have worked for me and others I have coached.

Firstly, if you really do lack strength and muscle, then basic weight training will start you off and build a strength base. But, if you are already at a stage where you are looking for more development to help your fighting skills, then the following things are essential:

1. Pull-ups and chin-ups. In my opinion the kings of total upper body strength. If I could only do one exercise for upper body power, strength and endurance, this would be it. It is the daddy. Also, triceps dips.

2. Next up, the best exercise for leg strength is squats. They are massive power builders. The 'old timers' used to refer to the legs as the second pair of lungs, and they were right. A hard-squat session will have you gasping for air. The whole-body frame is under stress when squatting, which is good. You will develop great power for lifting and slamming techniques by squatting regularly. If you find squatting with a barbell difficult, use a power bag. They are brilliant, and I use one all the time.

3. Deadlifts for overall body strength and clean and press, hang cleans and power cleans.

4. Dumb bell power snatches and cleans and presses from the floor are great for explosive upper body power. Again, they will also burst the lungs with exhaustion. I prefer dumb bell work to bar bell. It is much more functional for fighting, and you can use them in so many ways. They also equally strengthen both sides of the body and develop an iron grip. Kettle bells work on the same lines, but also put more work on stabilising muscles as well due to their shape.

5. Cable work is also worth putting in your workouts. The cables allow you to mimic fighting moves. With a little bit of imagination, you can come up with a lot of great functional stuff.

6. Bench pressing with dumb bells, again, is preferred to bar bells, and triceps dips are much better than triceps pulldowns or kickbacks. Three sets of triceps dips followed by three sets of pull-ups will give you the biggest arm muscle pump ever. It will also have taken care of a lot of your upper body work. Why bother with bicep curls or triceps pulldowns after? If you do the routine right, you won't want to do curls, etc. Look at gymnasts on the rings or parallel bars. They didn't get those awesome physiques from bench pressing or bicep curling!

As you will gather, I love pull-ups and their like. Hanging from bars, climbing around bars or ropes are brilliant for strength.

I have met professional climbers in the gym who showed me pull-ups off two short climbing ropes. It is incredibly hard to do these, but they will develop a grip of steel. This is functional for any grappler.

Look at the animal kingdom. Look at the strength of any primate. It's down to climbing, hanging and swinging, not lifting a bar bell. There must be something in it all!

When it comes to burning body fat, there are lots of schools of thought on this subject. There are literally thousands of books written on the subject. If you are fit enough, high intensity interval training is the way to go, not long hours of ponderous training.

Much can be achieved in a hard twenty-minute high-aerobic/anaerobic workout. I use, and have used, these methods for years, and I know they have worked for me. I manage to sustain my weight and body fat comfortably, although I don't train anywhere near as much as I used to do. For many of my training routines, check out my book 'Unleash the Beast', fitness and condition for the combat martial artist.

I have met some weird and wonderful people over the years in gyms. I have some remarkable stories, but because I am still in the industry, I feel it wouldn't be right to relate them now as I do still meet some of these characters.

One thing that does make me smile is that all gyms will have the group of males that believe by pumping heavy iron and flexing their pecs and biceps in the mirrors, this means they're 'hard men'.

I cannot count the times these boys have given out the evil eye and plumped themselves up like peacocks when I have passed them. They walk and strut around in their muscle vest with arms splayed as if they have mistaken their underarm antiperspirant for hairspray. You know those guys. They must shout and grunt when lifting a weight and, also, they have to drop it loudly so others might look around at them. They normally have a little following that hang on their every word and cough up the readies for some pharmaceutical enhancement that's on sale.

Lifting weights and having a bodybuilder physique doesn't mean or guarantee anything on its own. Take the world of cage fighting. Most champions are not muscle-bound or built like The Incredible Hulk. The champion's muscle is functional, not cosmetic. There is a world of difference.

The absolute best bodybuilders I have met are quiet, humble gentlemen. They will talk their trade if you ask them, and they are incredibly knowledgeable, but they won't bore you. My friend Tom Blackman, owner of the 'Ministry of Fitness' gym here in my hometown of Bristol, is one such guy. Also, the guys at 'Trojan Fitness' gym and Synergy know their stuff.

True bodybuilders don't all think that they are fighters (although some are, without doubt). I have the upmost respect for the genuine bodybuilder. I admire the dedication and discipline that they put into their training. Their mental resolve is incredible to keep doing what they are doing, day in and day out, in search of perfection. Being a combat athlete or fighter, you will need the same steely resolve and determination, but the physical training is worlds apart. The smart guys know this. The others? We will let them live in their fantasy world.

Below is my little rant about a few typical gym stereotypes about a few that will remain nameless.

You see, there is always more than one type of asshole in the gym, and you need to recognise this. They are not all the same. However, wherever I trained, there were at least half a dozen guys such as the following list of 'legends in their own lunchtime'.

A) The Hardman – This species believes in his pea-like brain that humping some weight around and getting a bit of a build somehow makes him a tough guy. You know the type. Strutting around, arms splayed, chest puffed out in a tiny micro-vest. He walks like he has just shit himself and hasn't quite finished yet. The hard stare, the glare, the snarl. Likes to grunt a lot and drop weights with a loud crash.

Now I know guys who lift a lot of weights and are tough. But the majority aren't. They are hiding behind their muscle-plated armour, hoping no one ever steps up for a look beyond the cosmetic steroid-pumped physique.

Lifting weights does not make you a fighter. Real fighters train to fight. Weights are a small part of their regime. Also, don't mistake big for hard. Never judge a book by its cover and never presume because you are bigger or have a better build then some other guy that you are somehow superior. Many have made that mistake in the past and paid a heavy price.

B) Bicep Curler – This guy spends hours sitting on a bench curling a dumbbell whilst checking himself out in the mirror. He believes big arms are the key to a great physique. He is a misguided soul wasting his time and energy. Day in and day out, he is doing the same thing and getting nowhere fast. His big arms come from mindless hours in the gym and lonely nights on his own. I mean how can there be a woman in his life when he spends more time in front of a mirror than her! I remember a lad coming to my MMA class once and telling me he thought he would be good at wrestling because he had big arms! "Of course, you will," I replied, smiling sweetly. Twenty minutes later, he was off the mat being sick after a gruelling blast of sprawls, mountain climbers and Hindu push-ups and having his ass handed to him.

My advice is, 'Do not sit on anything in a gym if it can be avoided.' Unless you are over fifty years of age or you have health issues, then stand up. Gym machines like a chest press, shoulder press, etc. were designed for victims of traumatic accidents that ended up with a psychological or physical impairment. Now, they have become the lazy trainer's staple diet.

We as human beings are dynamic machines built for movement, not sitting down. If you sit at a desk all day for work, why come into a gym after and sit? This also goes for doing your complete workout sitting on a bike or rower. No doubt you can get a decent session in, but why choose to sit on your ass when you can stand?

If you want to lift weights properly and get impressive results, do deadlifts, squats, clean and press, chin-ups, pull-ups, tricep-dips, one-arm rows, military presses and their like. Barbells, dumbbells, also kettle bells. Swing them, snatch them, rotate them and pull them. Be progressive, dynamic and move.

C) The Fat Boy – This lad poses around in a vest top and presumes he has a great build. He likes to refer to himself as big but in fact, he is fat.

He carries too high a percentage of puppy body fat and if he trained hard, worked up a sweat, lifted properly and cut out the carb overload, he would drop weight and body fat and look ripped and a whole lot better. But it probably won't happen. He is too far up his own ass.

He usually also has a bunch of weaselly, skinny little mates with him that look up to him as if he was Schwarzenegger himself. Usually, this person is a university rugby-type. He is a big fish in a little pond. He also likes to wear a weightlifting belt when he is squatting forty kilos. Unfortunately, he won't listen to sound advice; he knows it all and will remain fat.

D) Over Forties Bench Presser – This final species has come back to the gym after a twenty-year layoff, but in his mind, he still thinks that he's a young man. He has developed a beer gut and his tattoos are fading, but he struts around like a cockerel and still believes he is 'the Boy'.

Instead of beasting out some cardio to lose weight and burn fat so he doesn't have a heart attack, he spends the gym session laid under the Smith machine bench pressing. When he stands up, he will self-consciously suck his flabby belly in and pull back his rounded shoulders, believing he is still defying father time.

On this note, a bench press has always seemed to be the benchmark for strength. If this is the case, why isn't it in Olympic weightlifting? Just a random thought of mine.

These are the main gym pricks. While we are on the subject, let's recap. Unless you are physically or psychologically impaired or over fifty, don't sit on machines.

Also, unless you are the above-mentioned, don't sit on a bike pedalling and reading a book. That is a total waste of time. If I read a book whilst pedalling a bike, it would be turned into soggy pulp within thirty minutes. (Maybe this is where the term pulp fiction arose!)

Cut out posing in the mirror like a 'mincer', cut out talking bullshit, leching at the females and scratching your balls, and you can be more productive in less time. Amen.

Years ago, things like the above subject would make me angry, and I would be ready to confront these assholes and tell the person what I really thought of them. It was the same in the martial arts world. If I encountered an asshole, I was off the starter block to let them know that they were an asshole and to administer some pain! Now I'm more laid back and try to let it all go over my head. I have nothing to prove in that area any more. I like to take a more philosophical point of view. It takes a lot to wind me up these days. I do still hold strong views on certain issues, and I always felt I had a good sense of right and wrong bored through my upbringing and instilled in me by my parents. As a song lyric goes, 'haven't always been good, never really been bad.'

I don't like lack of respect or manners in training which, unfortunately, has found its way into the martial arts world more and more. In general, though, I keep a cork on the bottle with the demon in it and don't drift to the dark side very often, although it can sometimes be challenging.

I fondly remember a scene from an 80s' film called 'Stick' starring Burt Reynolds. In an early scene, Reynolds' character is released from prison and picked up by an old mate. They go to a beachfront bar (in Florida, I think). They both sit at the bar on stools. There is a drunken guy at the bar, and he keeps making crude comments about the pretty girl serving. He tries to bring Reynolds in on it, but he ignores him. The drunk then calls the girl to him. He leans over the bar to whisper something in her ear. Reynolds takes the opportunity to light a matchbook and put it on the stool. The guy sits back down, leering drunkenly at the girl and, then, his face registers burning! He suddenly leaps up out of his seat. This is when Reynolds grabs the back of his head and slams it a couple of times onto the bar. The guy hits the deck out cold. Reynolds' friend says, "Hey, what did you do that for?" Reynolds replies, "He was an asshole." His mate begins to rant at him, "Yeah, sure he was an asshole. Do you know how many assholes are in this world, eh? You going to bang every asshole's head you meet? You can't do that!"

It was a great scene, and it struck a chord with me. You are on a losing crusade if you are going to confront or challenge every asshole that crosses your path, because for every dozen you sort out, there will be another dozen waiting in line. In fact, I think there is a big factory somewhere in a town called 'Assholeville', and they must churn these people out regularly on a conveyor belt!

So, I've learnt. Walk away. Don't get involved and don't let it get to you. Unless this person is going to do me personal harm, then I forget it. When you do, it's like having a heavy load lifted from your back. You will feel better for it. As President Roosevelt said, "Walk softly and carry a big stick."

I am often asked how I have kept a high standard of fitness as I have got older. There is no secret to this; it takes a lot of challenging work and dedication.

From my point of view, I have always trained and have never had a long break or period away from it. So, over the years the hard base of fitness and conditioning has been built. It is down to me to maintain and preserve it the best I can.

Obviously, at fifty-four years old, you can't do what you could at twenty-three. You have got to adapt, so that you train smarter and not harder.

Your body obviously takes a lot of punishment over a period, particularly the joints. They get natural wear and tear anyway, but with constant punching, kicking and joint locking, they will take tremendous strain. I should discipline myself to a certain way of life if I want to still try being at the top in my field. This requires a vast amount of self-denial and self-control.

When you are in your youth, you can go out on a Saturday night, sink seven or eight beers, go clubbing, have a takeaway and tumble into bed in the early hours, and then get up and train the next day, no problem. You can also train every day with no after-effects and go balls out all the time. Now, I can't do this daily. I still train hard, but I pace myself and train at different intensities.

As a professional instructor and trainer, I still train or coach most days. I will have days where I will work at about sixty to seventy percent of my maximum, whether it is in the gym or on the mats. Nothing too intense. Just a nice, light workout, but keeping up my base level of fitness and conditioning. Twice a week, I will go for a harder workout, pushing up the pressure to maximum, working on my anaerobic fitness and explosiveness. This can be done with bag or pad work, or circuit like training in the gym.

To maintain my strength, I have one heavy weight session a week. I do this with my son Tom who takes me through the workout and makes sure I am not doing anything too crazy. I will work on strict and big compound exercises like squat, bench press, leg press, clean and press and dead lifts, etc.

I like to use the power bags and kettle bells a lot, as well as a staple diet of pull-ups, dips and push-ups. I find that with my other training, this is enough to maintain my strength. On my days for muscular endurance and explosiveness, this will include the battle ropes, sledgehammer striking on a lorry tyre, medicine ball slams, rope climbing and gymnastic rings. I don't do as much sustained plyometrics and callisthenics as I used to due to putting too much stress on my joints and overworking the muscles, which leave me stiff and sore (e.g. Hindu squats, Hindu push-ups, 'V' sit-ups, neck bridging, mountain climbers, burpees, star jumps, etc).

I realise now that I don't need to work my body to total exhaustion. When I was fighting, there was a need for these types of extreme and punishing regimes. Now, I must be smarter with what I do. It's not a question of could I still do it. I know that because I have a warrior's mentality, I would go at it until I dropped, but that doesn't make it right or good for me. So, I choose not to do it. After all, I am a grandad!

I no longer do any heavy sparring; in fact, I do little sparring at all. There comes a time when being punched in the face, kicked around the legs or being choked isn't your number one priority any more. I like to see myself today as an old lion. Content to know he has been there and done it and earned his stripes and now is happy to take a back seat and let the younger guys get on with it as they experience their journey. I have been the trailblazer but as the song goes, 'this train don't stop there anymore.' But if you persist to prod the 'old boy' with a stick, he still can bite if he has too.

As you get older, recovery time becomes longer between workouts, so you must get adequate rest, good food consumption and get in the right vitamin supplements. Food is your body's fuel. If you put crap in your system, you will get crap performance. I eat very little sweets and chocolate. I never had a sweet tooth. I do consume a small amount of alcohol. I can relax with a bottle of beer or a glass of wine. I keep down the intake of junk food, so if I have chips or a pizza, it is a treat rather than a weekly occurrence. I also watch my carbs and keep up a good protein intake as well. As I am not training as often or as intensely now, I don't need massive amounts of carbs for fuel.

I do let myself have treats. I deprived myself of them for a long time. I feel now I have earned it. I still believe everything in moderation is the way to go. Eating certain foods at the right times can help body recovery and replenish energy quickly.

I believe my generally good eating habits have kept me in shape and maintained my fitness as much as my training. But it takes willpower to resist or walk away from food you like.

Most people's concern about eating certain foods is becoming fat and gaining weight. Although I am wary of this, my main concern is being healthy on the inside, so my body is functioning correctly and can perform when required.

I have taken vitamin supplements on a daily basis for years. I take daily multivitamins (now for over fifties) with ginkgo biloba and ginseng for overall body and brain health. Glucosamine is taken for my joints, and Omega three and six for essential oily fats for cholesterol levels and a healthy heart. Vitamin D for overall health benefits.

Some people will say supplements are a waste of money, but in this fast-paced society, if you don't always get the opportunity to eat properly, supplements can help. Whey proteins mixed with amino acids and creatine can also be great sources of fuel for building muscle and endurance. But, get some expert advice before taking and make sure you have no allergies to these things.

There have been many debates over the supplement creatine. Does it really improve your strength or fitness capabilities? Can it damage your liver and have other side effects? Well, I can only give you my own personal view on this subject.

I took creatine for many years on and off. I feel that it has improved my strength levels in the gym and my performance on the mats.

I have taken many different so-called 'miracle' supplements (all legal) in the past, but creatine is the only one I can say that has given me positive results. The only side effects I have experienced are the occasional upset stomach. But in general, if you stick to the proper guidelines, I feel that creatine can enhance your fitness performance. I would usually go on it for a month to six weeks, then come off it again for the same period, and then start again. I have found this the best way to use the supplement. If asked, does creatine work, my answer would be, "Yes." But, you have also got to put the effort and work in whilst you train to gain the benefits.

Stretching is getting more and more important in my training. I have never been a massive fanatic of stretching, but I have tried to discipline myself to do more. Flexibility in the neck, back and hips are essential for grappling, and I feel a good stretching routine reduces a lot of stiffness and muscle soreness.

I read many years back in the autobiography of ex- footballer Tony Adams that he reckoned that when foreign coaches and players came into our British game, they brought the importance of pre- and post-stretching, and this extended his career and many others by years. I must agree on this fact. If your muscles are properly stretched, the likelihood of strains or pulls are greatly reduced as you advance in years.

Rest is also important. If you train hard, you must find time for adequate sleep. Staying up late all the time leaves you lethargic and listless the next day, and then you struggle to train.

I fully believe that all these things keep me going. As I said, there is no magic formula, but there are guidelines, and you must have a lot of willpower. Look at a man like the late Helio Gracie who well into his eighties would still get on the mat for a 'roll' with his sons. This was due to proper care and attention to his body. I hope that I can do this with my sons when I am that age! The bottom line is that you can't abuse your body and get away with it. In the end, the effects will catch up with you, and it will break down. Look at what happened to the football legend George Best who, in my opinion, was the best footballer on the planet. He never reached his full potential and threw this talent away.

It amazes me how people can utterly abuse their bodies and, let's face it, when it ceases to function, so do you.

Apart from my training, I want to be fit and healthy enough to enjoy my life. Do things with my family, go places and travel. I don't want my health or lack of it preventing me from doing this.

When you are young, you take fitness and health for granted. You take getting up out of bed as a God-given right. As you get older, you realise it is a precious God-given gift and one we must look after.

I am proud of my fitness. I am proud that I can still work out and do a bit with lads half my age. I can't take any of this for granted, and I must work sensibly to do this.

In 2013, after a catalogue of injuries, pains and niggles that had disrupted my training, I decided to look at what I had been doing in the way of exercise. After a lot of soul-searching and fighting with my inner voice, I concluded, regretfully, that a man of fifty-four just shouldn't be doing the crazy shit that I have carried on doing well past when I should have stopped it.

From the age of fourteen, the only way I knew how to train was 'balls to the wall'. It was all or nothing. No compromise. I set the bar high and continually moved it up in my quest for greater fitness.

My training sessions have been brutal at times and some would say crazy. Those that know me will know I don't bullshit. I have challenged myself in many arenas and pushed myself to the limits.

My body now tells me it is time to move on, so I am making changes albeit kicking and screaming, but I am making changes. Banging out one hundred sprawls, one hundred tuck jumps and one hundred push-ups and shit like that doesn't do it for me anymore. I have done it to death. Getting lumps knocked out of me sparring doesn't float my boat these days either.

You must remember that I have lived and breathed training way beyond the average person. I wasn't good at anything else. I have been through the 70s, 80s and 90s, and well into the 00s, training nearly every day like a man possessed. I have never quit training, nor taken time out or away from it. Training was my heart and soul.

When I became a full-time professional instructor, I was training and teaching eight to ten hours a day, six days a week without fail. In between this, I was reading, writing and watching training. I was obsessive. I trained in, around and through injuries with no moaning or complaint. No excuses. I carried on training when ill, when I was burnt-out, stressed and depressed. Excuses were for wimps. Looking back now, in some cases, I shouldn't have. It was dangerous, but I wasn't listening!

These days, my martial arts training is now based around a small core of tried and tested techniques that I can execute in a real-world encounter if the shit hits the fan. I don't need the fitness to run a marathon or fight six three-minute rounds any longer. I need cardio that will take stress off my limbs and make sure I am not a shambling cripple by the time I am sixty.

I remember in recent years going to a sports therapist who also happened to train in MMA under me. I went for some treatment on my knee.

He said to me that in general I needed a hell of a lot of other work done on me as well. But he also told me he was frightened to undo anything on my body in case it never went back again and I fell apart like an old car. Charming!

I did understand what he meant. Martial arts puts many rigours on the body and you do end up being bent into many weird and wonderful shapes. It is all bound to take its toll in the end.

Recently, I started my adventure back into swimming. I only swim on holiday occasionally. It is years since I regularly swam. I gingerly headed back to my local baths, feeling like a lost lamb. I had to deal with an unfamiliar sports centre, complex lockers, wristbands, mixed showers and all the swimming bath protocol I had forgotten. Not a punch bag or cage in sight. I was like a fish out of water, not in it!

It was lane swimming, and without ego or bluff, I went in the slow lane and relearnt how to swim. Coming from my background, it was hard to swallow the fact that in the fast lane, doing a great impression of Michael Phelps, were sixty and seventy-year-old men. Middle-aged housewives and a whole assortment of OAPs fucked past me. I felt quite inadequate. But I bit the bullet. This wasn't my territory. I was back to white belt, humbled and willing to learn. I did a forty-minute swim and felt quite pleased with myself. I got out with no back aches, no knee or elbow pain, no black eyes and no bloodied nose. I could get to like this. I am determined to put some longevity to my body that has been brutally abused over the years.

At the time, I had been seeing a physiotherapist for a trapped nerve in my neck which seems to be mercifully getting better. She was twisting my neck and arms in all directions and asking me, "Does that hurt?" I started laughing. When she asked me, what was so funny, I had to explain my background and tell her that my level of pain intolerance may be different to her usual clients.

I have now been swimming each week for a year or so, and it has been helping the joints immensely. Touch wood, the trapped nerve injury in my neck which has curtailed my training for the last six months seems to be on the mend. I hit the bags and grapple dummies today with no ill effects. It has been eight weeks since I have done this. It was a great feeling. I also managed some press-ups. Hooray!

I want to carry on the swimming and get into some serious hiking. The latter will keep a decent level of fitness, but it is also to discover more of Britain at the same time. I want to enjoy some fresh air and stimulate my senses with some beautiful views. I have been staring at breeze block walls, ceilings adorned with ventilation ducts and watching mindless MTV shit on TV screens for as long as I can remember. A big part of my life has been in gyms and dojos. Some of them good, others not so. That also goes for the people that inhabit them. I have met some wonderful individuals, and I have met some of the most narcissistic, self-important, fantasy-living, deluded assholes to walk the planet.

I have not, though, given up the gym totally. How could I, as I now have my own. I am now working on the 'train smarter, not harder' principle. Yes, I know I should have probably done it sooner, but we martial arts types are not always quick on the uptake and are set in our ways. Anyway, I have been researching the exercise principles called 'bursting'. It is like a lot of stuff I have done but not for the extreme periods of time that I have been used to.

I like the idea of fast-paced, high-intensity twenty to thirty-minute workouts as I have an urgent appointment with a local coffee house to get more writing time in, or to spend more time with my grandchildren.

When I was training to fight, or going for my belt grades or competing in some extreme challenge, my training had to mirror this. Dozens of hours of extreme training until you collapsed in a pool of sweat (and sometimes blood) on the floor. I would find it difficult to hold a teacup, knife and fork or a pen in my hands for hours afterwards, and would find myself dozing at the most inopportune moments. Basically, I had nothing left for the rest of my life outside of training.

As previously mentioned, I last had a professional MMA fight at the age of forty-three. I weighed in at 74.5 kilos. Today, I weigh seventy-six kilos. My problem was that after that fight, I knew in my heart that I wouldn't fight in that arena at that level again, but I carried on training as if I would for another ten years, even when I was being told by family and close friends to slow down.

In the end, the body makes that decision for you. Workouts become harder, recovery time takes longer, injuries don't heal as fast and some mornings, you crawl out of bed like an eighty-year-old. Not a good thing. Another piece of advice would be at the end of a year, always take time to review your training and note any progression or digression and then make the necessary changes.

When I worked as a gym coach, one of the standing jokes with some clients was that every year without fail come January, they would be back in the gym for another year of training just as they had for the last five or six years, and they still always looked the same. No change. Doing the same old thing for the same old return isn't smart.

I have done some crazy training over the years. These were mega sessions that have taken me to the brink and beyond. Not all of them good for me. Now, I have become more educated in when to train and when to rest. Yes, it has taken a while. When you get this balance and you can stay injury free, there is no reason why you can't go on training for as long as you wish.

Over the years, I have been lucky with injuries and not many have fully stopped me from training. I have broken toes, fingers, my nose, bones in my feet and fractured ribs. Also, the usual black eyes, chipped teeth and cauliflower ears. But in recent times, I picked up a few nasty injuries which I couldn't shift for long periods of time, and this worried me. The neck problem I spoke about was as painful as any I have experienced. I spent two weeks trying to sleep in an armchair as I couldn't lie down. I lost a lot of muscle and strength in my left arm due to this, and it has taken me a year once the injury finally went to get back to where I was before it. At one point, I couldn't even do one of my beloved pull-ups. Mentally, it took me to a dark place which I hadn't experienced and don't want to again.

I had to also get a cortisone injection in my right foot because the pain in it had got so bad that I couldn't walk down the road for five minutes, let alone train. The origins of this, I suspect, was from too much repeated plyometric jumping.

In a freak accident grappling with one of my then-fighters, my right eyelid got torn, so it was just hanging on by a thread of skin. I had to have it sewn back on with microsurgery. The surgeon who did this was amazing and did a wonderful job. I received five stitches on the inner side of the eyelid and seven outside. Being injected into the eyelid and eyeball is not a pleasant sensation. I had to return to the eye hospital a few times to check that my vision wasn't damaged. I was lucky the eyeball was okay.

These three injuries in the space of a very short time made me look at my training and adjust it before I ended up crippled. It was a bitter pill to swallow.

I feel that too much emphasis is put on age in the Western world, where in the Eastern climate people go on achieving amazing things to a ripe old age. It's all down to an attitude of mind. Tell somebody often enough that they are past it, and they will begin to believe you and act accordingly. Sir Steve Redgrave didn't listen and went on to win a fifth gold medal at forty, Evander Holyfield didn't listen and regained the heavyweight championship at thirty-nine, as did George Foreman at forty-two. Footballer Ryan Giggs didn't listen to talk about age barriers and won just about every honour in football.

I know that however old you get, you do not lose the fighters' mentality. Once a fighter, always a fighter. If you have lived the life of a fit, strong martial artist, it is very hard to relinquish that title. I fear the day I don't feel capable of looking after myself, and I pray it doesn't come too soon, but you realise you can't fight old Father Time. He is the one opponent that will beat you in the end. I just want to keep the bastard at arm's length for as long as possible! That's why I am not ready to give up the fight just yet. It's what keeps me alive, so that I don't lose my edge or spirit. I sincerely believe if you still want to compete at prominent level, your first goal is to stay fit and conditioned. You must have pride in yourself and look after your body. But, having said that, time will catch us all up, and you must be realistic. For all you veterans out there, train smart and keep heart and you can still cut it when needed.

"The iron ore feels itself needlessly tortured as it goes through the furnace. The tempered blade looks back and knows better."

The 'NAP' experience

A few years ago, I came across a DVD publishing company called NAP (New Approach Publishing). A friend of mine had received a newsletter through the post advertising some of their 'Reality Self Defence' productions. I saw a few names of instructors that I knew on the lists, so I thought that I would check out their DVDs.

NAP style back then was basically to film in its raw form (warts and all) to provide a degree of realism, plus to find some 'unfashionable' instructors who weren't in the monthly martial arts publications or, indeed, in the limelight. On viewing some of their work, I thought to myself, I'd like a crack at doing some stuff for NAP.

I really wanted to get my techniques, tactics and thoughts down on properly recorded discs so it was there for all that were interested to learn from them, no matter where they lived in the world. It is like laying down a blueprint for the future, so hopefully, when I am no longer on this planet, my ideas and teaching will carry on in some shape or form.

I remember many years ago buying Bruce Lee's long-awaited unfinished book 'The Tao of Jeet Kune Do'. I recalled thinking what a shame that the book hadn't been finished properly in his lifetime. We will never fully know what he wanted in it. It was pieced together from his many notes after his untimely death.

One of my main motivations for writing and, indeed, producing DVDs is to get my stuff down the way I see it and pass it on. I do not want to get too old or go to my grave regretting that I didn't find time to do this. My knowledge was hard-earned, but I am not a selfish man. I want others to learn from it if they are interested in it.

I wrote a letter to Ian Goehler, who is the main man there, and asked about the possibility of doing a DVD for them. Ian contacted me a few days later and informed me that he did, in fact, have my name down to approach about some film work. We agreed to meet up and discuss a few ideas.

NAP is based in Stockport. So, Ian came to Bristol, and we met up at Bristol Temple Meads train station for a coffee and a chat.

I must admit that I hit it off with Ian straightaway. He is a likeable and down-to-earth person who will listen and take your views on board. Ian, if you are reading this, you owe me for that quote!

I have done film work before for television, and a lot of those guys want you to do things their way, full stop. You can't have any input into it yourself. Since, Ian has become a good mate, and he has always delivered what he said he would. He is a total professional and a great guy to work with, as are his staff and colleagues.

Back at our first meeting, we discussed the possibility of putting together a two-disc DVD set on 'Joint Locks and Breaks'. It was an area they had yet to explore and because of my ju jutsu background, they thought it would be an excellent choice. I said, "Fine." I was more than up for that. I went away to devise the content, plus how I was going to present it. I found it exciting and challenging work.

Around six weeks later, we were on to film!

We filmed at UFC veteran Mark Weir's dojo in Gloucester over a day. The filming was practically non-stop. I knew what I wanted to do, so Ian let the camera roll and I got on with it.

Tony Watt and Corine Hines, two of my black-belt instructors, were great, especially Tony who was on the end of a barrage of finger, wrist, elbow, shoulder, hip, knee, ankle and spine locks! He was a trooper!

Much of it, we filmed on the first take. All the dialogue and explanations I had worked on, but teaching five days a week meant that it pretty much flowed naturally.

I think that I am some sort of frustrated movie star as I love being in front of the camera, and it doesn't faze me in the slightest.

On completion, we had around five hours' worth of technique. We had filmed longer, but it would all be edited down for the two discs. The set was entitled 'Kevin O'Hagan's Joint Breaking Secrets'. I was pleased with the final cut. It was filmed and edited much better than some of NAP's earlier DVDs, plus they had slow motion and a good opening sequence and music. I was happy to add a couple of high-quality good-production DVDs to my collection of work.

Later that year, NAP took a stall at SENI, the UK's largest martial arts trade fair and road show. It was held at the National Indoor Arena, Birmingham. I was asked to come up to work the stall and meet clients, sign autographs, have photos taken and generally promote the DVDs.

A large screen played my DVDs constantly throughout the day with other NAP products. I was proud to see it up there. It was a good weekend. I met many old faces and new ones, including my good mate Tony Downing (the walking oracle on all things martial arts) and also one of my old instructors, 'Mr Self Defence' himself, Dave Turton. On that day, I also met the film star/martial artist John Saxon, aka Roper from 'Enter the Dragon'. What a great moment that was. I watched that film so many times as a young man, and as outlined earlier, it was the first Bruce Lee film that I ever saw.

Six months down the line, I was contacted again. The DVDs had done well, and this time, Ian wanted to produce a five-disc box set. This was a bigger project for me. He discussed the possibility of a Military Unarmed Combat theme.

I have been fortunate to train with a lot of military and Special Forces guys. My first ju jutsu instructor was ex-SBS, a bodyguard and a close-quarter combat instructor. I have gone on to train with guys in the Paras and SAS reserve. As previously mentioned, I have also attended seminars with instructors of the Israeli anti-terrorist squad, Russian Spetsnaz, Israeli Krav Maga, South African mercenaries and some other 'exotic' individuals.

Ian wanted me to pool all that knowledge in a box set called 'Kevin O'Hagan's Special Forces Hand to Hand Combat System'. I was happy to do this if the marketing didn't make it appear that I was Special Forces. I have always tried to keep my integrity and the good name that I have built up. I pride myself on the fact that everything I write or teach is true. I don't tell tall tales or exaggerate the truth.

The DVDs had to come from the fact that I had spent a lot of time over the years training under and with these guys, but I was not military myself. With that issue cleared up, we were soon on our way back to Mark Weir's dojo for filming. This time, I was accompanied by my two sons, Tom and Jake. They were going to help me film. Both are good martial artists and, dare I say, rising stars of the future!

We put in two solid days of filming, covering all aspects of unarmed combat. I really crammed a tremendous load of techniques and information onto the five discs.

The subject content was unarmed striking techniques, escapes from holds, grabs, chokes, weapon defences, use of makeshift weaponry, ground combat and much more.

We were extremely proud of the finished discs. Tom and Jake did great. They were on the receiving end of some pretty hardcore techniques but took it all! I felt that I had upped the ante from the 'Joint Breaking Set' and Ian thought it would draw not only good interest in the UK, but also the States. The two days were tiring but rewarding. The Special Forces box set sold well. It has received some good, positive feedback and there are numerous clips up on YouTube at present.

When this was over with, I didn't envisage doing any more with NAP. I really had tried to put together the best techniques I could on 'Special Forces' because I thought that would be the lot. A year down the line, Ian was back again with another project.

When I met up with Ian once again, we threw a few ideas around and eventually settled on what would be called 'Kevin O'Hagan's One Shot System'. The idea was to film a four-disc box set on the fastest finishers I could come up with for a self-defence situation. The other idea was for a practical pressure points DVD. Ian emailed all his clients the ideas, and they voted on the internet overwhelmingly for the 'One Shot System'.

This time, my sons and I set off to Stockport and NAP's resident gym. It is a Muay Thai and Straight Blast Gym. It was spartan and fucking freezing, but try telling me something new. All real martial arts dojos are grim and freezing, aren't they? Character-building, I was always told. It snowed on and off during most of our time in Stockport, and things looked grey.

Once again, we had a tight two days filming schedule. But, by now, Ian and I knew each other well. We understood how we both worked, so it went to schedule. I am really interested in what goes on behind the camera as well as in front of it. The entire process is fascinating for me. The production on this box set, again, was higher quality and the editing and camera work was first-class (well done, Kim the camera man).

Tom and Jake also got to do some great MMA sparring on the end of the last disc. Everybody was happy.

I was once again pleased with the finished article.

I have gone on to further produce another box set entitled, 'The Weekend Warrior'. The idea of this one was to put together a programme of practical self-defence techniques that a novice could learn in a short space of time. I have had many clients that are business people going overseas to some potentially dangerous countries and come to me for some intense and condensed self-defence training. These discs mirrored this.

My most recent production is a massive eight-disc set called, 'The Horror Show'. This is extreme combatives. On these discs, I demonstrated the most nefarious of hand-to-hand combat from biting, flesh tearing, skin pinches, chokes, neck cranks, spinal locks and joint breaks. It was a huge project and this set is the most comprehensive that I have put together to date. The eight discs also come with two instruction manuals that we put together. Creatively, it really stretched me, but I loved the challenge. Massive thanks go to Lea Welsford, one of my instructors, who endured two days of being on the receiving end of some brutal techniques.

I have just finished filming another DVD collection entitled 'Samurai Soldier' where I hope to document in detail my combat ju jutsu syllabus. My good friend and training buddy Paul Bush helped me with these. He has been a loyal and dedicated fighter, coach and martial artist and an asset to my gym. Please keep an eye out on my website www.kevinohagan.com for updates for the release of 'Samurai Soldier'.

There is something immensely satisfying about planning and delivering the techniques you want and having then recorded for prosperity. It is a great way of reaching people across the globe that may never get a chance to train with you personally.

Some people commented that NAP's DVDs are pricey. I can't comment for other instructors, but I can one hundred percent guarantee that if you purchase any of my DVD sets, I have put as much as I could humanly cram onto them. They are loaded with information. Sixty pounds or seventy pounds or more may seem like a lot to part with for a set of DVDs, but I can't put a price on my experience and forty years of training. It would cost a hell of a lot more to learn that from me in private lessons.

NAP has an informative website and if you sign up to their 'Fight Lab UK' newsletter, you will get free self-defence information from all their DVD instructors, plus regular free fight clips from their collection.

I am proud that I have been voted top on one or more occasions in requests for my DVD clips. It is nice to know that people like my stuff.

When my friend first gave me that newsletter about NAP, it would have been easy to disregard it. But something drove me to contact them, and I am so glad that I did. I am a great believer in following your instincts and having a try. Nothing ventured, nothing gained. For me, it opened a whole new challenge and a great business opportunity. Also, you never know what other opportunities it may bring, as I was about to find out...

On the strength of my DVDs, Ian was contacted by a gentleman called Al Wharton who runs a large annual martial arts seminar every year in Bermuda. He asked if I would be interested in coming out there to headline it as the guest instructor... Surely, he's joking, isn't he?

"The distance doesn't matter; it is only the first step that is difficult."

The Bermuda 'Leg' Triangle!

October 17th saw my son, Tom and I fly out of Gatwick Airport bound for the island of Bermuda. It had become a reality. Over the previous months, arrangements had been made with Master Al Wharton, who was a karate instructor in Bermuda.

Al held two major international martial arts tournaments every year and would invite guest instructors to come over and teach on the three-day event. As I had mentioned earlier on, Al had viewed my DVDs which I had made with NAP Publishing and had liked what he saw. He contacted me directly about coming over, and the wheels were set in motion.

Master Wharton is a well-respected instructor of Uechi Ryu Karate and has been a member of their 'Hall of Fame' for over twenty years. He had brought well-known martial artists over to Bermuda for his tournaments in the past including Bill 'Superfoot' Wallace, the legendary American kickboxer.

I was the first UK instructor to get the invite, and I was excited and honoured to have been asked. Al was very interested in my combat ju jutsu and self-defence skills. My unconventional methods had struck a chord with him.

I must admit that before going, I had to refer to a world atlas to find out exactly where Bermuda was situated! Yes, I knew they had the 'triangle' and the 'shorts and shirts', but that was about it!

I soon grew to know more about the island. It was twenty-six miles squared. It had around thirty-six thousand inhabitants. The Queen was their sovereign. It took an exceptional amount of money to live there, and they had some of the best and most breathtaking beaches in the world.

We flew with BA, and it took around seven hours before we landed. One of Al's students, John O'Doherty, met us at the airport. We quickly dropped our bags at our apartment and then went to John and his lovely family's home for an excellent meal. It was very kind of them.

We then went to Al's dojo and met the man himself. We chatted briefly as it was late. We agreed to meet up tomorrow.

The jet lag soon kicked in and we retired early that evening. We were going to be met by another of Al's students in the morning for a whistle-stop tour of the island. That night, I briefly lay awake and listened to the relentless noise of the thousands of tree frogs outside in the foliage. Their screeching never let up till morning. It was a strange situation to be here. It was an unknown journey and one I looked forward to with anticipation. I was amazed where my boyhood passion for martial arts had now taken me. Sometimes, I had to pinch myself to make sure that I wasn't dreaming.

Next morning at nine a.m., Harry O, our guide for the day, picked us up. First up was a breakfast stop fit for a king at the Princess Hotel, one of the biggest and most exclusive hotels in Bermuda. It was an awesome experience! When we left, Tom and I were moving our trouser belts out a few notches with stupid grins on our faces!

We next visited 'Horseshoe Bay', voted the number one beach in the world! This was a brave claim but, when we saw it, we had to agree. It was an island paradise. Turquoise water lapped onto white sanded beaches. Lush green vegetation surrounded it. The sky was blue and the sun shone down.

This was a picture postcard experience. I made a mental note to try and get back sometime during our stay to swim in that beautiful water. We heard Michael Douglas and his wife, Catherine Zeta Jones, were apparently regular visitors to the beach.

We next stopped at Gibbs Hill Lighthouse. One hundred and eighty-five circular steps take you to three hundred and sixty-two feet above sea level. Stepping out onto the circular parapet gave you panoramic views of all of Bermuda, along with a little vertigo! It was a spectacular view from up there.

Harry O, then, took us to the capital, Hamilton. It is a little bustling town where most people work. It has no major chain stores or fast food outlets. Not a McDonald's or Burger King in sight.

We then went onto the old Town of St. George. It had a much more laid-back atmosphere. One thing which was very embarrassing for me was that everywhere I went; shop windows had posters of me in them advertising the tournament, which is a massive thing on the island. I had no idea how big it was. I felt uncomfortable with this celebratory status. After all, I felt that I was just an ordinary lad from Bristol, England.

Next, we visited Tucker's Point – home to the rich and famous. Michael Douglas owns a hotel in this area.

Tucker's Point boasts spectacular views, private beaches, immaculate golf courses, tennis courts and incredible houses. It is another world to behold. It is truly a millionaire's paradise.

Harry O was a brilliant guide, talking all of the time. He was a fountain of knowledge about everything on the island, and he looked after us superbly. He dropped us back at our apartment around three p.m. Both Tom and I still felt the fatigue from our journey from England, plus the heavy humidity drained us. We both rested again in preparation for our first teaching seminar at Bermuda College that evening.

I wondered how we would be received and whether they would like the stuff I was about to unleash on them. Oh well, I had come this far, and this is what I was there for. I wanted to give it one hundred percent and leave everybody in attendance with a good feel for us. I found it strange that here I was ready to go out on a world stage to teach when part of me saw myself still as the young, burgeoning kid from Bristol who wanted to learn martial arts. I was a proud man that day.

I taught a two-hour class. The emphasis of the training was the 'concepts' of street self-defence. I didn't want to talk about styles or systems. There was a variety of martial artists on the mats and also some novices. I wasn't there to make out what I did was the best. The concepts I taught could fit into any style. The big emphasis was on the modes of attack that somebody would come at you with on the street. I wanted to build techniques around scenarios with verbal dialogue, posturing and raw aggression.

It went down well, and it was certainly a learning curve for some people on the mat. I found the novices easier to work with as they were a 'blank canvas' so to speak with no previously programmed responses or techniques. The two hours shot by. Everybody there gave us positive feedback, so it was a good start.

In general, I found the Bermudan people lovely, very friendly and very helpful. They made Tom and me feel very much at home. I didn't feel any negative vibes during training, which was nice. They are so laid back. They just don't work to a schedule, which is hard when you come from a country governed by time.

Next day (Saturday), we taught two, two-hour seminars. I started with stuff from the previous day. Then, I taught principles of defending against a street sucker punch and some counter techniques. We also explored techniques against standing grappling situations and then street floor grappling. Tom and I kept up a good pace, drilling the guys hard. I tried to give them as much information as I could and taught and demonstrated continually. The humidity made you sweat buckets, and plenty of water needed to be taken in.

I found that most of the traditional practitioners struggled with my concepts of no stance, striking from where you stood and fence work.

It was something they hadn't done before. Also, most were karateka and they didn't have too much in the way of grappling skills. That said, they all took to it with great relish and enthusiasm. It was a long day, but another successful one. Sunday would see us close the tournament with a demonstration. But first, we had some free time, and we planned to hit the beach at Horseshoe Bay.

We got down to the beach at around ten thirty a.m. on Sunday. Incredibly, there were only a handful of people on it. No, Michael and Catherine weren't to be seen! If this beach had been in the UK, there wouldn't have been a pin's point of space to be found on it. The temperature was already up. The water looked inviting. Huge waves crashed onto the beach as Tom and I dived into the sea.

The water was clear blue and warm, which was a first for me on any beach! The sand was tinged with pink coral. The whole experience was surreal. Back in the UK at this time of year, it is well into autumn. Where we would by now be bringing out the jumpers, coats, hats and gloves, here we both were in shorts jumping around in the waves in eighty degrees! Crazy.

After, we took a leisurely jog along the beach. We took in the sumptuous surroundings and the warmth of the sun. Then, we had one last swim.

We later returned to our apartment and ate before making our way back up to the college.

The tournament was well under way by the time we arrived. There was a big crowd there watching. Many martial artists had come from all over the island for the event and some from the USA as well.

As I mentioned earlier, Tom and I were due at the end of the event to close with a demonstration. We sat and watched other demos. Taekwondo, karate, ju jutsu, aikido, weapons, breaking, etc. There was many karate fights and kata competitions as well. These went well on into the late afternoon.

We were going to do a mixed martial arts demo. MMA is not established in Bermuda, and I knew that the crowd were going to see something very different from anything else that day.

We had planned a five-minute 'fight', showing all aspects of MMA. From full contact strikes to wrestling, takedowns and submission with some 'ground and pound' thrown in!

It was a long wait. It was incredibly hot in the venue. We were sweating just sitting there. Eventually, the moment arrived. The adrenaline was flowing. This was certainly the biggest crowd I had demonstrated in front of in all the years I have trained.

We were given a good build up by Sensei Wharton, and then, we stepped onto the mats. We touched gloves and launched into a fast and frenzied five minutes of pure MMA.

We put it all in there. With Tom pulling off flying arm bars and triangle chokes. I put in some big slams and takedowns, and we exchanged flurries of blows and submission after submission! The crowd whooped and cheered throughout, and at the finish they stood up and applauded loudly.

Al presented Tom and me with two nice trophies as a memento of the demo and our visit. It had all gone down a storm.

After, many people wanted to ask about MMA and the techniques they had seen. Being in and around MMA for a long time, you tend to take what you do for granted, but for a lot of these people, this was new. They might have seen a bit of the UFC on television, but this was live, right there in front of them.

It had been a great end to the weekend, and I think that we went down well on all fronts. It certainly had been a brilliant experience.

Monday saw us briefly get into Bermuda's capital, Hamilton, to buy a few last-minute gifts. Then, we had a meal with Al and John at the 'Swizzle Inn', the oldest inn on the island. Al persuaded me to join him and John in sampling Bermuda's famous rum cocktails. I was quite relaxed on the trip to the airport for our flight home after that!

The hospitality and kindness we were shown was awesome. The Bermuda trip had been a once-in-a-lifetime experience and one I won't forget.

Standing in that university waiting to go on to teach, I realised just how far I had come on my journey and had dreamed as a young man about situations such as these and now there I was. Life can really throw some great stuff at you sometimes when you least expect it.

That trip all came on the strength of an email. What a great invention the web is! It opens so many doors and gives you opportunities you may not have thought possible in the past. I have had some great inspirational emails over the years. Two special ones in recent times, besides the Bermuda invite, stick in my mind.

The first one came from a US soldier serving in Afghanistan, who purchased some of my DVDs, and as a close-quarter combat instructor, he was teaching the troops my stuff!

Another one was from a Boston lawyer who shared my surname. John O'Hagan told me that every time he googled his name, he saw mine, so he considered what I did. He informed me that he would buy some of my DVDs as he dealt with some pretty nasty clients and might need a bit of protection. They were brilliant stories.

"You won't see all the doors of possibility until you start walking down the hall."

Old Friends and New Experiences

The British Combat Association was first established over some twenty years ago, and I was one of its early members. For me, the BCA is still *the* association to be associated with. It is the premier league of reality and combat-based training. It has access to a network of the best instructors in the UK, Europe and the world.

At its helm are the two originators of the association, Peter Consterdine and Geoff Thompson. These men were the pioneers in the early 90s of reality self-protection and have tirelessly worked since to keep their vision and beliefs growing.

World Combat Association, which they have recently got off the ground, will open a global network of the best of the best instructors!

Over the years, I have trained with Peter and Geoff on many occasions, and I am fortunate to call them my friends. I have also had the chance to train with some great instructors on their prestigious Instructors' courses. The names read like a who's who of martial artists. Neil Adams, Rick Young, Dennis Martin, Trevor Roberts, Bob Breen, Pete Robins, Mo Teague, to name but just a few.

I also got the chance to train and exchange knowledge with some of Geoff's early students and instructors such as Alan Peasland, Matty Evans, Tony Summers and Justin Grey.

In November 1996, I was asked to teach on one of their Instructors' courses. At that time I was no stranger to teaching as I had run my own classes since 1986, but I did feel it was a step up the ladder to teach in front of such fine company. It was an honour and one I remember fondly.

In November 2008, the BCA celebrated its fifteen-year anniversary with a four-day residential course at Lilleshall National Sports Centre in Shropshire. This prestigious seminar was open to BCA members.

Peter and Geoff were teaching and holding lectures and discussion groups. Over the four days, many different top reality-based UK instructors were invited to teach. Rick Young, Mo Teague, Iain Abernethy, John Skillen and yours truly.

Yes, I was back. Older, wiser and another twelve years' hard experience under my belt! I, again, was honoured to teach on this anniversary occasion for the BCA, and I looked forward to it with anticipation. It was a fantastic way to bring 2008 to a close.

On this seminar, I decided to bring my son, Jake as he had missed out on the Bermuda trip. Also, I asked him to invite his then-girlfriend (now wife) Soeli. I felt that I was bringing a good team with me, and I wanted to expose them both to the experience and build for the future.

We set off on the Saturday for the venue which is a fair journey from my home city of Bristol. By the time we got near Lilleshall, it was pitch-black and a dense fog had fallen. Lilleshall is right out in the countryside and it took an age to find it.

We got there and checked in our rooms and then made our way to the training hall. John Skillen was finishing off his class as we entered. There, we were warmly met by Peter Consterdine. Then, Geoff Thompson came over and his wife, Sharon. We chatted and caught up with things, and I introduced Jake and Soeli. Next, I met up again with Rick Young, Mo Teague, Al Peasland and a few other faces from the past. It really was like a 'who's who' of combat martial artists.

Peter informed me that I would be teaching the last session of the four-day seminar on Sunday morning.

The assembled crowd had trained hard over the four days, and now, I was going to close the show. Some were a little wary that I was going to beast them with a hard fitness routine. I promised the guys that I would go easy!

After dinner, we went to the lecture theatre where Geoff screened three short films that he had written. They were all extremely good. It was all real gritty stuff with a classic story behind them all. I know Geoff must have been proud to sit there watching them and take the huge applause at the end. I was extremely pleased for him. This man had come a long way from being a nightclub bouncer. He can be an inspiration to us all. Read his books if you haven't already. You will be enlightened.

Talk to people like Geoff and Peter, and you can't fail to be inspired by their drive and passion for their chosen professions. Yet, they are both humble enough to sit and listen to your plans and projects. Then again, all the best people that I have met do.

Next morning, I taught a four-hour session which went down well. Jake and Soeli were superb in helping me. Soeli got a loud round of applause led by Peter for her demonstration of punching on the pads. I think that it was a mixture of surprise, shock and disbelief. But as I stated earlier, don't judge a book by its cover.

We covered conditioning (of course!), takedowns, ground control and finishes. On the floor, I prefer striking and choking to anything else, plus I feel that it is the most efficient in any arena, the street

263

included. In all the competitive fight wins I have had, it has either been a strike or a choke that won it for me.

Jake worked well with me and showed great maturity beyond his then-twenty years when demonstrating and coaching. I was proud once more to have one of my sons teaching on the big stage.

It was great to see noted martial artists such as Ian Abernethy and his like on the mat, training and enjoying the session. With a question-and-answer session and photographs at the end, it was a great session and one I will remember.

Peter, Geoff and all the guys were highly complementary about the session and my teaching, and they promised to keep in touch for more courses.

The journey back didn't seem if we 'chewed over' the weekend and how it all went. The twelve-year gap had been well worth the wait! I hope to return sooner next time before I draw my pension!

"Don't stop believing."

Changing of the Guard

A few years ago now, I decided that for the clubs to keep running successfully and growing, I was going to have to have help. I had been a one-man band, so to speak, for as long as I could remember. In all the years I ran clubs, I was there at every session. Leading every warm-up and conditioning workout, teaching 'hands on' on the mats every week, come rain or shine. In between this, I had trained for my many fights and sparred endless rounds with other fighters. On top of this, I was running specialised courses for self-protection and conflict management, working with Mark Hewitt for PPTS and teaching weekend seminars. If I carried on this way, I knew that I would rapidly head towards 'burn out'. I needed desperately to find some balance and take some of the work load off my shoulders.

I have always had a tight hardcore group of black belts who have stuck with me through thick and thin. They have adapted along with me through all the changes I have made in my system and training over the years. I knew I had to push them on into coaching classes and taking that step up, which isn't always easy.

Over the many years I have taught, very few people made it to black belt. Some couldn't handle the pressure, others faded away and some just weren't good enough. I remember also many that had the talent to get the coveted black belt, but never quite got there. Each syllabus was tough and uncompromising, simply because I had witnessed people giving the grade for next to nothing in other arts. I didn't want to sell out for the pound signs. All the people listed here at one time or the other were first-class black belts under me, and all earned the rank and honour that went with it. It was a pleasure to teach you all.

Three of my ju jutsu guys were Tony Watt, Pete Dunn and Paul Hirst. They had been loyal trainers for years, and they had all helped me in my classes at one time or another. Now, I needed to know if any of them were interested in running some of my classes on a weekly basis.

Firstly, I wanted them to grade to their third Dan black belts. So I set them a training regime to follow and gave them a date for the grading. I had never graded anybody to third Dan in my system, so it was going to be a landmark occasion for us all.

Now, I would like to point out the fact that these three men were not, let's say, in their teenage years. They were all in their late thirties to forties. Their commitment to their training for this grade would put others half their age to shame. When they went to the changing rooms to put on their gis, it took them probably fifteen minutes each to put on various elasticised bandages and strapping over their injuries and aches and pains! That is dedication for you!

On the day of the grading, they gave their all. They worked their way through a very hard and comprehensive third Dan syllabus and they were all successful in achieving their grades.

They became the first third Dan black belts to date in my system. It was a proud moment. It had been a very long and arduous journey, but they had made it. They were all very different in their approach to teaching but that was good. They all had their own individual styles but kept the concepts of my ju jutsu system solid.

Also, I reached another landmark by grading my first female to black belt. Yes, in the twenty years plus that I have run classes, I have never had a lady stay the course to black belt. Now that's not for the lack of trying. I have had a handful of really promising females over the years training but, for several reasons, they didn't quite get to that coveted black belt!

Corine Hines came to my classes a quiet and shy young lady with no martial arts experience whatsoever. I didn't see anything in the early days to suggest that she might go on to achieve a high accolade in my clubs. She doggedly stuck to her training week in, week out. Even when her female training partner stopped training, she came herself and trained with whoever was available. In the end, she was regularly training with all the guys and beginning to hold her own and develop spirit and confidence. She worked her way up through the grades and totally changed herself around.

Corine, next, took the step of being the first female to come to my MMA classes. She came regularly to my infamous Sunday morning sessions! Without any moaning, whinging or tears, she sparred with all the guys there. Boxing, kickboxing, wrestling, ju jutsu, MMA and all in. She did the lot. She took a lot of knocks and tap outs, but came back again and again. I admired her tenacity and sheer willpower to succeed and test herself in a harsh and predominantly male arena.

When she was ready for her black belt, she trained extremely hard. She had to run through my whole ju jutsu syllabus (no mean task) and survive a Sunday morning conditioning, pad and sparring session. She did! With absolutely nothing left, she gave her last drop of energy to completing the task and achieving what she probably thought was unachievable. It really was a momentous achievement.

I was proud that I had finally guided a female right the way to the top. It had been a long road. Corine went on to help coach ju jutsu and self-defence.

Diane Jobling, who now lives in Australia, became my second female black belt and what an incredibly tough lady she was! Very quiet and reserved, but what a spirit she brought when she hit the mats!

My two present and active Combat ju jutsu coaches are Jay Newton (second Dan) and Lea Welsford (first Dan). Both have worked extremely hard to get to this level and are the future of my Combat ju jutsu system, if they want to be.

Jay has literally been with me man and boy and has been a loyal student and now coach. He has the potential to go on to bigger and better things and fly the flag for my system.

Lea is a close friend of mine and has had a tough journey with many twists and turns. He has faced much adversity in his life, and it is fair to say that martial arts saved him and gave him a new perspective. Lea refers to me as his mentor, and that is nice.

Ross MacKenzie, who was part of my early fight team has, in recent times, come back to training after a long absence. He has left his ego at the mat side and relearnt his skills, putting in many, many hours of training to gain his black belt first Dan and get his self-back to a point where we may see him in the cage again. Well done to him.

Both my sons are now also accomplished martial artists. Jake is, at present, co-director of our own training facility 'Impact Gym.' He is coaching MMA, conditioning and ju jutsu classes! He is a top-class coach and personal trainer. I have no doubt that he will go on to have a successful and lengthy career in this field.

At present, he is training for his qualification in wrestling. He has also been a founder member and fight promoter for 'Tear Up' MMA events and the hugely successful white-collar boxing shows. He is a burgeoning entrepreneur and business man with many great and innovative ideas. He has fought in many MMA and submission grappling competitions. He unselfishly put his fighting career on hold to help me set up our gym. He has taken a lot on his young shoulders. He is back fighting again in the cage and at the time of writing, he has just won his first comeback fight in style.

My other son, Tom, graduated from university with a First-Class Honours in Graphic Design. He is a talented guy. He has helped design so much for me. From leaflets, posters, DVD covers and my book covers. Also, he designed my whole new website. It was a massive job he took on, but he did it with patience and skill. Check out www.kevinohagan.com. Everything on there, he has put up for me and designed. He is at present running his own very successful personal training company, Apex Fitness. I wish him luck.

Tom is also an avid submission grappler, having much experience in the competitive arena. He has competed in 'Ground Control' and 'NAGA' – two of the biggest submission grappling tournaments out there at present. At the time of writing, Tom has just won a gold medal at the 'Sub Zero' grappling competition held by 10th Planet Ju Jutsu to add to his ever growing collection and achieved his blue belt in BJJ from Pedro Bessa.

He also teaches his own grappling and conditioning classes. It is good to see them both want to pursue their martial arts careers. I have never forced them to do so. They grew up with it and started training in ju jutsu when they were six years of age and have never really stopped. They are both first Dan black belts in my Combat Ju Jutsu system.

At ages seventeen and fifteen, they both came into my adult MMA classes and trained with me and the other guys. No favours were shown to them, and they learnt the hard way by many a nosebleed and a quick visit to the toilets to 'throw up'. Now, they can hold their own without any problems. Being my sons, they had to prove themselves twice as hard as anybody else, and I am extremely proud of them both.

My daughter Lauren is, at the time of writing, about to complete a PhD in Sociolinguistics. She graduated from university with a First-Class Honours degree in Modern Language Studies and a Masters in Applied Linguistics. She is a very talented girl. She wants to eventually be a university researcher. I know that she will do this. She has a fantastic love and a passion for her subject. She, at present, is teaching linguistics at Cardiff University. She can also throw a decent right cross as well, having grown up on the mats with her two brothers. I know that she will travel and her training will keep her in good stead.

Tina, my wife, is still my rock. Her belief in me makes anything possible. She still supports and encourages all that I strive to do and, at the same time, looks after all the family with a loving and caring attitude and has time for everybody. She gives selflessly. Anything I have achieved over the years would mean nothing without her. I feel I have a good level of mental strength, but she leaves me in the shade. Her positive attitude in the face of any dilemma is incredible, and I draw belief from her every day. I am a lucky guy and proud that she chose to spend her life with me. She is the lynchpin of the family.

I have trained hundreds of individuals in my time. Occasionally, I bump into some six-foot-plus young guy that will politely tell me that I taught them ju jutsu when they were a kid and influenced them greatly. That is immensely satisfying. Over the years, I have had feedback from many ex-students telling me how they successfully used the techniques I taught them to defend themselves on the streets. It is good to hear that they came out of these situations unscathed. Martial arts, in general, have enabled me to meet some truly fantastic people and a few oddballs. It has been a great learning experience and one I would never change.

When I think back to when I first set foot in a dojo in 1975, I had so many dreams to aspire to. But I also recall so many others that also had those dreams but, for whatever reason, they stopped training. They never quite made the grade.

My advice is: never, ever give up on your dreams. Keep pursuing what you want in life. Write the book, produce the DVD, teach that seminar, have that fight!

What made me do it? The answer is for the total and absolute love for the martial arts. That's why I have enjoyed each moment.

Through good and tough times, I have never really fallen out of love with the combat arts. They have shaped who I am, and they gave me discipline and purpose. I also kept a belief in myself when some didn't. I felt I had something to offer, and I never once wavered in that belief, even when I had many knockbacks and disappointments.

I also learnt that you haven't got to be the best at what you do. You have just got to have the tenacity to get out there and put yourself forward. You will get better by just doing it and having the courage.

A lot of people who have had success have been working under the radar for years, plying their trade. Each week they did a little more and a little more towards their goal. Sure, it's not easy but success isn't for everyone. Also, you must truly appreciate what you have to sacrifice for it.

If you are an instructor out there wanting to push on and achieve, then you must step outside of your comfort zone to do so. Nothing will come to you otherwise. You first have to go out and search for it. What you sow is what you reap.

To be recognised by your peers is probably the best measure of your success and in 2012, I was entered into the 'Martial Arts Illustrated Hall of Fame.'

"If you seek immortality, first you have to do something with your life."

Black Belt Students Family Tree

Below is a chronological list of students who have attained a Black Belt 1st Dan or above as part of Kevin O'Hagan's Combat Ju Jutsu to date.

1982 1st Generation

	Kevin O'Hagan 7th Dan	
Terina O'Hagan 1st Dan	Brian Baker 3rd Dan	Mark Fortune 1st Dan

1985 2nd Generation

Martin Williams 1st Dan	Mike Griffin 2nd Dan	Neil Bartlett 3rd Dan

1990s 3rd Generation

	Rob Cannon 2nd Dan	
Tony Watt 3rd Dan	Paul Hirst 3rd Dan	Andy Wintle 1st Dan
Bryan Watts 1st Dan	Mike White 1st Dan	Phil Davies 2nd Dan

2000s 4th Generation

Pete Dunn 3rd Dan	Ismail Kadi 1st Dan	Corrine Watt 1st Dan
Aaron Gilson 1st Dan	Dave Tanner 1st Dan	Rich Williams 1st Dan
Tom O'Hagan 1st Dan	Jake O'Hagan 1st Dan	Darren Sim 1st Dan
Dave Fredick 1st Dan	Diane Jobling 1st Dan	Lea Welsford 1st Dan
Ross MacKenzie 1st Dan	Jay Newton 2nd Dan	

At present, I am teaching a few people who may well become my next generation of black belts and instructors. Only time will tell if they have what it takes to go all the way.

The Ultimate Martial Art?

What is the ultimate martial art? This question has been put to me on many occasions and it's been one I pondered myself in my early martial arts career.

My answer to this question now is quite simple. It's not the art in the man, but the man in the art. There is no one art that has all the answers. Some come close but don't make it all the way. Every art has something to offer and can be adapted to work in a real situation.

Some will say that Shotokan karate is not a particularly practical art. Tell that to Sensei Terry O'Neil who has spent a lifetime in the art and adapted it for working on the 'doors' and for street combat. Indeed, the late and great 'daddy' of practical and realistic street fighting, Gary Spiers, was a traditional karate man.

These men and many like them looked beyond the traditional aspects of their arts and made it work. They were also not afraid to step outside of their art and experience other fighting systems.

Aikido has been knocked as an impractical art, but I can show you individuals who can adapt and make their technique work in the real world. You see, these individuals didn't run with the pack. They broke away to experience and experiment, so they had a practical and powerful fighting system.

Indeed, all the great masters and founders of the major martial arts systems were innovators and people who looked to improve, modify and develop their skills.

Is boxing better than judo? Is karate better than wrestling? Is Muay Thai better than ju jutsu? How can we determine this? They are all different and effective in their own way. If one boxer beats one judo man, can that be conclusive evidence of its dominance?

In the early days of the UFC, Brazilian ju jutsu was being hailed as the ultimate martial art. But three or four years down the line, Brazilian fighters were being beaten by kickboxers and wrestlers. Did this mean that Brazilian ju jutsu was no longer effective? Of course it didn't. It is down to fighters, not styles. There are good and bad in every art. At the top of the tree, most martial artists will agree. You need knowledge of more than one art to be a rounded fighter.

I honestly believe that at hand range, a pro-boxer is king. Their speed, power, reflexes and movements are awesome. But if a boxer is on the floor, the grappler becomes the master. It's a proven fact, and most of us know that by now. The MMA scene has gone a long way to hammering this home.

So if there is no ultimate art, is there an ultimate fighter on this planet? Sometimes, we hear of the heavyweight boxing world champion as the best fighter on the planet. In the realms of the boxing ring, yes, he is, but what about in the octagon of Mixed Martial Arts or on the pavement arena? Men like Frank Shamrock, Tito Ortiz and Rickson Gracie in their day have been called complete fighters and gone down in combat sport history. But this is referring to the arena they train in, not as a whole. The street arena, for instance, is a world apart from any sporting competition, no matter how few rules are involved.

I know men who may not fare too well in the ring or octagon but have literally stared death in the face and won. Men who have worked and fought on the streets all over the world in their capacity as security, bodyguards, forces or police. They have defeated attackers armed with knives, bats, axes, firearms and more. They have survived mass and multiple attacks and fought in dozens and dozens of real-world scenarios. Are they the ultimate warriors? See, it gets hard when you broaden your field of vision.

I feel that it's down to a specific person for a specific job. For example, a Ferrari is a fantastic example of a fast and powerful car. It's up at the top of its league, but if I was going to do some off-the-road driving, it would not be on my list of effective vehicles. See what I mean? It's horses for courses.

Over my years of training, I have met truly wonderful exponents of their given arts. Neil Adams' powerful and superbly executed throws, Kenpo Master Larry Tatum's awesome hand speed, John Machados's effortless ground grappling, Peter Consterdine's one-shot KO power, and so on, and so on. All have dedicated a lifetime to their chosen pursuit, but all would readily admit that as good as they are, they are not masters of every range of combat, although they may have a working knowledge.

I personally believe that there are not enough hours in a lifetime to be an ultimate fighter, but you can certainly gain a working knowledge of all ranges for your own self-protection. I do think, though, that you should have a base art to work from and then build upon it.

Ju jutsu has been my base art since the early 80s, but over an extended period of time, I have added other skills from different arts to my system. This didn't happen overnight. When I wanted to improve my ground grappling, I spent hour upon hour every day for eighteen months to begin to get to a decent standard to compete, but I was never the best. When I wanted to improve my hand technique for six months solid every week, I was in front of the heavy bag and floor-to-ceiling bag, sometimes five times a week, punching and punching. I could eventually box three to five rounds full-out amateur level, but I wouldn't have lasted long at pro-standard. These guys are a different breed.

You see, a lifetime is not enough to master everything. Not if you are honest with yourself and get your head out the clouds. I have seen people punching a heavy bag or the pads and believe that they are boxers. Reality check please. Get in the ring with a 'real' boxer, and you will see the difference.

You may spend years perfecting boxing skills, but what about kicking? And then we have throwing. Let's not forget ground grappling. See what I mean? Not enough hours.

Look at Manchester United. Without question, over the last decade or more they were the best football team in England. But would those players be also the best cricketers or rugby players after six months' training? Of course, they wouldn't. It's a different ball game altogether. You must view martial arts the same.

No matter how good you think you are, there will be someone better. As you improve and move up the ladder, there is always another ladder beyond that and beyond that with others, better, climbing it. How good you are depending on the kind of company you have kept. There are many big fishes in little ponds.

I have devoted a large chunk of my life to the arts, and I honestly will say to you that under extreme pressure of real combat, I am a moderate kicker, a reasonable thrower, a good puncher and a competent ground grappler, but not a master of any range. That's me being honest. To up the percentage on the different ranges, I have good conditioning and a tough mindset and fighting spirit. I believe that the ultimate fighter has not been born yet. Will there be such a person? I don't think so, but it certainly is fun debating and discussing the subject.

Finally, what we must be aware of is that there are people out there that really do believe they are the ultimate warriors. Beware of these characters. They believe their own hype and visualise themselves as the new Bruce Lee. The martial arts world is full of some weird, wacky and eccentric people, as well as would-be Ninja Turtles and Power Rangers! You only must check out YouTube to find these 'Walter Mitty' characters. I pray to God that nobody ever will view me in that light. If anybody out there does, I will have to tear out your heart with my secret iron claw killer Shaolin technique or tap you on the nose with my delayed death touch or, better still, knock you out from ten feet away with my projected Chi energy so, at least, you'll have time to finish this book before you die in terrible, screaming agony.

"No Ultimate Art, Just Ultimate Fighters."

'Random Weird and Wonderful Anecdotes from my Training Days'

As previously mentioned, through my years of training, I have experienced some weird and wonderful things as well as many humorous moments. In this chapter, I will touch on just a handful of these things to show what a mad and unpredictable world a martial artist can inhabit at times.

I have been lucky in the fact that I have received very few serious injuries whilst training and, touch wood, neither have any of my students. I do remember that on one occasion, one of my students came over to me and said that he thought he had 'done something' to his finger. I asked to look at it and, sure enough, he had. His middle finger was dislocated at the first joint so that the top of his digit was facing skywards, whilst the rest of the finger was horizontal. I told him that I could put it back in for him, but it may be a bit painful. He agreed for me to do it. I told him to look away, grabbed the finger and pulled sharply on the joint and in it popped! He was fine and pleased as punch. Off he went to train again. I was happy all had gone well.

Five minutes later, he was back to me, showing me the same finger pointing again skywards. He had caught it once more and dislocated it. I repeated the process and put it back. This time, I taped his finger to the next one and advised him that it was probably best to leave the training for the rest of the night. I laughed to myself at the likelihood of the same accident happening twice in such a small space of time.

I must hasten to add here that putting back dislocations are not medically recommended and can be unpleasant for both participants. But, sometimes, as an instructor, you have to think on your feet and improvise.

On another occasion, I had a lady join my class who told me that she had had a car accident a year previously, and because of her injuries, her shoulder had a habit of 'popping out' of joint. Somewhere in the back of my mind, I mentally made a note of this fact, and as it turned out, it was just as well!

Halfway through the session, I noticed her on her hands and knees cradling her shoulder with a concerned training partner looking over her. As I approached, the training partner said that they hadn't done anything and that the lady had just done a basic backward breakfall, and now, this had happened.

I could see that the lady was in some distress and pain. She told me that the shoulder was dislocated and pleaded with me to put it back in. Now, fingers I have done a few times, but shoulders, that is different. I said that it was probably better to call for an ambulance and get a professional to look at it, but she was in tears and begged me to give it a go. So, with a silent prayer and some basic idea, I held her arm at the elbow and elevated it up quickly. *Click.* The shoulder was back in. She was smiling, I was relieved and the class thought I was a hero. Result!

Some years later, Bristol-based Brazilian ju jutsu fighter and instructor Pedro Bessa came to train at my MMA class not long after he moved to the city. Within the first ten minutes, his shoulder dislocated due to an old injury. Once again, I was called upon to 'pop' it back in!

I am glad of my constant first-aid training and highly recommend every instructor to be trained in it, as you never know when it might come in handy.

In my capacity as a fitness instructor, I used to take clients in the gym for an induction to learn about the equipment. Usually, I did these in the mornings and some people may not have had breakfast before coming along (not the right move) and, consequently, whilst standing up and watching my demonstrations, they got lightheaded.

A few years back, as I was sitting on a hamstring curl machine, explaining to a group of about half a dozen people, a lady near the back just suddenly fainted and ungainly slid down the wall to a seated position. Luckily, she hadn't keeled over headfirst.

By the time I reached her, she suddenly came around and was more embarrassed than anything else. She didn't have any idea that she had fainted. It was so spontaneous.

On another occasion, as I supervised a group of fifteen- or sixteen-year-old school kids, a girl just fell off an exercise bike, where she had fainted whilst cycling. Again, fortunately, she wasn't hurt, but a bit confused and extremely embarrassed. A lot of young girls at this age skip lunch or eat very little, so any type of vigorous exercise is going to affect their blood sugar levels causing them to faint.

I must admit that I became a bit paranoid of standing groups on the induction for a while, as I expected another to keel over at any time.

As mentioned earlier, I also worked with people referred for exercise by their GPs. You really had to pay close attention to them as some had very bad heart problems, blood pressure or asthma, amongst other things. Again, you do get a little paranoid, waiting for every gasp, sigh or sudden movement. It really is an experience.

I have also witnessed some funny sights, although at the time you have got to be professional and deal with it. People falling off treadmills and rowing machines can be a hilarious sight, and you often wish that if you had a camcorder at hand, you could have made a fortune on 'You've Been Framed'.

I have been asked many strange, crazy and provocative things in the gym and dealt with all manner of people.

On one occasion, I was working out myself when a lady, whom I had seen in the gym on many occasions, approached me. We spoke and she told me that she was a physiotherapist at a local hospital, and she was teaching students in their last years of training. She asked if I would like to go along to a class and be a model so that they could make a real-life study of the muscles they had been learning about. Being the shy and retiring type, I immediately said, "Yes."

A few weeks later, there I am stripped to the waist with about twenty young ladies viewing my body from different angles and asking questions. I know it's a dirty job but someone's got to do it! I got paid for two twenty-minute classes as well. That certainly was an odd request.

Martial arts have also brought some strange and funny moments. I have taught all over the place from large sport centre venues to outdoors in the woods, an Indian restaurant, my living room, garage, private girls' school, school fêtes, village fares, scout clubs, TA centres, office blocks, prefab huts, prison, schools for behavioural problems, disabled centres, army bases, and so on, and so on. All in the name of martial arts.

I've trained myself, everywhere and anywhere. There is never an excuse not to train. I have fashioned and made training equipment out of any material to help me improve my skills. I believe that if you want to train, you will train anywhere. No excuses.

Wherever I worked in the past, I found somewhere to get some training in, even if it was only for twenty minutes or half an hour.

When I wanted to learn the nunchakus and the Filipino butterfly knife, I would get into work half an hour early, go to a quiet or empty part of the building and practise. I did this day after day until I began to get a feel for the weapon. I was lucky that I worked in timber yards, so I could find a deserted spot. I trained in the pitch-dark of an early winter's morning or when it was so cold my hands were frozen. I forget the amount of times that I lumped myself with the nunchakus or cut my fingers with the balisong knife, but I would carry on working at it. I must have looked a right madman if anybody had been watching me!

As mentioned earlier on, when Andy and I trained in our dinner hours, we used to go at it full out. Many a time, we were rolling on the floor, exchanging punches or attempting a choke or armbar when a member of the public came across us. There would be a look of disbelief and shock on their faces as they walked off. Many a customer in the timber yard had remarked to the other staff about some lunatics training upstairs!

Martial arts demonstrations were always fun moments, where you must expect the unexpected. Things never pan out the way you plan, and you suddenly must adapt and change tactics at the last minute.

I did a demonstration once at Leyhill Open Prison. One of my black belts, Mike Griffin, was a PTI there and got us a spot at their annual fair. It was a beautiful summer's day and three of us decided that it would be perfect to train on the grass. No mats needed. We were all prepared and ready to go when, half an hour before our time, a shower of rain came down. Now, this made the grass top very greasy and slippery. Our footing wasn't as sure as it should have been, and I can tell you that when we got to defending against weapons (knives, bats, chains, etc.), we had to be spot on as you couldn't afford to slip; otherwise, you were in danger of running onto one of those things!

Another time I did a demo for my kids' school fête. Again, it was a very hot June Saturday. My guys and I put down some PVC gym mats on the grass a little while before the demonstration time. Unknown to us, the sun was beating directly down on the mats and was nearly melting the PVC. We were training in bare feet, and after we had made the introduction and then stepped onto the mats, it was like walking on hot coals! We started off throwing each other around, and it was a blessed release to land on your back to get your feet off the floor. We ended up disregarding the mats and having to do the rest of the demo on the grass. I can tell you that the soles of my feet were blistered after that afternoon. You live and learn!

On another occasion, back in my aikido days, the clubs did a demo at another fête in Dursley, Gloucester. We performed the demonstration in a roped-off area with a good crowd watching. In the background were the Red Cross first-aid people idly watching and chatting. The close of the demo was that my fellow instructor and I demonstrated knife defences using a real but blunted knife. Up to this point, the Red Cross had been disinterested but when they saw this rather large knife flashing about, they were over and gathered right by the roped area and waiting eagerly in case one of us made a fatal mistake. Luckily, we didn't, but I think it ruined their day, as they were on the starter block with bandages at the ready!

Again, in my aikido days, my good mate Mark and I went to do a demonstration to open a new club. The instructor was Mike Narey, a well-known face in the aikido world. Mike basically bounced Mark and I around, showing the more dynamic techniques of aikido. Whilst doing this, he accidentally elbowed Mark on the nose. No problem, we all kept going. We stopped and, then, Mark and I had to face the class and go through some cuts with the bokken (wooden sword). As we started, Mark's nose began to drip blood. First slowly, then, as he increased the speed of his sword-cutting technique, it got faster. Now, Mark was one of those guys that just kept going unless he was told to stop. Mike was behind both of us, so he couldn't see what was happening. The assembled crowd watched, their eyes getting wider by the moment as a crimson fountain was spilling down Mark's white gi. I desperately tried to catch Mike's attention too. Eventually, he spotted it and told Mark to stop and clean himself up. I'm only glad he saw Mark when he did; otherwise, I had visions of his whole gi turning red and the whole crowd passing out!

As you can guess from earlier in the book, my old instructor, Mick Upham was an unpredictable force. Once, on a large multi-styled seminar, one high-graded instructor, whose name I don't recall, was teaching on one of the mat areas when suddenly he was called to the phone. Before leaving the mat, he looked around and spied Mick and asked him if he would take over whilst he was gone. Mick comes on, takes centre stage in front of all these eager people ready to train and says, "Right then, do you want to carry on with this shite or shall we get real?" The assembled group was gobsmacked. I had to stifle a laugh. Mick was a premier ball buster and didn't care what people thought of him. Many didn't like his methods but would not tell him to his face.

The late, great Gary Spiers was also a man who took no prisoners on his seminars. Once, on a seminar in Bristol, he spied a couple of young student lads not taking the training too seriously. He targeted in on one of these lads and said,

"What's that written on your forehead?" The lad was confused.

"What do you mean?" he asked.

Spiers replied, "Do you know what I can see on your forehead?" The kid shook his head.

"I'll tell you, son, fucking victim, that's what I see! It ain't your fault, lad, but if you don't do something to remove it, you are going to run into a whole lot of trouble." The lad was dumbstruck, and Gary patted him on the back and walked off. The moment was priceless.

You never know what to expect from people that join your classes. Most are great, but the minority can be strange. I remember in my early teaching career, I brought a class to an end, and whilst we knelt down, I asked them if they had any questions they wished to ask. Obviously, it was in relation to their training. One elderly guy put up his hand and said, "I have a problem, Kevin."

"Oh yes, what is it?" I asked, expectantly.

"Well, it's my cockatoo!"

I was momentarily thrown. "Sorry?" I replied.

"Well, whenever I practise my moves at home, it goes wild in its cage and makes a hell of a fuss."

By now the rest of the class were pissing themselves with laughter, but this guy I could see was deadly serious. Trying to control my own laughter, I said in my most serious of voices, "Maybe you should put a blanket over the cage so he can't see you."

He thought for a moment and then, quite seriously, replied. "Yes, I think I will do that, thanks!"

Sometimes the totally unexpected can occur. Once, I was on holiday with my family in Goodrington in South Devon. I was waiting outside a newsagents for my wife and children when a huge black four-by-four pulled up by the roadside. It captured my attention immediately, but the guy who got out of it captured it more. It was the legendary Shotokan karateka and film actor Terry O'Neill. I was in my twenties at the time, and I was gobsmacked. I couldn't work out why he was here in this little seaside resort. I had to introduce myself, and we talked. He was heading down the road a few miles to Paignton leisure centre to referee in a large annual karate tournament which, unbeknown to me, was held there each year. Now, Terry was also editor of 'Fighting Arts International' magazine. He asked me if I had this month's copy to which I answered no. So he pops back to his vehicle and comes back with a copy for me. He shook my hand and went on his way.

War stories? My God, there are so many books on the market with one person trying to outdo others in the 'I'm harder than you' department. I have read so much on tough guys that, in the end, the people involved all sound the same. Different name, different face, but same story. It all gets rather boring and repetitive.

I'm not about to glorify violence but at times I had to use my skills to defend myself and survive, especially when I was a younger man. In this chapter I will record a handful of accidents where I was grateful for my training.

Hard? Tough? We all have different ways of interpreting the words. At the end of the day, every city in every country has somebody ready to make a claim or tell a story. Every man involved in martial arts, fighting, or contact sports wants to believe that they are the best or the toughest. But it's all down to on the day and a bit of Lady Luck with you. Anybody can be beaten by fair means or foul, and when you live by the sword, you will die by the sword unless you can get away from that lifestyle. I don't tend to listen too much to all these stories. True or not, I'm not personally bothered. I don't want to have to have a street fight with anybody for the rest of my days. I believe that if somebody is pushed until their 'backs are to the wall', they will fight back no matter if they are good at it or not. I would only fight for survival, not for ego. Just because you don't want to fight doesn't mean you can't.

I grew up in a tough multiracial neighbourhood, and as a young man, I quickly devised many good self-defence plans to avoid and escape the local thugs. I became quite an expert at avoidance. But sometimes, no matter what you did, you were in the wrong place at the wrong time. I took a few beatings and I gave a few. I was mugged at knife point more than once. Fended off a few knife attacks. I was chased down by groups of youths baying for my blood on many occasions. Been attacked with bats, sticks and pool cues. Had bricks and stones hurled at me. Weapons of choice back then were sharpened steel combs, bike chains and pick axe handles and, then, it moved on to Stanley knives.

It was part of growing up. It was not a time of political correctness and ethnic groups didn't integrate a great deal, so if you wandered onto their patch, you had better be good at running or fighting.

In those early days, I wasn't great at either, hence my need to take up martial arts, as I was never going to be Usain Bolt! Also, I witnessed much violence at football matches where sometimes, unwittingly, you got caught up in it. Football violence was rife in the 70s, and clubs such as Manchester United, Leeds, West Ham and Millwall were all notorious. Crowd violence is dangerous and scary. After a few scary incidents, I even carried a knife for protection (never used it). Also, I have gone out with a pair of nunchakus in my coat pocket and even a stun gun.

I have been to pubs and clubs wearing a groin guard and had a gumshield in my pocket because they were so rough.

Doormen then were big, rough bastards that slapped you first and asked questions second. They had to be. The violence in nightclubs in the late 70s and early 80s was brutal. You would go out for a laugh and come home in stitches, as the old joke goes. Broken glass and blood on the dance floor was a normal weekend occurrence. Unbelievably, one of the worst places for trouble was the local ice skating rink! Great for meeting the girls, but shit for avoiding assholes. A kick in the nuts with a pair of ice skating boots is not a pleasant thing!

You guys that live in Bristol and are my age must remember the following clubs. The Locarno, Lords, Papillons, Tiffanys, The Dug Out Club and the Mandrake. They could be heaven or hell.

Also, from an Irish parentage, I returned to Ireland on a few occasions at the height of all the 'troubles' in the late 70s. The British Army were occupying Northern Ireland, and the war with the IRA was at its peak. Cities such as Belfast were like war zones, and it was a frightening place to be as a young man.

Some of the British troops were not much older than me. You were searched going in and out of shops and they stopped you at road blocks. I was told by my cousins when we went into town to not speak because if certain individuals heard my accent, I was going down big time.

I remember once spending the night at the house of one of my uncles' mother in Shankill Road, cowering with my sister and cousins under the bedclothes, listening to bombs exploding and machine gun fire on the streets. All this now seems surreal.

Again, whilst over there, I did my best to keep a low profile but, sometimes, shit happens. I recall that I was out with my cousins walking, and a group of youths confronted us. Many of my relatives live out in the countryside and it is a close-knit community. Word had gone around that my cousins had a visitor from England. These lads didn't like it, and they told me so in no uncertain terms. They were getting aggressive when one of my cousins thought it would be a good move to warn them that I did kung fu. If he thought that this would send the pack fleeing, then he was in for a shock.

One of them got in my face and said, "Come on then, want a fight, do you?" I didn't, but he suddenly punched me in the mouth. It didn't hurt that much, but it drew blood. This seemed to be a signal for them all to move in. I was scared, so I hit this guy with a knifehand strike on the side of the neck. I didn't know how effective it would be but he went down. I tried not to show surprise and sidekicked another in the knee, now warming to the task. Then, to my relief, they scattered and ran.

The word soon went around not to fuck with this English kid. I was feeling on top of the world and enjoying my new-found fame until one of my cousins kindly informed me that they might come back with their older brothers and shoot me!

When I was younger, as I mentioned previously, I enjoyed going to football matches, but in the 70s and early 80s violence was high on the menu and rivalry was extreme. I had many incidents at matches where I was grateful for my fitness to run and also grateful for some fighting skills.

Normally it was gang violence. I must emphasise here I was not a football thug, but sometimes because of the colour of the scarf you wore, you became a target.

One of the worst cases I recall was me and a few mates being chased down the road by a large group of rival fans baying for our blood. I was shitting myself, I can tell you. Running around a corner to a dead end isn't the best of moves. A large padlocked gate faced us, and we all started to climb it rapidly.

My bad leg prevented me from being as swift as my mates, and I was pulled down by the mob who proceeded with a beating.

One thing I knew was I wasn't going down to the floor, or I was finished. I used my aikido footwork to spin and turn from their grabs and punches, then front kicked the nearest one in the balls and then wrist locked another who grabbed my coat. I heard his wrist crack as he fell away. I was pushed up against the fence, and I knew I was in trouble.

I double thumb gouged this guy's eyes and nutted him, but I was running out of strength as somebody punched me in the ear.

Suddenly two police cars skidded to a halt by the mob, and they dispersed. I managed successfully with a spurt of new-found energy to get over the gate and disappear. I had been lucky. I lived to fight another day.

When others know you trained in martial arts, you were always in for a challenge. I tried to keep it a secret, but my mates liked to brag and tell everybody.

Once I was at a youth club when this black lad approached me and said he did karate and that he heard I was some sort of kung fu expert. Before I could reason with him that wasn't particularly true, the challenge was thrown down and peer pressure saw me in the car park with him. My asshole was twitching but I had come too far. I had to save face.

This guy was bigger than me, and through his tight t-shirt I could see the outline of his muscular frame.

I breathed deeply and held my 'bottle'.

He dropped into a stance and then came at me with a barrage of kicks and punches. Most didn't connect. I hit him with my then-favourite spinning back kick in the stomach, and he went down.

I thought it was over, but the game bastard got back to his feet. I didn't give him another chance. I ran in and hit him with a backfist on the nose and swept his legs. This time he didn't get up. I helped him to his feet, and we shook hands. It was over.

I took the congratulations of my mates and went back into the youth club. I excused myself to the toilets and was violently sick. The aftermath of adrenaline.

Back in those days if you trained in martial arts you were regarded either as some deadly killer or a bit of a weirdo. Certain individuals that felt intimidated by you were always calling you out.

I fought guys in the local parks or playing fields on more than one occasion. It was a bit like fight club. Nobody really got seriously hurt. It was just 'young bucks' testing themselves with these 'new and mysterious' techniques. There were many 'would-be Bruce Lees' out there.

I remember a friend of mine walking down the local street in broad daylight when, quite unprovoked, another lad produced a pair of nunchakus from his coat and proceeded to beat on him.

Another fellow martial artist and friend, who shall remain nameless, once took a fleeing assailant down by throwing a ninja star in his back.

I went through a phase of collecting a huge amount of exotic weaponry. Back then you could get hold of practically anything if you had the sources. I had dozens of incredible combat knives and replica guns. Extendable batons, PR-24 side-handled batons, nunchakus of many shapes and sizes and a few Filipino butterfly knives. I had knives that were concealed as belt buckles, credit cards, pens and keyrings. Many Kubotans, brass knuckles, stun guns and pepper sprays. I hasten to say I didn't go around trying these weapons out on people. I just loved training with them and sparring weapon against weapon, finding out their strengths and weaknesses. Also from personal experience, I don't advise you to see what a stun gun or pepper spray may feel like if exposed to either. Yes, not a clever move and both fucking painful.

I also loved training with makeshift weapons. Everyday items that could be used as a weapon in an emergency.

I was grateful of this one night when I was making a call in a phone box (remember those), and a guy pulled open the door to mug me. I instinctively hit him with the telephone receiver right between the eyes, and he ran off. Result.

All this said, to be honest, I had more fights on the mats than ever off them. As a young man in his twenties, I relished at any opportunity to test my skills. On any seminar I went to, I always seemed to encounter somebody who wanted to mix it, and I was only happy to oblige. I wouldn't let anybody take liberties with me, and if they did, they were in for some fun.

A few moments, in particular, stick out in my mind, although at the time, they were far from humorous.

Again, in my aikido days, I was training at my club with a guy who we will call Melvin. He wore a hearing aid, and everybody always made allowances for his lack of hearing, and I felt he played upon this. We were doing Jo techniques (four-foot wooden staff), one for one. After a few goes, Melvin brought the Jo crashing down on my head, and it bloody hurt! He mumbled that he was sorry, so I let it go. A few minutes later, he did it again. Was it lack of control or was he just trying it on? I told him this time to control it and be careful. Lo and behold, a couple of seconds back into drilling, he did it once more. This time, I was angry and felt the anger rise inside me. Did I notice a glimmer of a smile on his lips? I took a deep breath. My head was throbbing with three distinct lumps rising on it. I was not a happy man. This Jo staff was made from solid Japanese red oak and was bloody heavy. I waited for my turn, deflected Melvin's Jo and brought mine down with considerable force squarely on his skull. Take that, you fucker, I thought to myself. He went down like a pack of cards, stunned, in a heap. Unfortunately, my instructor was passing and saw me do it, and I was admonished for dangerous practice. Still, it was worth it. I didn't have any trouble from Melvin again!

I had so many similar incidents over the years that I forget more than I remember. I know that I went through a proving stage and seemed to always be in conflict. For me, martial arts training was a serious business. I didn't do it in any half measures, and I expected others to be like-minded. Of course, this wasn't always the case, and I am sure that over the years, people thought that I was too hard or severe with my training.

I recall, once again, in my aikido days as an orange belt when this guy, who had come from America, joined the club. He was also an orange belt and had gone to great lengths to tell me how he had been training with Chiba Sensei and other top Japanese instructors. My initial thoughts were, great. Another good person to train with. The first time I paired off with him, I realised he could talk the talk but not walk the walk! After I had thrown him over two or three times in my usual style, he started telling me how he had a back problem and could I go easy. Then, he was using stalling tactics by doing up his belt or fixing his gi. This all served to infuriate me as I felt he was a fraud to his grade and couldn't have worked as hard as me to earn it. After this, and on every possible occasion, I tried to partner him and give him some stick. For all his shortcomings, he was still training and trying to bullshit us with name-dropping and tales of his training. In the end, he would do his utmost to avoid me and would skirt around me as I approached him to train. One night, after training, we were all having a drink, and he opened up and admitted when he came to our club that it had frightened him. He said that he hadn't trained nowhere near as intensely as we did, and he had struggled badly. He turned to me and said that I had literally given him nightmares, and he had avoided me like the plague. I admired, at least, his honesty; we shook hands and I agreed to help him out. From then on, we got on all right, but some months later, he returned to the USA. About six months after this, I heard that he had received his Dan grade, which was incredible. Luckily, he never came back to train at our dojo; otherwise, I would have helped him out via the window!

I have met so many people like the above man, who are in love with the idea of training in martial arts, but are living in a fantasy realm, visualising themselves as some great warrior or fighter.

I have knocked them out, choked them out and twisted their joints until they screamed, but I have never done anything to the other person that I wasn't prepared to have done to me.

Here is another crazy incident. I had a guy train with me for a while; let's call him 'Joey'. Now, Joey was a tough man. A street fighter with hands like shovels and a face like a robber's dog. He asked one evening in a class to box with me. At first I didn't want to, but he persisted so I relented.

"I want you to go hard, full out and don't pull your punches. I want to test myself," he told me.

So be it, I thought, so off we went. He wasn't a great boxer, and I am no 'Sugar' Ray Leonard. He was a fighter though, hard as nails and a brawler, plus he could punch. He came in, head down like a bull, swinging hard. I covered up and hit him with a hook to the body and then doubled it to his head. The punches were hard, and he went down to one knee. Then he sprang up and bored forward again. Once more I hit him hard to body and head, and he was down again. He sprang up yet again and swung some big punches, then dropped his head into my face. I now saw red and unloaded a flurry of punches to his head and down he went again. "That's enough, Joey," I said.

He got up, his nose was bleeding. "No, I want some more, come on, I ain't giving up yet," and he steamed in again. I kid you not and this is honest. If I knocked him down another twenty times it would not be an exaggeration. This went on for around fifteen minutes. I finally stopped it. Firstly, because both his eyes were closing over, and he was bleeding heavily from his nose and mouth and, secondly, because my fucking hands hurt from punching him. He had a head as hard as a bowling ball.

When it stopped, he shook my hand and said, "Fucking great, I enjoyed it, but I have had enough now, cheers." He then just wandered off.

I shook my head in disbelief. Part of me didn't feel good that I dished out this beating, but that was the way it went.

I didn't see him for a week, and I began to worry that he was in a hospital bed with tubes sticking out of him, or I was going to read about him in the obituary column of the local newspaper. Thankfully, he did return and no worse for wear apart from telling me that his head had hurt for days and, oh yes, his face looked a bit like the fucking 'Elephant man's'!

One of my pet hates is an individual who will have watched you train your balls off and maybe sparred and grappled several people whilst they have been sitting on their ass, and then they ask if you want a 'roll'. I have experienced this many times, where the said individual knows you are tired, and they are going to try and take advantage of that fact.

On one such occasion I encountered a guy who did this. He asked me for a grapple. He wasn't a novice and knew what he was up to, which made it worse.

I was tired and was at the end of my training, but it pissed me off that he did this, so I took up his offer.

As usual he steamed in trying to take the piss. But this was like a red rag to a bull for me. I got angry which I shouldn't have, but he was going at it hard.

I got him to cross body top and locked it in and smashed two big knees into his ribs; I didn't pull them. I then slammed his arm down into a figure-four elbow lock (Americana) and pulled it down tight. I was ready to rip his elbow up hard, that would have broken it, but at the very last second, I stopped and regained my composure. I suppose his shout of fear jolted me back to reality.

I walked off into the changing rooms, angry that he had taken me to that point where I really wanted to hurt him badly. Martial arts on the mats is all about control, but on that occasion I almost lost it. That is not the Warrior way.

On another occasion, I was grappling with a guy who was mega-aggressive but also really awkward and clumsy. Whilst passing his guard he pulled up his knees erratically and one of them smashed me in the face. The loud crack told me instantly the idiot had broken my nose. It hurt like hell, but I carried on and passed his legs and got to mount position straddling his chest where I beat down on his head with punches. He rolled to his stomach and I locked in a strangle and squeezed hard. He tapped instantly but part of me wanted to hold it on a little longer, seeing he had stupidly ruined my film-star good looks!

Training was uncompromising in the very early days. We didn't have any protective gear and even if you wore a groin guard, you were viewed as a pussy. Forearms and shins bruised purple was a normal occurrence. They were badges of courage. Being choked out, brought back around and choked out again was a rite of passage. There was no such thing as health and safety and all that human rights stuff. You were training in a martial art, so man up and get on with it!

Most weekends, I would travel to broaden my knowledge on various seminars and trained in many diverse arts to sample them and see what they were all about.

I mentioned earlier about going on a seminar in ninjutsu, where senior instructors were impressing upon all who were present about how they wanted their art to be taken seriously and that they didn't want to be comic-book figures hiding in the dark and performing exotic tricks and techniques.

Then, in the lunch break, I watched two guys clad in black from head to toe trying to 'capture' each other with weighted nets and swords. There seemed to be some sort of paradox going on here!

Sometimes, while teaching, things don't always go according to plan, and you just must improvise and go with the flow. On one occasion, I was teaching on a seminar, and I called one of my lads out to throw a punch at me so I could demonstrate a certain counter. This lad had a terrific and very awkward right hook, which caused us a lot of problems.

I was flowing on a high and getting a good response from the gathered group. I asked him to throw the punch, but I wasn't concentrating fully. The hook went around my cover-up guard and connected hard with my jaw. Luckily for me, it was high up on the jaw and not on the chin. It connected with a sickening dull thud, and I felt the blow. I was suddenly seeing double, and my legs felt slightly rubbery. I shook it off and said, "See how difficult it is to block a punch. You can't afford to let that happen." I, then, just carried on showing it correctly. The group must have thought that that was one hell of a graphic way to get your point over!

At another seminar, I called out a young lady who used to train with me called Rachael. She was a tough girl and would mix it with any of the men and hold her own. Sometimes, though, she could be full on and not pull her punches. At this course, I brought her up to show how a lady can defend herself if grabbed from the front. I wanted the scenario to look as real as possible, so I steamed in and grabbed her hard and forcefully in a bear hug around the waist.

Her adrenaline must have kicked in and without an ounce of control, she headbutted me in the face, sunk her teeth into my shoulder (bloody hard) and kneed me in the testicles. The watching group was stunned, but not as much as me! I could easily have gone to my knees from the groin shot, but I gritted my teeth and working to my full professional capacity, I turned to the group and just said, "See, that's how it's done!" (Spoken in a rather squeaky voice!)

I always enjoyed demanding training and one of my black belts that I mentioned earlier, Mike Griffin, was always up for this, and we had some wars together. One of the things that we would do regularly at the end of a class would be to attack each other randomly, one for one with grabs, holds, punches, kicks or weapons, standing or on the ground. It usually started off sensibly, and then deteriorated into each of us trying to come up with a worse and more awkward type of attack. One evening, we had pretty much exhausted our repertoire and Mike had pinned me up against a wall in a frontal body hold, crushing the air out of my lungs. He was grinning and saying, "Come on then, how are you going to get out of this?" I waited till the moment was right and then clamped my hands firmly to his face and kissed him long and hard on the mouth! I tell you, he dropped me faster than hot coals and was gagging and spitting and rubbing his mouth. While he was doing this, I shot a kick to his groin and a following elbow to the spine and retorted, "That's how!" He was never the same again!

As mentioned elsewhere, our rituals for fooling about knew no bounds. My all-time classic came when I was invited to Mike's 'wedding do' on the evening after he had got married. Mike had hired a delightful hotel, and all his family, relatives, work colleagues and friends were there. I arrived with a few others from my club and mingled in and had a drink. I asked where Mike was, and I was told that he was up on the dance floor doing karaoke. He had had a few to drink and was doing his George Michael impression.

Now, Mike wasn't a drinker, but hey, it was his big day so he was celebrating. I hunted him down, and he had drawn quite a crowd with his singing. There he was, still in morning dress, giving it stick. He hadn't noticed me, so I crept up behind him and grabbed him by the balls! I lifted him and took him to the floor. Mike was, to say the least, taken by surprise! The assembled family and friends were in shock, thinking, who is this bald maniac attacking Mike? I loved every minute and caught him good and proper. We laughed about it later, but at the time, I don't think he found it too funny.

Now, Mike had been pestering me about grading for his second Dan, and I kept telling him that he wasn't ready, but at every opportunity, he kept on and on. I thought up another little 'surprise' for him on his wedding day.

At the night party, there was a table laden with wedding gifts which Mike and his wife would open when they returned from their honeymoon. This all gave me the idea. I wrapped up, in special wedding paper, a brand new white belt and labelled the present, 'To Mike from Kevin, Something I knew you've been waiting for'. I put this amongst the other gifts. Now, I knew Mike was desperate for his second Dan, and I also knew that when he read the label, he would think his grade had arrived. Can you imagine his face when he frenziedly tore off the wrapping paper to find a white belt! I just wish I could have been a fly on the wall at that moment. He gave me some stick when he later caught up with me, but it was worth it!

Sometimes, I feel you can get obsessed with training. When I was really going through a mad stage of ground grappling, I found it started to overlap into other areas of my life. On one occasion, I was having a moment of romantic passion with my wife I even started to pass the guard! I tell you, that was bad enough, but the finishing armbar really pissed her off! These are all only jokes, folks, honest!

To put the record straight, I never really was a ground fighter until I got heavily into MMA and was fortunate to train with some great people such as Renzo Gracie, John Machado, Erik Paulson, Neil Adams and many others over the years.

Another incident that happened recently, I remember, clearly illustrated to me that no matter how good a fighter you are, there will be a time when you feel completely vulnerable and all the macho big-man stuff counts for nothing.

I was on holiday in Lanzarote with Tina. We had also taken her dad as a treat for his eighty-second birthday. We stayed in a villa and from day one, I was a little uneasy about how open it was and how easily the garden and pool area could be accessed.

I thought that maybe I was overreacting and taking my awareness skills a little too seriously. But from being a veteran of those skills, I should have trusted my senses.

One night, we were asleep in bed when Tina woke up and said to me, "I think Dad wants something. He's in the room."

Stumbling from a deep sleep, I half woke to answer her and then I heard the tone of her voice change as she said, "It's not Dad, there is a man in here."

I clicked awake and saw a shadowy figure standing over me by the side of the bed. I instinctively shot up and dragged back the bedclothes as the figure turned to exit the room.

I knew that there was a light switch on the wall by the door, but in the darkness, I couldn't find it. I reached out fumbling along the wall and at the same time, keeping my eye on the figure's fleeing back.

By the time, I hit the light switch; he was out of the room. I went down the hallway into the living area, flicking lights on as I went. The place was empty.

I was beginning to think that I had dreamt the whole thing. Then, I saw the patio doors swinging open in the breeze and the realisation hit me like an icy cold hand.

I suddenly went into code red and span around scanning the room. Was he still in here hiding?

I, then, thought of my father-in-law. I crept silently down the hallway, instructing Tina to stay in the bedroom. I quietly pushed open his door and to my relief, he was sleeping undisturbed.

I now went and searched every nook and cranny of the villa. I knew that in my heart, he had probably gone, but I had to be sure.

I, then, went outside and scanned the area, but there was no sign of him. By this point, my adrenaline was coming down and I felt weak. The whole thing seemed so surreal.

We contacted the villa rep, and they, in turn, got the police, but nothing came of it. It totally unnerved us. To think that somebody had opened the patio doors so silently and had the balls to walk right into our bedroom undetected was scary.

He had been reaching to open my bedside drawer, looking for money. It was still partially open. My t-shirt lay on the floor. He had used it to hide any fingerprints. He had been a pro, no doubt. The way he had unhurriedly just walked back out of the villa confirmed this to me.

The thing, though, that really got to me was the fact that if he had wanted to stab or shoot me, he would have had no problem. If Tina hadn't woken up, fuck knows what would have happened.

It was the first time in my life for a long while that I really felt vulnerable and exposed. I tell you, I didn't like it. Big tough black belt or not, this was one occasion I had to accept that I would have been in trouble.

This illustrated to me something I always preach. Self-defence skills are scenario-based. You will never know where or when you will need them. One thing is for sure: you won't be warmed up, stretched out and have your MMA gloves on!

Awareness is the vital key to survival. All the fighting skills in the world won't help you in a situation like the above. But, hey, don't we feel safest when we are in our house tucked up in bed.

Although it happens we probably wouldn't even consider it happening to us. So there is a lesson learnt. Sometimes when we feel we are at our safest is when we can be at our most vulnerable. Life teaches us a lot.

"Life is all about living experiences and making memories."

More Memories from the World of MMA

I have many fond memories of my time in the world of MMA. I have seen and experienced so much in this great combat sport. I have also met some fantastic people. Guys that stand out for me in my neck of the woods are the likes of Richard 'Shaky' Shore and his Tillery Combat team from Wales. All of them are true warriors and, a great bunch of lads. 'Shaky' has worked tirelessly to put MMA on the map big time in Wales. Much respect to him. I also have fond memories of grading him for his second Dan in ju jutsu.

Team Trojan and Paul Sutherland are another great bunch of fighters. Paul and I go back a long way to the early days of MMA.

Stu Pike of Dragonslair has also blazed a trail here in the South West.

Many individuals I have met stand out over the years for varied reasons and here, I give a few honourable mentions. Dale Adams, Paul Jenkins, Mark Woodard, Alex Owen, Mark Weir, Leigh Remedios, Ian Freeman, Sol Gilbert, Neil Hall, Mark Goddard, Howard Hughes, Mick Broster, Mark Spencer, Ian Rossiter, James Thompson, Paul Reed, Wes Murch. These are but a small selection of the many top people.

Here are some stories from that time.

Way back in March 2002, 'Ultimate Combat' had their first MMA show in Chippenham, Wiltshire, and I was kindly invited to go along and be a guest on one of their VIP cage side tables. It was the first professional MMA show I had been to, and it was a cracking experience and event.

Bruce Buffer, the legendary UFC fight announcer, was invited over to introduce the show. It was brilliant to see him here from the States opening a local event and quite an achievement for Dale Adams and all who were involved in running with the show.

The event opened with an exploding canister of ticker tape in the centre of the cage. It was impressive, along with the lights, dry ice, music and Buffer doing his famous welcoming intro.

Once the dust, or in this case, ticker tape, settled, the organisers suddenly had a problem about how to rid the cage of it before the first fighters came in. Brushes were issued with no effect. No vacuum was to be found. It was panic stations, until old 'pro' himself Bruce Buffer took a towel and started vigorously to wave it to and fro to blow the ticker tape out of the cage. The crowd gave him an enormous ovation, and I am sure that he thought, "Yeah, the yank has saved your 'limey' asses again." What a hilarious start to a truly great event and the pathway for many more UCs, of which I was proud to have fought on two of the shows.

Ultimate Combat shows were always top-notch, and I have been privileged to be involved in fighting or cornering on a great many of them. So many great fighters were on the shows. Guys that were trailblazers for the sport of MMA. Here are just a few. Damien Riccio, Pierre Guillett, Lars Besand, Marc Goddard, Alex Owen, Dave McLaughlin, Mick Broster, Ross Mason, Paul Jenkins, Pat Carr, Sol Gilbert, Matt Unwin, Zelg Galesic. The names just go on and on. I have many great memories from some memorable nights. They were incredibly exciting times.

As I am writing, this weekend, one of my good mates and former fighters Nad Narimani is fighting in London on 'CWFC 64'. Nad has the ability, with the right coaching and guidance, to go all the way to the top in this sport. I would, someday, love to see him enter the octagon at the UFC.

Nad came to me back around 2009-10 to train in ju jutsu and I soon recognised that he had a raw talent and great spirit to become an MMA fighter. I am proud to have started him on his journey and under my 'Impact' fight banner, he boasted a record of 7-0 in the cage, as well as winning a gold medal in four tap out fights at the 'Spartan Grappling Challenge.'

He was one of the hardest-training students and fighters I ever had the pleasure of training, and I remember our sparring bouts sort of fondly until he just became a juggernaut, and the 'old boy' here had to call time on them to preserve what was left of his good looks!

I have many great memories and stories of my time training Nad, but here are a few funny ones.

Nad fought on a fair few 'Knuckle Up' shows in Bath and became a firm crowd-pleaser. His seven fights with me were all wins by KO, stoppage or tap out. He was a force to be reckoned with and still is, by the way.

The shows were run by Matt Hand and also Dane Bowers of 80s boy band 'Another Level.'

Dane always did the after-fight interviews in the cage.

At 'Knuckle Up 4' in November 2010, Nad won his fight in great style. The show was being televised, and everybody beforehand had been told how to conduct themselves in front of the camera.

So, Dane Bowers holds the mike in front of Nad and asked him how the fight went. Nad really is a guy who lets his fighting talk for him. He was pumped up after the win, and the adrenaline was still coursing through his body when he replies to the question, "Well, I just went out and fucking done it!"

Dane Bowers' jaw dropped for a second, knowing that this was all going down on film. Then, like a true 'pro', he laughed and said something along the lines of, "Well, thanks, Nad, for that candid answer."

All the corner crew and crowd were laughing their heads off. Nad hadn't even realised he had sworn until after when we told him behind the scenes. What a great showstopper that was... but not as good as his next stunt on the following show in March 2011.

Again, Nad had a great win, and Dane was back in the cage with the mike. Obviously wary of the last interview, he subtly mentioned, "Don't forget that we are on film, Nad," before he began his post-fight interview.

Now, earlier in the day, Nad, myself and the corner team of 'Impact' joked about what he should do if he won this time. We said that he should lift and slam Dane Bowers in the cage. Little did we know that he was going to do it. So, his interview went well without incident, and no doubt, Dane was breathing a sigh of relief. Suddenly, Nad steamed forward, lifted him as if he was a feather and slammed him to the cage floor. Dane went one way and his microphone the other. We all took that as a sign to run over from the corner and give him a bit of a 'kicking'. It was a priceless moment and fair play to Dane, once he had found his composure, and probably his spinal cord again, he took it in good sport. A few people commented that it was probably the biggest hit he ever had!

Great memories of a truly great fighter and also outside of the cage, a lovely guy. Although he now fights under 'Iron Man MMA', he is always welcome at 'Impact Gym Bristol' where his grass roots were. All the best for this weekend, my friend. Do what you do best, and I am sure that you will have another win on your record.

I have seen some great fights in MMA. Epic battles, quick knockouts or submissions and major upsets. Many of my fighters have been involved in a few. My own sons, Tom and Jake, Dale Utting, Ross Mould, Dan Bond, Mark Skidmore, Matt Law, Stuart Mowling, Paul Bush, Billy Gibbs and Chris Fone. Back before this generation was, Matt Sperring, Ross MacKenzie, Nick Orchard, Paul Croft, Matt Stone and Steve Devine, to name but a few.

One fight that stands out in my mind was one of my then own fighters from 'Team Impact' way back in 2009. The show was 'Tear Up', a local Bristol event, and my fighter, Ross Mould, was matched against Harvey Dines of 'Gracie Barra Bath' coached by Salvatore Pace. It was a decent match-up, and I knew that Harvey was very capable on the ground. Ross was as durable a fighter as I have ever worked with. What he may have lacked in overall skill, he made up for in spirit, guts and a dogged determination. He had an uncanny resilience at that time to not be submitted easily because of his super bendy rubber limbs.

The fight was an epic battle. To say Harvey dominated it was an understatement. He took the fight straight to Ross from the off, gaining mount many times and raining untold punishment down on Ross. But, somehow, Ross covered and worked escapes and basically hung in there when others would have surely tapped. The referee was poised on many occasions to step in but just as that seemed to be going to happen, Ross would work and move and do enough to keep in the fight. After two rounds, he was looking worse for wear and I couldn't believe that he was still in there and up for it. I told him that he had to stop Harvey as he was too far behind on points. I checked if he wanted to go out for this third and final round, and he said, "Yes."

Again, he was taken down and battered. Harvey had poured so much into this fight that he was very tired. I am sure that he couldn't believe that Ross was still in it. No one could. But in it he was. As Harvey continued his tired assault from Ross' guard, he just seemed to run out of gas and leaned in too far. That was all it took for Ross to secure a tight leg triangle and tap Harvey out.

We went crazy. It was one of the best turnarounds to a fight I have ever seen and just goes to show you how unpredictable MMA can be. Harvey was gutted, Ross elated and the corner and I over the moon. What a night!

Ross never ever had a dull fight when he was with me. Each one held its own drama. Ross is now establishing himself as a MMA referee and has retired as an active fighter. I shared many highs and lows with him, but I personally think this was his best win ever. Much respect to a true warrior.

I mentioned Paul Jenkins earlier on, and what a good fighter he was. He was also a great comedian and always up for a laugh. Here are just a few of the things I remember about him.

I recall him on a show where all the fighters would go out for a parade around the cage before the show started. In the early days of MMA, we all wore the brief and tight Vale Tudo trunks. On the way out of the dressing room for the parade, Paul took a banana from a fruit bowl and shoved it down his trunks. I watched from the wings, crying with laughter as he paraded around the cage, his arms aloft with a sizeable bulge on display!

I judged on the 'Cage Rage 2' show in 2003 in Bethnal Green, London. Paul was fighting another notable talent, Gaz Roriston. Paul came into the cage and spotted me at the judges' table. He ran over and proceeded to shower me from his water bottle.

I remember that he fought a great fight, and in the break before the final round, Gaz was kneeling in his corner getting instructions from his team when Paul crept over and sat down behind him listening as well. The poor old referee didn't know what to do.

When Paul was on the fight card, you just didn't know what to expect from entering the cage in a Borat-style mankini to riding in dressed as an ostrich. It was always funny. There was never a dull moment when he was in your corner room/warm-up area.

I have really witnessed the weird and wonderful in the world of MMA. One of my early fighters, Nick Orchard, didn't have a lot of luck in his short career. Two major moments stand out with him that stick in my mind are when he fought on an 'Anger Management' show in Weston-super-Mare. As I walked him to the door of the arena and we were waiting for his entrance music to start up, a mass fight broke out in the crowd, which spilled right out of the doors right in front of us. As the security got stuck in to break it up, I had to shield Nick and tell him to keep focused. A pretty tall order when there are bodies all around you swinging punches and throwing chairs!

On another occasion, between seeing his opponent at the rules reading to getting in the cage, his opponent was changed for a 'lookalike'. We had no knowledge of it and we weren't told. It was only after the fight that it came to light that this wasn't the same man we had met to fight earlier on!

I have seen the legendary Royce Gracie referee the top of the bill fight on 'Cage Rage'. He spent most of the time gazing out into the crowd and forgetting he was refereeing at all. Suddenly, it would dawn on him, and he would then try to make head or tail of who was winning and what was going on. It was a strange moment.

Being involved in MMA was an incredible experience. I experienced it as a fighter, coach, cornerman and judge, and enjoyed it all.

I was the first person in Bristol to start up an MMA class way back in 1998. At the time, the phrase MMA wasn't even coined. The classes were rough and ready and very tough. The lads that came to my door were all new to it and we all worked hard to progress the sport. In a little room under a gym with just some mats, I developed my first real generation of MMA fighters. We had no ring, no cage and no proper kit to speak of, but we all had spirit, heart and ambition.

We had no branded fight wear like there are these days. It was speedos or board shorts and a pair of bag gloves.

I can recall getting my first pair of Harbinger gloves (then used in the UFC) and a pair of Bad Boy fight trunks. I thought I was the business.

It would be fair of me to say that nearly all of the MMA fighters and grapplers from my area that went on to good things in the sport trained with me at one time or another, and I am proud to have given them a start at grass roots levels.

Men such as James Thompson, Paul Reed, Greg Knapp, Jason McCauley, Steve Devine, Wes Murch, Matt Sellars, Nad Narimani and many more, graced my mats as young and up-and-coming fighters.

I have been fortunate to meet, associate and train with the world's best in this sport, and I am honoured to have been a part of the evolution of the most exciting combat sport on the planet.

I got to play a big part in its development here in the UK and enjoyed every minute of it. It was a very special time in my life, and I will always remember it fondly and all the wonderful people I met through it.

"The cage is not the place for wannabes and dreamers. When the door shuts you either put up or shut up."

Heroes and Influences in the World of Combat.

My heroes and influences in the martial arts have been many and also varied depending on the stage I was at in my career. For anybody who started martial arts in the 70s, Bruce Lee must be a massive influence and a hero. The image of this icon on the front of a magazine today, some thirty-five-plus years after his untimely death, can still boost its sales. His films are still avidly watched over and over, and there always seem to be a new book in the offing about his life. This goes to show what a phenomenal influence he was, and still is, so many years down the line. Stripping away all the razzmatazz and bullshit about him, he truly was a man ahead of his time in the martial arts. In the 60s, he was training and experimenting with what we know today, forty years on, as cross training and mixed martial arts. If he were alive today, I'm sure he would fully support the MMA scene and been a big part of it. I believe this was his vision for martial arts training.

Chuck Norris was also another great example of a true martial artist and his story of his rise to fame is truly inspirational.

Dan Inosanto is also a martial arts legend who has been top drawer for decades and is still out there breaking new ground. How can you not be influenced by these men?

On a personal level, one of my first instructors, John Bennett, is a man I greatly respect. He took time with me to give me the best of instruction, but also advice when I was a young man. He became a close friend, and I admired his straightforward manner, honesty and integrity. When you are a young man in your teens, you think you know it all, and nobody can tell you anything. Well, I always had time to listen to John and heed his advice. It takes a special kind of person to do this, and that was John. I bumped into him recently. He is now in his 70s, still as fit as a fiddle and training to run yet another marathon. Truly inspirational. He is a little man in stature but a big, big influence.

Mickey Upham will always be the man that opened the door to what I call 'real' combat ju jutsu. He changed the way I viewed ju jutsu forever and planted the seeds that took me to where I wanted to be.

Dave Turton is another who keeps the flag flying for 'old school' combat training. These guys are all in the minority these days.

People are buzzing now about systems such as Kapap and Krav Maga. Great systems, no doubt, but the guys just mentioned and their like have been doing this stuff for decades. They are unsung heroes. There is nothing new out there. It has just been re-packaged and resold. Disarming knives and firearms was always part of our training. It isn't something new or exclusive to the new boys on the block! I remember going out in the woods to train with deactivated guns and live blades on more than one occasion.

I have always been a big boxing fan, and in the 1980s, men like Hagler, Leonard, Duran and Hearns were my boxing heroes. Thomas the 'Hitman' Hearns was particularly my favourite. I even named my oldest son, Thomas, after him. Hearns was a legend at welter, light middle, middle, super middle and light heavy – five world titles! I have never seen a faster or more accurate jab than the 'Hitman's', and although we bear no resemblance body-wise, I tried hard to emulate his moves. Duran was also a hero, a fantastic and underrated boxer known more for his brawling techniques. He was a superb fighter and body puncher. These men inspired me greatly as I was training. Also, guys like Aaron Pryor, Alexis Arguello and Mike McCallum. The list is endless. I loved to watch Julio César Chavez fight. He could have fought his bouts in a telephone box or on a handkerchief laid out on the ground. He was a relentless boxer/puncher and one of the cruellest body punchers in the world.

Our own Nigel Benn was a legend along with Eubanks and Watson. Classic fights and let's not forget Barry McGuigan.

Evander Holyfield is also a hero of mine. I have never known a more dedicated boxer with such strong belief in himself. He defied critics so many times and pulled off unbelievable results. Also, he is an incredibly humble man and a true champion.

I was a big boxing fan and a bit of a historian. I loved reading about the bare-knuckled champs like John L. Sullivan through to Jack Dempsey, Bob Fitzsimmons, then later Marciano, Liston, Ali, Frazier, etc.

In the big wide world of martial arts, I have immense respect for Royce Gracie. He put the world of MMA on the map with superb technical performance of his Brazilian ju jutsu. People have been too quick to knock 'this man', but let's remember that he won three UFC shows in a row when you had to fight three or four times on the night. Most of his victories were against bigger and stronger men. Plus, let's also remember that he wasn't the best of the Gracie family clan. He took the Gracie challenge squarely on his shoulders and must have been under unbelievable pressure to uphold his family's honour. He is a true martial arts warrior and, in my eyes, a hero.

Another martial artist that I highly rate is Erik Paulson. This guy has got to be one of the most well-rounded fighters in the world, plus a superb technician, not only in the striking and kicking arts but, also, grappling and submission. His training tapes are fantastic and motivational. He is also a down-to-earth guy with no ego.

All the early 'Pride' fighters were also a massive influence on me in the burgeoning days of MMA. They were trailblazers. Giants in their sport and incredibly tough men. Coleman, Kerr, Randleman, Cro Cop, Sakuraba and Nogueira, amongst many others. All were absolute monsters of their day.

Bas Rutten is another guy I absolutely love. A monster of a fighter and such a funny man.

Finally, no round-up of inspirational men would be complete without my friend, Geoff Thompson. I have never hidden my admiration for this man, and he has constantly inspired me to greater things. Geoff is a man who, whilst climbing the ladder of success, has always had time to reach out and help others up a few more rungs. This is the mark of a great person. What I admire most about Geoff is that he was the first martial artist who openly, in public, admitted that it was all right to be scared and feel fear, and he spoke quite candidly about this. He made a whole lot of people feel better about themselves when he disclosed this.

Up to that time, martial artists were all totally machismo. No fear, no pain, indestructible and immovable. None would admit to fear, as they would see it as a sign of weakness. So, all others in their wake followed suit.

Geoff changed all this and opened many new doors and horizons for a lot of people. He has booked his place in martial arts history, and I am proud to be a friend. There are many others in the martial arts that I respect, admire and like. Too many to list, but the people I have previously mentioned are high on my list.

I have all the time in the world for 'real' instructors. Guys who have plied their trade relentlessly, year in, year out, without selling out to the McDojo money-making machine. Also, guys who have not elevated themselves onto a pedestal where they are living in a 'Walter Mitty' fantasy land.

I have witnessed too many of the above-mentioned. These people believe that they are some sort of Jedi Knights. They take the money, demonstrate how deadly they are but are not really concerned about teaching a student and helping them achieve.

As a novice on the mats, a few minutes of any of my instructors' time were like gold dust, and you would leave your training feeling ten foot tall.

I don't want people just to remember me for my techniques. I want them to remember my teaching, my approach and my enthusiasm for them to learn. I love teaching martial arts, but I also love training in them. There is not a week that goes by when I am not working with my students. I am a hands-on instructor. I am always on the mat, which is my domain. It's what I do best. On the mats, I can switch on and perform. Just like an actor or singer in front of a camera or walking onto a stage. It's where they belong and come into their own. The mats are my stage, and I want to be active on them for as long as possible. If you don't train regularly, you lose your edge, sharpness and hunger, and you will be fooling yourself if you think otherwise. Other instructors still blazing a trail in my home city of Bristol and have been in their arts many years are the likes of, Simon O'Brien, Martin Hurd, Jon Munden, Paul Moylett, Stuart Davies, Mike O'Connor, Andy and Chris Davies, Phil Allen, Sean Viera and Pedro Bessa. These guys have been around the block and still can do a bit. All should be inspirations to any up-and-coming youngsters. I take my hat off to you and am proud to call you my friends.

I have always been a firm believer in practise what you preach and, in the same token, preach what you practise. If I tell you that I have experienced boxing, full contact training, hard submission grappling and MMA, I have, and I will teach from those experiences. If I put you through an arduous programme of conditioning and exercise, it will be nothing I haven't experienced. That's how I am.

I will not tell tall tales, exaggerate the truth or make out I'm something I'm not. What you see is what you get. I don't class myself as a master, but I have got vast knowledge and experience in the martial arts. I don't consider myself to be a premier fighter or killer Ninja Turtle, but I have talked the talk and walked the walk. For all I have achieved, I know there are others who have achieved more, and I am not so wrapped up in my own abilities that I can't learn from somebody else. I hate frauds, bullshitters and those that promise but don't deliver.

Dedication and commitment are the key things that most great martial artists have in abundance.

I am a great believer in both above-mentioned things. I have always tried to give one hundred percent in my training or teaching, and I respect others that do the same. In my time, I have been let down on many occasions by students who could not show the desire or commitment to push themselves that little bit further, or individuals who took but couldn't return the favour and give back. It saddens me that these people that I spent so much time and effort with, so easily throw you into touch when something more important comes along or when their enthusiasm begins to fade.

There are many times, as a professional instructor, that I have wished I had the night off or cringed at the thought of having to teach, but I've carried on and done it, and to the best of my ability. I don't think it's too much to ask for a bit of the same commitment back but, sadly, this isn't always the case.

I really do get pissed with individuals telling me how they want to pass this grade or that grade, or how they want to compete, or how they will try to get to certain classes, and then let you down time and time again. I often wondered how many classes I would have had if I had the same attitude and approach to teaching.

The excuses I have heard over the years have been many about why a person isn't training or can't make it. Sure, some are genuine; others are laughable. I have heard so many that I now let them go through one ear and out the other.

We can all find excuses for all our shortcomings. Most come down to commitment and dedication.

It is easy to find a reason not to do something. It takes great courage and tenacity to find a reason to get up and do it.

It all boils down to how much you want something. If you want to be a great musician, artist, actor, footballer, fighter or black belt, you have got to be prepared for a lifetime of sacrifice and dedication. If you aren't prepared to do this, you will not make it.

If you want to dabble or be a recreational trainer then don't be surprised with the return you get.

If you deposit a penny in the bank, what will you see as your return? If you deposit one hundred thousand pounds, the return will be substantially different.

Many people are looking for big returns without any noticeable deposits. It doesn't work like that.

Yes, it's hard work but if it was easy we would all be doing it. If you want something in life, the bottom line is you must ask yourself, "How bad do I want this, and what am I prepared to sacrifice to achieve it?"

Anything is achievable but it will come at a price.

"To know what life is worth, you have to risk it sometimes."

Dark Days

As I stated at the start of this book, I wanted to document my entire career, the good and the bad. This chapter was difficult to write, but it was essential to my story and where I am now.

The year 2011 heralded my half-century on the planet. It is a sobering thought that you have lived through fifty years of your life and seen and done most things. I have experienced the good and the bad that life can throw at me and, somehow, I am still standing. This chapter outlines dark times that pushed my will and resolve to the brink. A bad time in my life where I was ready to chuck in the world of martial arts that had shaped my very being. It was a time when I fell out of love with my passion and was lost for a while. It is a place I never want to go back to again, and I thank God that I had the strength to pull myself back.

I speak about this period of my life not for sympathy but to rather illustrate that sometimes your opponents are intangible ones. The kind of opponent that a kick or punch won't defeat.

As I tried to lead the life of a warrior, I realised that there is so much more to it than physical skills. You must also be incredibly mentally strong to overcome the invisible enemies that sometimes invade your life. If you are not prepared for them, they will take you down.

I will confess here, at this time in my life, that I was down but not out. They say the mark of a true champion is to get up off the floor and fight back and win. It is hard for me to write this chapter, but I need to show you that no matter how terrible things get human beings are incredible with so much untapped potential. It is not until your back is firmly against the wall that we truly find out about ourselves.

But I am getting ahead of myself. Let me reveal the good and bad as I bring you up to present day…

January 16th 2011 started a black period in my life. My father passed away. It was a sudden and massive heart attack that claimed him. He was eighty-four years of age.

My sister Brenda and I were at his house when the incident occurred. We stood powerless watching the paramedics working hard for thirty minutes to resuscitate him. I knew in my heart that he was gone. I had to help lift him onto the stretcher, and I just remember looking at his shoes as he was covered over and thinking how new they looked. Strange how you remember the craziest things.

The hardest thing was the fact that for many years, he had cared for my mother who had had two debilitating strokes and now had developed the onset of dementia. She just sat there on the sofa while all this was happening around her, not realising she had lost her husband and I, her son, my dad.

From the moment I was told officially in hospital that my father was dead, something shifted in me. I was now the head of the family. The buck stopped with me, and I felt a great and driven sense of responsibility for all my family. I went on autopilot addressing all the pressing matters that had to be dealt with when something tragic like this happens.

I knew, in that instant, that fear was rapidly coming. I know this because I have been trapped in the spiral of worry, anxiety and fear more times than I care to remember. As a boy, a teenager and a young man, I suffered more than my share of the dreaded spectre of fear tapping on my shoulder, usually when I least expected it. Yes, fear still likes to gate crash my party and piss on my parade. No one is immune, sorry to say.

Firstly, fear that I had lost my father. Fear that he had been my mother's sole carer. He had been stubborn and refused all help and support from any official source. He wanted to do it all with help from the family.

I now knew that Mum would have to go into a home. The family house would have to be sold to go towards her care. All my father's and mother's finances would have to be sorted out, and a will would have to be read. Funeral arrangements had to be organised. Along with managing my own business and family, we were just in the process of looking to sell our own home. Also, my father-in-law was just convalescing from a major heart operation, my brother-in-law was seriously ill, my youngest son was getting married and I was going to celebrate a fiftieth birthday. Apart from that, nothing much was fucking happening in my life!

Here, in England, were just my sister and my wife as direct family, as my parents were from Ireland. The buck stopped well and truly here. Overnight, and for the next few years, my life was bedlam.

I never really had time to mourn my father's passing. I deeply regret that. But I felt I couldn't. I believed if I let myself lose control everything else would come tumbling down. I had to suck it up and get on with it.

Did I feel scared, anxious, stressed and worried? Yes, you fucking bet. Could I cope with it, be strong, come through the turmoil? Who knew? But I did know that I was equipped with the tools and knowledge to deal with it. Now, it was down to me. Sink or swim time.

I have faced adversity in my training life many times and faced it down, but this was going to be tougher.

Once more in my life, I had to embrace fear and make it work for me.

I could not envisage how all these things would completely turn my life on its head. I couldn't think of my loss. I had to think of my mum, the house and the finances.

I had to battle with bureaucracy, red tape and bullshit of councils, solicitors, estate agents, pensions and care homes. It was an unending stream of faceless people all wanting their pound of flesh. Every day brought a fresh challenge. Most days, I felt like I was banging my head against a brick wall. One step forward and two back. I felt like I was trying to hold the tide back like King-fucking-Canute, and I didn't know how much strength I had left. I felt alone.

While this all went on, I still had to deal with my own business and keep my classes, etc. going. My sons did help me, and I am grateful for that, but eventually, you have got to resume your role. I had to put on my professional face and get on with my coaching but, inside, unknown to anybody else, I was unravelling.

It was against all my nature, but I couldn't stop it from happening. I felt the walls closing in on me. I found that I had a glass in my hand too often and was sitting up late at night on my own, watching mindless shit on the television to escape the life around me. I had never been like this before. I loved life and was always looking for the next challenge. I had always been optimistic and mostly positive. I had always prided myself on my fitness and strength and, deep down, I knew I should break this cycle but, unbeknown to me at the time, I was slipping into depression.

Through this, I still managed to operate on some level. Looking back, I am not sure how I did it. Deep inside, I still believed I held a responsibility to all around me, and I guess this kept me in the game. I have never been a big sharer of problems. I always got on with stuff myself and didn't want to burden anybody else with my shit. I said nothing and battled on myself.

Sometimes I felt like another person looking down, watching me going through the motions of life. I felt detached. I was like a zombie on the inside but still functioning to all intents and purposes on the outside as normal.

I knew though from helping others over the same problems that the answer lay within me, not in the bottom of a bottle, a fucking pill from the doctor or lying on some shrink's couch. If my old man had been alive he would have told me to shape up or ship out.

I knew all this but just didn't seem to have the resolve to do something about it. The fire of ambition that had driven me for so long was now just smothering embers. Whether those embers kept burning was down to me. But time was running out.

Tina was there every step of the way for me, but I don't think she even knew how far I was sinking. Without her by my side, fuck knows what would have happened.

Every time I felt I was slipping, I somehow managed to get my ass back in gear, but it was very much a day-to-day thing. I was up and down like a yo-yo.

As my fiftieth birthday approached, I had set in my mind the previous year that I wanted to do something significant to mark it. Now, I needed to do this more than ever for my sanity.

One of my long-time unfulfilled ambitions was to perform a stand-up comedy routine, and I had decided that my birthday would be the perfect time to do it.

I loved the old-school comedians. Guys that used to walk out on stage with no props and just stood there and made a room erupt in laughter. I thought they were incredibly brave. I loved especially Bob Monkhouse. He was a genius.

I had captivated a room with my martial arts ability, could I do it with humour? It was a big ask. I felt the fear but with many things in my life now, instead of running from it I was going to face it head on.

So amongst all the things I was going through, I started trying to focus on putting a routine together and rehearsing it whenever time permitted. It was a tough project that took me, again, out of my comfort zone, but I thought at the time, what the hell. How much worse can it get? Let's face it, I needed a fucking laugh.

Every day, time permitting, for six weeks I rehearsed the routine. Early in the morning or late at night, I worked on it, determined to give myself a project away from dealing with all the other shit going on in my life.

Sometimes I was standing for two hours or more running the routine. I would make mistake after mistake, forget jokes, forget the running order or just stumble over my words. It wasn't fucking good enough. I wanted perfection. I had to get this right.

I had set a date, and I was determined I would be up on that stage and ready. It became an obsession.

I was running jokes in my mind lying in bed, in the bath, in my car, on the toilet, practically everywhere. It consumed me.

But it was giving me much-needed focus and that was good.

In the end, I cracked it and didn't need a script. It was all in my head.

My party was held at a local Labour Club and a big gathering of family and friends were there to see the performance. As you can tell by now, I am never one to do things in half measures. Let's crank up the pressure another few notches. Why not?

I recall one moment vividly. I was standing on this small stage, microphone in my hand, alone. Everybody was in another part of the building and I was just going to practise run a few jokes. Suddenly, I went totally blank. I couldn't remember anything. Panic rose in my body. What the hell was I going to do now? But then, I called on all my knowledge and experience of fear control and breathed deeply a few times, and it all came flooding back. What a relief.

I went on to perform a flawless forty-five-minute routine with no notes to prompt me. I was over the moon because I had run through it dozens and dozens of times alone over the previous months and, now, it had all come to its fruition. The feedback was great and everybody loved it. It really is a satisfying feeling to make people laugh. Somebody even offered me a spot at the local comedy club if I wanted it!

As a birthday present, my students presented me with a beautiful samurai sword in a presentation box. It still holds pride of place in my house. It was a wonderful night, and just what I needed. For a few hours, all seemed good.

Getting my mother into a care home and trying to sell the family house and my own at the same time was proving an uphill task. Also, I had to manage all my father's and mother's affairs. My father's, obviously, because he was no longer around; my mother's because, God love her, she was no longer capable. To get official power to do this is the most long, drawn-out and frustrating process ever. I was juggling too many balls and, on a given day, I wasn't sure who I was talking with. Was it my estate agent or my mother's? Was it my solicitor or hers? Was I talking to probate, pensions, disability allowance, care workers, council officials or 'Uncle Tom Cobley' and all!

The year eventually melted away, and I had managed to sell my father's home and by the skin of my teeth, move into my new home as well just a week before Christmas. But the run-up for this had been a nightmare, resulting in me and Tina being out of our house and living with my father-in-law for six weeks with all our worldly goods in storage until we could move into our new home. The unravelling slowly kept going.

The year 2012 kicked off with the continuing sagas of the previous year. If I thought I was out of the woods, I was sadly mistaken.

I was still training and teaching throughout this time, but relying too much on a drink to get me through the crisis I was in. I told no one. I bottled it up (no pun intended). A little habit I learnt from my father. I found it difficult to ask for help.

During this period, I brought a team of fighters down to a local grappling tournament. Whilst watching them weigh in, I decided on impulse to enter myself. I was off on holiday to the USA the following day and injury would have been unthinkable. My wife, Tina, needed the holiday as much as me, yet, I didn't think. I just wasn't functioning properly.

I had had a few drinks the night before and wasn't exactly at my best, but I just needed to do it. Maybe to prove I hadn't slid too far down the pan and that I could still hack it if need be.

All this said, at the ripe old age of fifty-one, and certainly the oldest guy at the competition, I went on the mats and won a silver medal in my weight category. I won my first two fights and narrowly missed out on gold, losing to my old friend and fellow MMA and grappling competitor Alex Owen who is a superb technician.

I was amazed how relaxed I felt. In my first fight, I recall working guard against a very game opponent, but knowing I had control. Yet, at the same time, I was conversing with the timekeeper, asking him whether the time was up, as I was getting 'knackered' and a man of my age needed his rest!

Arriving home, I was feeling pretty good about myself, until Tina found out and soon brought me back down to earth with a bump, lecturing me about being irresponsible. She was right, of course. It wasn't the smartest thing to do but… I am still proud of that medal. Once a fighter, always a fighter, I suppose. I knew in my heart that I hadn't totally lost my passion for martial arts, but I still couldn't quite rekindle the feelings of yesteryear.

When you have done something this long and with such passion you begin to fear when you can't do it anymore. After all, this is who you are. This is your whole substance. What the fuck were you going to be when it was gone? It is hard when you stand at a crossroads in your life and question one of the things you have loved most. Something that made up your very fibre. Dark times that everybody will come to face someday. Therefore so many boxers return to the ring. They don't need the money, they need an identity!

Looking back now, I was suffering from a deep depression, but I was never going to admit to it at that time. I had been taught to get on with things in life and stop moaning, so I just dealt with it myself.

I didn't really have a fucking clue what to do. But the resolve I had built up over the years through my hard training was the glue that kept me together.

I hated feeling the way I did. I didn't want to hate the life I had been so passionate about. I guess my father's death had hit me harder than I realised. But at the time, I just didn't have the time or head space to sit down and reflect on this.

Slowly, I did begin to fight back. I had fought all my life, but this was an intangible opponent. One I hadn't faced before. It was an unknown quantity. First, I had to get its measure, understand it and then, with every ounce of my resolve, I had to crush the fucker!

A ray of light helped me immensely: the birth of my grandson, Logan. This little lad was the turning point of me. I wanted to be there for him and have him proudly look up to me.

I was on my way back out of the fog. I had dragged my sorry ass up and was ready for another round. As the old saying goes, 'You can't keep a good man down'!

"What does not kill us makes us stronger."

Making an Impact

For quite a few years, my son, Jake and I had talked about getting our own premises. He had come into a business partnership with me, and as time went on, I began to realise that the only natural step for me was to get my own place. I couldn't go on indefinitely teaching classes, week in, week out. I needed a plan. My own place seemed the only solution. Plus, it would leave a legacy in time for my family.

I had grown tired of being out every night teaching at different venues, and I also hated the time used up travelling to these places. I had been doing this for twenty-plus years. Even with the best will in the world, you get jaded. Now in my fifties, it was time to take stock of my life to date and look at where I wanted to go.

As 2012 was ending, we came across a place that we thought might be suitable. Well, Jake, my son did. I just couldn't see it myself, but he was convinced this was it. We had viewed so many other places that either didn't come up to scratch or the deal just fell through. I just presumed this would be another of those… but, boy, I was wrong.

My son, Jake found what was to become 'Impact Gym'. When he showed me the place and spoke about his vision, I wanted to walk away. It was too ambitious and too big a project. It would be a massive risk, and it had no guarantee of success. Businesses were going to the wall in that present climate, not prospering.

Also, I was still suffering internally and not properly focused on life. Something I had longed for, for many years, had come along and I didn't want it.

But what was the alternative? Give up, go and stack shelves in a supermarket? Sell my ass on the streets?

It took much thought and soul-searching to finally agree, but the reality, for me, was where I was going to be heading now in my life if I didn't take this risk.

I had been teaching and paying rent at various premises for as many years as I could recall. I always had to abide by the rules of these establishments and couldn't really put my own stamp on them.

I didn't have a place I could truly call my own and, deep down, I wanted something not just for me but for my family and the O'Hagan name. I wanted to leave a legacy in Bristol where I had first started out on my martial arts journey forty years previously.

I knew that I didn't have the energy or desire to do this alone, but with Jake with me, maybe we could make it work. So, we went for it.

To say the project nearly finished us both off would be an understatement. The pressure we put ourselves under and the huge task we set was going to stretch our resolve, patience and sanity to breaking point and beyond. Also, our father-and-son bond was tested to the full. If I thought things had been tough in the previous few years, this venture was about to take me far into the reserves of belief and spirit I never even knew I had in me.

So February 2013, we began work on making the dream come true. We worked relentlessly day and night on the project. We were there right on ground level getting stuck in with our builders. Big thanks to Mark Lomand and his guys for a top job.

We cleared mountains of rubbish that had accumulated in the space before we could even get to the refurbishment. This took weeks. Next, came the knocking down of existing walls and building new ones. New doors going in, skirting, windows, toilets, showers, kitchen and then, scrape the brick walls, treat and paint and paint and paint, then paint again. Gallons of the fucking stuff.

Tower scaffolding was brought in so the ceiling could be boarded and painted, as too was the endless pipework and metal girders, pillars and posts way up in the 'gods'.

This wasn't a bog-standard unit where you could slap some emulsion paint on the walls and a few mats on the concrete floor and get going. Oh no. This was something much grander and, fucking scarier.

Jake managed the project overall as I was keeping my existing clubs that I had running at other venues. It was tough going in this transitional time. We were burning the candle at both ends.

It took up all our days, a lot of evenings and many weekends. At one stage, we just thought the project was too huge for us. Yes, we could have got a smaller unit somewhere and a lesser project, but we wanted to build something unique. We wanted something more ambitious. Something that we thought would make a difference. As Del Boy might have said, "

The foot injury I mentioned earlier was at its worst in this period, and I was on my feet literally all day and well into the evening. The pain was excruciating, but I couldn't lie down and cry about it. I had to carry on and worry about it later.

In amongst this entire chaos, Jake's wife, Soeli, gave birth to our beautiful grandson Logan Joe O'Hagan. His middle name, Joe, was in memory of my dad, which was a lovely touch. He was the one little bright light in amongst all the stress and worry. He kept me sane. He is wonderful. A proper little boy. I love him dearly.

Having a new born baby enter the world at this extremely busy time increased the pressure on us all. Jake, Soeli, Tina and I worked hard to juggle responsibilities. We didn't always get it right, but somehow, we kept going and even in the darkest hours, found the reserves of strength to battle on.

We had come too far to go back. The refurb caused us many problems. We ran into crisis after crisis. It was so bad I was contemplating giving Kevin McCloud a ring from Grand designs!

A project this big <u>bled </u>money like it was going out of fashion, and we became the bank manager's best friend. We had problems with the landlord, council, the neighbours, suppliers, builders, planning, and change of business and just about everybody else as well who seemed determined to fuck us over and not let us follow our dream.

After all, we were trying to do something productive for the community, yet in the eyes of the powers that be, you would have thought we were opening a lap dancing club. There were days when I thought it would be easier for me to put a G-string on and learn to hang off a pole, like the guy in the advert on television.

But bit by bit, the vision that Jake had sold to me began to take shape.

Many of our friends popped in and gave us a welcome hand when they could. That was great. I thank you all for that. Gradually, we were getting there.

Our idea was to have everything under one roof. *The complete package.* So that anybody joining wouldn't have to also be paying to go to other establishments as well.

'Impact Gym' wanted to provide martial arts, fitness, nutrition, massage treatment and sports psychology all in one place.

Through Jake's many connections, we were sponsored by energy drinks giant 'Rockstar' and our striking area/bags, etc. were sponsored by 'Triumph United.' Many thanks to Matt Law for this.

We invested in a full-size boxing ring and a custom-made cage, as well as a fitness rig and strongman kit, made and supplied by Trojan Fit. We had a full-size matted area and a matted studio sponsored by Zebra mats.

There was also a functional fitness area with the rig as mentioned, Olympic weightlifting kit, sledges, tyres, battling and climbing ropes, kettle and dumbbells, medicine balls, power bags, etc.

'Impact Gym' wanted to offer fitness classes instructed by the best coaches so members knew how to use all the kit safely and correctly.

Martial arts-wise, we could offer classes in boxing, wrestling, Thai boxing, MMA, submission grappling and Japanese combat ju jutsu and Brazilian ju jutsu.

We have a top in-house nutritionist with us from 'Apex Fitness' – Matt Cooper, and Soeli has her treatment and therapy room. We also added yoga to the timetable.

Our planned opening day kept getting postponed as we ran into problem after problem.

Eventually, we had to decide on a date and go for it whatever the circumstances.

Come the midnight of the opening day on the Saturday, Jake and I were on our hands and knees cutting mats to fit into the cage. When we eventually left, we were all exhausted, not only physically but mentally. The project had been draining, and it had taken its toll on us all, but the day had come and 'Impact Gym' was ready to go.

Anybody out there running a full-time gym will know that 'living the dream' is not all plain sailing.

Coaching is one thing, but that is just one of the many jobs that are required to make a gym successful. Adapting to these things can be a big learning curve. But, basically, the buck stops with you. Training in somebody else's gym and then just leaving when you have finished is easy. You don't really think or question how the place actually runs or functions. It is a big eye-opener. Lots of hard work goes on behind the scenes to keep the place operating smoothly. Also, it doesn't always all go according to plan. Respect to all guys out there running their own gyms or dojos.

When the gym opened, on a personal note, I made the decision that I wanted to take a backseat from coaching MMA. I felt I had gone as far as I could with it and wanted others to take over the mantle led by Jake.

I decided to start teaching combat ju jutsu once more and see what the response was like. The class took off and students, old and new, turned up to train.

The children's ju jutsu was taken over by Jake and another of 'Impact Gym's' coaches, Paul Bush. It is thriving.

You learn by trial and error. Some classes worked; others didn't. But we try to swap and rectify this. Some coaches are unreliable; others are great fighters but not great coaches. Coaching is a lifetime pursuit, not something you can just jump into because you have a black belt or a championship title.

As I write this, we are two years into running 'Impact Gym' and I am pleased to say that we are keeping our heads above water and hopefully, the future is bright.

Both my sons have grown and excelled as martial artists. It is great to see them both running their own successful classes at the gym. It seems that no time ago, they were toddlers playing with their toys on the edge of the mats whilst their 'old man' was putting somebody through their paces. Now, it is them who are doing it. Both are skilled all-rounders, but if pressed, I would say that Jake is at his best in wrestling range and Tom on the ground leg locking somebody.

Also, my daughter-in-law, Soeli, is blazing a trail with her Amazon workout. Her classes are going from strength to strength, and I know she has some big plans for the Amazon coming soon. I wish her all the luck in the world. In recent years, she has fought through a catalogue of injuries, illness and setbacks, but she is still out there kicking ass.

We have had some great coaches on board with us over the years. Charlie Menter coaches Olympic weightlifting and crossfit, Dan Woodsford a striking coach for MMA and one of Mark Weir's top coaches, Paul Bush, a great pad man. We also have had Danny Butler, English middleweight boxing champion coaching in the gym and kickboxing champion, Ryan Edmundson and top-level wrestling coach Saeed Ismael and Paul Croft, all-round endurance athlete.

We keep an open mind to training and love to invite coaches from different disciplines to come and teach at Impact. From BJJ to Krav Maga, from Muay Thai to judo, we have had them all. In recent times, an old name from the past, Andy Davies, who I trained with way back in my kung fu days has been in touch and has brought his 'Elite Academy' taekwondo and kickboxing into the gym. How ironic is that?

All that said, the nucleus of Impact is the O'Hagan name, which I am extremely proud of.

When the place is packed and everybody is training, it is an inspiring sight. I watch new members starting their journey with wide-eyed enthusiasm. It reminds me of when I was that green, freshfaced lad standing in my first class raring to go way back in 1975.

Sometimes, last thing at night or first thing in the morning, when the gym is empty and I look around, I do stand and take a moment to give myself a little pat on the back and say well done.

At the time of writing, we are coming up to celebrating our second-year anniversary.

Last year, we topped a fun day off at Impact with a few 'wrestling' matches heralding the 'golden age' of TV grappling. It was great. I found a new alter ego in the shape of 'Diablo, the Masked Assassin', who entered the ring and wrestled for the 'championship' belt against his arch enemy, Paul 'the Bloodbath Butcher' Bush and won the belt. This year, we are on for a rematch, and as I speak, we are training hard together for the big day. 'Worked' match or not, I am still sore and stiff from being chucked around the ring. I must be mad, but it is all for a compelling cause.

As a family, Jake, Soeli, Tina and myself have our important roles to play in the daily running of the gym and we all bring something to it. But Jake was responsible for selling me the dream and working hard to see it happen. Hopefully he can take this on to bigger and better things in the future.

We have some great people training at Impact gym. They are the heartbeat of the place and we love them all.

It is great to finally have somewhere to call home after all these years. I hope my family keep the tradition going for many years to come.

"Ambition is the path to success. Persistence is the vehicle you arrive in."

My Opinions on Self Defence, Ju Jutsu, the Black Belt and Real Fighting.

Self Defence

I read a lot of posts on Facebook these days about the age-old question, "What is the most practical and effective fighting system for self-defence?" I hear shouts for Krav Maga, BJJ, boxing, Thai, etc., etc.

One of the things we must take into consideration first is that fighting is not self-defence.

Fighting or having a fight is about two participants agreeing to engage in mutual combat or facing off against each other. This is, and never will be, self-defence.

Self-defence is about one party minding their own business, getting on with their life when, unfortunately, violence comes their way, usually when they least expect or anticipate it.

These are two totally different things. If you are prone to fighting in the street, you will have a very short shelf-life. You will either be spending a good percentage of your life behind bars or, eventually, six feet under.

Fighting on the contest mat, in the cage or the ring is by the consent of all parties involved. It will be done according to weight, experience, rules and duration. There will be a referee present to see fair play and step in to stop the fight if and when needed.

Self-defence is about being targeted for an unprovoked attack. It can be split into two distinct areas. There is confrontational and ambush. That's it. A match fight is not in the equation.

In self-defence, if the situation warrants physical response and isn't dealt with in three seconds, it will deteriorate into a type of match fight, but that is a rarity. Normally, the first person to land a shot wins.

Self-defence isn't about sparring up and feeling out your attacker before you launch your deadly attack. It is about somebody sucker punching you in the head before you even realise it, or pushing a glass in your face or a knife in your guts. There will be no posturing and twirling of the weapon or any bad-ass film dialogue before this happens.

It is about somebody grabbing you around the neck whilst you are checking your iPhone or jogging with headphones on. It is being held at knife point at an ATM machine.

It is about being chased down like a zebra and having a pack of animals kick ten bells out of you. No tap outs here or referee's stoppage. You may not ever see daylight again, or if you do, you may be confined to a wheelchair.

Forget all this macho posturing and bullshit that make up the big percentage of shit on the internet. Any time two people are facing off with each other, whether it is on the pavement or the ring, it is a fight. Whether you are wearing a gi with more patches than some Girl Guide or camo trousers and boots, it is a fight.

In the world of self-defence, the only time you may have to face up to somebody is because you can't talk or walk your way out of the situation, or you may be shielding your family or loved ones from harm. Otherwise, it will mean that you are mutually agreeing with some asshole to be an asshole as well.

In the world of match fighting, it has been proven, beyond doubt, that the 'big boys' that stand up under pressure are Western boxing, wrestling, Thai and BJJ/submission wrestling. Why? Because now they are mainly practised as combat sports in this day and age.

Self-defence is situational and scenario-driven. It is a totally different world. It's not to say these combat sports can't make the changeover, but they need to be adapted greatly. This is a huge topic on its own. The combat sports' right cross, leg kick, double leg takedown or rear naked strangle will work in any situation when adapted and practised for that arena. But in the main, combat sports are combat sports.

Having a row outside the chip shop or pub isn't, and never will be self-defence, if you have willingly engaged and not tried to find another solution.

Self-defence also includes legal and moral issues, and they can't be separated. The ethics and the code you live by will determine and justify your actions.

Teaching self-defence and teaching fighting is not the same thing. When it comes to self-defence, engaging in the physical is the last-resort option. If your only option in self-defence is hit them in the mouth, then you will get plenty of time to perfect that technique in the showers at one of Her Majesty's hotels. Teaching awareness, tactical positioning, spatial awareness, the 'shield or fence' position, de-escalation and escape routes are all essential stuff before you hit the physical skills. Then, as mentioned, it will be an in-your-face confrontational attack, or it will be an ambush when you are switched off and not prepared. You won't be attacked after leaving your dojo after twelve rounds on the pads and some sparring. It won't be after

318

you just got your record number of tap outs. It won't be when you are stretched out, warmed up and ready to rock. If only...

No, it will be when you are out for a nice, quiet dinner with your partner, when you are in the park with your children, when you are walking with your elderly parents. It will be when you are cold and wet, tired, under the weather or preoccupied.

Rarely, will it be one person and, if it is, there will probably be a weapon involved. Reality says that it will be more than one with weapons.

When you see these 'Martial Arts superheroes' standing ground in fighting stances against two or more attackers, you know it is bullshit. I have been targeted by gang attacks more than once in my younger days. I was grateful for the mystical and magical techniques of running, climbing and fucking hiding over any combat moves. No pressure point knockouts or invisible force field energy in sight!

These situations are very scary. This is not about fighting for a medal or a trophy and a chance to impress on your mates what a beast you are. This is about survival and possibly having to defend your very life. Hiding under a car, pasty-faced, shaking like a shitting dog and doing your upmost not to piss yourself isn't so glamorous, and it won't get a viewing on YouTube. Nor will you be giving it the 'big one' to your mates about it. But it fucking works.

By now, I hope you are getting the picture. I admire and salute all who go into the combat sporting arena. I have been there many times myself. It is, no doubt, a hard and tough environment to be in and a tougher one to earn a living from. But, at the end of the day, it is just 'fighting'. It is not combat. Barring something terrible and tragic, you will walk back out of that arena again.

Self-defence on the streets doesn't guarantee you that. Neither does fighting on the streets. If you mistakenly bring a knife to a gun fight, you will lose. If you have built a reputation for being a fighter on the street, don't be naive enough to think that the next person looking for you is going to be coming to fight you under the Queensberry rules or BJJ format. They don't want a fair fight; they just want to beat you. So if a bat, knife or firearm will do the job, they will bring it. So, please be careful what you wish for. You might just get it.

Save your 'fighting' for the competitive arena, and try to live a good life outside of it and stay safe.

Ju Jutsu: A brief history.

When people talk about ju jutsu currently, they refer to Brazilian ju jutsu as their point of reference. A lot of them wrongly presume that this is the only form or source of ju jutsu. Many also refer to it as "that ground stuff". Others talk about grappling in a gi as if it was something unique and only for the chosen few.

BJJ is, no doubt, a huge art worldwide and has proven itself not only on the contest mats, but also in the cage and in many 'no holds barred' fights. But it is a far cry away from what ju jutsu originally was. Japanese ju jutsu was trained for a different purpose and with a different mindset.

To explore these differences, we need to have a look at its history. This is a brief overview and not meant to be comprehensive. I am not a historian, but I do have a big interest in the background of the martial art I chose to study many years ago.

Ju jutsu can be traced back to over two thousand five hundred years ago, when legend tells that two gods punished the lawless inhabitants of a village using its techniques.

Arguably, Buddhist monks of India and China were the first to study what was to be eventually called ju jutsu. However, it is well known and documented that ju jutsu flourished greatly in Japan and was adopted by the fearsome Samurai warriors who were, in feudal times, the private bodyguards of the ruling warlords.

The Samurai are one of history's most celebrated warriors. They were highly trained in bujutsu, the art of weaponry, and masters of unarmed close-quarter battle. Not unlike our Special Forces and black ops of today. In fact, these military groups still use the hand-to-hand combat skills of ju jutsu even today.

In the years of AD 1192–1573, these periods in Japan were known for bujutsu (classical military training including 'old style' ju jutsu). At this time, it was named Kumi Uchi, Yawara or taijutsu amongst others. Kumi Uchi translated means 'grappling in armour'.

Back then, the Samurai fought in armour. Fighting was mainly done on horseback with bow and arrows and spear. They were master marksmen. On foot, they would use their swords – long sword (the katana), short sword (wakizashi) and knife (tanto).

Unarmed combat skills ensued when weapons clashed and went to grappling range, or if a weapon was broken or dropped. Unarmed skills were mainly trips, throws and sweeps to down an opponent to finish them. Stomps and kicks to the knees were administered for destruction and unbalancing. Joint locks, twists and breaks were also used to disarm weapons and disable the enemy. Chokes, strangles and neck cranking, along with knee drops and stomping, were used to kill the enemy.

Strikes were mainly used to unbalance or open the opponent up to get them to the floor for a quick kill. Many strikes were ineffective against armour, although there were weaknesses which certain types of strikes exploited. The throat, armpits and groin areas were vulnerable, not only to blades, but also strikes with the edge of the hand or fingertips.

Ground wrestling would have been nearly non-existent. It would have been too cumbersome and dangerous and would only be used as a last resort.

At this time, Ju Jutsu was purely an art of warfare and its techniques were used to kill, period. Remember, these were wild and lawless times, and it was kill or be killed.

Practise of ju jutsu technique back then was to hone these skills to apply in combat, not sport. Many ju jutsu techniques were probably tried out on the battle fields for the first time against a resisting opponent. If they failed, you didn't get a chance to tap out and have another go. The consequences probably resulted in your death. Therefore these warriors trained constantly for perfection. Every day may have been their last. Their mindset was not that of a sporting competitor. Their techniques reflected this.

"A Japanese Samurai's only goal in combat was to fight well, kill many enemies, survive or die with honour." Not unlike our forces of today.

Grappling for trophies or points was not on the agenda.

The Edo period of 1603-1868 saw more strikes being introduced, as armour wasn't always being worn, especially out of battle. The strikes were taken from Chinese Kempo (roughly translated as 'law fist'). They were circular and linear strikes with the closed fist and open hand, as well as kicks, knees, etc. Without the handicap of armour, strikes to vital points could be more effective. The way ju jutsu was being trained was slowly changing.

The year 1890 saw the end of the feudal era and effectively, the end of the Samurai as we knew them. They became nomads without masters, who hired themselves out as mercenaries.

As Japan became more westernised, the brutal killing arts of ju jutsu were frowned upon. Many schools of bujutsu went underground or disbanded. Japan wanted to become more civilised to the world. The sword was no longer the law. Policing now began.

Ju jutsu techniques changed greatly to be used for law enforcement, hence more locks, restraints and hold downs were introduced. Pressure points and nerve centres were manipulated, as well as the use of the steel baton (jutte) and roping and tying skills. These methods prevailed over hard-line Kempo strikes and strangulations.

This is where the controlling techniques of ju jutsu flourished. Striking was used now mainly to stun and 'soften up' an attacker before they were pinned or restrained. Not unlike the skills of the modern police force.

As the level of threat increased, so did the level of force. That is why ju jutsu kept the techniques of vital point striking and choking in its arsenal.

Ju jutsu roughly translates as 'pliable art'. This principle relied on using the opponent's force against them. Body movement was emphasised for throwing. The hard and direct jutsu part of Kempo and Atemi Waza was not used so much.

The techniques of ju jutsu were also now being trained for civilian self-defence. The more nefarious combat techniques were eliminated.

The year 1882 saw a ju jutsu practitioner, Jigoro Kano, begin to modify some of the more combative techniques of old-school ju jutsu to eventually develop what we know as judo.

Jigoro Kano worked to combine and preserve the ancient martial traditions of Japan. Kano refined the techniques he had learned primarily from two traditional systems, the Tenshin Shin'yo Ryu and the Kito Ryu, and founded his own style, Kodokan Judo. One of the most important innovations in Kano's judo was the emphasis placed on 'randori', or non-cooperative free sparring practice. Most of the ancient ju jutsu styles based their training on pre-arranged sequences of attack and defence known as 'kata' as their techniques were purely designed to kill and were difficult to practice safely. It is said that Samurais used prisoners and peasants to practice their killing techniques on. Although Kano acknowledged the value of kata practice (kata training is present in judo training to this day), he also realised the absolute necessity of learning to apply techniques in the most realistic manner for the era's needs. Randori allows the practitioner to develop the mindset and technical proficiency needed to apply techniques against fully resisting opponents as safely as it would allow.

Kano's modern style was put to the test in the famous tournament of 1886, hosted by the Tokyo Police. Of the fifteen matches pitting Kodokan judo fighters against fighters of various classic styles of ju jutsu, the Kodokan won thirteen matches and tied the other two. Kano's hybrid martial art and revolutionary methods of training had proven most effective. In the late nineteenth century, although the name ju jutsu still existed, it was all but now judo being practised.

Many books written from that time carried the name ju jutsu, but they were a far cry from the Samurai art and were really judo.

In 1914, judo was introduced to Brazil but still under the name of ju jutsu. Mitsuyo Maeda, a student of Kano's and an expert fighter versed in classical ju jutsu and judo, passed his skills on to Carlos Gracie, and he, in turn, passed them onto his family. The Gracie family will always be linked with introducing BJJ to the world.

Is Brazilian ju jutsu really judo? I am sure many would argue the point, but the techniques are extremely similar even today. I would say that back in the late nineteenth century, judo emphasised more leverage breaking and throwing than it did groundwork. But many exponents also had classical ju jutsu skills which did involve some floor work, so they sort of got fused together.

Kosen Judo was a refinement of Kodokan judo which put emphasis on *newaza* (groundwork). Their competitions allowed unlimited time on the floor until submission was found. It also allowed pulling in an opponent to take them down. Does this sound more like the style of judo brought to Brazil? The pulling-in bit would certainly encourage guard and working off the back. A lot of the old-school ju jutsu masters preferred this type of contest, as it was taken to its conclusion the same as it would be in real combat. There was certainly a friction between the two schools on what they deemed to be right. Either way, it allowed some of the more acceptable skills of ju jutsu to be used in a more sporting light rather than just becoming obsolete.

It is recorded that when old-school ju jutsu practitioners went to train their art, they had a meal with their family beforehand as they didn't know whether they would return. That was how brutal it was. Obviously, this is not the practice today.

There are subtle differences between judo and BJJ, but you would really have to be an exponent of one or the other to really appreciate them. BJJ now is known predominately as a ground-grappling art. Its strengths are the ability for a smaller person to defeat a larger one by using tactical positioning and strategy. At least ninety percent of its practice is on the ground wearing a gi and only ten percent standing. It is also mainly now used for the sporting arena, and it is even different from the early days of its introduction into the States and the UFC. It has proven itself effective in no-holds-barred fights but maybe its image has now changed to be a more widely accepted martial art that is not just linked with 'cage fighting'.

Just like Kano's vision of judo, its product is for it to be used against a live resisting opponent and not to be drilled in kata fashion.

It has become a worldwide phenomenon, initially through the Gracie family and mixed martial arts. Although it has proved itself a highly effective art, it is a world apart from Japanese Samurai ju jutsu, where its emphasis was ninety percent standing and ten percent on the ground. Modern-day combat ju jutsu holds the same view with the motto, 'Learn to fight on the ground, but do not go to the ground to fight'.

The old saying that ninety percent of fights end up on the floor may be true. But also, nearly one hundred percent start standing up. Remember that self-defence skills are not about a 'match fight.'

In the early twentieth century, elements of 'old school' ju jutsu were used effectively by troops in both world wars. Classic text books such as Fairbairn's 'Get Tough', Applegate's 'Killed or be Killed' and Styers' 'Cold Steel' amongst many more used the unarmed skills of ju jutsu. Ju jutsu, once again, went back to its roots as an art of warfare and proved every bit as effective as it did two thousand years previously.

It was also adopted by police forces throughout the world, especially for control and restraint. Even now in the world of policing, security and body guarding, the techniques of ju jutsu are still taught and used.

In the 1950s, karate became the new kid on the block in the Western world, but ju jutsu never really died. In the late 60s, it received a rebirth and had a massive stronghold, especially in the north of the country under legendary instructors such as Blundell, Clark, Morris and Steadman. I was fortunate to train with some of these men and many of their second generation instructors.

I began my formal ju jutsu training in 1984. My first instructor, Mike Marshall, who has now sadly passed on, was a member of SBS and a bodyguard. His ju jutsu was very orientated to real-world combat. It was taught for the environment it was to be used in. Other instructors I trained with such as Mickey Upham, Trevor Roberts, Dave Turton and they're like all worked in security 'on the doors' and their ju jutsu suited their needs. This is what I term 'Combat Ju Jutsu and this was/is my main style of ju jutsu and to which I hold a seventh Dan black belt.

I have blended the many elements of old- and new-school ju jutsu into a practical art that is as effective now as it was on the battlefields two thousand years ago.

I love ju jutsu's traditional roots, and I teach to preserve its lineage with a bit of a modern spin, as the enemy of today is no longer a Samurai on horseback. But with my heavy involvement in MMA, I also embraced the modern art of BJJ and Japanese submission wrestling, and I have been fortunate to train with many great instructors and respect their place in the evolution of ju jutsu as a whole.

For me, the 'combat' element of my ju jutsu was pressure testing it in the 'full contact' arenas. Making sure it stood up to the rigours of modern combat, and if it didn't, refining and adapting it so it did. I embrace the origins and work hard to preserve them, but I am also astute enough to move with the changing times.

But I must make it clear to the new generation that you haven't got the patent on an arm bar or 'invented the wheel'. These techniques have been around a long time and sometimes, it is good to see where they have originated from and how they were being practised back in the day.

The manner of ju jutsu practice has also changed over the years.

Japanese ju jutsu was taught in a very militaristic and harsh manner. Training was very strict and hard. Countless repetitions were done of throws, joint locks, strangles, etc. Every technique had to be executed fully with contact. You became hardened to this type of practice.

As I moved into modern combat ju jutsu, it was still hard training, but it was a little less formal on the mats.

Now, BJJ welcomes this relaxed and informal type of training.

I like to teach somewhere in the middle of both ends. I don't have people calling me mate on the mats or wander on wearing their socks, for example, but I will not teach like a drill sergeant.

There is a time to be tough and a time to have a bit of a laugh and not take yourself too seriously.

I have met some teachers that act as if they are God and think they can walk on water. Most can't. Stay humble is my motto, no matter what skills you have.

Sometimes, I am asked about how I think Samurai/combat ju jutsu would hold up against BJJ in a fight? Personally, I am not interested in fighting. A true warrior keeps his sword sheathed until he is facing death. Competition and having a roll are fun fighting. Combat ju jutsu is for a life or death situation. It is worlds apart. This 'combat' is a whole different animal. The emphasis is not holding positions or tapping somebody out; it is about tearing them a new asshole. Win or lose, in combat you will come out with something missing. It is a different mindset and a different objective.

Both combat ju jutsu and BJJ have their place. They have both proven themselves in real fighting situations. I see the relevance for both.

For me, ju jutsu is a martial arts chameleon. It has lasted through the ages and had rebirth after rebirth from Samurai battlefield art and art of law enforcement to modern-day military, security personnel usage and the world of mixed martial arts.

I love the art and all its facets, but I do urge people to train in its many aspects and not just one. It is good to look to learn from the present and also train for the future, but we can also learn from the past and from the men who went before us and blazed a trail.

The Black Belt

Does a black belt hold any value currently? This is always a good subject for debate. In these days of MMA and reality-based fighting, we don't see much of the traditional black belt worn, and for today's young and rising stars of the martial arts world, a black belt doesn't seem to be at the top of their list of priorities. Certainly, when I was a youthful martial artist, my goal was a black belt achievement. But, in many ways, over the years, it has been devalued by greedy money-orientated associations that gave out these belts like Smarties. It seemed, at one stage, that everybody I met had a black belt in one art or another. In some quarters, the black belt became a joke.

Black belts at ten years of age or second Dans at twenty years of age just don't cut it with me. Yet, there are hundreds of them out there.

Back in my era and earlier, the black belt was the Holy Grail that was achieved by a chosen few. You had to sweat blood and tears for it and be able to show a high level of ability, as well as fighting spirit and fitness.

But, somewhere in the 80s, large associations raped and pillaged the belt for big bucks. It became the ultimate bargaining tool for greedy instructors. With this greed went the integrity, and with the integrity went the value and the standards that the black belt stood for.

In the event of the grappling explosion and reality fight scene, many a black belt was taken down to earth by lesser grades that could have a fight or combat sports fighters who measured their ability in the ring, cage or on the mats. People were drawing conclusions from this and coming up with the answer that the black belt was, in fact, worthless. My thoughts on this are as follows.

Firstly, there is certainly truth in this but, also, let's not forget that these individuals who set foot in the cage, etc. may not have been the best examples of a black belt, but they must be applauded for having the balls to do it, no matter how misguided or disillusioned you may think they were.

No doubt, if your black belt was just gained on learning techniques and not pressure testing them, then you have a flaw there. But the black belt isn't just a sign that you are supposed to be a 'ninja warrior'.

A black belt is an individual and personal thing. What it means to you, how you carry it and what you do with it is down to that individual. Some arts, you can receive a black belt for your technical ability and understanding of the system without ever having to test yourself. A lot of martial arts have little or no combat value; others do. It will depend what art you have trained in and what you achieved the black belt for. A black belt certainly doesn't mean you're an 'expert' or a 'master fighter'. That idea has been sold to the public by the media. It does show a measure, though, of your achievements within your chosen system. It's the same with any job, pursuit, sport or pastime. You will always have awards and marks of your achievements or dedication to that pursuit. Why should the martial arts be any different? Let's be realistic. Can a sixty-five-year-old eighth Dan compete against a twenty-three-year-old blue belt in a contest? Answer: very unlikely. But does that mean that man has nothing to offer? Of course it doesn't. He can offer vast experience and knowledge that he can pass on to the younger man and coach and groom him. Look at some of boxing's greatest coaches. Many were either poor or average fighters themselves, but they had a talent to coach. Are they thought any less of for that? Dan grades in martial arts reflect the time you have given to your system and the knowledge you have achieved, not whether you are a 'Karate killer' or not. I do feel, though, that every black belt has a responsibility to themselves to be a good or a poor black belt.

To me, being a black belt is a way of life. You try to live by certain values and ethics. You aspire to live a life of discipline like a warrior. You carry the black belt mentally on and off the mat.

Outside, in the real world, you don't walk around with a black belt around your waist, but you should still try to act like one.

When it comes to physical skills, you are only as good as the last time you stepped on the mats. Some individuals reach the high levels, then take their foot off the pedal and relax back on their achievements; others will see it as another rung on the ladder and adjust accordingly.

I look back and like to think that I earned my black belts the right way, and put them and the reputation they carried on the line on many occasions. I never hid behind them.

When I graded any of my students to black belt, they got it the hard way. No favours, no concessions. Money was not my motivation. Whilst we are on this subject, how can some instructors charge hundreds of pounds to grade a student for their black belt? That is ludicrous.

In recent times, Brazilian ju jutsu has brought some integrity back to the black belt. I can honestly say that I have never seen a poor BJJ black belt. The reason for that is that you have to earn it the right way. But as BJJ gets ever more popular and more money gets made from it, we will have to monitor whether those standards begin to slip. I hope not.

My advice is that if you grade for belts in a syllabus, make the syllabus full and challenging and make sure people earn that belt honestly. To me, gaining black belts in two years is not an option. That span of time will not give you the knowledge or experience to carry that grade. If certain quarters believe the black belt is worthless, it is down to instructors to make sure it isn't and give it back the status it deserves. But at the same time, clarify what it signifies and what it doesn't.

I am proud of my black belt and still wear it with pride. The standards stop with you, the instructor, and if you don't sell out, you can make the black belt something worth achieving again.

A swift lesson in street fighting techniques

Why does every man think that he can fight? Ask any average guy on the street and he feels that when it comes down to it, he will know how to handle himself.

Well, the sad truth is the vast majority of males couldn't fight sleep, beat an egg or, for that matter, batter fish. They are deluded. Their fighting knowledge comes from watching fake fights on film and TV. They believe they are Bruce Lee, Chuck Norris, Steven Seagal and Van Damme all rolled into one.

What is this stupid and naive attitude based on?

The bottom line is, ninety percent of men couldn't punch a hole in a fucking wet paper bag.

There can be a lot of posturing, front and mouth from many, but when it comes down to supplying the goods most come up short.

How do I know this fact?

Well, firstly I have invested a lifetime in the combat arts, and if you practise something every day, year in, year out, you are going to certainly get better at it than Mister Joe Public.

It amazes me to see guys posturing violently in front of one another when they have the fighting ability of a five-year-old child. What is their confidence built on?

Probably by intimidating somebody so they back down, so they never actually have to take it to a physical level.

Another reason I know most men can't fight is because I have spent a lifetime around real fighters. Real professionals that do this stuff for a living and are fucking good at it.

These guys' everyday work is based on how to give another human being as much pain as possible in as many ways as they can.

They can punch with the power of a runaway train and the accuracy of a cruise missile. They can kick you as hard as a mule. They can bend you into knots, choke you, break your limbs and mangle your internal organs so they resemble spaghetti.

They can put you to sleep faster than Ovaltine or a Coldplay record.

These people are the real fucking deal. They are in the minority. To see these guys in action is pure violent poetry. *Truly a beautiful but deadly thing.*

But they have invested a lifetime to achieve this perfection.

The average person will not have the time, inclination, patience or fitness to achieve these elevated levels of skill.

I will outline here a condensed crash course on how to kick ass if you or your loved ones' lives are threatened and you are in danger. It has taken me forty-plus years to come to these conclusions; you, the reader, are getting it a lot quicker and without all the pain and expense!

Fighting Myths

As I already stated, most guys' fighting knowledge is from the films. Hence, they are not real. They will do more harm than good.

Here are a few reality checks:

1. Being covered in tattoos, body piercings and pumping a bit of iron doesn't make you a fighter. No matter how much you posture, swagger and practise your one-thousand-yard mean stare, it still won't cut it. Being a legend in your own mind is cruising for a heavy fall. I know guys you would not give a second glance to with pipe-thin arms, weighing nine stone, soaking wet that could tear you a new arsehole without raising a sweat. Looking the part doesn't mean you are the part. So, ditch the film-star machismo and stop being a twat. Real men and real fighters don't walk around dragging their knuckles and snarling at everyone that crosses their paths but bullies and arseholes do!

2. If you get smashed over the head with a blunt instrument you won't be up in five minutes running around like a two-year-old. The fact is you will bleed a lot, probably be concussed. Possibly have a fractured skull, be unconscious or, at the very least, feel dizzy and nauseous. You will definitely not be in the mood to fight.
If you are unconscious for a length of time when you wake up you will have pissed yourself, maybe even shit yourself. You don't see that in the Bond movies!

3. If you get kicked in the nuts, you will lose the will to fight and, again, you will not be up and recovered in a few minutes. If you are down from the nutshot, you will be in danger of being kicked to death.

4. Street fights are very fast and ferocious, a lot faster than you can imagine. There will be no sparring or dancing around like Muhammad Ali. Somebody will get up in your face and hit you without warning. If you are not switched on, you will be out of the fucking fight before you know you are in it. Normally the person who lands the first blow, unless he is totally useless, will win the encounter.

There is no block and parry shit, no ebb and flow with a sprinkling of cheesy dialogue such as, "Is that your best shot, motherfucker." It is a three-second assassination when done correctly.

5. You can't smash a beer bottle on the side of the bar and have a neatly jagged weapon at hand. Firstly, it takes a lot to break a bottle and, secondly, when it does break, it smashes all over the place and will probably sever your hand. Movie bottles are made out of sugar glass.

6. You will not be executing complicated and fancy moves like Liam Neeson in 'Taken'. The body will go into survival mode, and you will be working on gross motor skills: e.g. one repetitive movement over and over until you win or lose or just get plain exhausted.

7. Punching a person in the bony head means you will probably break bones in your hand, especially if you have been pushing a pencil and shuffling paper all your life. If you are not used to the exposure of full-contact sparring, when you get hit, it will fucking hurt, even with the adrenaline pumping in your blood stream.

8. Most people have forty-five seconds of fight in them, and then they are fucked.

9. If you can't fight on the floor, you are fucked.

10. If you can't land an accurate and hurtful blow in the first few seconds, you are fucked.

11. Most young guys on the street will either attack you as a group or use an edged weapon on you. If you have no training in either of these areas you are fucked.

SO LISTEN UP...

Here is the first rule:

If you are about to be beaten on by one or more individuals, do not wait to be hit. If you can't escape, hit fast. Hit the biggest and ugliest one. Scream like a lunatic, look like a bloodcurdling killing machine even if, inside, you are shitting yourself. Play psycho. But, inside, be in control.

If you want to bring a big bastard down to his knees, here are a few combat proven moves:

Stomp with the sole of your boot into their kneecap – this will bring them down to size and crying like a baby.

Smash your fist or knee up into their balls. Ouch!

Slap both your open palms over their ears for a concussive knockout.

Ram the heel of your hand up viciously under their chin or nose – the heel of the hand is the preferred method of hitting the bony head, not your more fragile fist.

If your life is on the line, attack the throat. Slash the edge of your hand (the classic karate chop) into the windpipe or thrust the web of your thumb and forefinger into the throat.

Smash the fleshy base of your fist down like a hammer onto the bridge of the nose.

Spread your fingers like a claw and drive them into the eyes or grip the windpipe hard and squeeze and rip.

Headbutt the nose with the dome of your forehead. The rule is headbutt with every part of your head above the eye line to everything below their eye line. The nose is the prime target.

Elbows are like close-range baseball bats: they can hit from all angles and wherever you strike, it will have an effect. Swing it across, back up or down to do some severe damage.

Swing your forearm like a bat into the side or back of an attacker's neck, and they will hit the floor fast. When they are down on their knees, a shot to the ribs or head will make sure they stay down! Brutal? Yes. But we are fighting for our lives here, not for a parking space in Asda.

If grappling:

Seize the testicles and squeeze.

Bite anything you can latch onto.

Stick a thumb in an eye or drill it into the cavity behind the earlobe.

You can thrust your fingers into the indentation at the base of the neck and the joint of the collarbones or up the nostrils.

Pull and twist the hair, moustache or beard, etc.

Hook a finger into the mouth, avoiding the teeth and rip.

Grab the head and pull it down into a rising knee to the face or into the body.

If grabbed in any shape or form from behind, use one or more of the following:

Smash the rear of your head into their face.

Stomp the insteps.

Back elbow their body.

Hammer fist or seize the groin.

Reach up and find a little finger and bend and snap.

If you are on the floor with an opponent standing over you:

Kick out at their shins and knees until they back off and you can get up.

Do not let your attacker get past your legs.

If they do and they are kicking you, curl into a protective ball protecting your head. Look to grab their ankle and roll your body right through their knee or latch onto their calf with your teeth and bite through it.

Against weapons, your first option is to fucking run! If this is not an option, pick up an equaliser that you can use. Preferably something big and scary.

Put a barrier in the way – table, chair, dustbin, car, etc.

Use anything in sight such as a stick, brick, briefcase, laptop bag, shopping bag, umbrella, etc. as a weapon.

If you have no choice and you must fight barehanded, then attack the attacker. Run in and close them down, grab their weapon hand and beat the fuck out of them with your other free hand.

Remember, the body's weapons are the head, teeth, hands, elbows, knees and feet. Don't forget your best weapon – your brain!

Once you have incapacitated the attacker, run! Don't wait and admire your handiwork.

Avoid violence and confrontation. Real men can talk then walk from a fight. Self-defence is different. Your only choice may be to defend yourself by fighting back.

If you believe your life or your loved ones are in jeopardy, fight back with a hundred percent commitment and ferocity. Give no quarter and no mercy.

Remember, *it is not the size of the dog in the fight; it is the size of the fight in the dog*. Also, don't be an asshole and pick fights, or don't associate or go where assholes go. No matter how hard you think you are, there is someone out there harder.

If you choose to settle disagreements with your fists, you will go to jail. You won't pass Go or pick up a hundred pounds. You will, however, be sharing a cell with an eighteen-stone, tattooed biker named Alice who will keep you company on dark, lonely nights. Also, it won't be Head and Shoulders shampoo you will be taking into the showers. It will be Alice!

Beware. Fighting is for playgrounds and mugs. Real men defend themselves when all other options run out.

It takes a bigger man to walk away from a fight or have the verbal skills to talk your way out of a fight.

Our most powerful weapon is our brain. That's what separates us from the animal kingdom. That's what gives us an edge.

Put us naked up against any animal and we come a pretty poor second. We have no claws, big fucking teeth, armour, scales, venom or stings. But we do have our brain. Use it, avoid violence. It is an unpleasant thing but also know what to do when the shit hits the fan.

It is a man's responsibility to look after himself and his loved ones. Not cower behind a wall praying it will all go away.

Do not be a bully or abuse your fighting skills. I am a great believer in Karma and what goes around comes around. Conduct yourself like a gentleman and shit will normally bypass you. But don't be naive. Trouble can raise its ugly head anywhere, simply because there are a lot of arseholes around.

Most want to posture and bad-mouth you. They are bullies and probably won't step over the line if you don't play their stupid games. But some are predators. They are sociopaths that cannot be reasoned with. They are a rare breed, but if you come across one and you can't escape, you will be fighting for your life. So, get some training in beyond a fighting game on the Xbox.

Real men also teach their ladies, children and loved ones how to defend themselves, and if they can't, they will be man enough to send them to somebody who can.

"You cannot just tell people you're committed; you cannot just say you're dedicated; you cannot simply talk about your strength, your gift, your perseverance. You have to prove it."

On a Personal Note

This book has very much been about my experiences, thoughts and opinions on martial arts. Away from that arena, I am a private person and don't usually mix the two. My family knows my love, passion and dedication for the arts and when it also became my living, they accepted that I would have to devote a large percentage of my time to it. But when I am away from training, teaching, etc., my family gives me the balance in my life. Sometimes, dealing with reality combat fills you with the loathing that one human being can inflict terrible violence on another, and you do get immersed in the dark side of human nature. My family is the light, the good side and the positive side, and I count myself a lucky man to have this.

Tina, my wife, has always supported my training when things have been good and bad. We went through some tough times when I first started out as a professional instructor and we had very little income. We learned to live without many things and budgeted to do so. Through all this, we kept the faith (isn't that a song?) and never doubted that things would get better. She hasn't always agreed with some of the things I've embarked on (fighting MMA), but never stood in my way. For this, I am deeply grateful.

As mentioned, away from the 'mats', I am not a martial arts bore. If I am in the company of fellow combat practitioners, I can talk on the subject all night long. If I'm not, I don't mention it unless somebody asks me about my work or pastimes. I have encountered too many 'Martial artists' who go around trying to impress upon anybody who wants to listen about how deadly they are and how supremely skilled they may be. I know how boring and utterly pathetic it sounds. Also, I find that if a person who is not involved in the martial arts hears that you are, they still come out with the old clichés such as, "I wouldn't want to meet you in a dark alley," (why do they presume I would be in one?), or "I won't upset you then, mate," (as if I was going to tear their throats out if they disagreed with me). It wears a bit thin sometimes. Plus, I find many men suddenly put up their mental guard and subconsciously start posing because I presume they feel I'm a threat. Therefore, I keep quiet and try to avoid the subject.

Another classic remark will be, "Oh, I used to do karate or whatever, but I had to give it up because I hurt my back, or knee, or foot, etc., etc." There are oh-so many fallen or would-be warriors on the planet.

Their excuses get trotted out and can border from lame to highly ridiculous.

When I'm relaxing from training, I love to read. I am a voracious reader, and I always have a book or two on the go. Some reading I use to educate and inform myself; others to entertain. I like autobiographies and books on achievement or endurance through hardship. I find them inspirational and informative. I also love books on travel. Bill Bryson is brilliant. If I'm on holiday and just want to totally unwind, I may read horror or crime fiction, which I have had a penchant for since childhood. Authors like Shaun Hudson, James Herbert and Richard Laymon are the top men in the horror genre. Michael Connelly, Lee Childs, Richard Montanari, C.J Box and Simon Beckett are just a few of the crime writers I enjoy.

I am not an academic reader and although I have aspired and bettered myself, I am still proud of my working-class roots. You won't find me reading Dickens or Bronte because I feel I should!

These crime and horror writers inspired me to write and have published two books of short urban horror stories by Olympia Publishers – something that I have always longed to do. I am proud of 'A Sting in the Tale' and 'A Short Sharp Shock'.

I grew up reading horror and ghost stories and loved TV programmes such as 'Thriller', 'Tales of the Unexpected' and 'Hammer House of Horror'. I loved the work of screenwriter Brian Clemens. His imagination for a story was truly genius. I was sad to learn, as I write this, that he has passed away. Another immense talent has gone.

Another British writer I also admired was the late James Herbert. I was fortunate enough to have a copy of my book, 'A Sting in the Tale' personally signed by him with a lovely message. Something I fondly cherish.

I have a profound sense of humour and love comedy shows, especially those that mirror real lives. Those close to me know my wicked and dry humour well. This inspired me to develop my alter ego 'Clinton Steele' to pen the book 'Real Men Don't Wear Pink' in 2014. It was a tongue-in-cheek no-holds-barred look at where all the real men of my era had disappeared to and how they had been replaced by the dreaded metrosexual. 'Clinton' certainly pulls no punches, and it is nice to let him off the leash now and again. Normally, I keep him well buried and in check while I'm at my 'day job'.

These days, I am a disciplined performer who tries to be professional in his whole approach to his training and coaching, but every now and then, when I am relaxed, the 'Other Kev' can appear. He can he funny but also dangerous. That's why I keep him in check.

Those who know me from old will know what I mean. There is a time for seriousness and damn demanding work, and a time for fun. I think I now have the balance. When I'm 'at the office' so to speak (the training hall or gym is my office), I give one hundred percent in all I do and can be intense. I do the business. But away from that, I can chill out a bit.

I also like to get away to peaceful settings like the countryside or by the water. I find this helps me recharge the batteries and removes me from the rush of city life. I have also got the travel bug over the last twenty years and would very much like to do more of this in the years to come.

Some years back, I achieved a long-time ambition to visit the USA. It was a wonderful experience. The West Coast is my favourite. It is fabulous. It has a rich mixture of cultures and scenery. Totally breath taking. I have been fortunate enough to revisit the States many more times, and I dream of seeing as many of the fifty states as I can.

I have seen some incredible places such as Niagara Falls, Grand Canyon, Golden Gate Bridge, Statue of Liberty and Mount Rushmore amongst many more. The world is a big place. It is a fascinating one and a world that demands to be explored.

If God spares me I want to see as much of it as I can. There is still much I want to see and do.

Those of you who know me well will know that two weeks prior to the tragedy of September 11th, my family and I stood marvelling at the colossal size of the World Trade Centre Twin Towers in New York. When the news broke later of the devastation, death and mayhem, we were deeply affected by it all. We have friends and relations in America, and I felt for them all. I am not into preaching politics or religion. I just know that from my own first-hand experiences, I have found the people of America fantastic, and I wish them all my best for the future. We shouldn't confuse them with the politicians.

My spiritual writing home is Lanzarote. I really do love this island, and every year I will try to travel there to 'chill' out and write. I seem to get inspired there with ideas and projects that sometimes I can't always produce at home.

If I were asked to give out a piece of advice to you, the reader, that has helped me in my career, I would have to say that it is important to have goals. Without them, you wander through life aimlessly, letting opportunities pass you by. You will not have progression and you will, instead, be wandering, lost.

It is like being abandoned in a desert without a clue in what direction to head. As you get to the top of one sand dune, all you will see ahead are countless others. In the end, you won't even bother climbing the dunes because you will know what will await you. You must plan your goals carefully and map them out so you know where you are heading and what you need to do. Have purpose in your life. Don't be the sort of person who is looking forward to their summer holiday in February with nothing in between, or the person who at eight a.m. Monday morning in work is already waiting for five p.m. Friday afternoon. Don't wish your life away. Take something positive from each and every day. Don't go to your grave with your best song still inside you.

Around fifteen years ago, I decided that before every New Year, I would sit down and write down my goals for the coming year. Once they are on paper, they are set and can be worked towards. Some goals were long-term, large ones, which may take more than a year to achieve, but at least I could start on them; others were short-term and quite achievable; others were immediate goals, something that I could change about myself or my life straight away.

I also kept a diary of these goals, so that each day, I could monitor my progress. Remember, a small step in progress is better than none. During the year, while working towards those goals with targets and direction, I was surprised at what could be achieved. It really works, but you must be single-minded and dedicated to achieving. Take, for example, a man like Richard Branson, a self-made millionaire and a very successful businessman. People can be envious and jealous of his achievements, but his success and wealth didn't come overnight. From an early age, he worked tirelessly through goals, direction, targets and great vision for what he wanted. He had hardship on the way and failure, but he refused to give up and tried and tried again. As he completed one project with success, he was onto another one straight away. His life story is an inspirational one. You may not have the goals that Branson has, but it all works on the same basis. If you want to improve in an area of your life, first, you have got to accept that it needs improving and do a complete character X-ray of yourself. It's not always pleasant, but it has to be done.

I did this some ten years ago and began to totally change myself for the better. I changed a lot of my unhealthy habits, weaknesses and personality traits. I started to re-educate myself and set many goals in my martial arts career and private life. My reward was achievement in things I never thought I could gain. I have met and associated with great people I otherwise wouldn't have met. I pushed myself to new levels of skill and ability in martial arts and basically became a better person. I also believe firmly in having time for others. What you give out you reap back twofold somewhere along the line. Success can't always be measured in monetary gain, although that is desirable. Satisfaction of having achieved or completed a lifetime ambition is just as rewarding, if not better.

When you set goals, they must stretch you but not to totally unrealistic levels. You need to know that there are three types. Understanding these will help you achieve the desired results.

The three types are:

Ultimate goal
Product goal
Process

continue to help people through the lessons I have learnt. Ultimate goal is what you want to be remembered for in years to come. What would people say about you if you were being honoured at a special awards ceremony? What would be your epitaph?

Product goal is result-orientated. Set yourself three things that you want to improve on or achieve over the next twelve months.

Process goal is about understanding and working on a particular thing to help you towards your product goal. How are you going to achieve the above? What steps do you need to take?

When it comes to motivation, there are two types.

Firstly, there is the desire to move towards certain thoughts, feelings and state of mind.

Secondly, there is the desire to move away from certain thoughts, feelings or state of mind.

Are you success-driven or fear-of-failure-driven?

Currently, people have little or no time for others. It's a selfish society. Learn to give and doors will open for you, and you will get much spiritual refreshment. My friend Geoff Thompson taught me this, and it works.

Through all these experiences, I recently set up my 'Winning Minds' programme that helps others work to achieve their goals and dreams. So far it has been received well, and I would like to

I am no superman or all-knowing guru, but I have been there and done a bit. I have overcome my fears and many obstacles to be the person I am now today, and I want to do the same for others.

Whether you believe in God or a higher universal power or energy, it doesn't matter. I believe that something or someone is looking down on you, and they will guide you and give you choices. It's what you do with those choices that determine how you live your life.

Lastly, remember that your life is now. Not tomorrow, next week, next month, next year. It is now!

So, start working towards what you want out of it. You only get one shot and this is it. The one thing that none of us have loads of is time. The clock is ticking. What have you done today to plant a seed or take a step nearer your dreams?

Some of my goals took five years or more to achieve, but what a sense of fulfilment I got when I reached them. To some, many of my goals may not seem great, but to me, each and every one was significant. I came from very humble beginnings and worked relentlessly to better myself. Go on, you can do whatever you want and be the person you want to be.

The formula is goals, targets, destinations, vision, belief, dedication and tenacity.

I wish you all well for the future. I hope you have enjoyed my story and found it inspiring enough to reach for your dreams.

I chose the path of the warrior. What path will you choose?

God bless.

Kevin O'Hagan.

"On the long journey from A to Z, you learn an awful lot about B to Y."

Epilogue

'They think it's all over...'

The year is 2015. I am two months shy of my fifty-fourth birthday. I have worked my way back to a decent level of fitness and health again. The gym is speeding towards its second-year anniversary, and I think we have turned a corner. It has been an extremely tough few years, but I am coming out of the dark. I am feeling more positive and energised.

At the end of 2014, I got involved with a challenge organised by my son, Tom where we collectively trained a group of people to survive a 'Zombie Apocalypse'. The result was to compete in the only full-contact zombie challenge in the UK. It is run by a company where all these guys are ex-paras, foreign legion and other military groups. To say it was physically and mentally tough would be an understatement. I don't think that anybody who entered the challenge realised how full contact it would be. Especially me!

The team we entered were all ushered into a warehouse complex and kitted out in full riot squad gear. Then, we were briefed on the two missions we had to complete.

The first one was to be driven to an unknown location full of rage zombies, and we were to use riot shields and batons to keep them off us and make it back to the van at a designated spot. Otherwise, we would be left behind at the mercy of the flesh-hungry undead.

Our second mission, armed this time with the highest legally powered M16 paint ball machine guns, was to go into a pitch-black warehouse and clear it of zombies and, once again, get back to the van. This was going to be an adrenaline-fuelled hardcore day.

For our first mission, we had to be trained correctly on how to work as a team whilst using the riot shields. This was the exact training that would be given to the military or the police. The only difference was that we would have rubber batons.

We went collectively through the drills. The large riot shields are surprisingly heavy and locking them in together to form a wall is not as easy as you might think.

Also, we were taught to use the smaller, lighter shields. If you were on the end of the riot team's wall, you could break away and attack the zombies.

To illustrate, this trainer asked for two volunteers. I went immediately out, presuming that I and a partner would drill a bit with the batons and shields. But no!

The trainer informed us that in thirty seconds' time, a full-on rage zombie was going to be coming through the door, and we had to take him down! The other volunteer was a slightly built female (most of our team were females), and no disrespect, but I knew that I would be targeted hard.

There was a loud slamming on the metal door and my adrenaline kicked in. The door burst open, and then, a huge zombie ran in screaming.

I knew I had to go to him but with a flimsy rubber baton and Perspex shield, it was no contest. This guy must have been around one hundred and seven kilos against my seventy-six kilos. He slammed into me like a truck and knocked me flying onto the concrete floor. I was shaken by the ferocity of the attack. As I picked myself up from the floor, I knew I was in a fight and that this guy was going to target me as a message to the assembled team that if you fucked with them or thought this mission was going to be a walk in the park, you were dead fucking wrong.

Behind my riot helmet and flak jacket, he had no idea that he was ragging around a fifty-three-year old granddad!

I went in again, shield and baton pounding him. This time, he grabbed me with both hands on my jacket and threw me headlong into a pile of sand bags and riot shields. I had to thank my ju jutsu breakfalling skills from preventing me from breaking an arm, leg or my fucking neck. Half a dozen more times I dragged my ass up and went in to be smashed down again. On the last occasion, I went down with my shield covering my head, and this guy smashed down relentlessly on it with his fists. In the end, my training took over, and I kicked him in the guts. I threw the shield down. Enough was enough. I was going to have to double leg this bastard down!

But, at that moment, he backed off a little and allowed me and my female companion to beat him down to bring this little exercise to an end. I must admit that it took all of my self-control not to stomp or knee drop the bastard!

Well, that certainly marked everybody's card. This wasn't going to be no picnic.

My lungs were bursting after that little encounter. I had adrenaline shakes, but I sucked it up and carried on with the rest of the training.

The next training was on how to operate our guns and how to work as a team to clear a building.

We went into a pitch-black building and had to shoot at life-size targets. Some civilians and some zombies. It was a massive adrenaline rush, and I have total respect for the forces or police who have done this sort of thing for real.

In the last section, we had to down the firearms, pick up a rubber baton and go into the final room of the building and fight off a group of zombies hand to hand.

My son, Tom and I were first in and started smashing everything we saw with our batons.

At one stage, Tom got into a bit of a standing wrestle with one of the zombies, so I rushed in from the blind side and double leg lifted him and put him on the deck where we both then smashed him with our batons. As we ran out of the building, he shouted, "I will fucking remember you two!" He wasn't impressed.

For the first mission, we were split into two teams. The first team were bundled into the back of a van and driven off in pitch-blackness. We were told that as soon as the van stopped, we were to jump out, pick up the riot shields, form a wall and get ready.

The van squealed to a halt, and we jumped out into what looked like a movie set. There were disused buildings, abandoned cars, some on fire. It was like a bad moment from 'Night of the Living Dead' or '28 Days Later'.

We all locked shields and walked forward into the biggest chaos I have ever seen. The bastards came lumbering from everywhere. Every time you thought you were clear, more appeared. We were smashed from pillar to post. The big zombies came down hard on you. Smashing you with no mercy. One of the male members of our team was, unceremoniously, thrown head first into a car door!

At one point, Tom and I went down under a pile of zombies. They were smashing at our shields and crushing us against a few abandoned cars. From his back, Tom got one of them in a omoplata (a shoulder lock using your legs). The zombie yelled out in pain and relented.

Another highlight for me was being propelled by the largest zombie there across the tarmac to land face first in a big fucking muddy rain puddle.

I must admit part of me thought what the fuck are you doing. This is a Sunday afternoon. You should be at home, feet up after a Sunday roast watching 'Flog it'. But no, you are out battling zombies. Story of my life.

At last, the van pulled up and we were urged to run for it. Tired and battered, the adrenaline kicked in once again to get us to smash through the remaining group of zombies and dive into the van. Nobody wanted to be left behind. First mission accomplished.

The second mission was with the firearms. We were to go into a pitch-black warehouse and clear it of zombies. It was like the practise run we did earlier, but now it was live zombies, not cardboard targets.

The guys training us said that this would be as near as it got to a real mission, and they would lead us through it just the way they would do it.

Stepping into that pitch-black sparked the adrenaline once again. There were obstacles in the way and debris on the floor to make the going tough. Somewhere in there hiding was a group of flesh-hungry zombies ready to pounce on you.

We went into a maze of corridors and rooms, and at intervals, zombies would appear, but you now got the opportunity to blast them down, providing your gun didn't jam or you ran out of ammo by overzealously firing.

On two occasions, while watching ahead, I was attacked from the back. The first time, a zombie came up behind me and grabbed me around the neck. My ju jutsu training instantly kicked in, and I back elbowed him and took him down.

On the next occasion, I was shoved to the ground from behind. I fell, spun around and unloaded six rounds into my attacker, dropping him. Chuck Norris would have been proud of me.

It was an incredibly intense experience, and I felt like Stallone, Schwarzenegger and Willis rolled into one.

Finally, through smoke and sirens, we exited the warehouse and had to wait and form two lines like in the film 'Zulu'. As the remaining zombies came out of the building heading towards us, we had to wait and hold fire until they were in range, which was about six feet away, and then, blast them.

That was the hardest part. Letting them get that close and not panicking and wasting your shots.

Again, we ran to the van and dived in. We had made it and the second and final mission was complete.

I was very tired, sore and bruised, but I was in one piece and survived a very tough and unique experience. All the team did great. I seriously suggest that if you want to test yourself in a unusual way, check these guys out. But be warned. You have got to be in shape and be up for a fight!

We are nearly up to speed, guys. April 2015 gave me my final challenge to date.

I decided to look for something else to test my fitness and give me a goal to train to. I hadn't intended to, but an opportunity arose, and I know from past experience that if you feel you have got it in you to try something, then don't let that opportunity pass you by.

So, I decided to enter NAGA (North American Grappling Association) – a premier submission grappling competition.

They come to the UK once a year, and they are one of the biggest grappling competitions in the world.

They also allow all types of submissions including neck cranks, heel hooks and twisting ankle locks.

For me, this is real submission wrestling without the limitations that other competitions put on competitors. The emphasis is on tapping your opponent out and not just lying on them and scoring points.

This year's competition was to be held at Crystal Palace in London. Seven hundred competitors entered from all over the world.

I entered the Executive Masters division for over-fifties. I hoped that there would be somebody my age up to have a fight. To be honest, there aren't many.

I entered the no-gi division, as this is what I enjoy most. I did a lot of training and fighting in the gi many years ago, and I am currently thinking of going back to training in it. Maybe BJJ. I would love to achieve my black belt in another style of ju jutsu with this battle weary body before I am too old. We will have to wait and see.

Up to the day, I trained for six weeks with my son, Tom who was also competing.

I was coming back to good fitness, but competition fitness is another thing.

I religiously worked a couple of disgusting circuits and a heavy weight session plus grappling sparring every week.

I worked up to sparring six times six-minute rounds standing to floor submission wrestling. I never dreamt, as the weeks went on, that I could get myself back into this top shape. It was fucking hard and, at times, I questioned my sanity in doing this again. The old body protested but held up. I was determined to do this. Tom was supportive and positive. He believed I could do it.

Apart from a few close friends and family, nobody even knew I was in training, let alone going to fight again. It was all under the radar. This test was just for me.

A week or so before the event, I pulled a muscle in my back. At first, I dismissed it as nothing. But it got really tight to the point that when I was grappling, it would go into spasm and literally stop me in my tracks. I was gutted, but I was desperate to fight.

Deep heat, massage and Ibuprofen were administered, but even going up to the event, it was still tight.

We arrived in London the night before to weigh in, and the traffic had been heavy, making us run late for the weigh-in.

We rushed up finally to be weighed. I quickly bent down to take off my shoes and my back went. I mean, I couldn't move. How I straightened up and stood on the scales, I don't know.

The competition was this close. I couldn't not do it.

After the weigh-in, I was concerned and that night and the next morning, I had hot baths, administered deep heat and took Ibuprofen to try and get it mobile.

On the day, the spasm released but it was still tight, and I knew that it would affect how I would fight. I knew that 'shooting in' or any explosive twisting movement would put pay to me, but there was no way I was pulling out!

On the day, I did have another guy in my age category enter to fight me (Terry Doyle, Darlington 10th Planet ju jutsu). I weighed in at seventy-six kilos. He was around eighty-four kilos. But we both had worked so hard to get here that we just wanted to fight regardless of the weight difference.

I felt chilled in spite of my back, and we fought for the championship belt in our division.

I felt that I dominated the fight and had a few submission attempts and controlled things, but it was a close call. My opponent knew his stuff. If you don't get the finish, you will be scored on points.

I don't fight this way and just didn't think of points for positions. I went all out for the finish. Points-wise, it was two versus two (which I didn't know). Late in the fight, my opponent passed my guard to half guard and scored a point making it three versus two.

Although I reversed the position and ended up attacking, the time was up and he pipped me to the belt by one point. I was slightly gutted as I thought I had won. It was still nice to stand on the podium and get a silver medal put around my neck, though. At fifty-four years of age, I never thought I would get another opportunity to compete. But I had. Now, next year if I went back… THE BELT WAS IN TOUCHING DISTANCE…

Appendix

Competing and fighting in the combat sports arena was a small part of my martial arts journey, but for the record, here is my official fight background for those interested.

Kevin O'Hagan MMA Fight History
Pro fights

Result	Fighter	Event	Method/Referee	R	Time
win	Sami Berik	UC 9 - Rebellion Mar / 28 / 2004	Submission (Rear-Naked Choke)	1	4:28
loss	Kasan Hipkiss	G&P 1 - Ground & Pound 1 Oct / 12 / 2002	Submission (Heel Hook)	1	3.42
win	Andy Proctor	UC 2 - World Warriors Jun / 09 / 2002	Decision	2	5.00

Amateur Fights

Result	Fighter	Event	Method/Referee	Time
loss	Gareth Roberts	CSNC - Combat Sports National Championship 2 Nov / 25 / 2001	Submission (Knee Bar)	4.52
win	Suley Mahmoud	CSOT 4 - Combat Sports Open Trials 4 Sep / 30 / 2001	(decision)	4:00
win	James Stitfall	CSOT 3 - Combat Sports Open Trials 3 Jul / 28 / 2001	(neck crank)	0:42
loss	Charles Hallewell	CSOT 3 - Combat Sports Open Trials 3 Jul / 28 / 2001	(guillotine)	0:33
win	Mark Woodard	CSOT 3 - Combat Sports Open Trials 3 Jul / 28 / 2001	(guillotine)	0:50
Draw	Paul Jenkins	CSOT 2 – Combat Sports Open Trials 2 Feb / 25 / 2001	(distance)	4:00

Draw	Lee Gibson	CSOT 1 - Combat Sports Open Trials 1 Nov / 26 / 2000	(distance)	4:00
Draw	Gareth Roberts	CSOT 1 - Combat Sports Open Trials 1 Nov / 26 / 2000	(distance) N/A	4:00

Kevin O'Hagan. Ju Jutsu/grappling fight history

1997	Gold Medal Middleweight Vets Champion	National Ju Jutsu Kumite Championships, Worcester
1998	Silver Medal Middleweight Vets Champion	National Ju Jutsu Kumite Championships, Worcester
1998	Silver Medal (Blue Belt Division Vets) Brazilian Ju Jutsu	International European BJJ Championship London
April 2001	Combat Sports Submission Wrestling Trials, Lightweight Division	Bath
April 2001	Draw against Max Bateman	Bath
April 2001	Lose by armbar to Roger Woodward	Bath
July 2011	Silver Medal Welterweight Vets	Spartan Submission Grappling Championships, Nailsea
May 2015	Silver Medal Executive Masters Division	NAGA Championships, Crystal Palace, London

Kevin O'Hagan Martial Arts Qualifications

7th Dan black belt Masters Grade in Combat Ju Jutsu.
7th Dan Senior Self Protection instructor (BCA).
5th Dan black belt in Goshin Ryu/Goshin Kai Ju Jutsu.
1st Dan black belt in Japanese Ju Jutsu.
1st Dan black belt in Karate Jutsu.
3rd kyu Aikido.
Orange sash Pak Mei Kung fu.
British National Martial Arts Association award for 'Contribution and Development of Martial Arts' (BNMMA Hon)
Certified Conflict Management trainer. (BTEC Advanced Award, Edexcel)
NHS Certified Conflict Resolution trainer (NHS CFSMS)
Specialist advisor to accreditation panel for the first accredited awards for control and restraint, flashlight defence tactics, conflict management and personal safety. (Open College Network)
Inducted into the MAI Hall of Fame for 'Contribution to the Martial Arts'

Additional Coaching Qualifications

REPs Fitness Instructor Level 2
NCFE Sports Coach Certificate
NCFE Diploma in Sports Psychology
Diploma in Neurolinguistics Programming (NLP)
MASTARR NTP Coaching Certificate in Health and Safety
MASTARR NTP Coaching Certificate in Child Protection
MASTARR NTP Coaching Certificate in Instructing Module
MASTARR NTP Coaching Certificate in Coaching
BWLA Leader's Award
Diploma in Exercise for Special Populations (Premier Training International)
COPD Certified trainer
Certificate in Strength and Advanced Strength Training Creator of the Gladiator Total Body Workout

Some Empowering Statements

When life is not going to plan, don't look for excuses; look for solutions.

You can choose how much a situation bothers you. Decide what is important and what isn't. If you don't want something to be important, it need not be.

Ask yourself how long you want to brood over something and what good it will do.

Learn to laugh at yourself and keep a good sense of humour. If you take yourself too seriously, your happiness will diminish.

Don't just react to other people's moods or wishes. Decide what you want and negotiate, but don't become a passive victim.

Try to deal with the cause of the situation, not the symptom.

Sometimes, yelling and getting something off your chest may be beneficial, but make sure that it solves the problem, not makes it worse.

Learn to love yourself, and don't be too critical of yourself. Unhappy people are their own biggest critic. Happy people will accept and support themselves.

Do at least one good and positive thing every day.

Get out of bed like it's your last day on earth.

If you had a year to live, list all the things you would like to do. Then, live your life as if you have that much time.

Don't waste time listening to negative people. They will drag you into their world and steal your energy.

Don't waste time and energy worrying about things you can't change. Accept them and put your energies into the things you can change.

If you are anxious and worrying about something that may happen, it is evidence that it hasn't. So don't waste your energy. If it does happen, you will then deal with it.

Growing old is inevitable. Growing old, lonely, miserable and unfulfilled is a matter of choice.

Some Favourite Motivational Quotes

I love motivational quotes. They inspire you to push for greater things and reach your goals. Do not underestimate the power of the written word. I hope the following quotes will get you through your training when the going gets tough.

"Strength does not come from physical capacity. It comes from indomitable will." Gandhi

"A warrior knows that it is impossible to live in a complete state of relaxation." Coelho

"Energy and persistence conquer all things." Benjamin Franklin

"Working hard does not mean that you are working productively." Anon

"Success is the ability to go from one failure to the next with no loss of enthusiasm." Churchill

"Success is a journey, not a destination." Anon

"When one has much to put into them, a day has a hundred pockets." Nietzsche

"Courage is resistance to fear, mastery of fear and not, absence of fear." Mark Twain

"Work to live; don't live to work." Anon

"Failing to prepare is preparing to fail." Anon

"It doesn't matter how slowly you go as long as you don't stop." Confucius

"God helps those who help themselves." Anon

"Our greatest glory is not in never falling, but rising every time we fall." Anon

"A man who has never made a mistake has never done anything." Anon

"A lot of people have gone further than they thought they could because someone else thought they could." Anon

"Pressure is nothing more than the shadow of great opportunity." Anon

"Tough times don't last; tough people do." Anon

"Some of the world's greatest feats were accomplished by people not smart enough to know they were impossible." Doug Larson

"There are no shortcuts to any place worth going." Beverly Sills

"You cannot dream yourself into a character; you must hammer and forge yourself into one." Henry D. Thoreau

"Success is the sum of small efforts repeated day in day out." Anon

"Success is the good that comes from aspiration, desperation, perspiration and inspiration." Evan Esar

"Pain is temporary; pride is forever." Anon

"Only the weak attempt to accomplish what he knows he can already achieve." Stella Juarez

"Strength is the product of struggle." Henry Rollins

"Quitters never win and winners never quit." Anon

"Thou shalt not NOT train." Anon

"You can't fake endurance." Anon

"Fatigue makes cowards of us all." Shakespeare

"Training is habit forming. Form the habit." Anon

"Train hard, fight easy." Alexander Suvorov

"The only place success comes before work is in a dictionary." Anon

"The man who hasn't tasted defeat has not done anything." Anon

"Fear and discomfort, means you are growing." Anon

"Big does not equal tough." Anon

"Our best friend and worst foe is our mind." Anon

"There is little you can learn by doing nothing." Anon

"It takes a brave man to step out of his comfort zone and seek pastures new." Anon

"Success is not a destination, it's a journey, and it's the direction in which you are travelling." Anon

"There are no gains without pain or wisdom without adversity." Benjamin Franklin

"Our greatest glory is in never failing, but in rising every time we fall." Confucius

"Real strength is internal, not external." Anon

"It's not the size of the dog in the fight; it is the size of the fight in the dog." Mark Twain

"Nobody achieved success overnight. They have been working under the radar for a long time." Anon

"I am not successful despite my pain; I am successful because of it." Geoff Thompson

"Happiness is a state of mind." Anon

"When you were born, your life was a blank canvas. It is up to you what you paint on it." Anon

"We are born to die; it is what you do in between that is important." Anon

"He who is not courageous enough to take risks will accomplish nothing in life." Muhammad Ali

"While most are dreaming of success, winners wake up and work hard to achieve it." Anon

"No matter how slow you are moving, you are still lapping everybody on the couch." Anon

"Do a little more each day than you think you possibly can." Lowell Thomas

"Every time you stay out late, sleep in, miss a workout and don't give 100%, you make it easier for me to beat you." Anon

If you enjoyed my story, then keep up-to-date with my blogs, thoughts and products at, **www.kevinohagan.com**

For more information about classes and training facilities, go to, **www.impactgymbristol.com**